PAP

M000073561

ELVIS

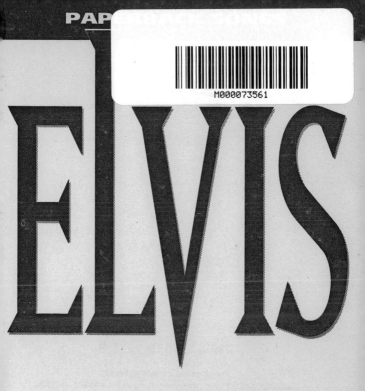

MELODY LINE, CHORDS AND LYRICS
FOR KEYBOARD • GUITAR • VOCAL

HAL•LEONARD®

ISBN 0-7935-7342-4

For all works contained herein:
Unauthorized copying, arranging, adapting, recording or public performance is an infringement of copyright.
Infringers are liable under the law.

Visit Hal Leonard on the internet at http://www.halleonard.com

Elvis and Elvis Presley are registered trademarks of Elvis Presley Enterprises, Inc., Copyright © 1997.

This publication is not for sale in the E.C. and/or Australia or New Zealand.

HAL•LEONARD®
CORPORATION
7777 W. BLUEMOUND RD. P.O. BOX 13819 MILWAUKEE, WI 53213

Welcome to the PAPERBACK SONGS SERIES.

Do you play piano, guitar, electronic keyboard, sing or play any instrument for that matter? If so, this handy "pocket tune" book is for you.

The concise, one-line music notation consists of:

MELODY, LYRICS & CHORD SYMBOLS

Whether strumming the chords on guitar, "faking" an arrangement on piano/keyboard or singing the lyrics, these fake book style arrangements can be enjoyed at any experience level – hobbyist to professional.

The musical skills necessary to successfully use this book are minimal. If you play guitar and need some help with chords, a basic chord chart is included at the back of the book.

While playing and singing is the first thing that comes to mind when using this book, it can also serve as a compact, comprehensive reference guide.

However you choose to use this PAPERBACK SONGS SERIES book, by all means have fun!

CONTENTS

6 Ain't That Loving You Baby
7 All Shook Up
10 Always on My Mind
12 An American Trilogy
18 Any Way You Want Me
20 Anything That's Part of You
22 Are You Lonesome Tonight?
24 As Long As I Have You
26 (You're So Square) Baby, I Don't Care
28 Baby, Let's Play House
30 Big Boss Man
15 A Big Hunk O' Love
32 Bitter They Are, Harder They Fall
38 Blue Christmas
40 Blue Hawaii
35 Blue Moon of Kentucky
42 Blue Suede Shoes
44 Bossa Nova Baby
46 Burning Love
48 Can't Help Falling in Love
50 Change of Habit
52 Charro
54 Clean Up Your Own Back Yard
58 Crying in the Chapel
60 Don't
62 Don't Ask Me Why
64 Don't Be Cruel (To a Heart That's True)
67 Don't Cry Daddy
70 Don't Leave Me Now
72 Doncha' Think It's Time?
74 Fame and Fortune
76 Flaming Star
78 Follow That Dream
80 Fool
82 (Now and Then There's) A Fool Such As I
84 For the Good Times
86 G.I. Blues
88 Girls! Girls! Girls!
91 Good Luck Charm
94 Good Rockin' Tonight
98 Green Green Grass of Home
100 Hard Headed Woman
102 The Hawaiian Wedding Song (Ke Kali Nei Au)
104 Heartbreak Hotel
106 Help Me Make It Through the Night
108 His Latest Flame
114 Hound Dog
116 I Beg of You
111 I Feel So Bad
118 I Got Stung
124 I Gotta Know
126 I Need Your Love Tonight
128 I Want You, I Need You, I Love You

130 I Was the One
132 I'm Leavin'
134 I'm So Lonesome I Could Cry
136 I've Got a Thing About You, Baby
138 I've Lost You
121 If I Can Dream
140 If You Talk in Your Sleep
142 In the Ghetto (The Vicious Circle)
148 It Hurts Me
150 It's Now or Never
152 Jailhouse Rock
145 Kentucky Rain
154 King Creole
156 Kissin' Cousins
159 Little Sister
162 Lonely Man
164 Love Me
183 Love Me Tender
166 Loving You
168 Mary in the Morning
170 Mean Woman Blues
172 Memories
174 A Mess of Blues
176 My Baby Left Me
178 My Boy
180 My Way
184 One Broken Heart For Sale
186 One Night
188 (There'll Be) Peace in the Valley (For Me)
190 The Promised Land
196 Puppet on a String
198 Return to Sender
200 Rock-A-Hula Baby
193 Separate Ways
202 She's Not You
204 Spinout
206 Steamroller (Steamroller Blues)
208 Stuck on You
210 Surrender
216 Suspicious Minds
218 (Let Me Be Your) Teddy Bear
220 That's All Right
222 Too Much
213 Treat Me Nice
224 T-R-O-U-B-L-E
228 Unchained Melody
230 Until It's Time for You to Go
232 Viva Las Vegas
236 Walk a Mile in My Shoes
238 Way Down
243 Wear My Ring Around Your Neck
246 The Wonder of You
248 You Don't Have to Say You Love Me
250 You're the Devil in Disguise
240 You've Lost That Lovin' Feelin'

AIN'T THAT LOVING YOU BABY

Words and Music by CLYDE OTIS
and IVORY JOE HUNTER

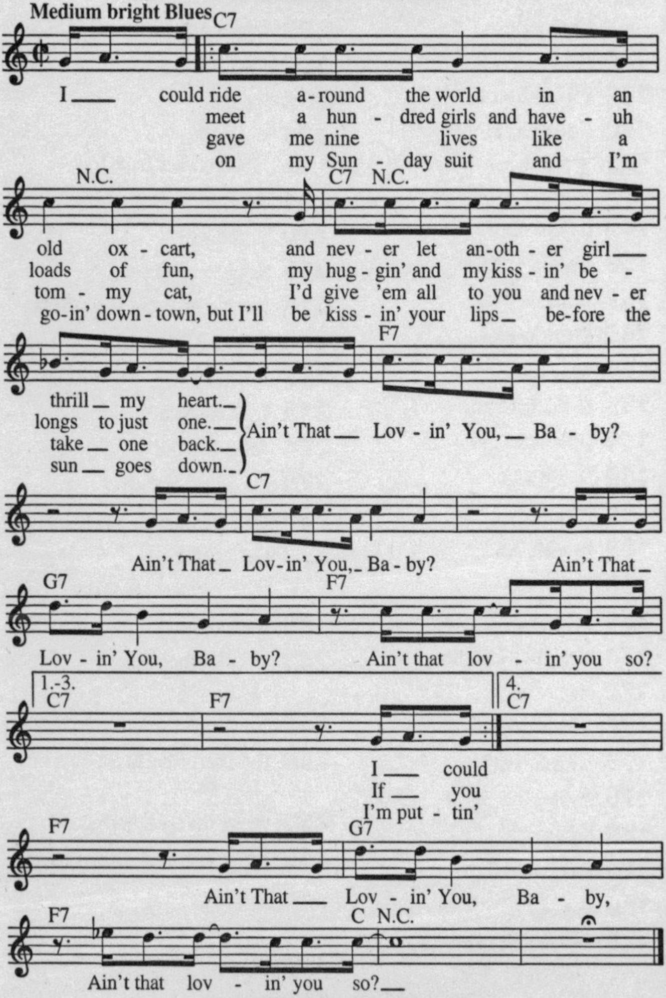
Medium bright Blues
C7
I ___ could ride a-round the world in an
meet a hun - dred girls and have - uh
gave me nine lives like a
on my Sun - day suit and I'm
N.C.
C7 N.C.
old ox - cart, and nev - er let an-oth - er girl ___
loads of fun, my hug - gin' and my kiss - in' be -
tom - my cat, I'd give 'em all to you and nev - er
go-in' down - town, but I'll be kiss - in' your lips ___ be-fore the
F7
thrill ___ my heart. ___
longs to just one. ___
take ___ one back. ___
sun ___ goes down. ___
Ain't That ___ Lov - in' You, ___ Ba - by?
C7
Ain't That ___ Lov-in' You, ___ Ba - by?
Ain't That ___
G7
F7
Lov - in' You, Ba - by?
Ain't that lov - in' you so?
1.-3.
C7
F7
4.
C7
I ___ could
If ___ you
I'm put - tin'
F7
G7
Ain't That ___ Lov - in' You, Ba - by,
F7
C N.C.
Ain't that lov - in' you so? ___

Copyright © 1959 by Elvis Presley Music, Inc.
Copyright Renewed and the interest of Clyde Otis
assigned to Elvis Presley Music (Administered by R&H Music)
International Copyright Secured All Rights Reserved

ALL SHOOK UP

Words and Music by OTIS BLACKWELL
and ELVIS PRESLEY

Medium Shuffle rhythm

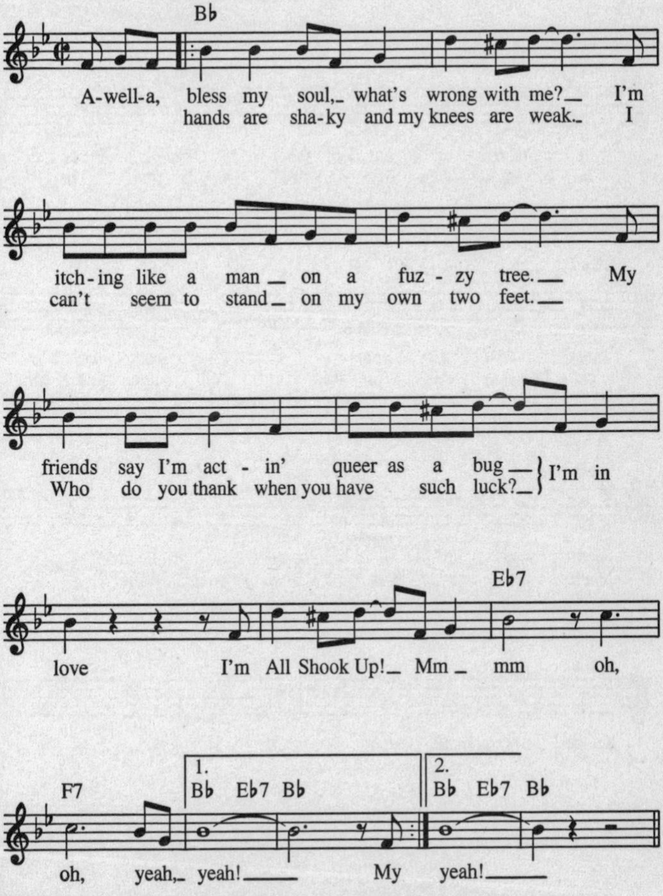
Bb
A-well-a, bless my soul,_ what's wrong with me?_ I'm
hands are sha-ky and my knees are weak._ I
itch-ing like a man _ on a fuz - zy tree._ My
can't seem to stand_ on my own two feet._
friends say I'm act - in' queer as a bug _
Who do you thank when you have such luck?_
I'm in
love I'm All Shook Up!_ Mm _ mm oh,
Eb7
F7
1.
Bb Eb7 Bb
2.
Bb Eb7 Bb
oh, yeah,_ yeah!_ My yeah!_

Copyright © 1957 by Shalimar Music Corporation
Copyright Renewed and Assigned to Elvis Presley Music (Administered by R&H Music)
International Copyright Secured All Rights Reserved

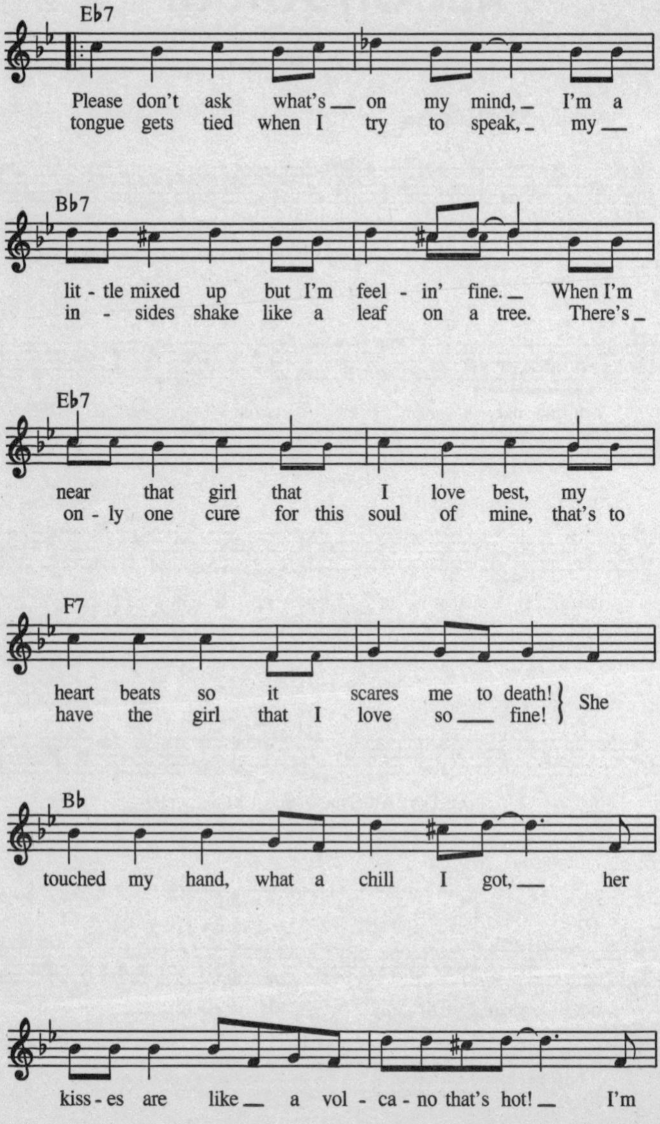
E♭7
Please don't ask what's __ on my mind, _ I'm a
tongue gets tied when I try to speak, _ my __
B♭7
lit - tle mixed up but I'm feel - in' fine. _ When I'm
in - sides shake like a leaf on a tree. There's _
E♭7
near that girl that I love best, my
on - ly one cure for this soul of mine, that's to
F7
heart beats so it scares me to death!
have the girl that I love so __ fine!
She
B♭
touched my hand, what a chill I got, __ her
kiss - es are like _ a vol - ca - no that's hot! _ I'm

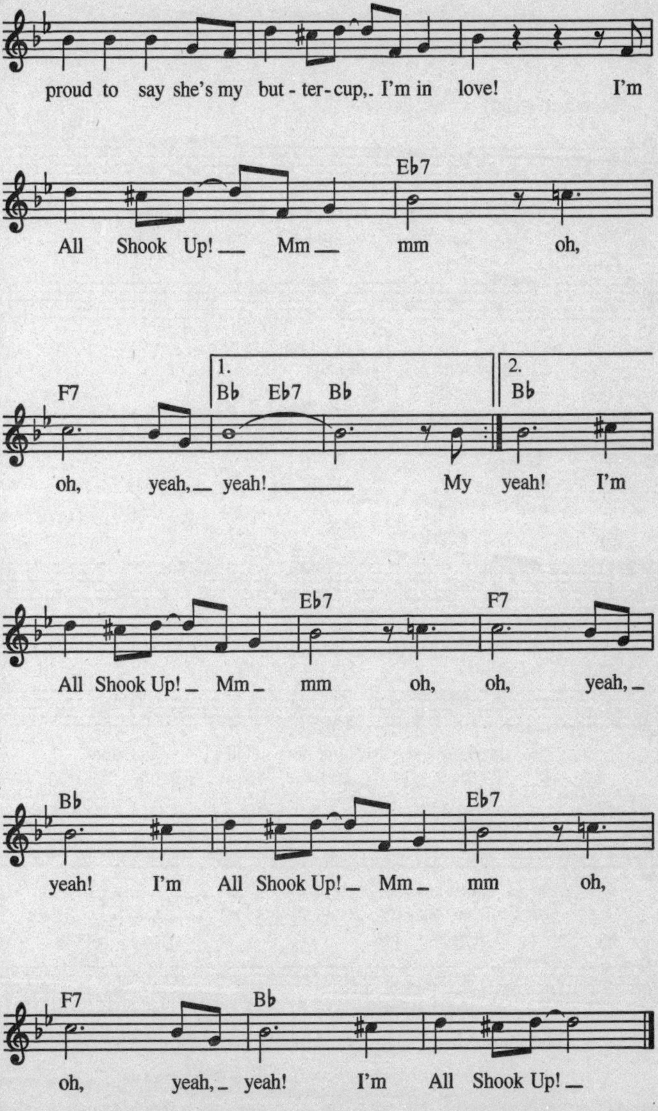
proud to say she's my but - ter - cup,. I'm in love! I'm
Eb7
All Shook Up! Mm mm oh,
F7
1.
Bb Eb7 Bb
2.
Bb
oh, yeah, yeah! My yeah! I'm
Eb7
F7
All Shook Up! Mm mm oh, oh, yeah,
Bb
Eb7
yeah! I'm All Shook Up! Mm mm oh,
F7
Bb
oh, yeah, yeah! I'm All Shook Up!

ALWAYS ON MY MIND

Words and Music by WAYNE THOMPSON, MARK JAMES and JOHNNY CHRISTOPHER

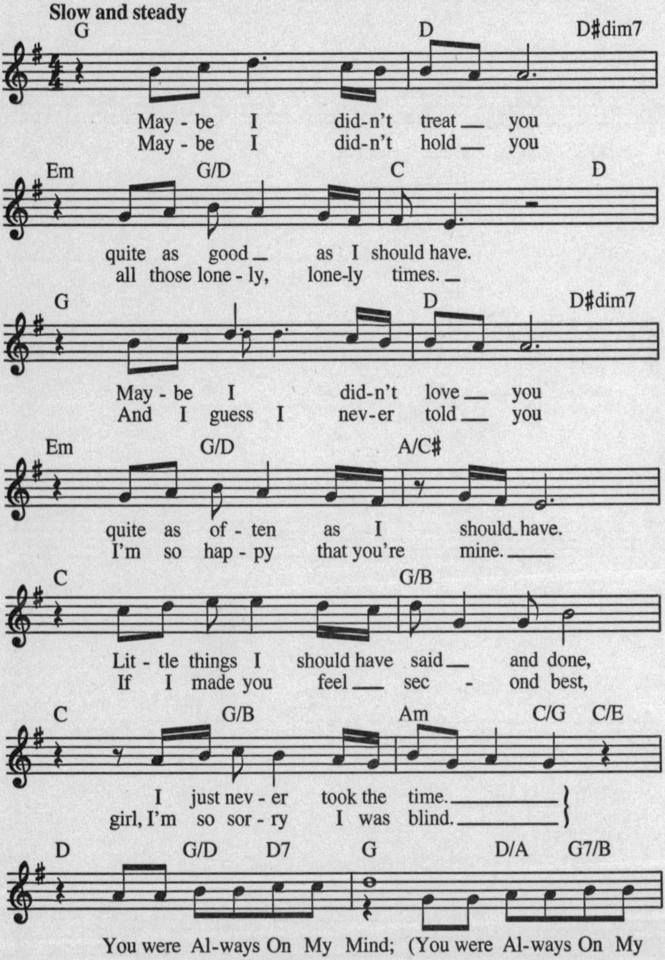
Slow and steady
G D D#dim7
May - be I did-n't treat you
May - be I did-n't hold you
Em G/D C D
quite as good as I should have.
all those lone - ly, lone-ly times.
G D D#dim7
May - be I did-n't love you
And I guess I nev-er told you
Em G/D A/C#
quite as of - ten as I should have.
I'm so hap - py that you're mine.
C G/B
Lit - tle things I should have said and done,
If I made you feel sec - ond best,
C G/B Am C/G C/E
I just nev - er took the time.
girl, I'm so sor - ry I was blind.
D G/D D7 G D/A G7/B
You were Al-ways On My Mind; (You were Al-ways On My

© 1971,1979 SCREEN GEMS-EMI MUSIC INC. and BUDDE SONGS INC.
All Rights Controlled and Administered by SCREEN GEMS-EMI MUSIC INC.
All Rights Reserved International Copyright Secured Used by Permission

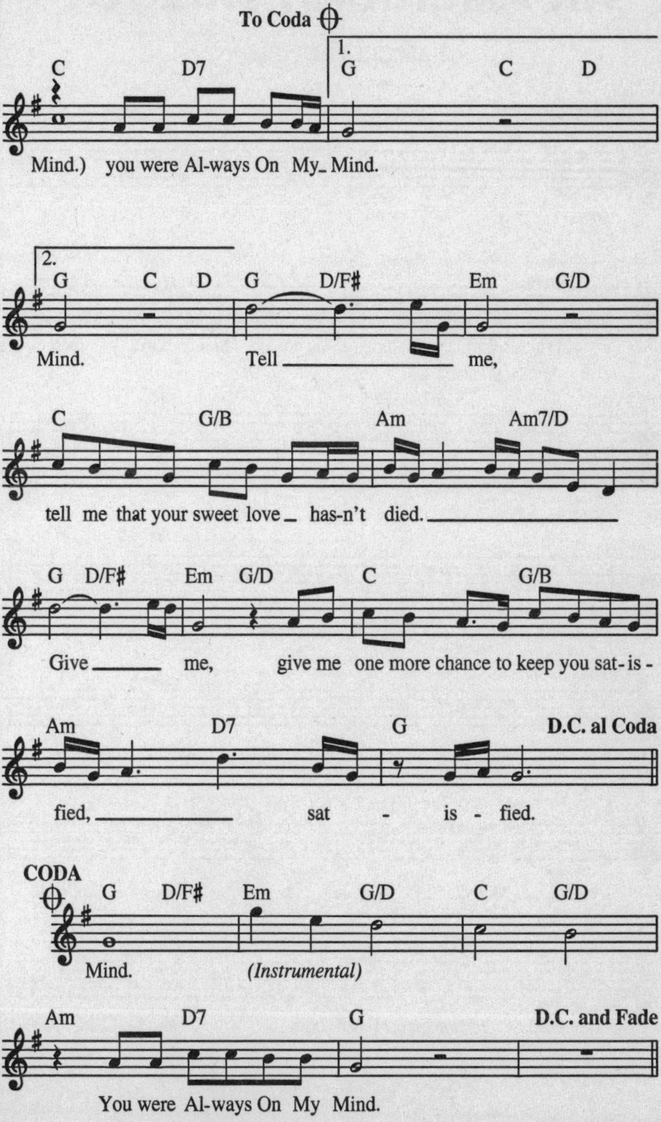
To Coda
1.
C D7 G C D
Mind.) you were Al-ways On My_ Mind.
2.
G C D G D/F# Em G/D
Mind. Tell me,
C G/B Am Am7/D
tell me that your sweet love_ has-n't died.
G D/F# Em G/D C G/B
Give me, give me one more chance to keep you sat-is -
Am D7 G D.C. al Coda
fied, sat - is - fied.
CODA
G D/F# Em G/D C G/D
Mind. (Instrumental)
Am D7 G D.C. and Fade
You were Al-ways On My Mind.

AN AMERICAN TRILOGY

By MICKEY NEWBURY

Moderately slow

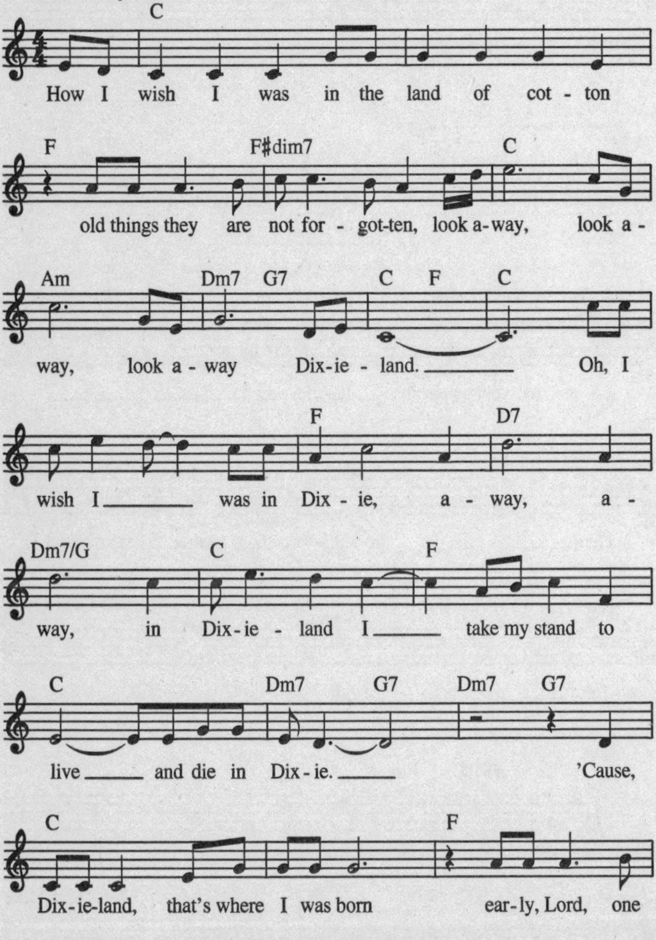
C
How I wish I was in the land of cot - ton
F F#dim7 C
old things they are not for - got-ten, look a-way, look a -
Am Dm7 G7 C F C
way, look a - way Dix-ie - land. Oh, I
F D7
wish I was in Dix - ie, a - way, a -
Dm7/G C F
way, in Dix-ie - land I take my stand to
C Dm7 G7 Dm7 G7
live and die in Dix-ie. 'Cause,
C F
Dix-ie-land, that's where I was born ear-ly, Lord, one

Copyright © 1971 by Acuff-Rose Music, Inc.
All Rights Reserved Used by Permission

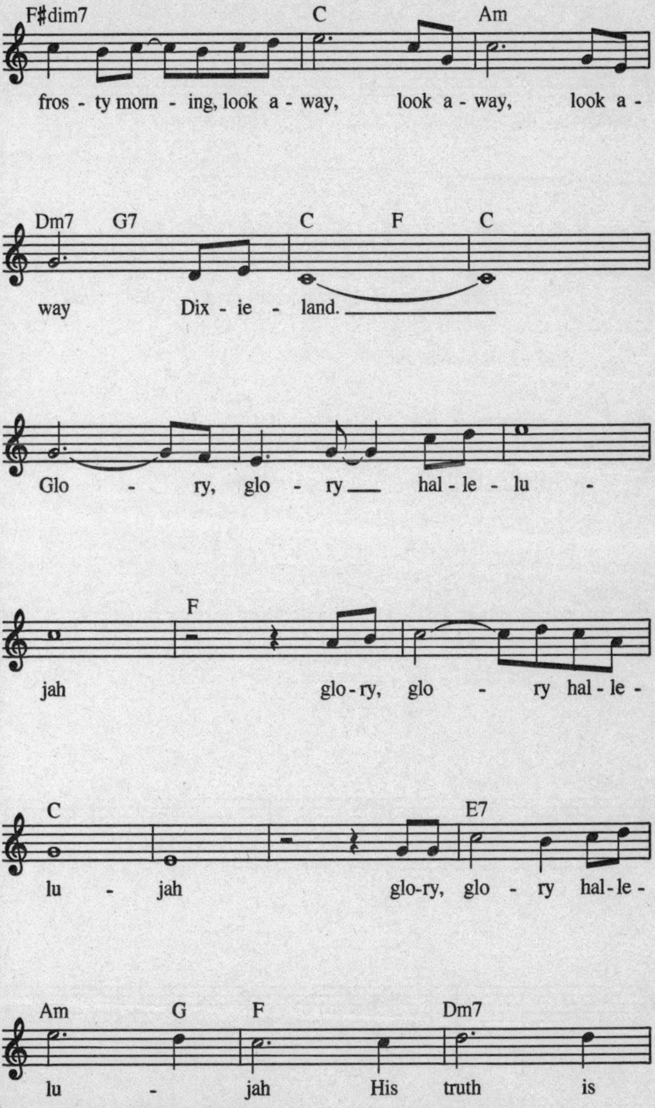
F♯dim7 C Am
fros - ty morn - ing, look a - way, look a - way, look a -
Dm7 G7 C F C
way Dix - ie - land.
Glo - ry, glo - ry hal - le - lu -
F
jah glo - ry, glo - ry hal - le -
C E7
lu - jah glo-ry, glo - ry hal - le -
Am G F Dm7
lu - jah His truth is

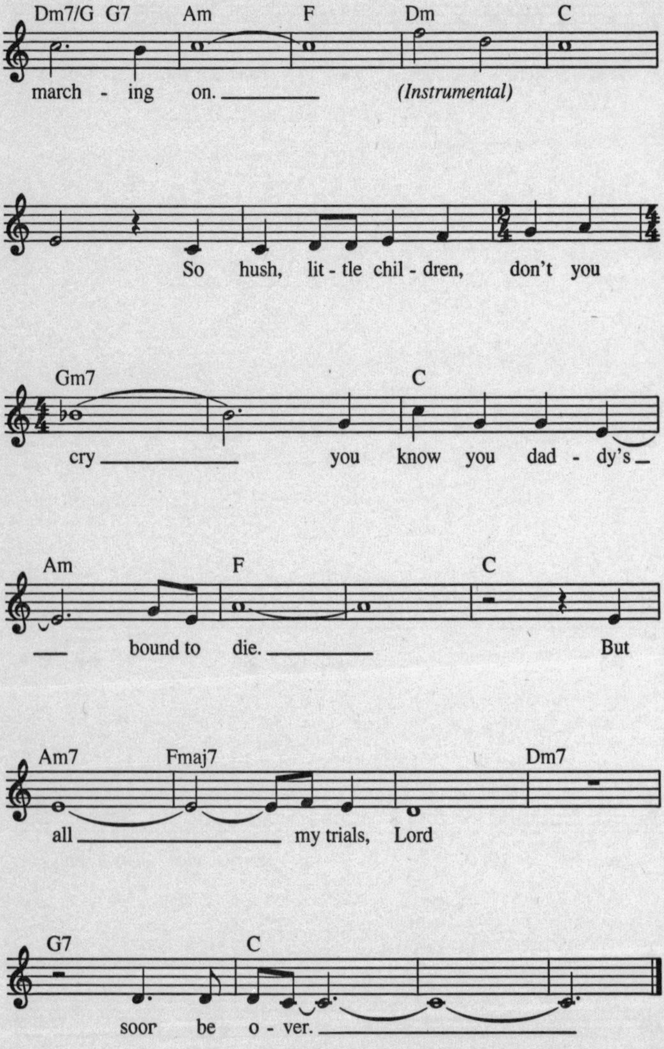
Dm7/G G7 Am F Dm C
march - ing on. (Instrumental)
So hush, lit - tle chil - dren, don't you
Gm7 C
cry you know you dad - dy's
Am F C
bound to die. But
Am7 Fmaj7 Dm7
all my trials, Lord
G7 C
soor be o - ver.

A BIG HUNK O' LOVE

Words and Music by AARON SCHROEDER
and SID WYCHE

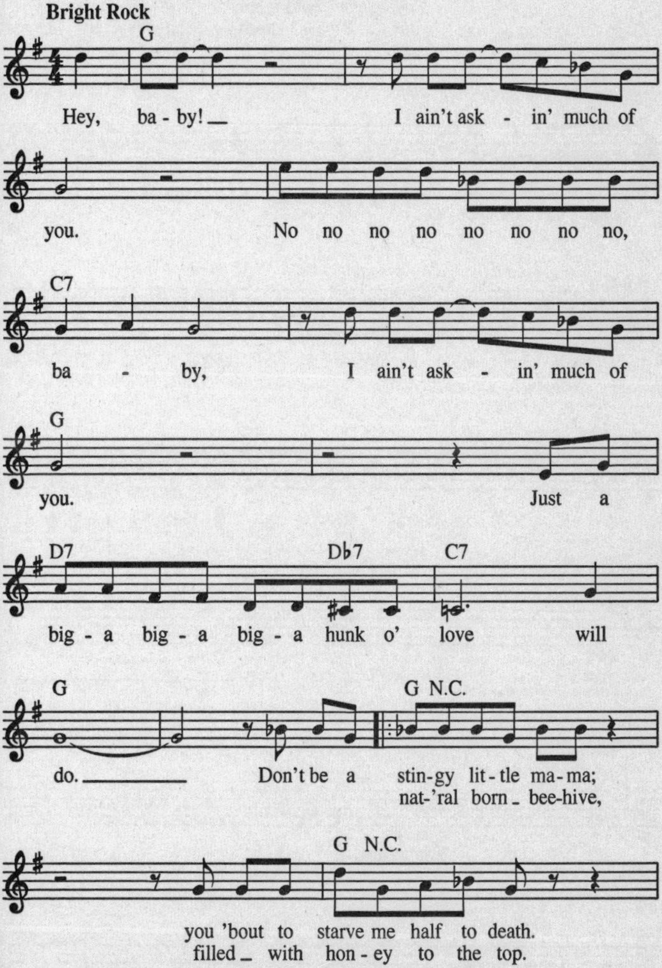
Bright Rock
G
Hey, ba - by! I ain't ask - in' much of
you. No no no no no no no no,
C7
ba - by, I ain't ask - in' much of
G
you. Just a
D7 Db7 C7
big - a big - a big - a hunk o' love will
G G N.C.
do. Don't be a stin-gy lit-tle ma-ma;
nat-'ral born bee-hive,
G N.C.
you 'bout to starve me half to death.
filled with hon - ey to the top.

Copyright © 1959 by Elvis Presley Music, Inc.
Copyright Renewed and Assigned to Elvis Presley Music (Administered by R&H Music)
and Rachel's Own Music (Administered by A. Schroeder International Ltd.)
International Copyright Secured All Rights Reserved

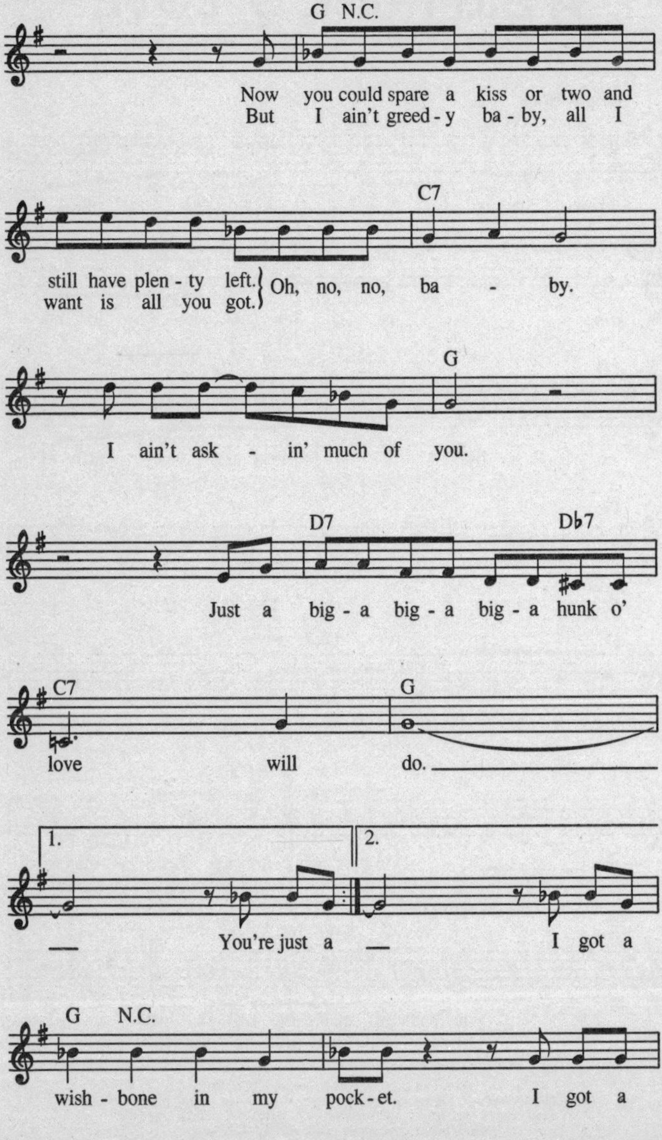
G N.C.
Now you could spare a kiss or two and
But I ain't greed - y ba - by, all I
C7
still have plen - ty left.
want is all you got.
Oh, no, no, ba - by.
G
I ain't ask - in' much of you.
D7
Db7
Just a big - a big - a big - a hunk o'
C7
G
love will do.
1.
2.
You're just a
I got a
G N.C.
wish - bone in my pock - et.
I got a

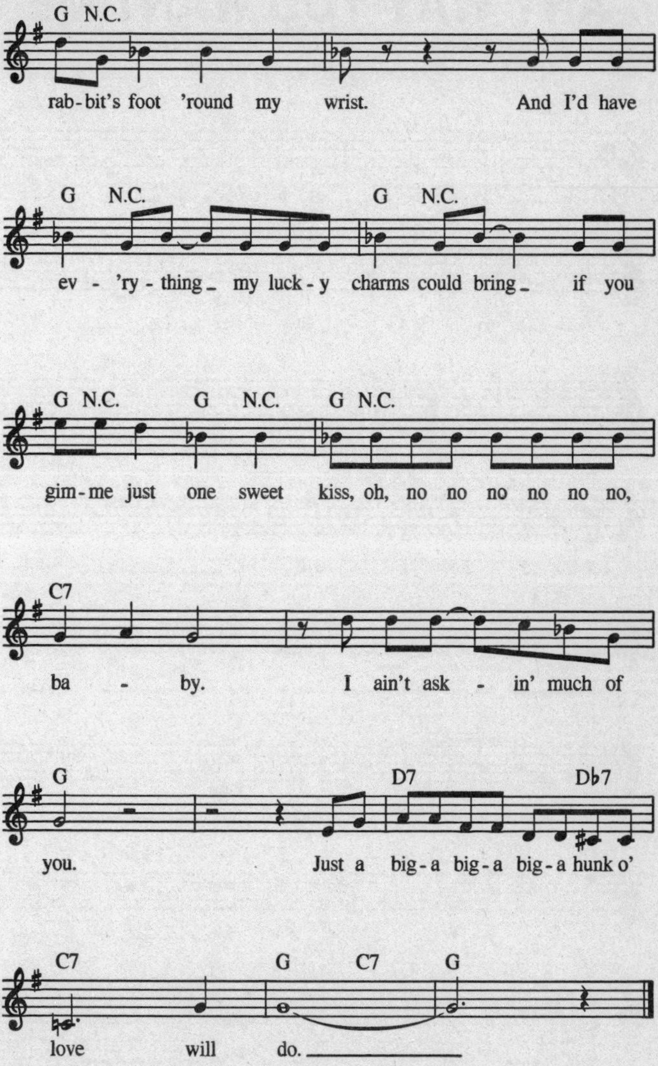
G N.C.
rab-bit's foot 'round my wrist. And I'd have
G N.C. G N.C.
ev - 'ry - thing my luck - y charms could bring if you
G N.C. G N.C. G N.C.
gim-me just one sweet kiss, oh, no no no no no no,
C7
ba - by. I ain't ask - in' much of
G D7 Db7
you. Just a big-a big-a big-a hunk o'
C7 G C7 G
love will do.

ANY WAY YOU WANT ME

Words and Music by CLIFF OWENS
and AARON SCHROEDER

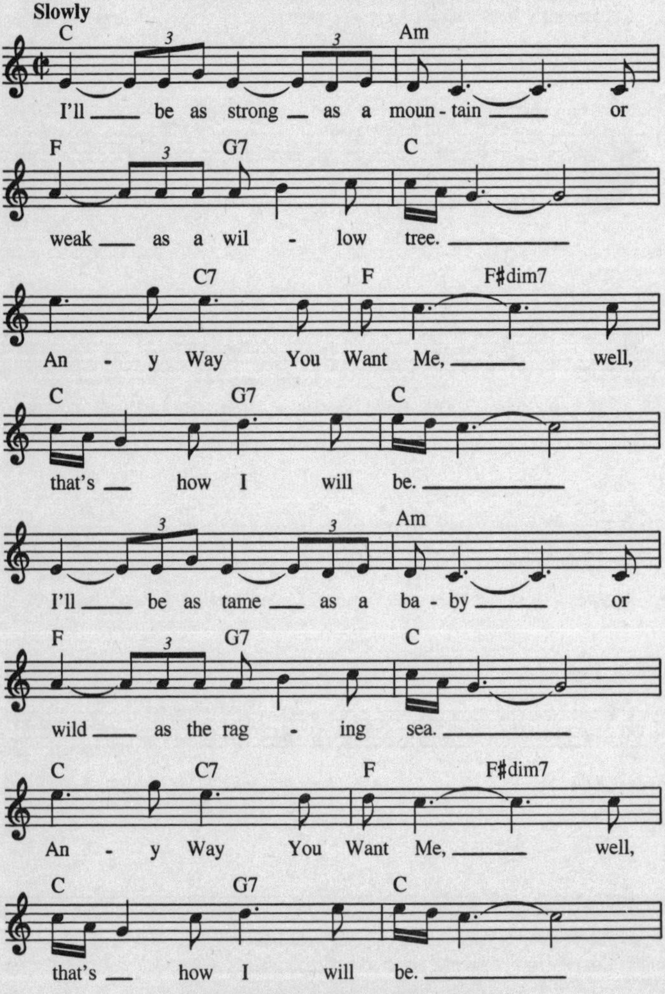
Slowly
C Am
I'll ___ be as strong ___ as a moun - tain ___ or
F G7 C
weak ___ as a wil - low tree. ___
C7 F F♯dim7
An - y Way You Want Me, ___ well,
C G7 C
that's ___ how I will be. ___
Am
I'll ___ be as tame ___ as a ba - by ___ or
F G7 C
wild ___ as the rag - ing sea. ___
C C7 F F♯dim7
An - y Way You Want Me, ___ well,
C G7 C
that's ___ how I will be. ___

Copyright © 1956 by Chappell & Co. and Rachel's Own Music
(Administered by A. Schroeder International Ltd.)
Copyright Renewed
International Copyright Secured All Rights Reserved

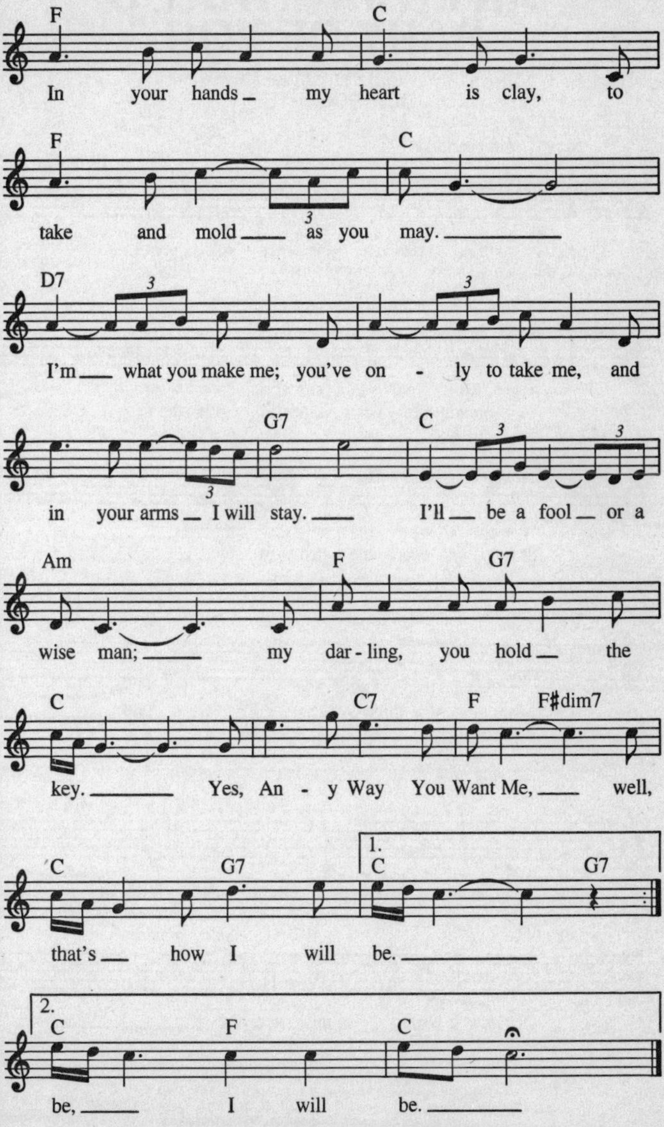
F C
In your hands my heart is clay, to
F C
take and mold as you may.
D7
I'm what you make me; you've on - ly to take me, and
G7 C
in your arms I will stay. I'll be a fool or a
Am F G7
wise man; my dar - ling, you hold the
C C7 F F#dim7
key. Yes, An - y Way You Want Me, well,
C G7 1. C G7
that's how I will be.
2. C F C
be, I will be.

ANYTHING THAT'S PART OF YOU

Words and Music by
DON ROBERTSON

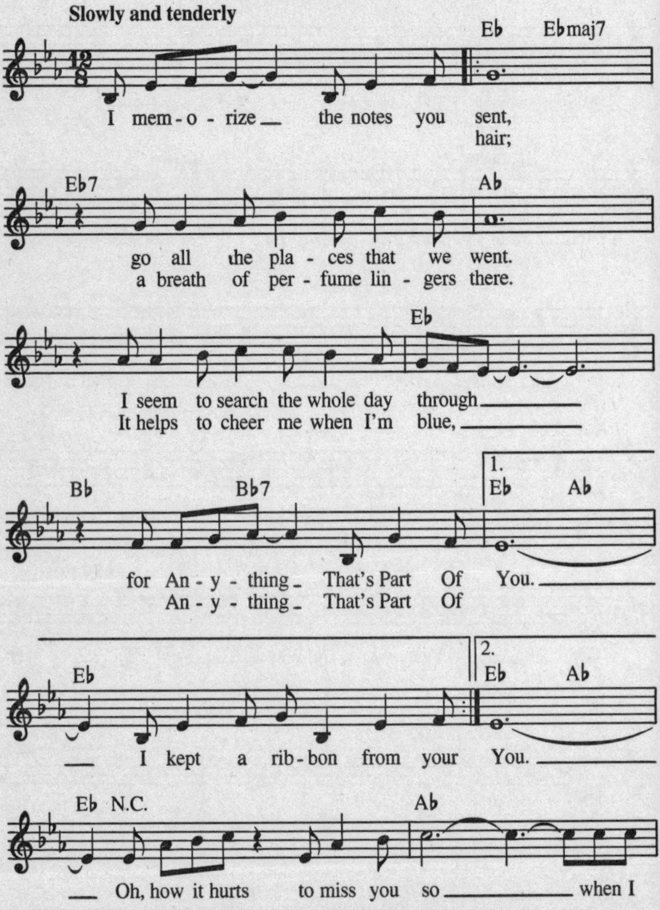
Slowly and tenderly
Eb Ebmaj7
I mem - o - rize the notes you sent,
hair;
Eb7 Ab
go all the pla - ces that we went.
a breath of per - fume lin - gers there.
Eb
I seem to search the whole day through
It helps to cheer me when I'm blue,
Bb Bb7
1.
Eb Ab
for An - y - thing That's Part Of You.
An - y - thing That's Part Of
Eb
2.
Eb Ab
I kept a rib - bon from your You.
Eb N.C. Ab
Oh, how it hurts to miss you so when I

Copyright © 1962 by Gladys Music, Inc.
Copyright Renewed, Assigned in the United States in 1991 to
Don Robertson Music Corporation, P.O. Box 4141, Thousand Oaks, CA 91359
International Copyright Secured All Rights Reserved

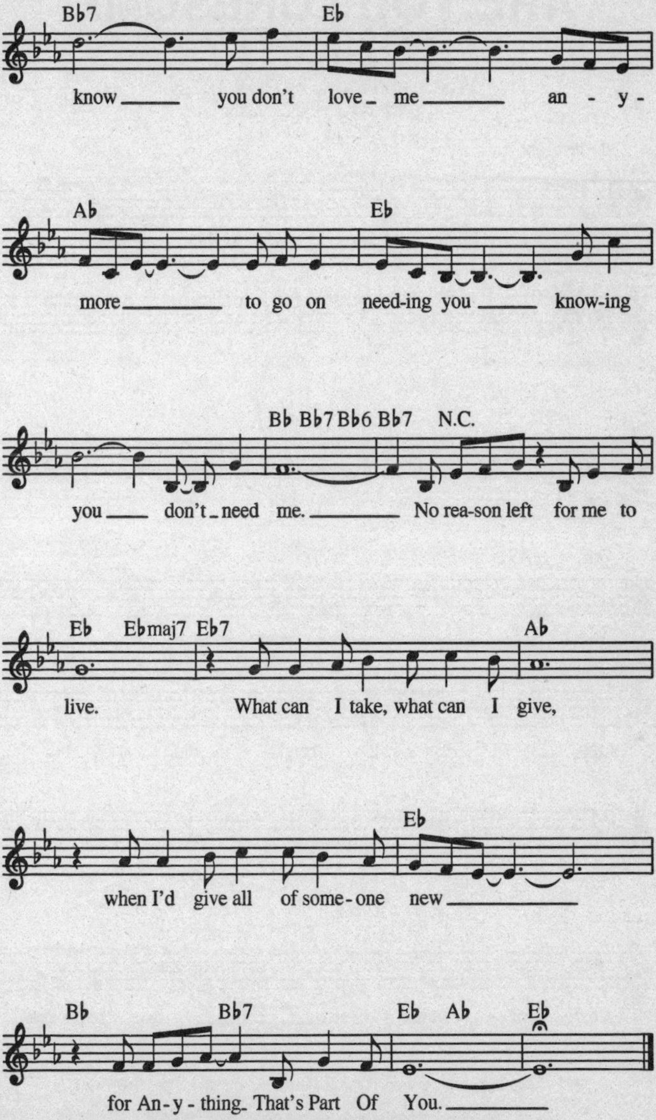
Bb7 Eb
know ___ you don't love _ me ___ an - y -
Ab Eb
more ___ to go on need-ing you ___ know-ing
Bb Bb7 Bb6 Bb7 N.C.
you ___ don't _ need me. ___ No rea-son left for me to
Eb Ebmaj7 Eb7 Ab
live. What can I take, what can I give,
Eb
when I'd give all of some-one new ___
Bb Bb7 Eb Ab Eb
for An-y - thing That's Part Of You. ___

ARE YOU LONESOME TONIGHT?

Words and Music by ROY TURK
and LOU HANDMAN

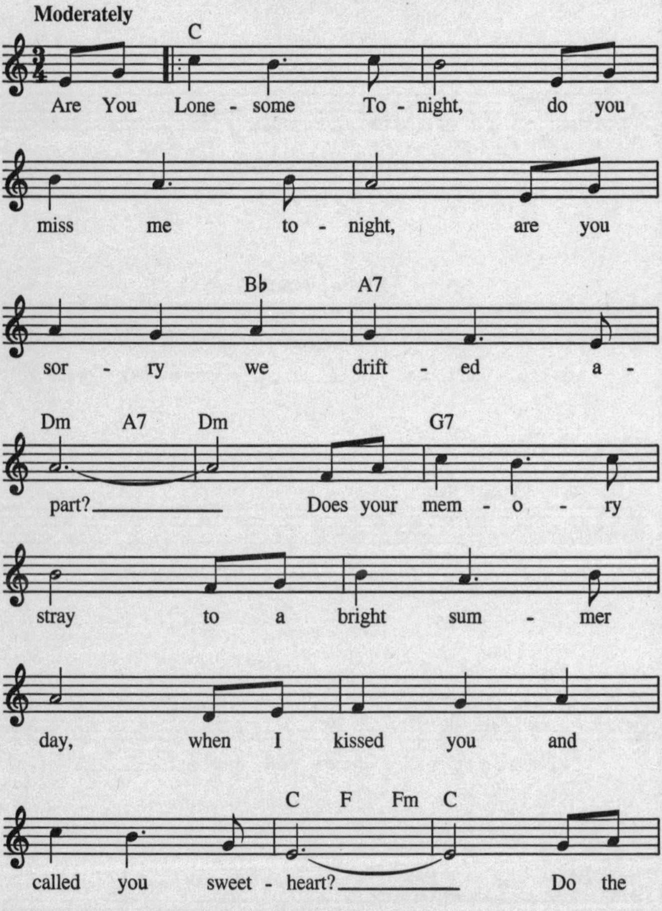
Moderately
C
Are You Lone - some To - night, do you
miss me to - night, are you
B♭ A7
sor - ry we drift - ed a -
Dm A7 Dm G7
part? Does your mem - o - ry
stray to a bright sum - mer
day, when I kissed you and
C F Fm C
called you sweet - heart? Do the

TRO - © Copyright 1926 (Renewed) Cromwell Music, Inc. and Bourne Co., New York, NY
International Copyright Secured
All Rights Reserved Including Public Performance For Profit
Used by Permission

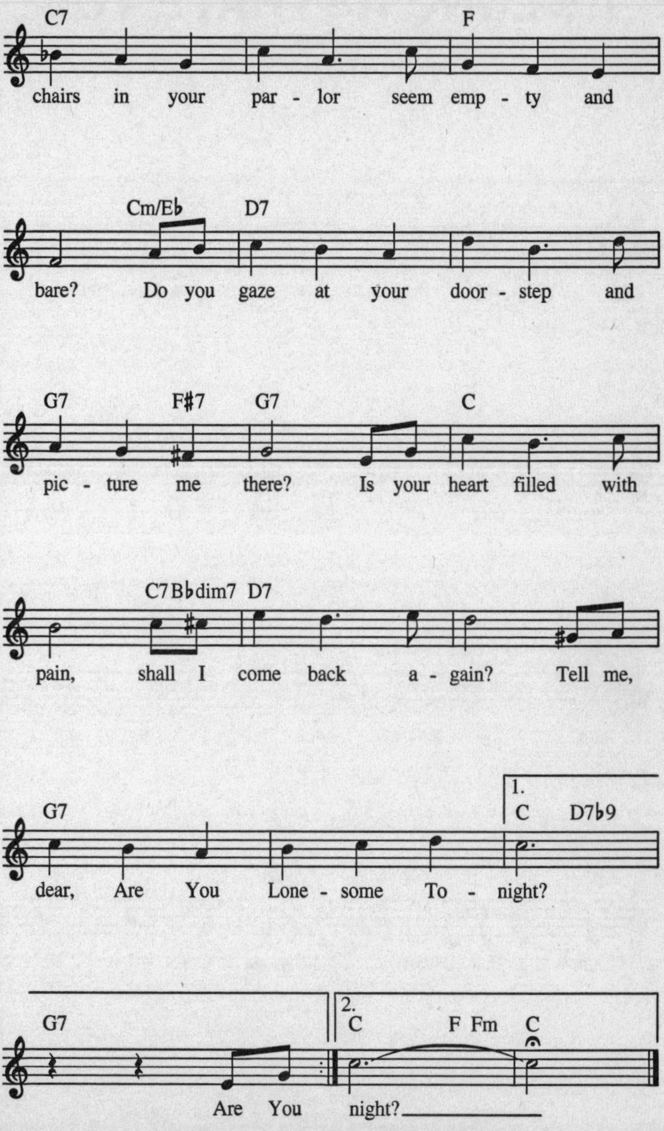
C7 F
chairs in your par - lor seem emp - ty and
Cm/E♭ D7
bare? Do you gaze at your door - step and
G7 F♯7 G7 C
pic - ture me there? Is your heart filled with
C7 B♭dim7 D7
pain, shall I come back a - gain? Tell me,
G7 1. C D7♭9
dear, Are You Lone - some To - night?
G7 2. C F Fm C
Are You night?

AS LONG AS I HAVE YOU

Words by FRED WISE
Music by BEN WEISMAN

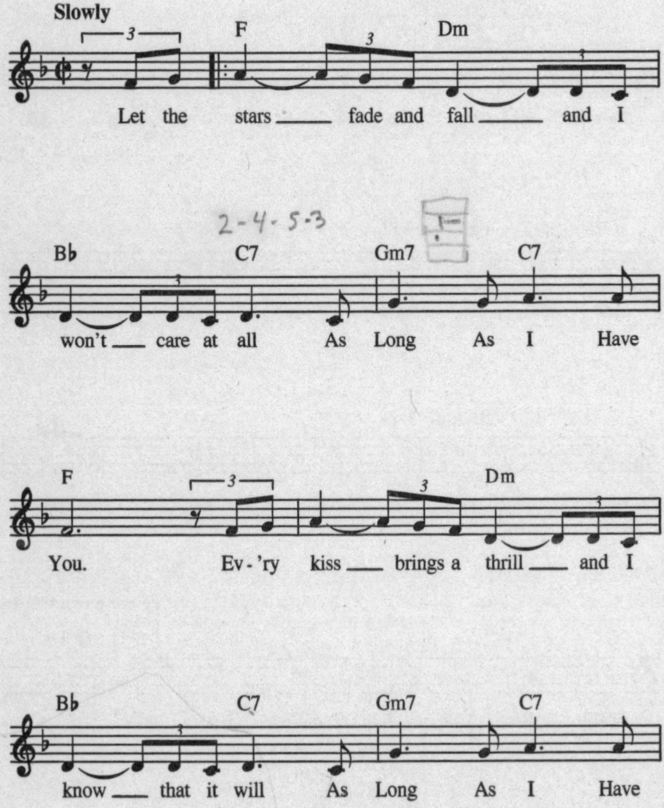
Slowly
F Dm
Let the stars fade and fall and I
Bb C7 Gm7 C7
won't care at all As Long As I Have
F Dm
You. Ev-'ry kiss brings a thrill and I
Bb C7 Gm7 C7
know that it will As Long As I Have

Copyright © 1958 Gladys Music, Inc.
Copyright Renewed, Assigned to Chappell & Co. and Erika Publishing
International Copyright Secured All Rights Reserved

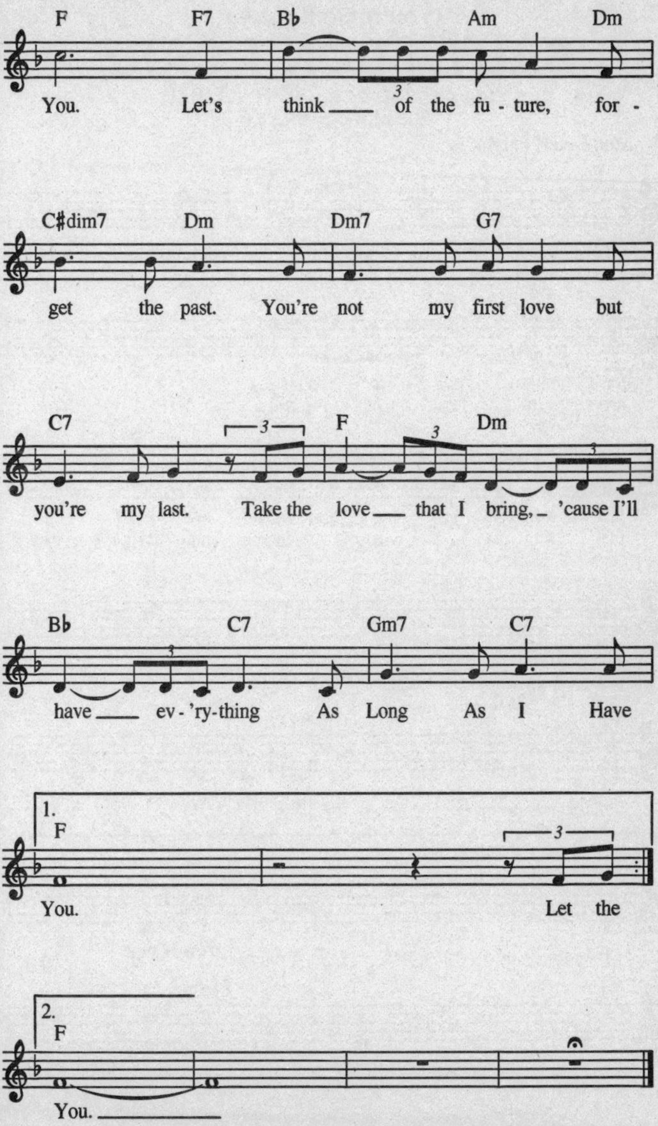
F F7 Bb Am Dm
You. Let's think of the fu - ture, for -
C#dim7 Dm Dm7 G7
get the past. You're not my first love but
C7 F Dm
you're my last. Take the love that I bring, 'cause I'll
Bb C7 Gm7 C7
have ev - 'ry-thing As Long As I Have
1.
F
You. Let the
2.
F
You.

(You're So Square)

BABY, I DON'T CARE

Words and Music by JERRY LEIBER
and MIKE STOLLER

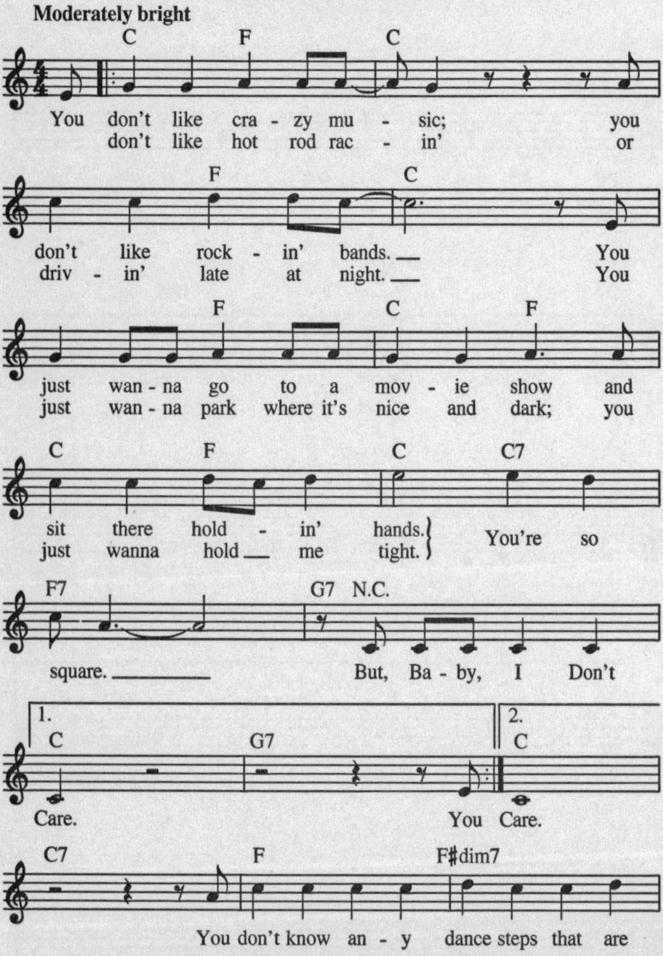
Moderately bright
C F C
You don't like cra - zy mu - sic; you
don't like hot rod rac - in' or
F C
don't like rock - in' bands. You
driv - in' late at night. You
F C F
just wan - na go to a mov - ie show and
just wan - na park where it's nice and dark; you
C F C C7
sit there hold - in' hands.
just wanna hold me tight.
You're so
F7 G7 N.C.
square. But, Ba - by, I Don't
1. C G7
Care. You
2. C
Care.
C7 F F♯dim7
You don't know an - y dance steps that are

© 1957 (Renewed) JERRY LEIBER MUSIC and MIKE STOLLER MUSIC
All Rights Reserved

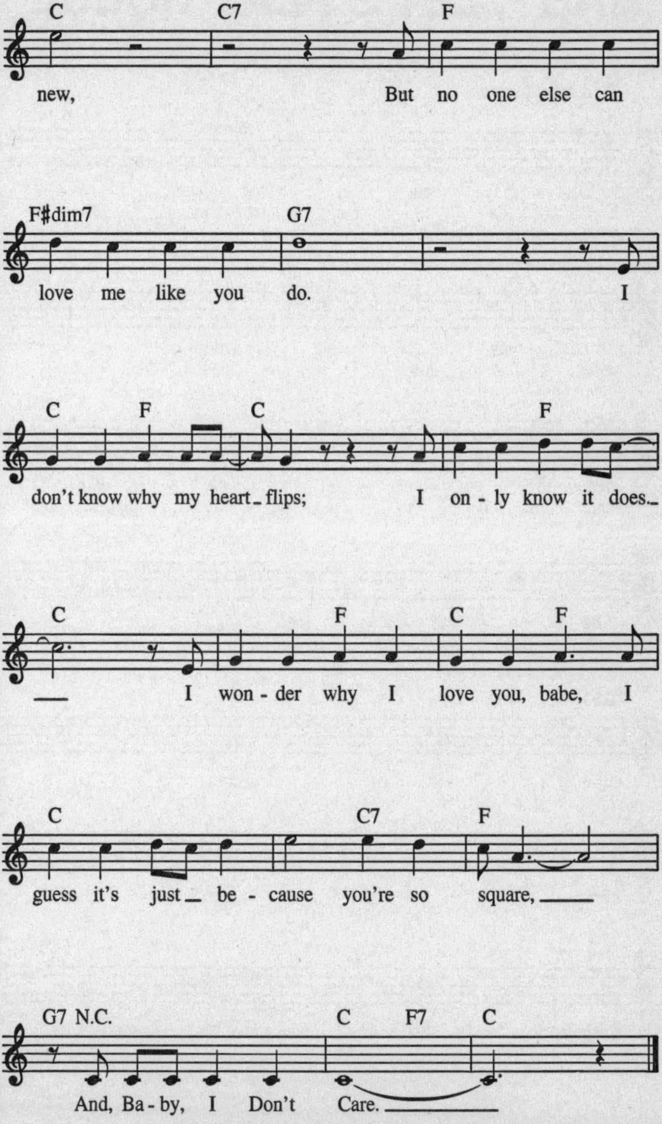
C C7 F
new, But no one else can
F#dim7 G7
love me like you do. I
C F C F
don't know why my heart _ flips; I on - ly know it does._
C F C F
__ I won - der why I love you, babe, I
C C7 F
guess it's just _ be - cause you're so square, ___
G7 N.C. C F7 C
And, Ba - by, I Don't Care. ___

BABY, LET'S PLAY HOUSE

Written by
ARTHUR GUNTER

In a solid four

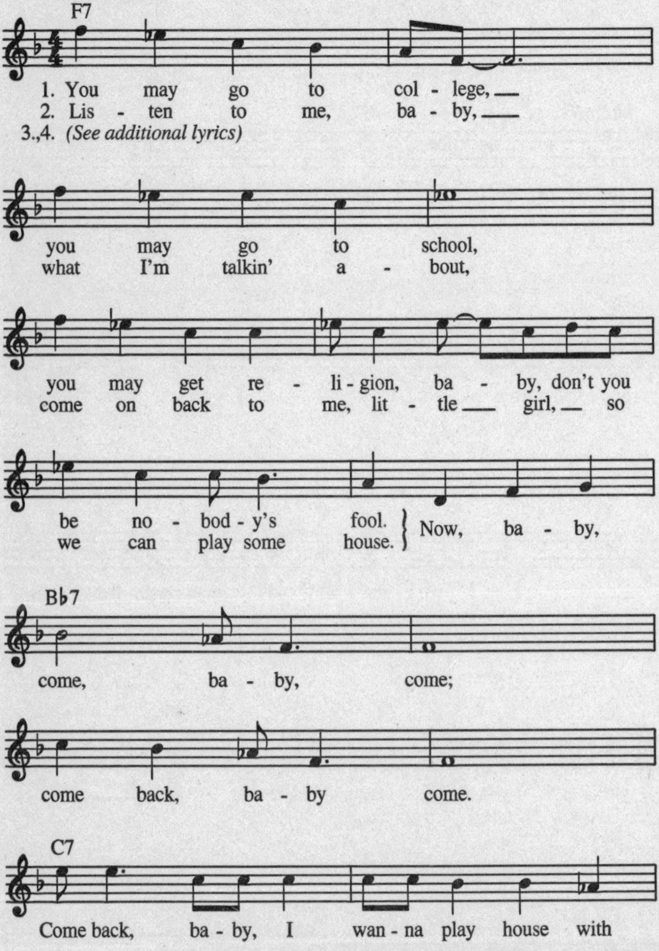
F7
1. You may go to col - lege, __
2. Lis - ten to me, ba - by, __
3.,4. (See additional lyrics)
you may go to school,
what I'm talkin' a - bout,
you may get re - li - gion, ba - by, don't you
come on back to me, lit - tle __ girl, __ so
be no - bod - y's fool.
we can play some house.
Now, ba - by,
B♭7
come, ba - by, come;
come back, ba - by come.
C7
Come back, ba - by, I wan - na play house with

Copyright © 1954 (Renewed) by Embassy Music Corporation (BMI)
and Excellorec Music, a division of AVI Music Publishing Group, Inc.
All Rights Administered Worldwide by Embassy Music Corporation
International Copyright Secured All Rights Reserved

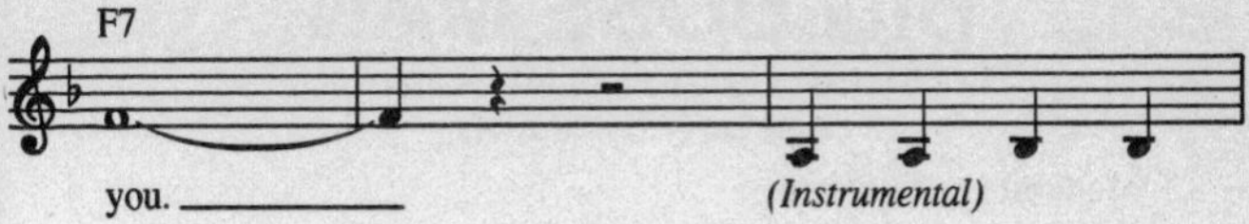
F7
you.
(Instrumental)

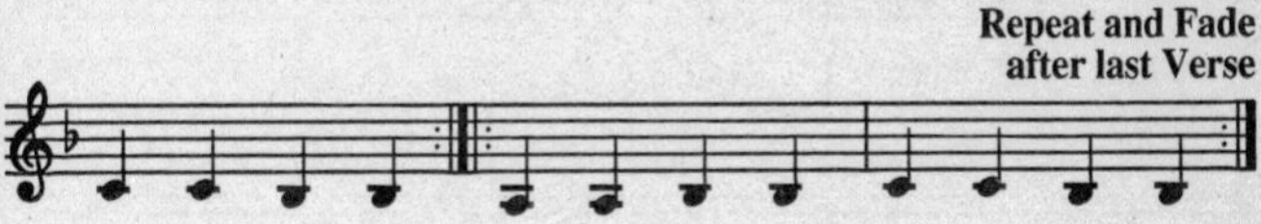
Repeat and Fade
after last Verse

Additional Lyrics

3. This is one thing, baby
   What I want you to know:
   Come on back and let's play a little house
   So we can do what we did before.
   Now, baby, come, *etc.*

4. Listen, I'm telling you, baby,
   Don't you understand?
   I'd rather see you dead, little girl,
   Than to be with another man.
   Now, baby, come, *etc.*

BIG BOSS MAN

Words and Music by AL SMITH
and LUTHER DIXON

Moderate Rock tempo

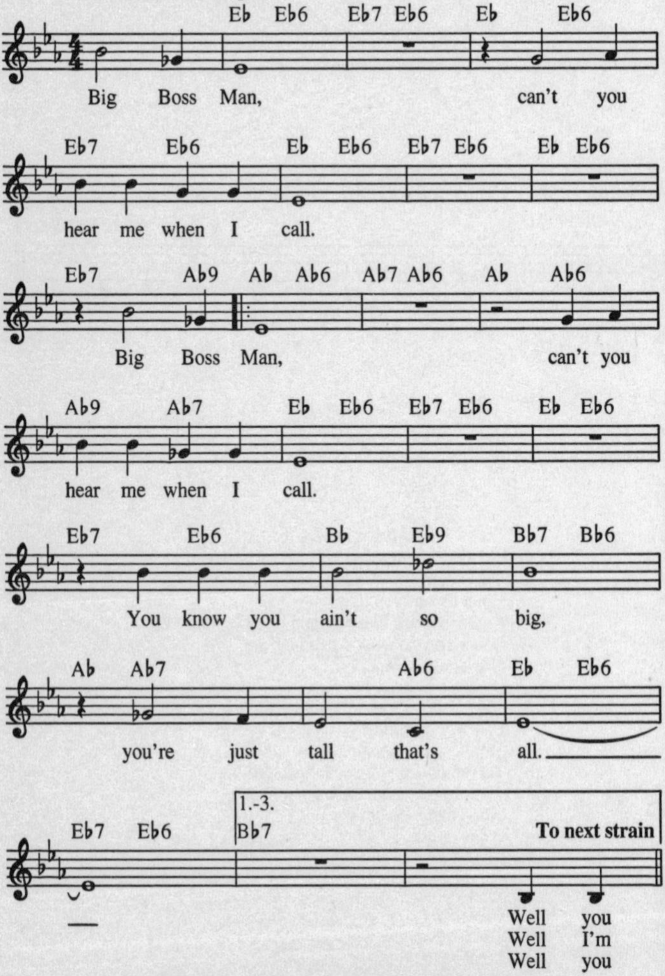
Eb Eb6 Eb7 Eb6 Eb Eb6
Big Boss Man, can't you
Eb7 Eb6 Eb Eb6 Eb7 Eb6 Eb Eb6
hear me when I call.
Eb7 Ab9 Ab Ab6 Ab7 Ab6 Ab Ab6
Big Boss Man, can't you
Ab9 Ab7 Eb Eb6 Eb7 Eb6 Eb Eb6
hear me when I call.
Eb7 Eb6 Bb Eb9 Bb7 Bb6
You know you ain't so big,
Ab Ab7 Ab6 Eb Eb6
you're just tall that's all.
Eb7 Eb6
1.-3.
Bb7
To next strain
Well you
Well I'm
Well you

Copyright © 1960, 1967 by Conrad Music, a division of Arc Music Corp.
Copyright Renewed
International Copyright Secured All Rights Reserved

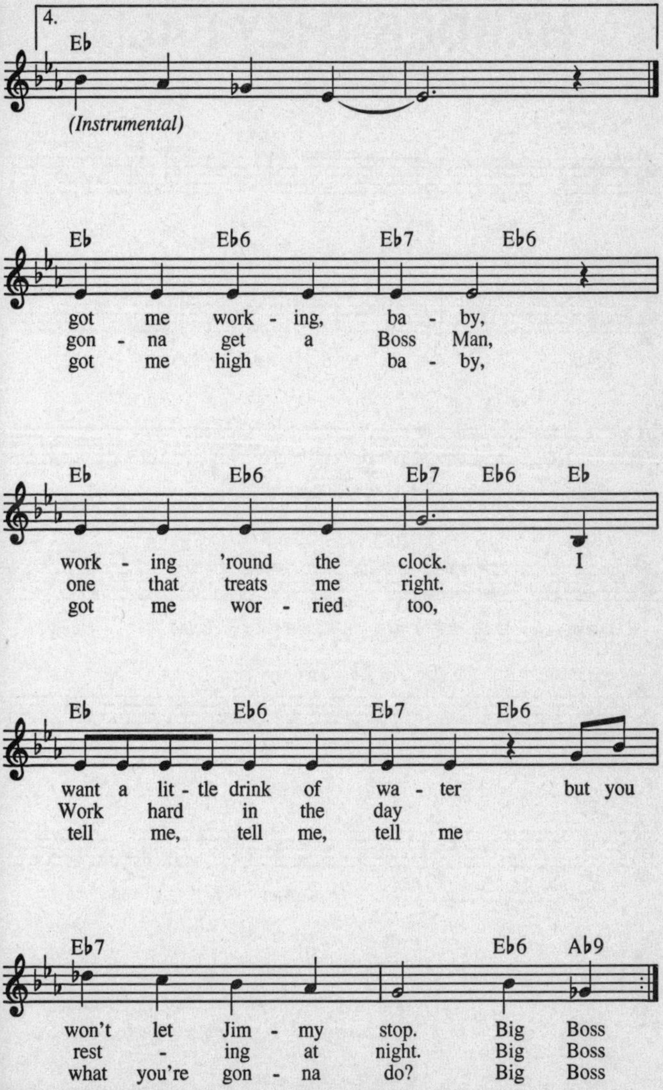
4.
Eb
(Instrumental)
Eb Eb6 Eb7 Eb6
got me work - ing, ba - by,
gon - na get a Boss Man,
got me high ba - by,
Eb Eb6 Eb7 Eb6 Eb
work - ing 'round the clock. I
one that treats me right.
got me wor - ried too,
Eb Eb6 Eb7 Eb6
want a lit - tle drink of wa - ter but you
Work hard in the day
tell me, tell me, tell me
Eb7 Eb6 Ab9
won't let Jim - my stop. Big Boss
rest - ing at night. Big Boss
what you're gon - na do? Big Boss

BITTER THEY ARE, HARDER THEY FALL

Words and Music by
LARRY GATLIN

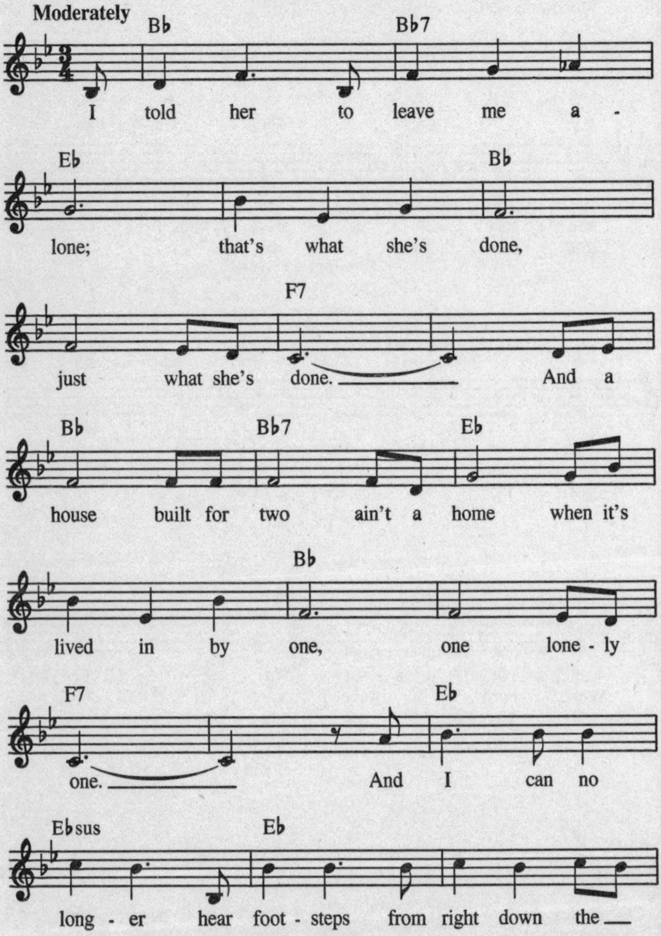
Moderately
Bb Bb7
I told her to leave me a -
Eb Bb
lone; that's what she's done,
F7
just what she's done. And a
Bb Bb7 Eb
house built for two ain't a home when it's
Bb
lived in by one, one lone - ly
F7 Eb
one. And I can no
Ebsus Eb
long - er hear foot - steps from right down the

© 1973 TEMI COMBINE INC.
All Rights Controlled by COMBINE MUSIC CORP. and Administered by EMI BLACKWOOD MUSIC INC.
All Rights Reserved International Copyright Secured Used by Permission

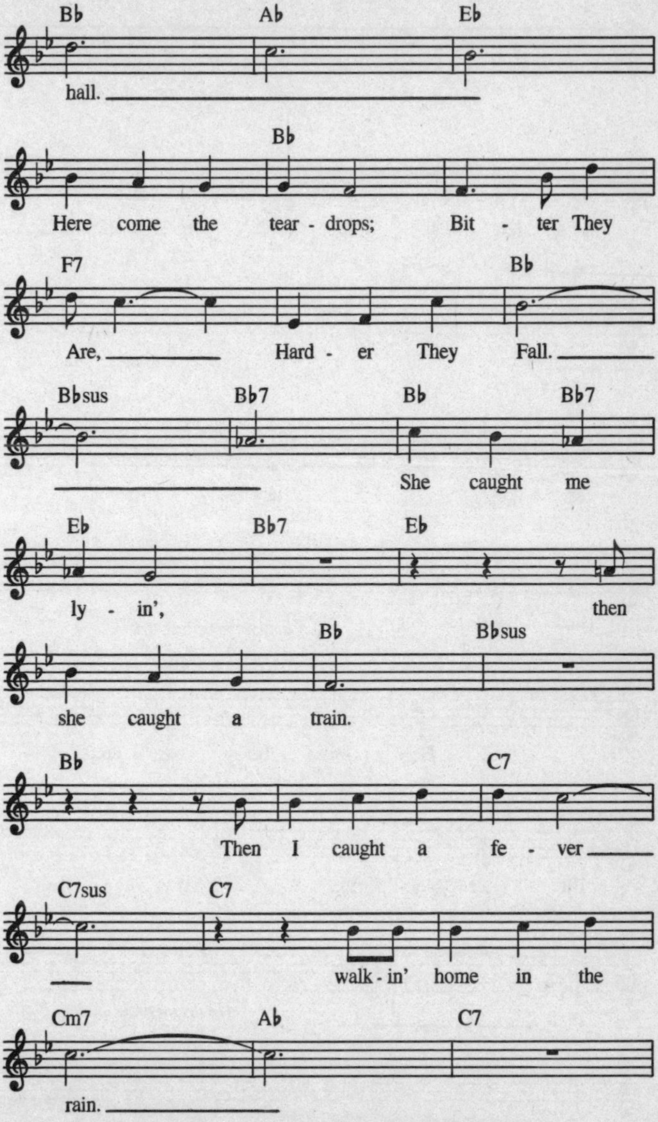
B♭ A♭ E♭
hall.
B♭
Here come the tear - drops; Bit - ter They
F7 B♭
Are, Hard - er They Fall.
B♭sus B♭7 B♭ B♭7
She caught me
E♭ B♭7 E♭
ly - in', then
B♭ B♭sus
she caught a train.
B♭ C7
Then I caught a fe - ver
C7sus C7
walk - in' home in the
Cm7 A♭ C7
rain.

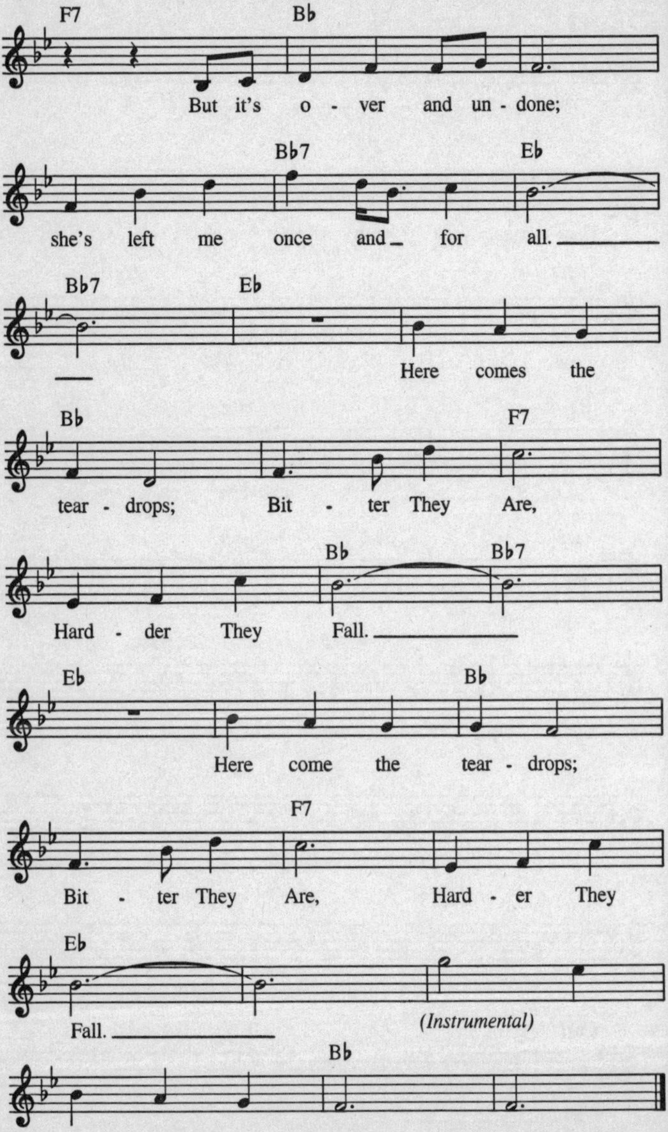
F7
Bb
But it's o - ver and un - done;
Bb7
Eb
she's left me once and for all.
Bb7
Eb
Here comes the
Bb
F7
tear - drops; Bit - ter They Are,
Bb
Bb7
Hard - der They Fall.
Eb
Bb
Here come the tear - drops;
F7
Bit - ter They Are, Hard - er They
Eb
Fall.
(Instrumental)
Bb

BLUE MOON OF KENTUCKY

Words and Music by
BILL MONROE

Bright Jump tempo

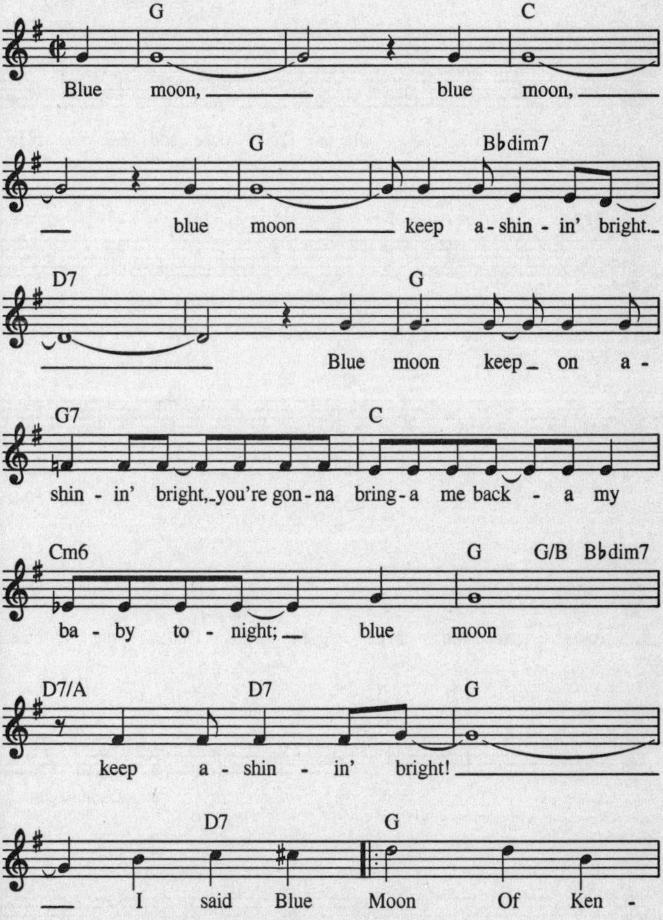
G C
Blue moon, blue moon,
G B♭dim7
blue moon keep a-shin-in' bright.
D7 G
Blue moon keep on a-
G7 C
shin-in' bright, you're gon-na bring-a me back-a my
Cm6 G G/B B♭dim7
ba-by to-night; blue moon
D7/A D7 G
keep a-shin-in' bright!
D7 G
I said Blue Moon Of Ken-

Copyright © 1947 by Peer International Corporation
Copyright Renewed
All Rights Reserved Used by Permission

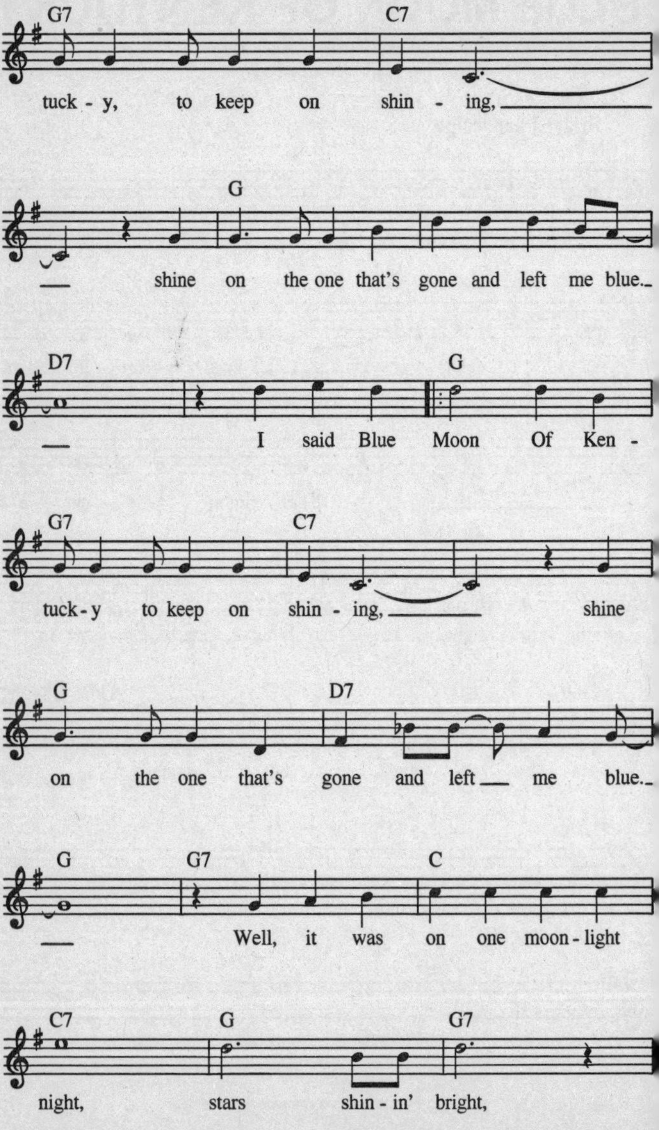
G7 C7
tuck - y, to keep on shin - ing,
G
shine on the one that's gone and left me blue.
D7 G
I said Blue Moon Of Ken -
G7 C7
tuck - y to keep on shin - ing,
shine
G D7
on the one that's gone and left me blue.
G G7 C
Well, it was on one moon - light
C7 G G7
night, stars shin - in' bright,

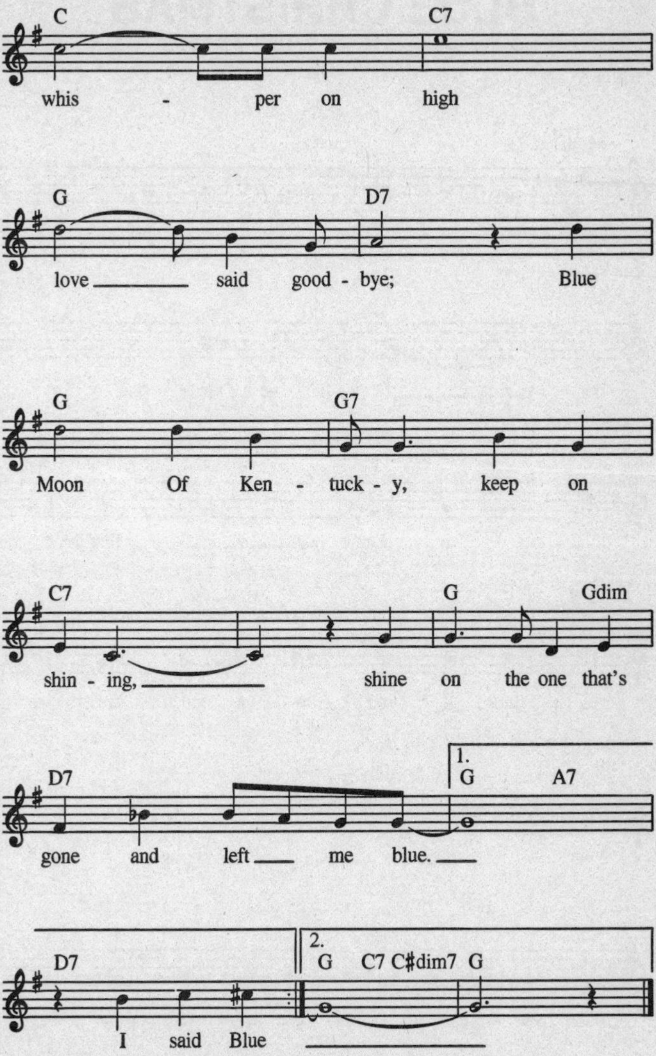

C
C7
whis - per on high
G
D7
love said good - bye; Blue
G
G7
Moon Of Ken - tuck - y, keep on
C7
G
Gdim
shin - ing, shine on the one that's
D7
1.
G
A7
gone and left me blue.
D7
I said Blue
2.
G C7 C#dim7 G

BLUE CHRISTMAS

Words and Music by BILLY HAYES
and JAY JOHNSON

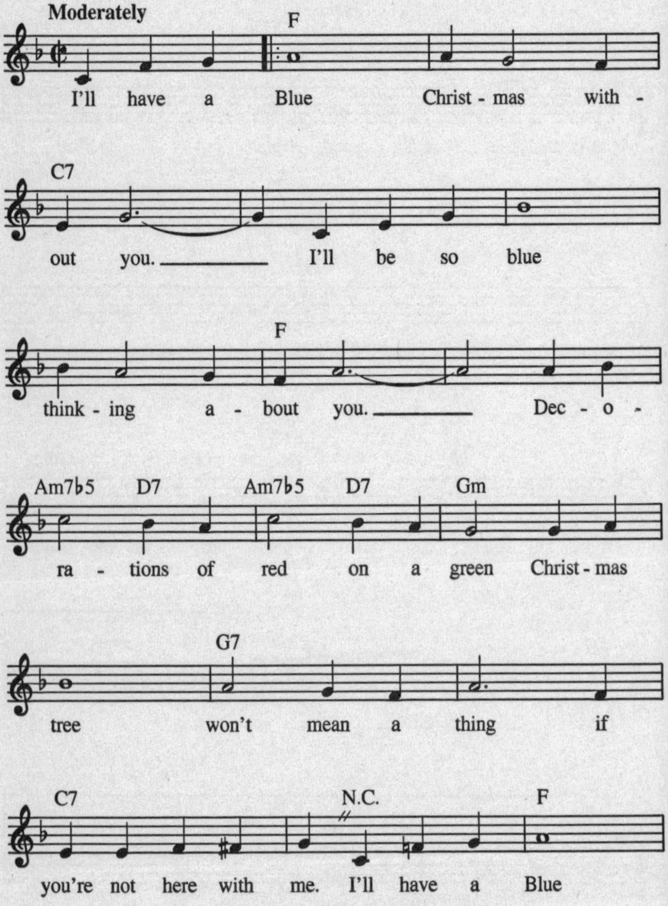
Moderately
F
I'll have a Blue Christ - mas with -
C7
out you. I'll be so blue
F
think - ing a - bout you. Dec - o -
Am7♭5 D7 Am7♭5 D7 Gm
ra - tions of red on a green Christ - mas
G7
tree won't mean a thing if
C7 N.C. F
you're not here with me. I'll have a Blue

Copyright © 1948 PolyGram International Publishing, Inc.
Copyright Renewed
International Copyright Secured All Rights Reserved

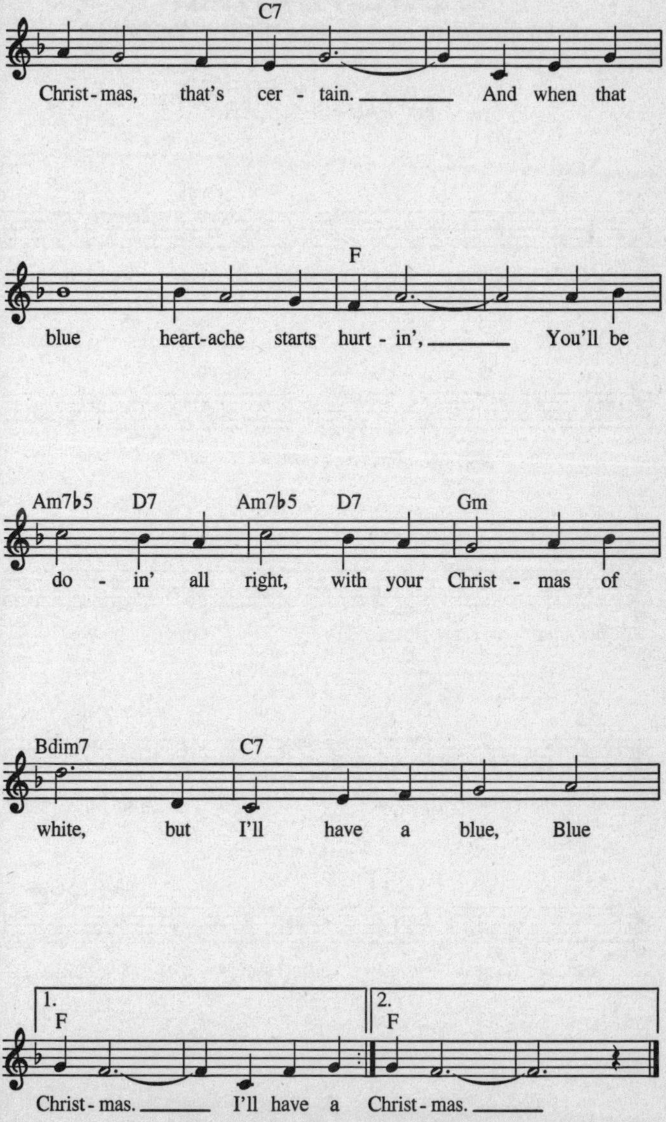
C7
Christ-mas, that's cer - tain. ___ And when that
F
blue heart-ache starts hurt - in', ___ You'll be
Am7♭5 D7 Am7♭5 D7 Gm
do - in' all right, with your Christ - mas of
Bdim7 C7
white, but I'll have a blue, Blue
1. F
Christ-mas. ___ I'll have a
2. F
Christ-mas. ___

BLUE HAWAII

from the Paramount Picture WAIKIKI WEDDING

Words and Music by LEO ROBIN
and RALPH RAINGER

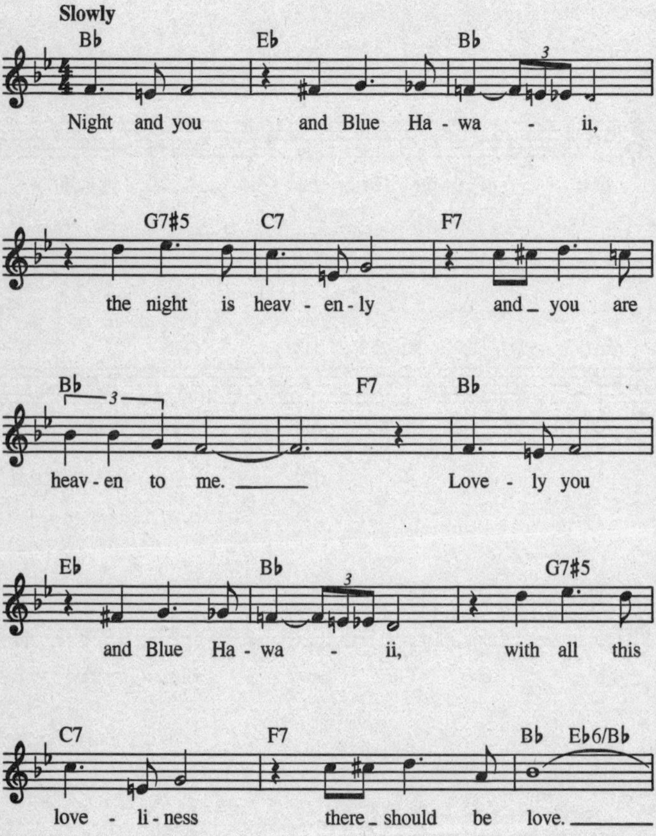
Slowly
Bb Eb Bb
Night and you and Blue Ha - wa - ii,
G7#5 C7 F7
the night is heav - en - ly and _ you are
Bb F7 Bb
heav - en to me. _______ Love - ly you
Eb Bb G7#5
and Blue Ha - wa - ii, with all this
C7 F7 Bb Eb6/Bb
love - li - ness there _ should be love. _______

Copyright © 1936, 1937 (Renewed 1963, 1964) by Famous Music Corporation
International Copyright Secured All Rights Reserved

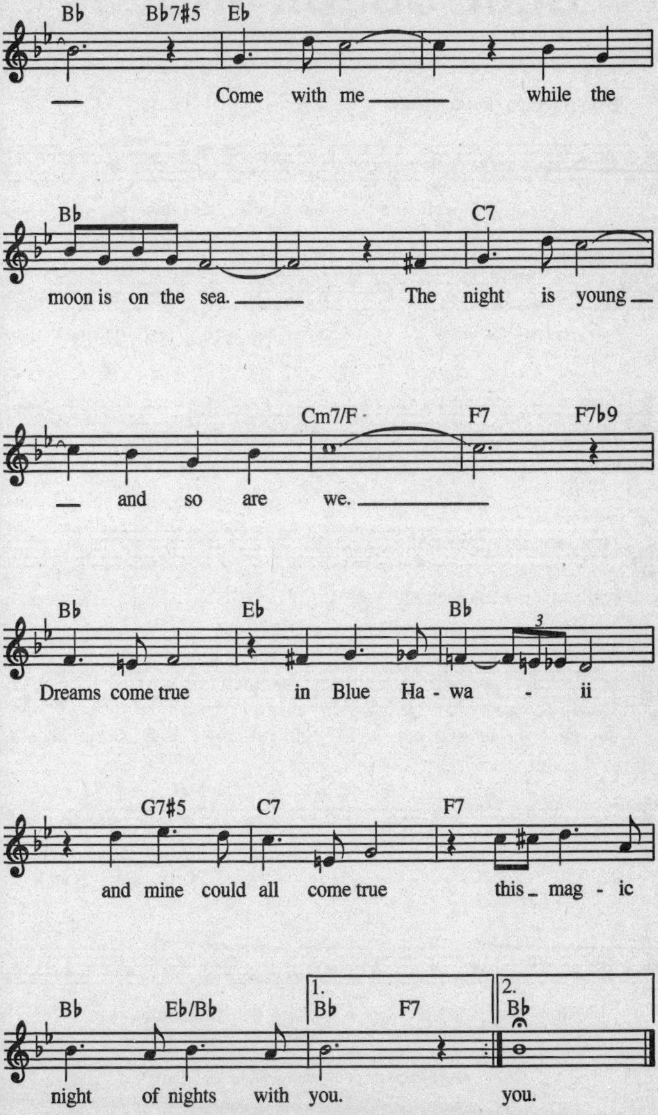
Bb Bb7#5 Eb
Come with me while the
Bb C7
moon is on the sea. The night is young
Cm7/F F7 F7b9
and so are we.
Bb Eb Bb
Dreams come true in Blue Ha - wa - ii
G7#5 C7 F7
and mine could all come true this magic
Bb Eb/Bb
night of nights with you.
1. Bb F7
2. Bb
you.

BLUE SUEDE SHOES

Words and Music by
CARL LEE PERKINS

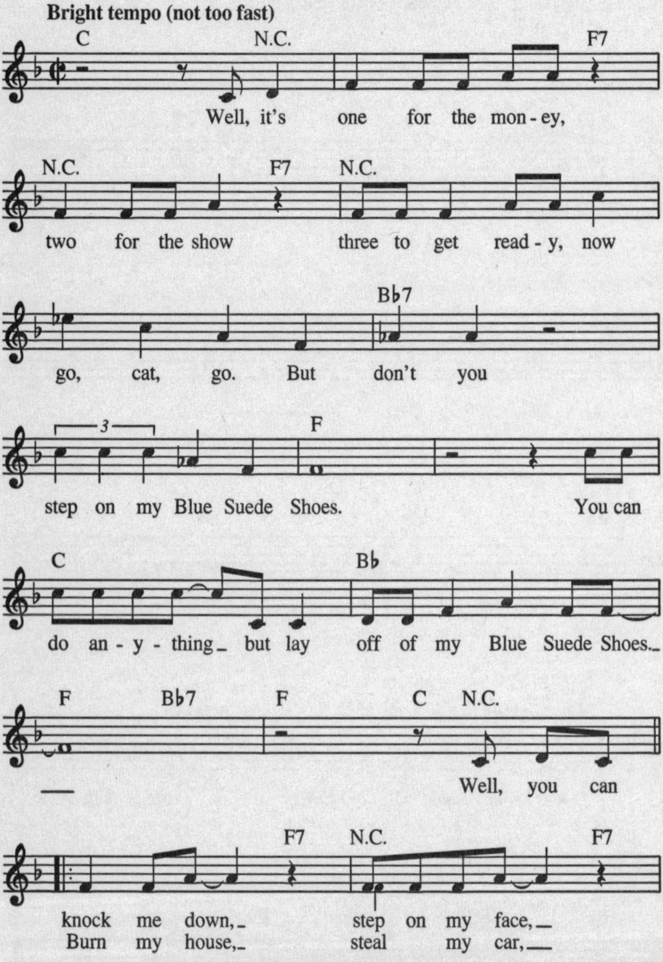
Bright tempo (not too fast)
C N.C. F7
Well, it's one for the mon - ey,
N.C. F7 N.C.
two for the show three to get read - y, now
Bb7
go, cat, go. But don't you
3
F
step on my Blue Suede Shoes. You can
C Bb
do an - y - thing but lay off of my Blue Suede Shoes.
F Bb7 F C N.C.
Well, you can
F7 N.C. F7
knock me down, step on my face,
Burn my house, steal my car,

Copyright © 1955 by Carl Perkins Music, Inc.
Copyright Renewed
All Rights Administered by Unichappell Music Inc.
International Copyright Secured All Rights Reserved

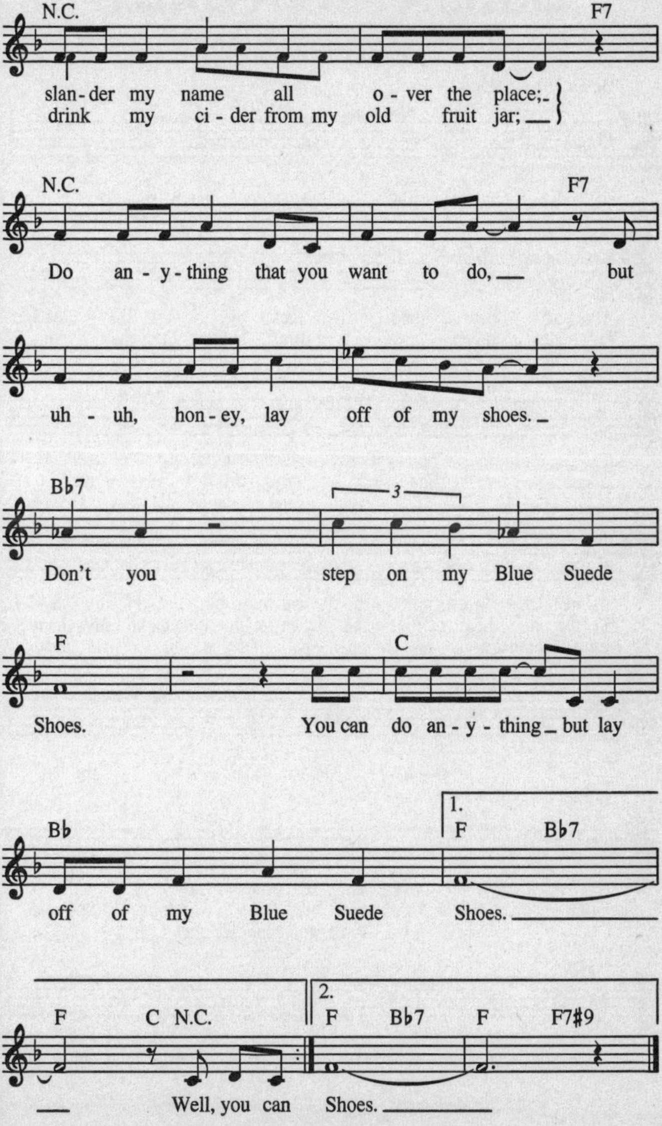
N.C.
F7
slan-der my name all o-ver the place;
drink my ci-der from my old fruit jar;
N.C.
F7
Do an-y-thing that you want to do, but
uh-uh, hon-ey, lay off of my shoes.
Bb7
3
Don't you step on my Blue Suede
F
C
Shoes. You can do an-y-thing but lay
Bb
1.
F
Bb7
off of my Blue Suede Shoes.
F
C
N.C.
Well, you can
2.
F
Bb7
F
F7#9
Shoes.

BOSSA NOVA BABY

Words and Music by JERRY LEIBER
and MIKE STOLLER

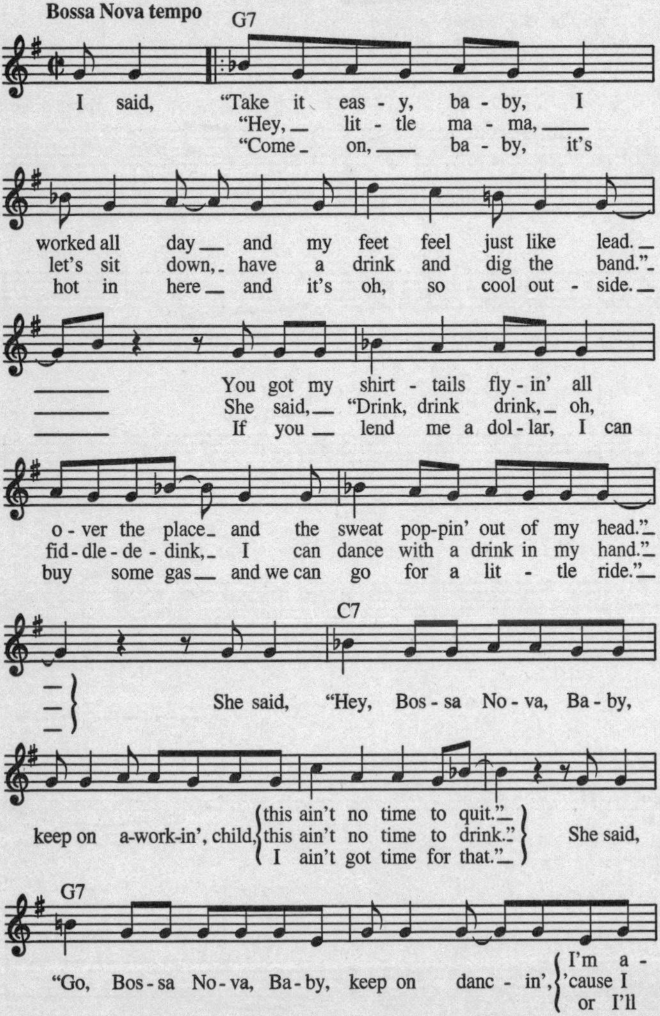
Bossa Nova tempo
G7
I said, "Take it easy, baby, I worked all day and my feet feel just like lead. You got my shirt-tails fly-in' all o-ver the place and the sweat pop-pin' out of my head."
"Hey, lit-tle ma-ma, let's sit down, have a drink and dig the band." She said, "Drink, drink drink, oh, fid-dle-de-dink, I can dance with a drink in my hand."
"Come on, ba-by, it's hot in here and it's oh, so cool out-side. If you lend me a dol-lar, I can buy some gas and we can go for a lit-tle ride."
C7
She said, "Hey, Bos-sa No-va, Ba-by, keep on a-work-in', child,
this ain't no time to quit."
this ain't no time to drink."
I ain't got time for that."
She said,
G7
"Go, Bos-sa No-va, Ba-by, keep on danc-in',
I'm a-
'cause I
or I'll

© 1962 (Renewed) JERRY LEIBER MUSIC and MIKE STOLLER MUSIC
All Rights Reserved

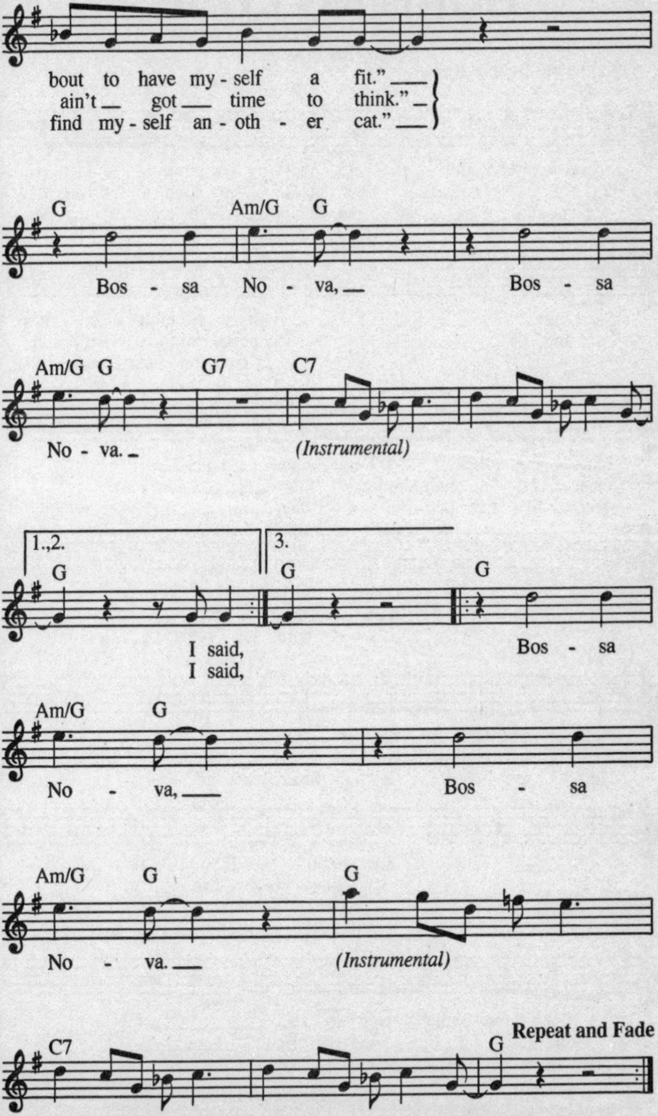
bout to have my - self a fit." ___
ain't ___ got ___ time to think." ___
find my - self an - oth - er cat." ___
G Am/G G
Bos - sa No - va, ___ Bos - sa
Am/G G G7 C7
No - va. ___ (Instrumental)
1.,2.
3.
G G G
I said,
I said,
Bos - sa
Am/G G
No - va, ___ Bos - sa
Am/G G G
No - va. ___ (Instrumental)
Repeat and Fade
C7 G

BURNING LOVE

Words and Music by
DENNIS LINDE

Moderate Boogie-Rock

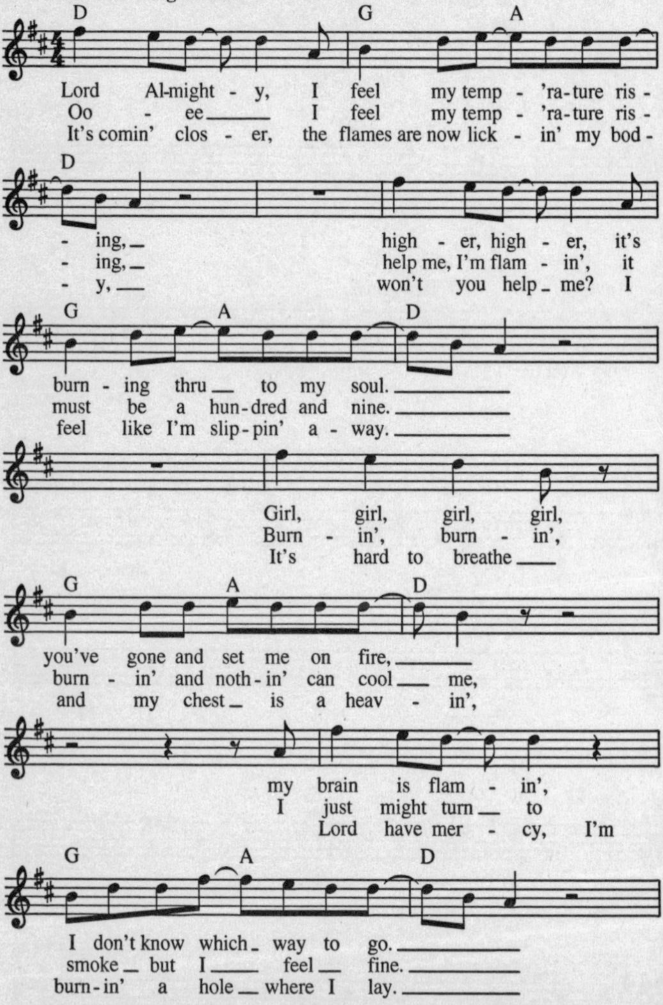
D G A
Lord Al-might - y, I feel my temp - 'ra-ture ris -
Oo - ee ___ I feel my temp - 'ra-ture ris -
It's comin' clos - er, the flames are now lick - in' my bod -
D
- ing, ___ high - er, high - er, it's
- ing, ___ help me, I'm flam - in', it
- y, ___ won't you help _ me? I
G A D
burn - ing thru ___ to my soul. ___
must be a hun-dred and nine. ___
feel like I'm slip-pin' a - way. ___
Girl, girl, girl, girl,
Burn - in', burn - in',
It's hard to breathe ___
G A D
you've gone and set me on fire, ___
burn - in' and noth-in' can cool ___ me,
and my chest _ is a heav - in',
my brain is flam - in',
I just might turn ___ to
Lord have mer - cy, I'm
G A D
I don't know which _ way to go. ___
smoke _ but I ___ feel ___ fine. ___
burn-in' a hole _ where I lay. ___

© 1972 TEMI COMBINE INC.
All Rights Controlled by COMBINE MUSIC CORP. and Administered by EMI BLACKWOOD MUSIC INC.
All Rights Reserved International Copyright Secured Used by Permission

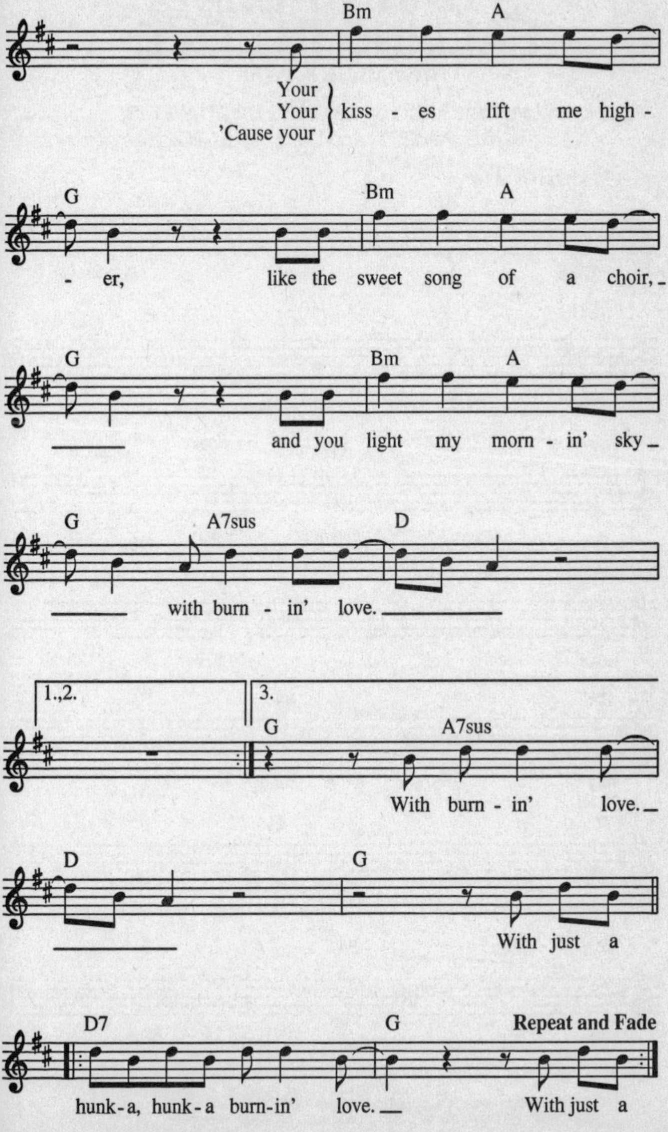
Bm A G Bm A G Bm A G A7sus D
Your / Your / 'Cause your kiss - es lift me high - - er, like the sweet song of a choir, and you light my morn - in' sky with burn - in' love.
1.,2.
3.
G A7sus D G
With burn - in' love. With just a
D7 G
Repeat and Fade
hunk-a, hunk-a burn-in' love. With just a

CAN'T HELP FALLING IN LOVE

from BLUE HAWAII

Words and Music by GEORGE DAVID WEISS, HUGO PERETTI and LUIGI CREATORE

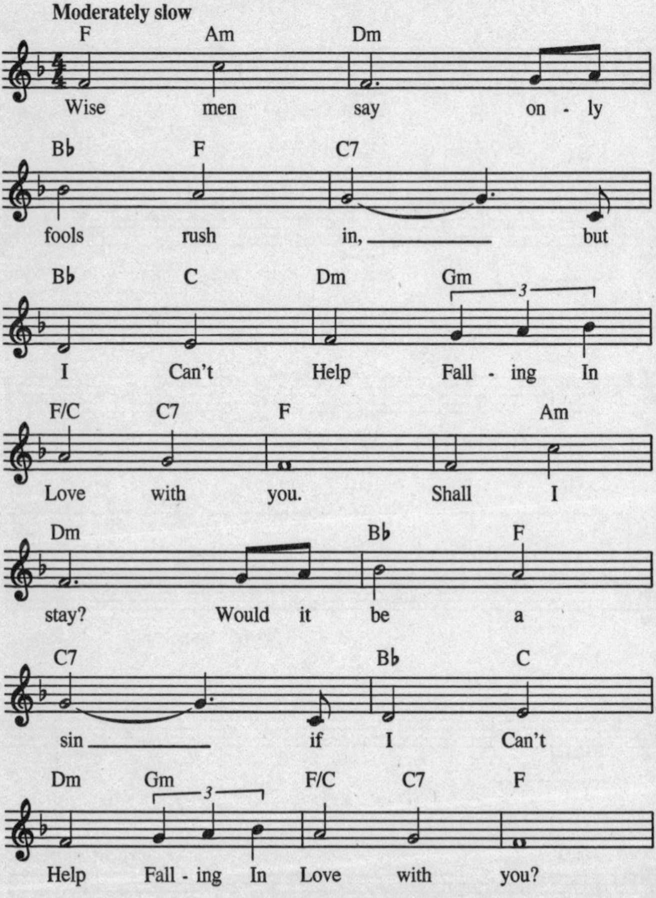
Moderately slow
F Am Dm
Wise men say on - ly
B♭ F C7
fools rush in, but
B♭ C Dm Gm
I Can't Help Fall - ing In
F/C C7 F Am
Love with you. Shall I
Dm B♭ F
stay? Would it be a
C7 B♭ C
sin if I Can't
Dm Gm F/C C7 F
Help Fall - ing In Love with you?

Copyright © 1961 by Gladys Music, Inc.
Copyright Renewed and Assigned to Gladys Music (Administered by Williamson Music)
International Copyright Secured All Rights Reserved

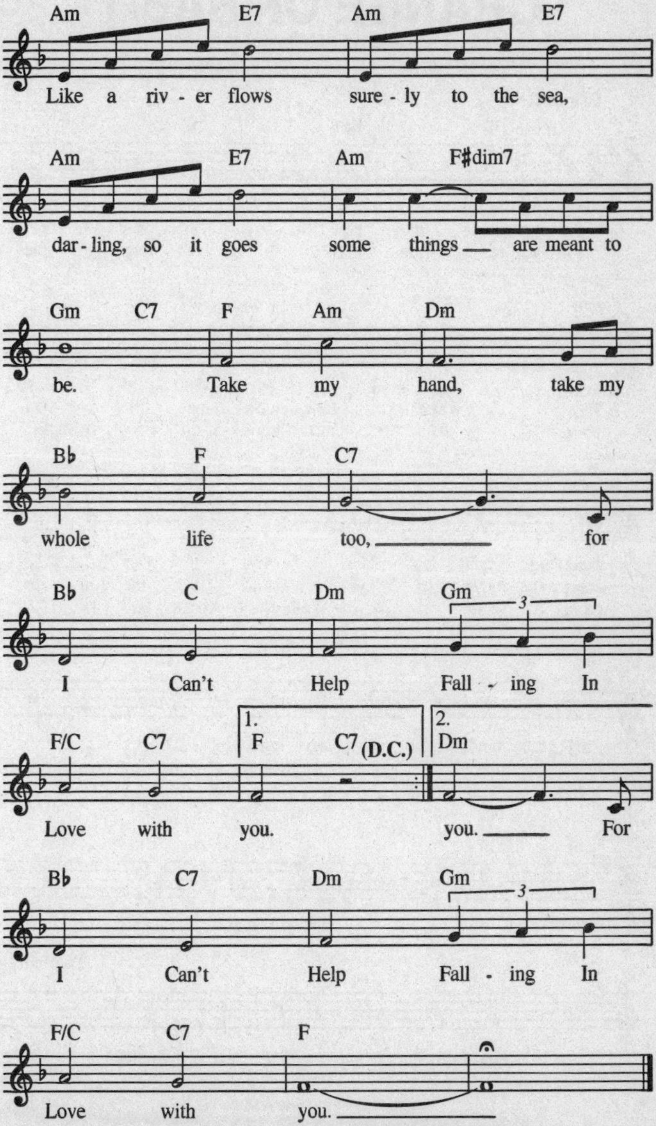
Am E7 Am E7
Like a riv - er flows sure - ly to the sea,
Am E7 Am F#dim7
dar - ling, so it goes some things are meant to
Gm C7 F Am Dm
be. Take my hand, take my
B♭ F C7
whole life too, for
B♭ C Dm Gm
3
I Can't Help Fall - ing In
1. 2.
F/C C7 F C7 (D.C.) Dm
Love with you. you. For
B♭ C7 Dm Gm
3
I Can't Help Fall - ing In
F/C C7 F
Love with you.

CHANGE OF HABIT

Words by BUDDY KAYE
Music by BEN WEISMAN

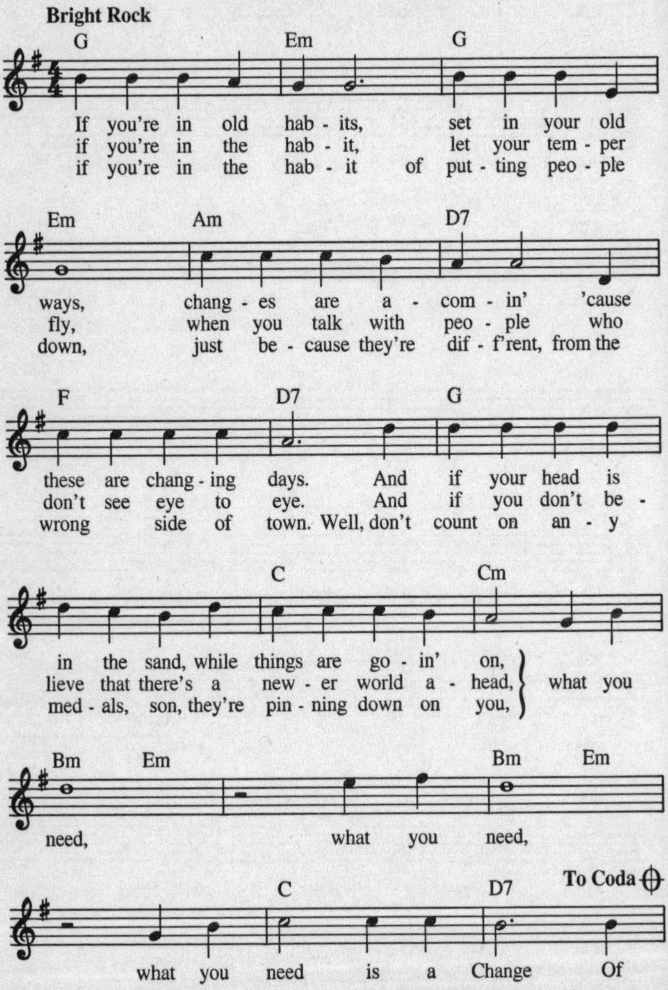
Bright Rock
G
Em
G
If you're in old hab - its, set in your old
if you're in the hab - it, let your tem - per
if you're in the hab - it of put - ting peo - ple
Em
Am
D7
ways, chang - es are a - com - in' 'cause
fly, when you talk with peo - ple who
down, just be - cause they're dif - f'rent, from the
F
D7
G
these are chang - ing days. And if your head is
don't see eye to eye. And if you don't be -
wrong side of town. Well, don't count on an - y
C
Cm
in the sand, while things are go - in' on,
lieve that there's a new - er world a - head,
med - als, son, they're pin - ning down on you,
what you
Bm
Em
Bm
Em
need, what you need,
C
D7
To Coda
what you need is a Change Of

Copyright © 1970 by Gladys Music, Inc.
Copyright Assigned to Gladys Music (Administered by Williamson Music)
International Copyright Secured All Rights Reserved

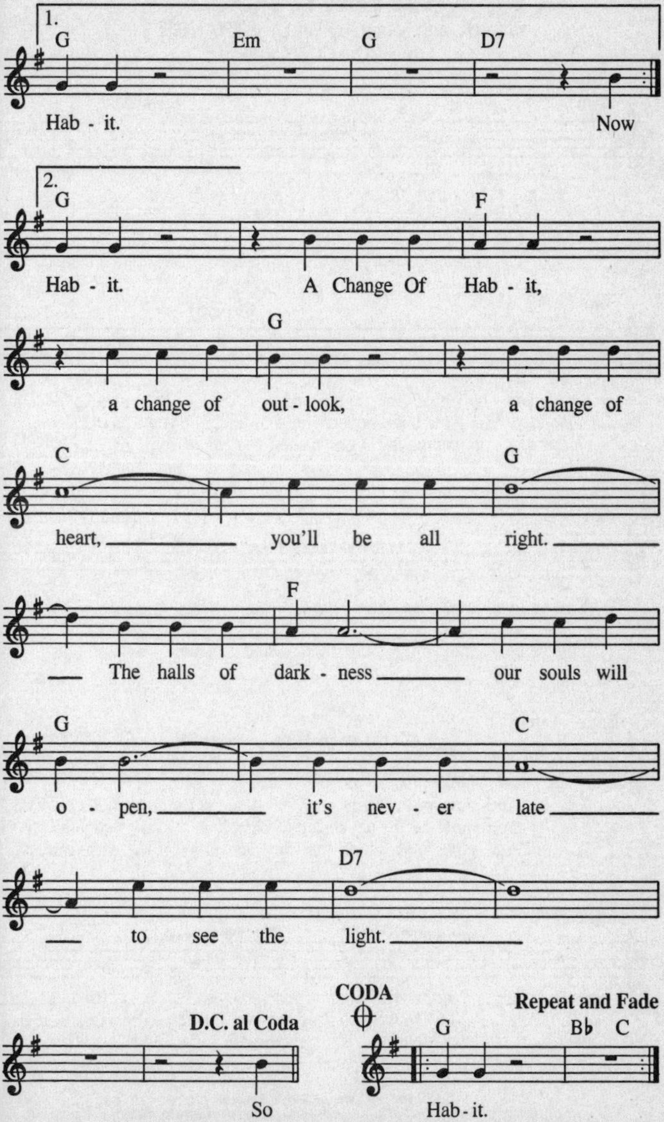
1.
G Em G D7
Hab - it. Now
2.
G F
Hab - it. A Change Of Hab - it,
G
a change of out - look, a change of
C G
heart, you'll be all right.
F
The halls of dark - ness our souls will
G C
o - pen, it's nev - er late
D7
to see the light.
D.C. al Coda
So
CODA
Repeat and Fade
G B♭ C
Hab - it.

CHARRO

Words and Music by BILLY STRANGE
and SCOTT DAVIS

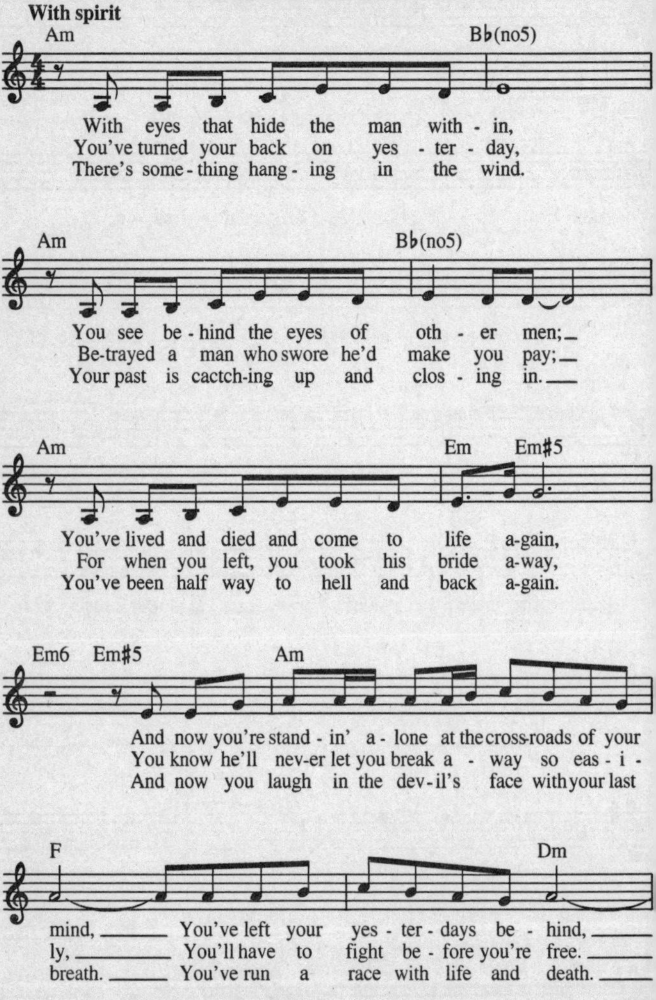
With spirit
Am
Bb(no5)
With eyes that hide the man with - in,
You've turned your back on yes - ter - day,
There's some - thing hang - ing in the wind.
Am
Bb(no5)
You see be - hind the eyes of oth - er men;
Be-trayed a man who swore he'd make you pay;
Your past is cactch-ing up and clos - ing in.
Am
Em
Em#5
You've lived and died and come to life a-gain,
For when you left, you took his bride a-way,
You've been half way to hell and back a-gain.
Em6
Em#5
Am
And now you're stand - in' a - lone at the cross-roads of your
You know he'll nev-er let you break a - way so eas - i -
And now you laugh in the dev - il's face with your last
F
Dm
mind, You've left your yes - ter - days be - hind,
ly, You'll have to fight be - fore you're free.
breath. You've run a race with life and death.

Copyright © 1969 by Gladys Music, Inc.
Copyright Assigned to Gladys Music (Administered by Williamson Music)
International Copyright Secured All Rights Reserved

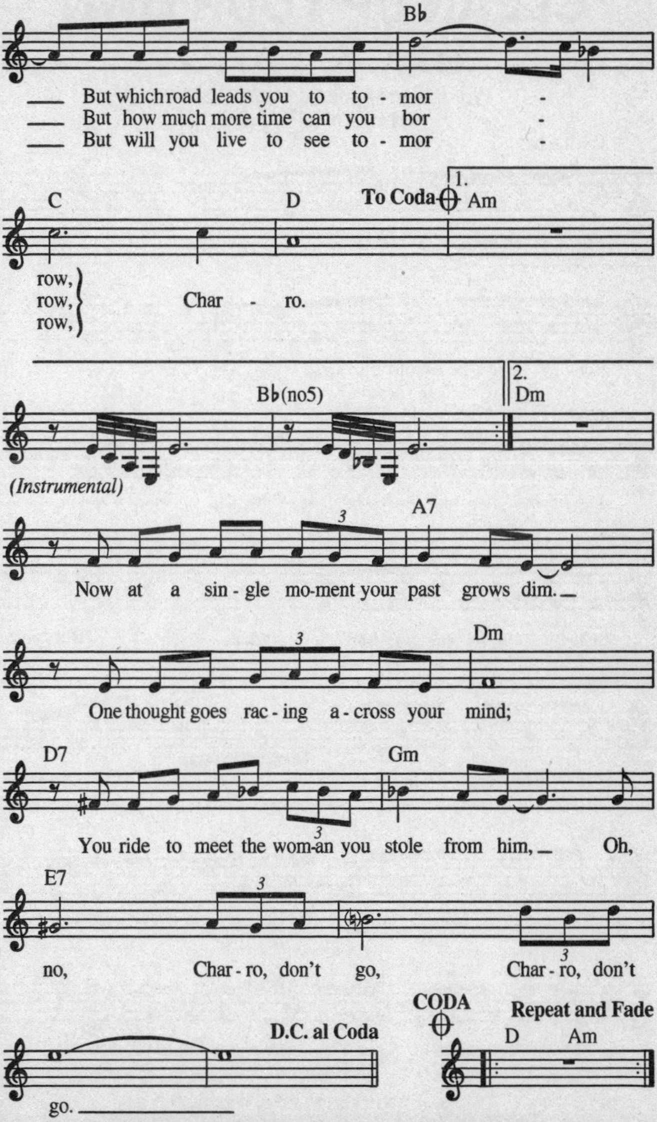

B♭
But which road leads you to to - mor -
But how much more time can you bor -
But will you live to see to - mor -
C
D
To Coda
1.
Am
row,
row,
row,
Char - ro.
B♭(no5)
2.
Dm
(Instrumental)
A7
Now at a sin - gle mo-ment your past grows dim.
Dm
One thought goes rac - ing a - cross your mind;
D7
Gm
You ride to meet the wom-an you stole from him, Oh,
E7
no, Char - ro, don't go, Char - ro, don't
go.
D.C. al Coda
CODA
Repeat and Fade
D
Am

CLEAN UP YOUR OWN BACK YARD

Words and Music by SCOTT DAVIS
and BILLY STRANGE

With a beat

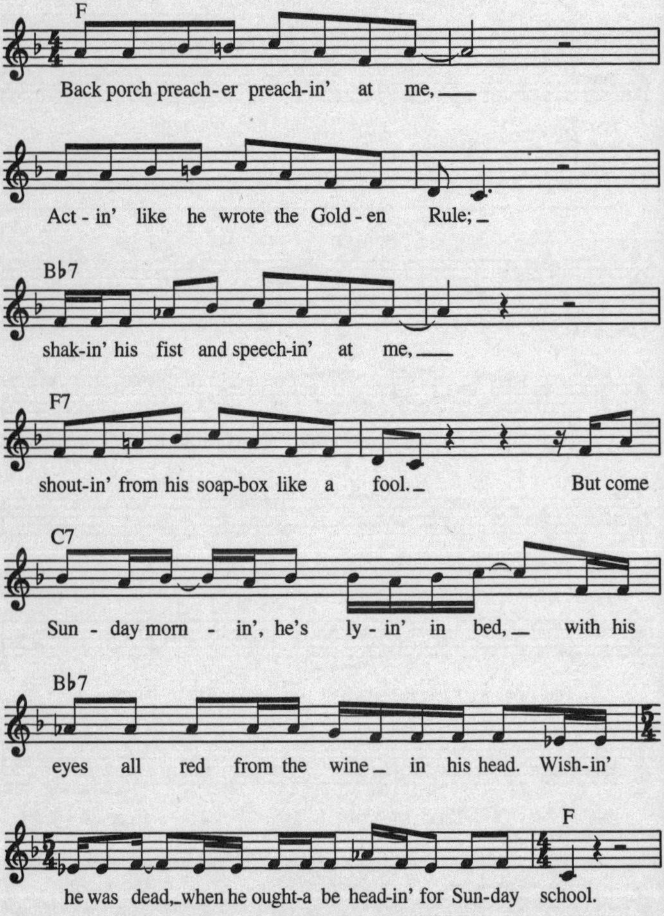
F
Back porch preach-er preach-in' at me,
Act - in' like he wrote the Gold - en Rule;
Bb7
shak-in' his fist and speech-in' at me,
F7
shout-in' from his soap-box like a fool. But come
C7
Sun - day morn - in', he's ly - in' in bed, with his
Bb7
eyes all red from the wine in his head. Wish-in'
he was dead, when he ought-a be head-in' for Sun-day
F
school.

Copyright © 1969 by Elvis Presley Music, Inc.
Copyright Assigned to Elvis Presley Music (Administered by R&H Music)
International Copyright Secured All Rights Reserved

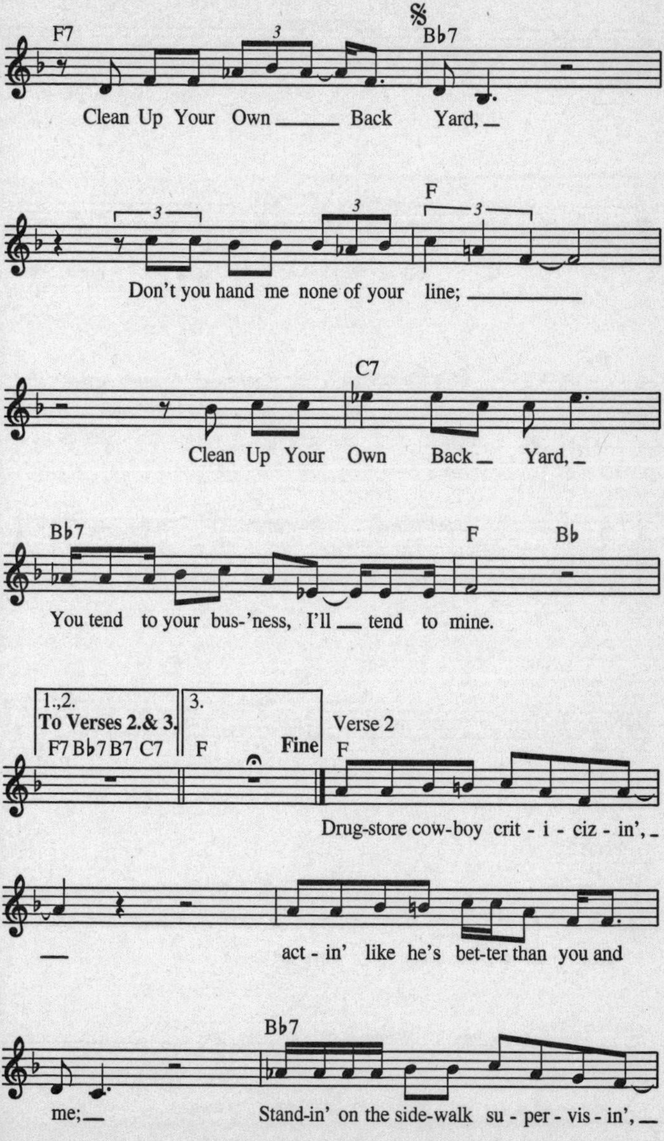
F7
Bb7
Clean Up Your Own Back Yard,
F
Don't you hand me none of your line;
C7
Clean Up Your Own Back Yard,
Bb7
F
Bb
You tend to your bus-'ness, I'll tend to mine.
1.,2.
To Verses 2.& 3.
F7 Bb7 B7 C7
3.
F
Fine
Verse 2
F
Drug-store cow-boy crit - i - ciz - in',
act - in' like he's bet-ter than you and
me;
Bb7
Stand-in' on the side-walk su - per - vis - in',

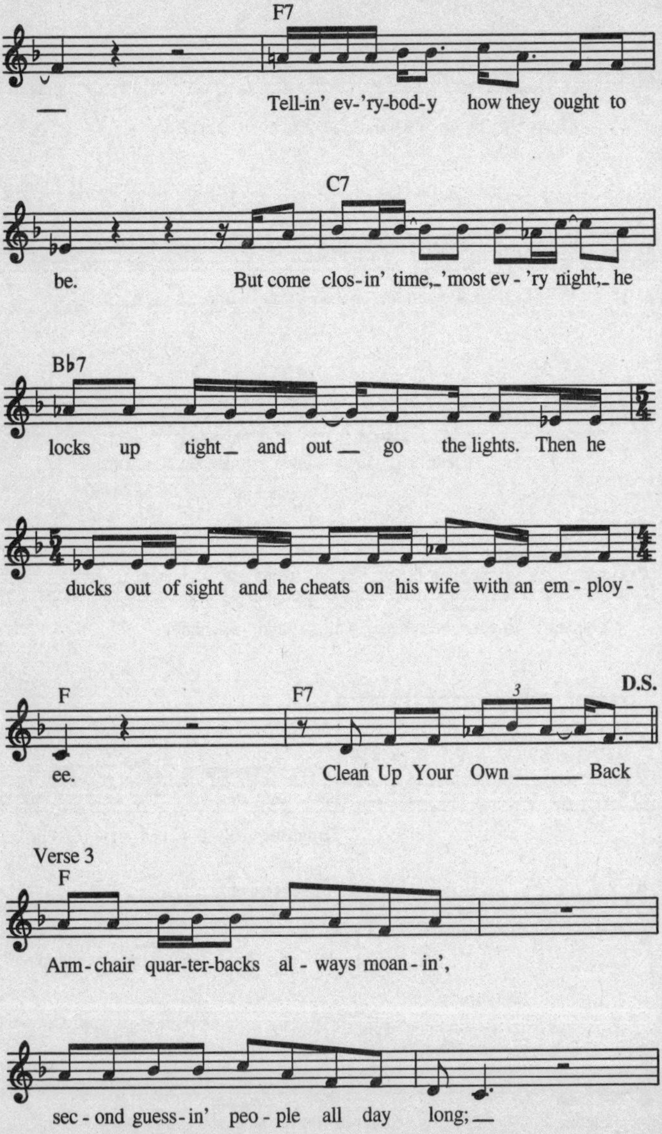
F7
Tell-in' ev-'ry-bod-y how they ought to
C7
be. But come clos-in' time, 'most ev - 'ry night, he
B♭7
locks up tight and out go the lights. Then he
ducks out of sight and he cheats on his wife with an em - ploy -
F
F7
D.S.
3
ee. Clean Up Your Own Back
Verse 3
F
Arm - chair quar-ter-backs al - ways moan - in',
sec - ond guess - in' peo - ple all day long;

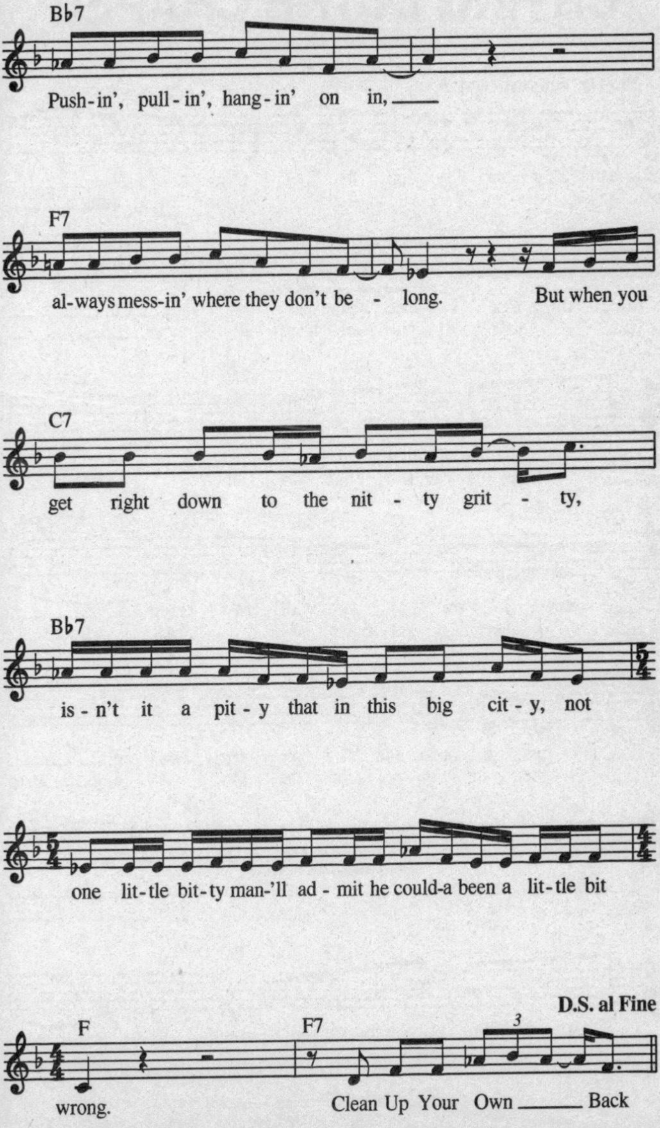
Bb7
Push-in', pull-in', hang-in' on in, ___
F7
al-ways mess-in' where they don't be - long. But when you
C7
get right down to the nit - ty grit - ty,
Bb7
is - n't it a pit - y that in this big cit - y, not
one lit-tle bit-ty man-'ll ad - mit he could-a been a lit-tle bit
F
F7
D.S. al Fine
wrong. Clean Up Your Own ___ Back

CRYING IN THE CHAPEL

Words and Music by
ARTIE GLENN

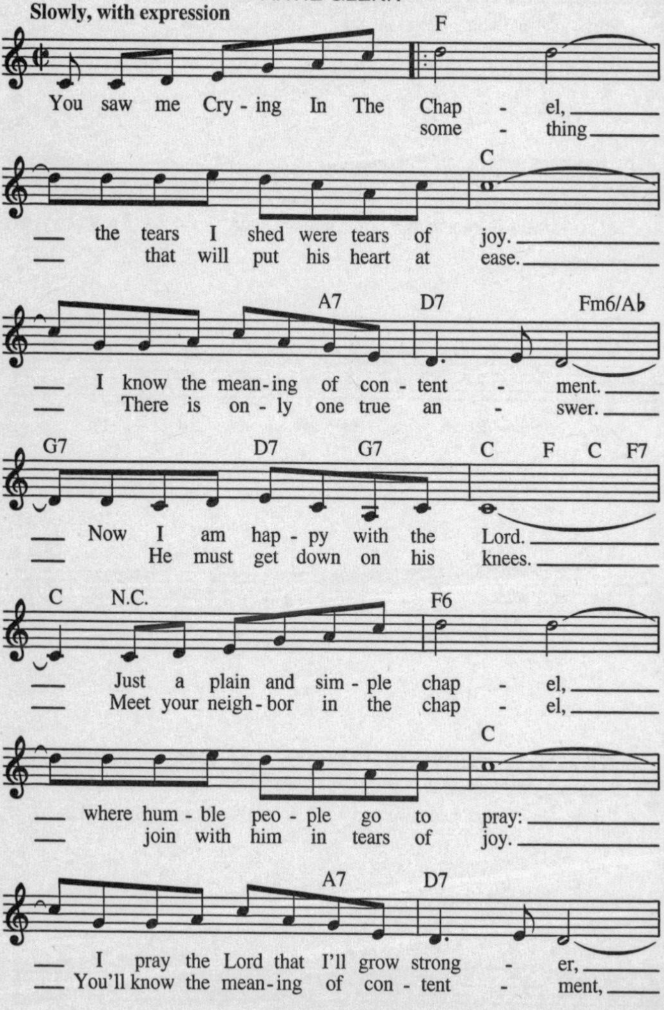
Slowly, with expression
F
You saw me Cry - ing In The Chap - el,
some - thing
C
the tears I shed were tears of joy.
that will put his heart at ease.
A7 D7 Fm6/A♭
I know the mean-ing of con - tent - ment.
There is on - ly one true an - swer.
G7 D7 G7 C F C F7
Now I am hap - py with the Lord.
He must get down on his knees.
C N.C. F6
Just a plain and sim - ple chap - el,
Meet your neigh-bor in the chap - el,
C
where hum - ble peo - ple go to pray:
join with him in tears of joy.
A7 D7
I pray the Lord that I'll grow strong - er,
You'll know the mean-ing of con - tent - ment,

Copyright © 1953 by Unichappell Music Inc.
Copyright Renewed
International Copyright Secured All Rights Reserved

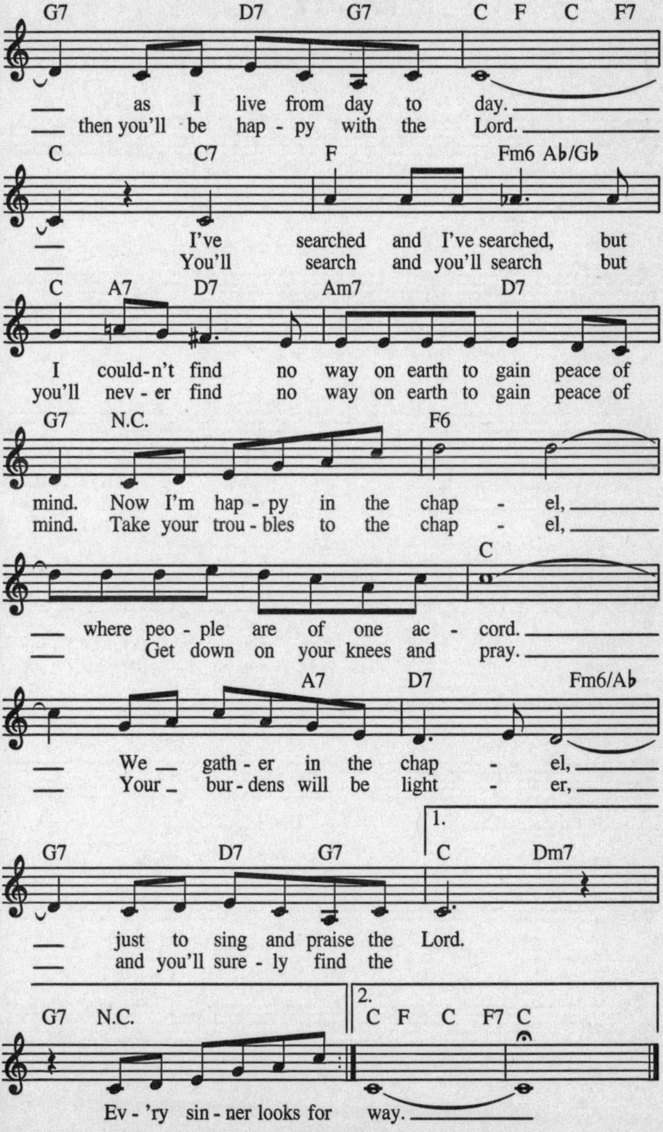
G7 D7 G7 C F C F7
as I live from day to day.
then you'll be hap - py with the Lord.
C C7 F Fm6 Ab/Gb
I've searched and I've searched, but
You'll search and you'll search but
C A7 D7 Am7 D7
I could-n't find no way on earth to gain peace of
you'll nev - er find no way on earth to gain peace of
G7 N.C. F6
mind. Now I'm hap - py in the chap - el,
mind. Take your trou - bles to the chap - el,
C
where peo - ple are of one ac - cord.
Get down on your knees and pray.
A7 D7 Fm6/Ab
We gath - er in the chap - el,
Your bur - dens will be light - er,
1.
G7 D7 G7 C Dm7
just to sing and praise the Lord.
and you'll sure - ly find the
2.
G7 N.C. C F C F7 C
Ev - 'ry sin - ner looks for way.

DON'T

Words and Music by JERRY LEIBER
and MIKE STOLLER

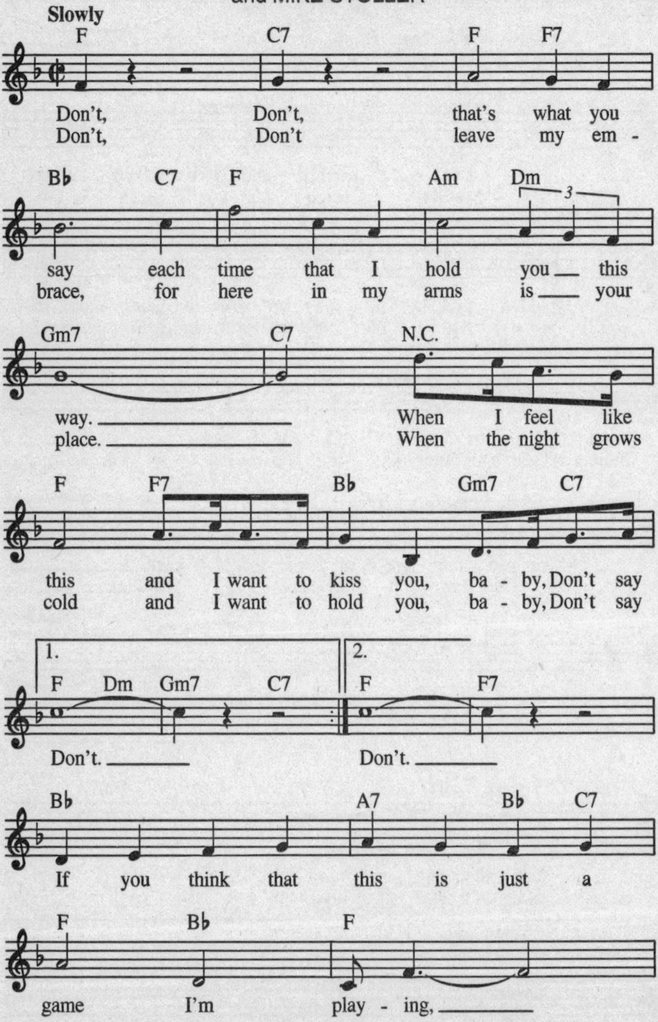
Slowly
F C7 F F7
Don't, Don't, that's what you
Don't, Don't leave my em -
B♭ C7 F Am Dm
say each time that I hold you __ this
brace, for here in my arms is __ your
Gm7 C7 N.C.
way. __ When I feel like
place. __ When the night grows
F F7 B♭ Gm7 C7
this and I want to kiss you, ba - by, Don't say
cold and I want to hold you, ba - by, Don't say
1. F Dm Gm7 C7
Don't. __
2. F F7
Don't. __
B♭ A7 B♭ C7
If you think that this is just a
F B♭ F
game I'm play - ing, __

© 1957 (Renewed) JERRY LEIBER MUSIC and MIKE STOLLER MUSIC
All Rights Reserved

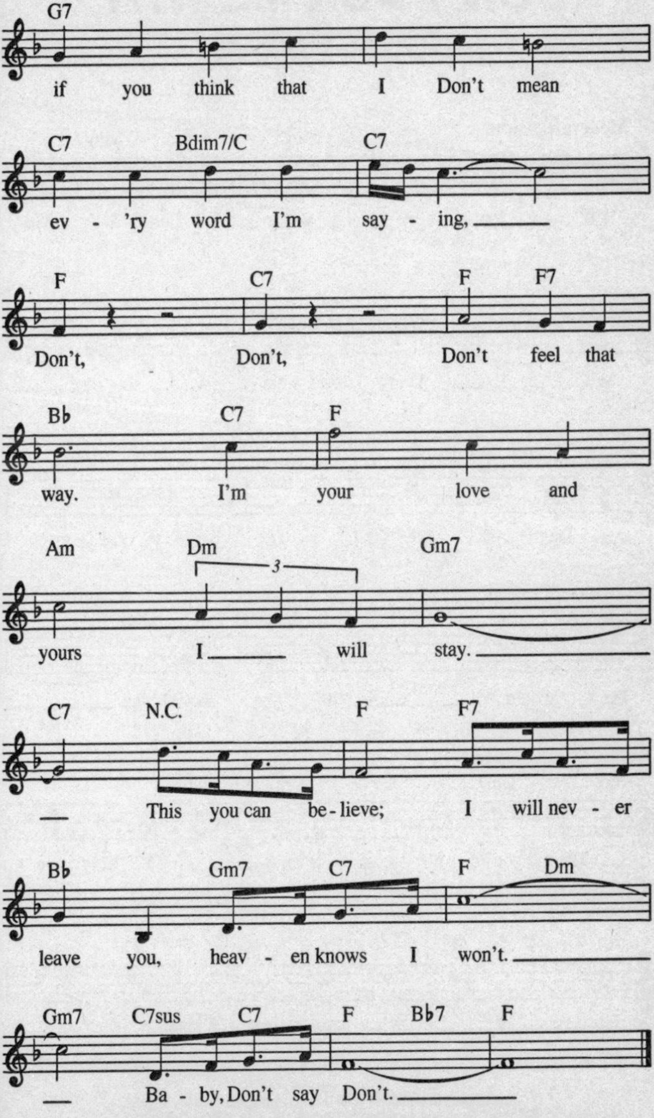
G7
if you think that I Don't mean
C7 Bdim7/C C7
ev - 'ry word I'm say - ing,
F C7 F F7
Don't, Don't, Don't feel that
B♭ C7 F
way. I'm your love and
Am Dm Gm7
3
yours I will stay.
C7 N.C. F F7
This you can be - lieve; I will nev - er
B♭ Gm7 C7 F Dm
leave you, heav - en knows I won't.
Gm7 C7sus C7 F B♭7 F
Ba - by, Don't say Don't.

DON'T ASK ME WHY

Words by FRED WISE
Music by BEN WEISMAN

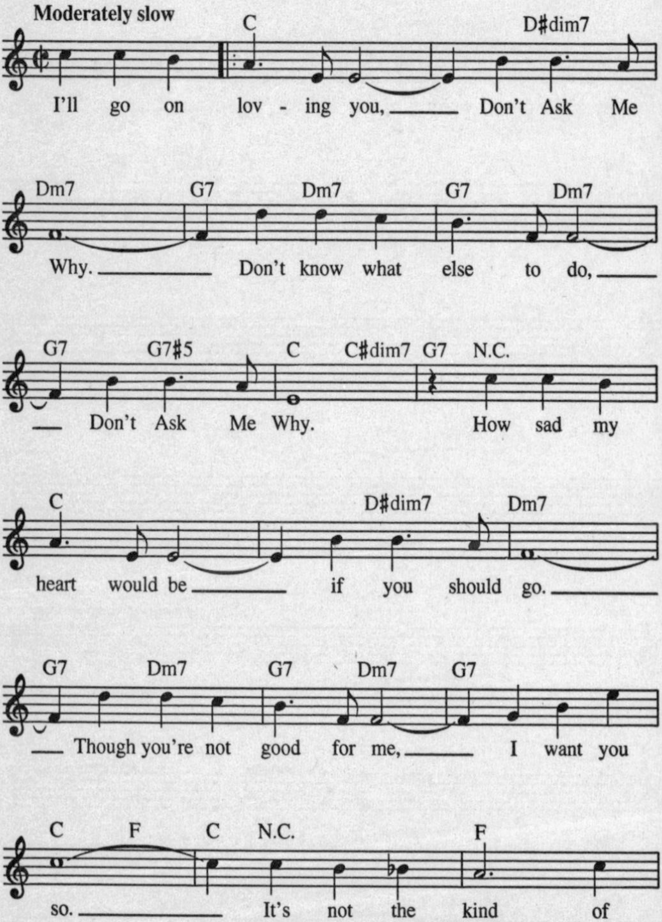
Moderately slow
C D♯dim7
I'll go on lov - ing you, Don't Ask Me
Dm7 G7 Dm7 G7 Dm7
Why. Don't know what else to do,
G7 G7♯5 C C♯dim7 G7 N.C.
Don't Ask Me Why. How sad my
C D♯dim7 Dm7
heart would be if you should go.
G7 Dm7 G7 Dm7 G7
Though you're not good for me, I want you
C F C N.C. F
so. It's not the kind of

Copyright © 1958 Gladys Music, Inc.
Copyright Renewed, Assigned to Chappell & Co. and Erika Publishing
International Copyright Secured All Rights Reserved

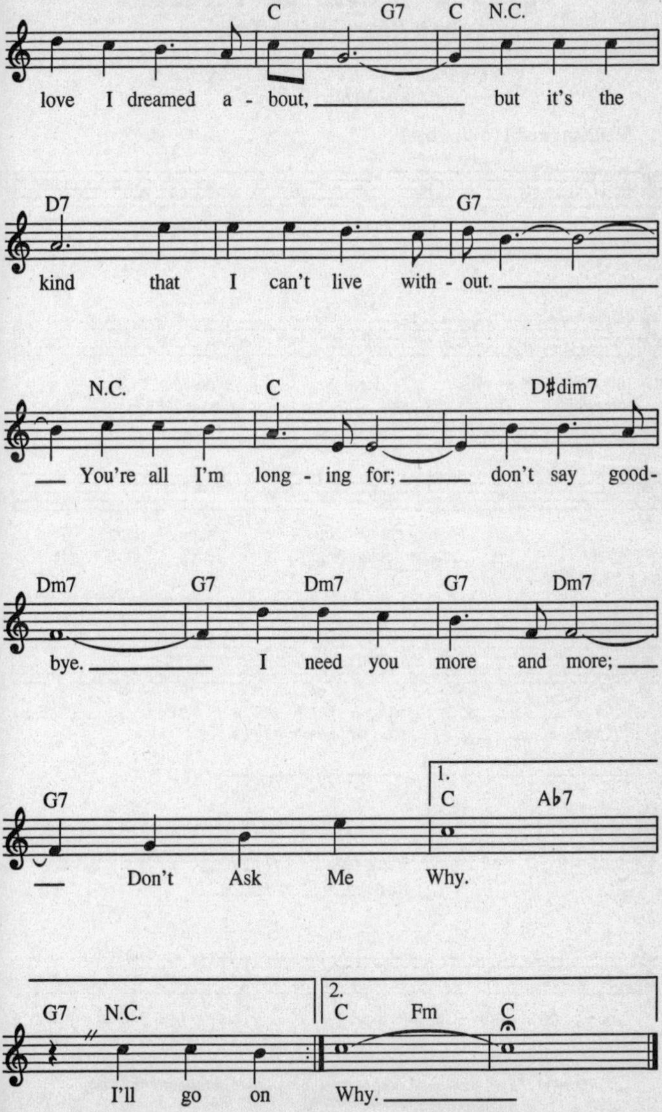
C G7 C N.C.
love I dreamed a - bout, but it's the
D7 G7
kind that I can't live with - out.
N.C. C D♯dim7
You're all I'm long - ing for; don't say good-
Dm7 G7 Dm7 G7 Dm7
bye. I need you more and more;
G7 1. C A♭7
Don't Ask Me Why.
G7 N.C. 2. C Fm C
I'll go on Why.

DON'T BE CRUEL
(To a Heart That's True)

Words and Music by OTIS BLACKWELL
and ELVIS PRESLEY

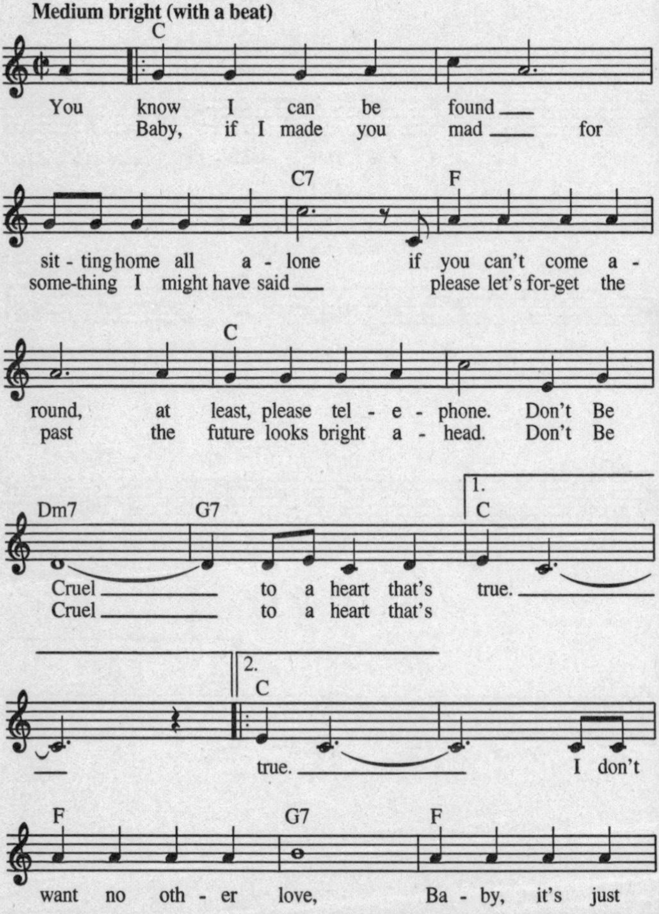
Medium bright (with a beat)
C
You know I can be found
Baby, if I made you mad for
C7 F
sit - ting home all a - lone if you can't come a -
some-thing I might have said please let's for-get the
C
round, at least, please tel - e - phone. Don't Be
past the future looks bright a - head. Don't Be
1.
Dm7 G7 C
Cruel to a heart that's true.
Cruel to a heart that's
2.
C
true. I don't
F G7 F
want no oth - er love, Ba - by, it's just

Copyright © 1956 by Unart Music Corporation and Elvis Presley Music, Inc.
Copyright Renewed and Assigned to Elvis Presley Music (Administered by R&H Music)
International Copyright Secured All Rights Reserved

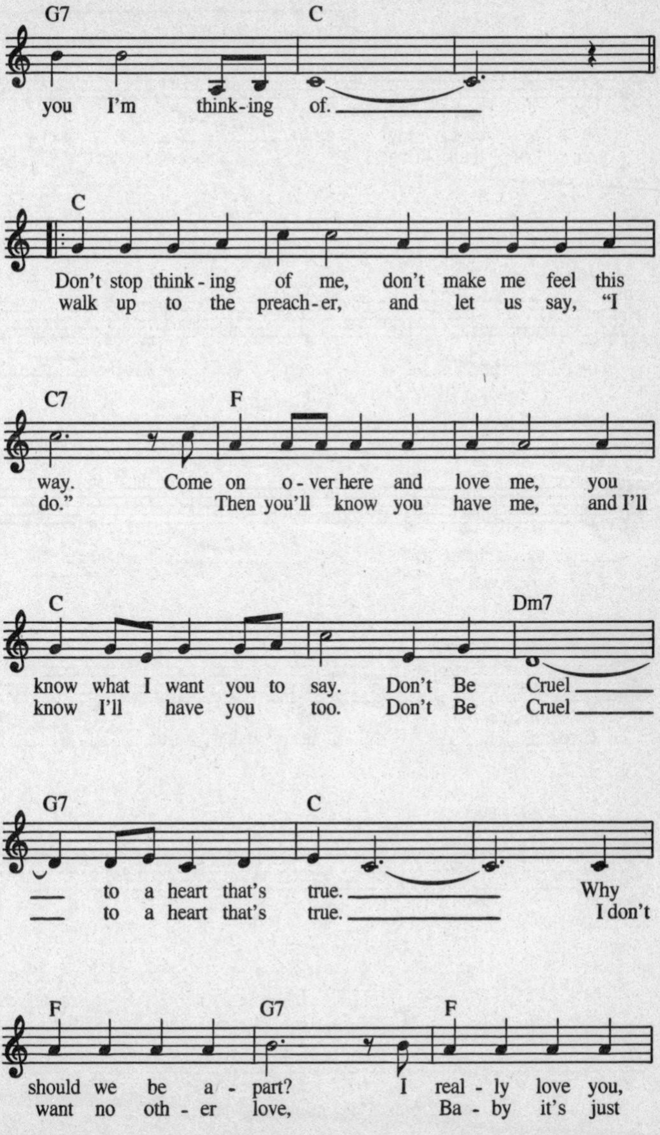
G7 C
you I'm think-ing of.
C
Don't stop think - ing of me, don't make me feel this
walk up to the preach - er, and let us say, "I
C7 F
way. Come on o - ver here and love me, you
do." Then you'll know you have me, and I'll
C Dm7
know what I want you to say. Don't Be Cruel
know I'll have you too. Don't Be Cruel
G7 C
to a heart that's true. Why
to a heart that's true. I don't
F G7 F
should we be a - part? I real - ly love you,
want no oth - er love, Ba - by it's just

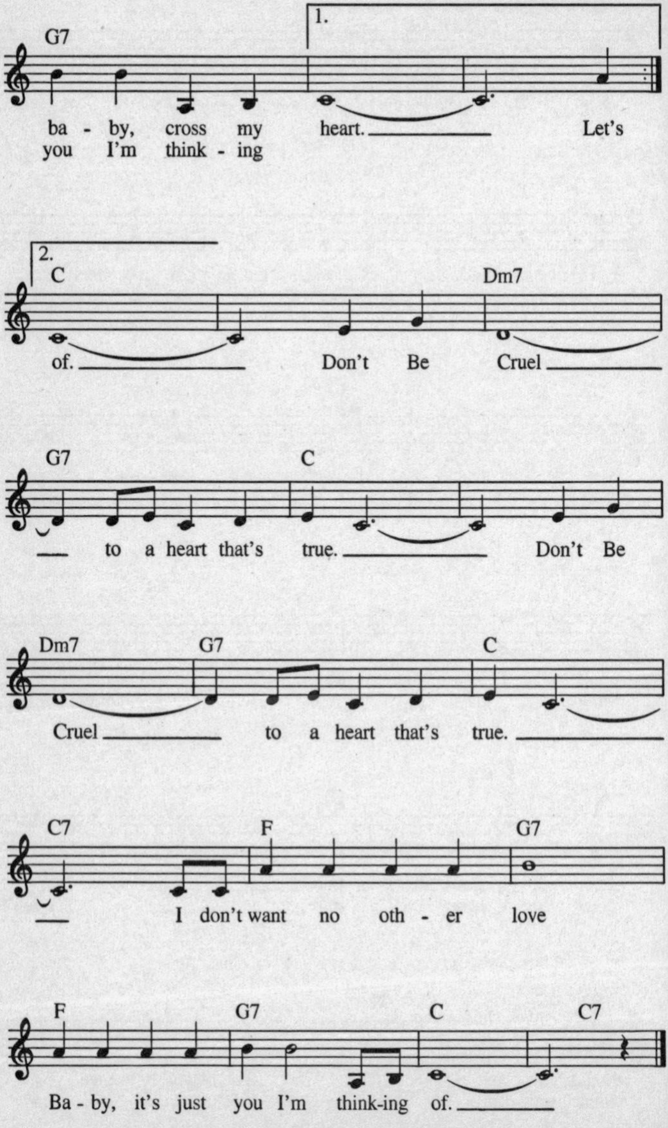
G7
1.
ba - by, cross my heart. Let's
you I'm think - ing
2.
C
Dm7
of. Don't Be Cruel
G7
C
to a heart that's true. Don't Be
Dm7
G7
C
Cruel to a heart that's true.
C7
F
G7
I don't want no oth - er love
F
G7
C
C7
Ba - by, it's just you I'm think-ing of.

DON'T CRY DADDY

Words and Music by
MAC DAVIS

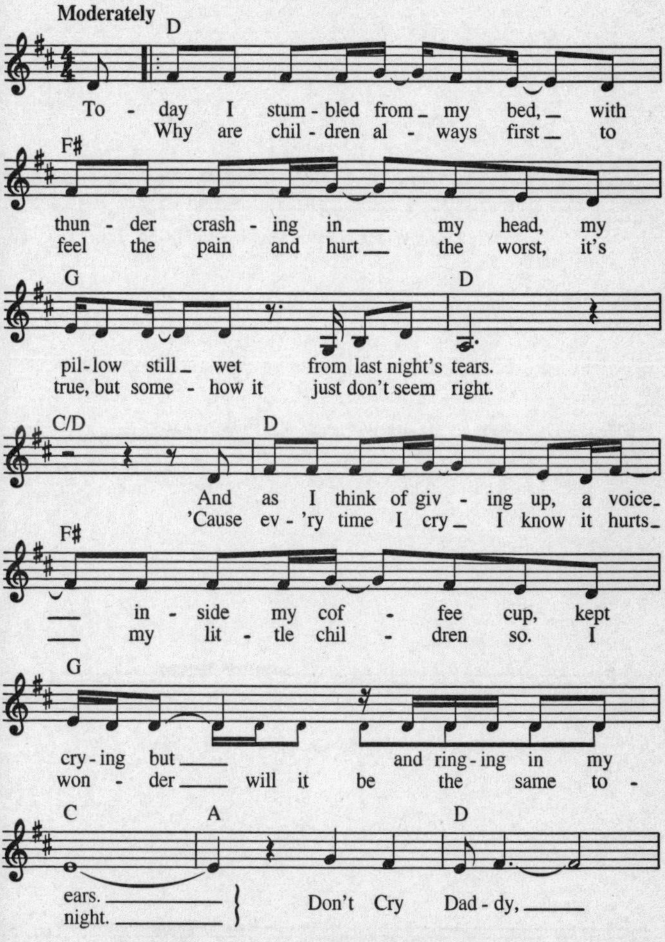
Moderately
D
To - day I stum - bled from my bed, with
Why are chil - dren al - ways first to
F#
thun - der crash - ing in my head, my
feel the pain and hurt the worst, it's
G
D
pil - low still wet from last night's tears.
true, but some - how it just don't seem right.
C/D
D
And as I think of giv - ing up, a voice
'Cause ev - 'ry time I cry I know it hurts
F#
in - side my cof - fee cup, kept
my lit - tle chil - dren so. I
G
cry - ing but and ring - ing in my
won - der will it be the same to -
C
A
D
ears.
night.
Don't Cry Dad - dy,

© 1969 SCREEN GEMS-EMI MUSIC INC. and ELVIS PRESLEY MUSIC
All Rights Controlled and Administered by SCREEN GEMS-EMI MUSIC INC.
All Rights Reserved International Copyright Secured Used by Permission

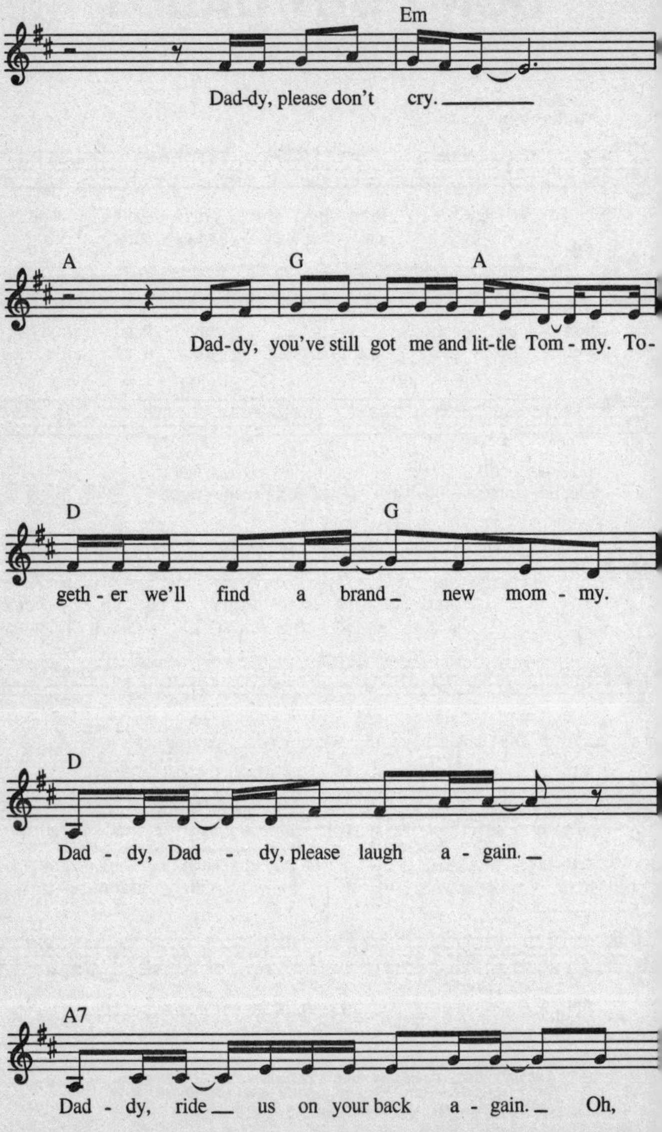
Em
Dad-dy, please don't cry.
A G A
Dad-dy, you've still got me and lit-tle Tom-my. To-
D G
geth-er we'll find a brand new mom-my.
D
Dad-dy, Dad-dy, please laugh a-gain.
A7
Dad-dy, ride us on your back a-gain. Oh,

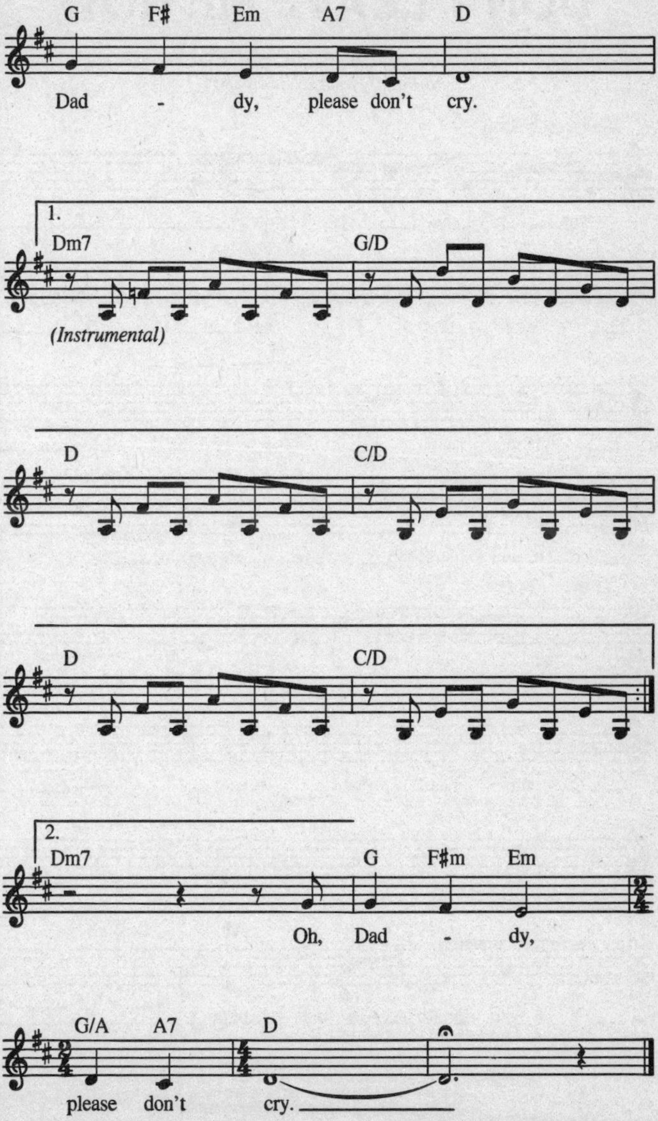
G F♯ Em A7 D
Dad - dy, please don't cry.
1.
Dm7 G/D
(Instrumental)
D C/D
D C/D
2.
Dm7 G F♯m Em
Oh, Dad - dy,
G/A A7 D
please don't cry.

DON'T LEAVE ME NOW

Words by AARON SCHROEDER
Music by BEN WEISMAN

Moderately slow

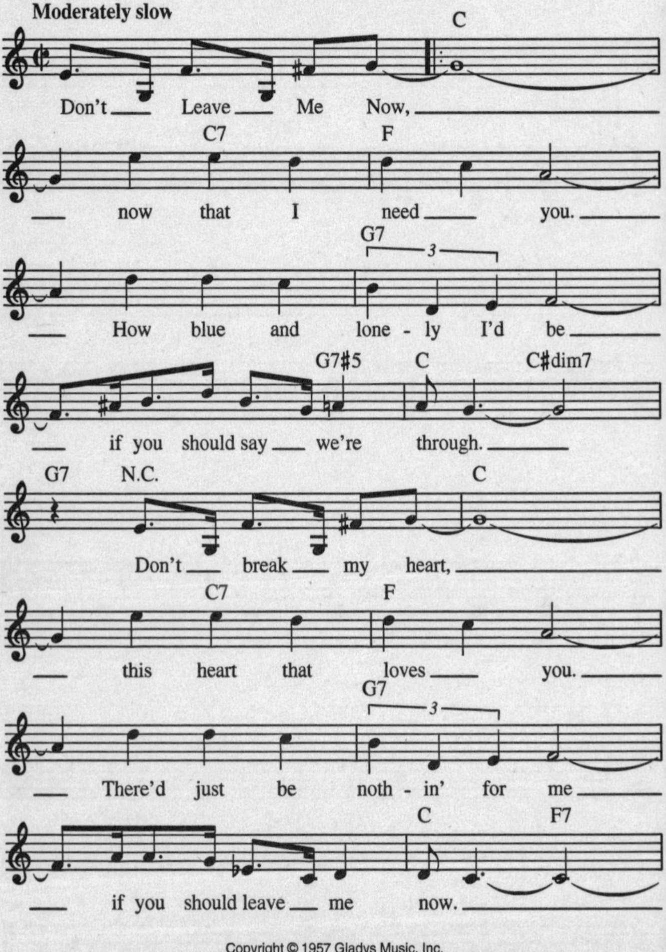
C
Don't Leave Me Now,
C7 F
now that I need you.
G7
3
How blue and lonely I'd be
G7♯5 C C♯dim7
if you should say we're through.
G7 N.C. C
Don't break my heart,
C7 F
this heart that loves you.
G7
3
There'd just be nothin' for me
C F7
if you should leave me now.

Copyright © 1957 Gladys Music, Inc.
Copyright Renewed, Assigned to Chappell & Co. and Rachel's Own Music
(Administered by A. Schroeder International Ltd.)
International Copyright Secured All Rights Reserved

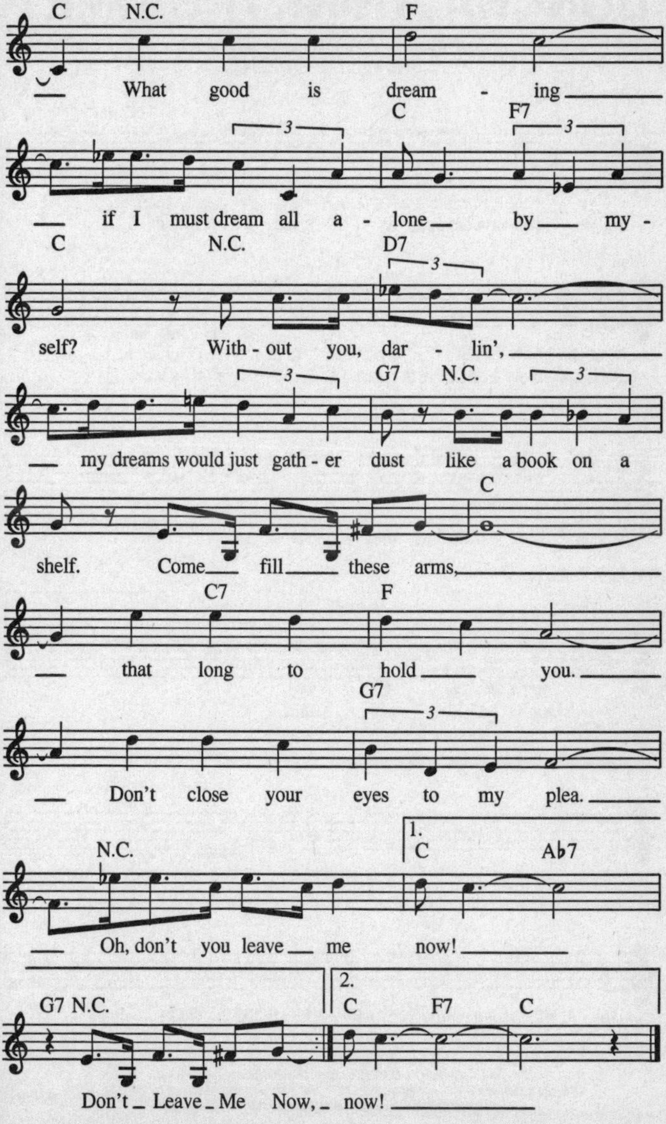
C N.C. F
What good is dream - ing
C F7
if I must dream all a - lone by my -
C N.C. D7
self? With - out you, dar - lin',
G7 N.C.
my dreams would just gath - er dust like a book on a
C
shelf. Come fill these arms,
C7 F
that long to hold you.
G7
Don't close your eyes to my plea.
N.C.
1.
C Ab7
Oh, don't you leave me now!
G7 N.C.
2.
C F7 C
Don't Leave Me Now, now!

DONCHA' THINK IT'S TIME?

Words and Music by CLYDE OTIS
and WILLIE DIXON

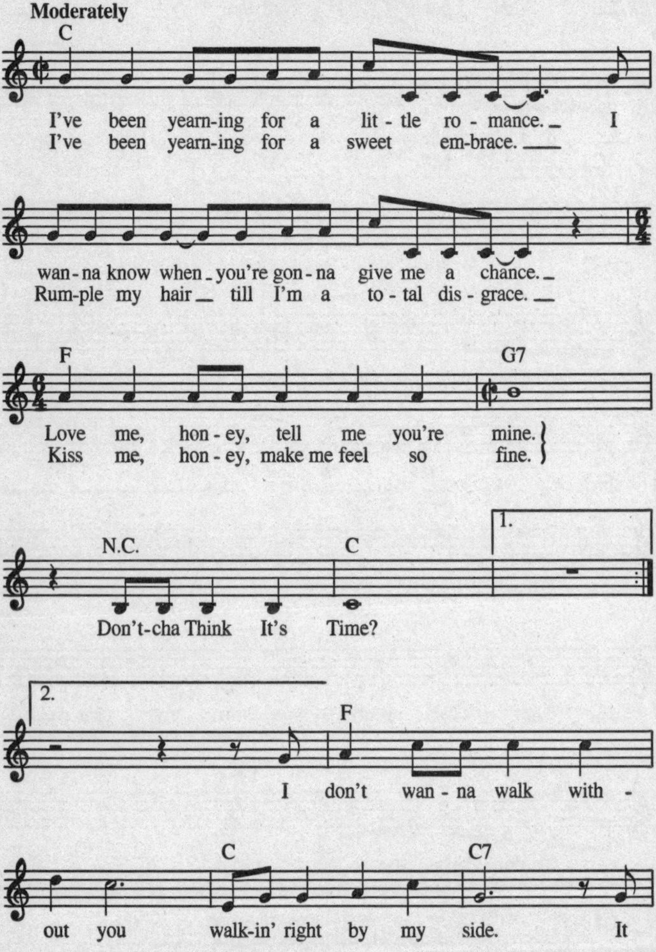
Moderately
C
I've been yearn-ing for a lit - tle ro - mance. _ I
I've been yearn-ing for a sweet em-brace. ___
wan - na know when _ you're gon - na give me a chance. _
Rum-ple my hair _ till I'm a to - tal dis - grace. _
F
G7
Love me, hon - ey, tell me you're mine.
Kiss me, hon - ey, make me feel so fine.
N.C.
C
1.
Don't-cha Think It's Time?
2.
F
I don't wan - na walk with -
C
C7
out you walk-in' right by my side. It

Copyright © 1958 by Elvis Presley Music, Inc.
Copyright Renewed and Assigned to Elvis Presley Music (Administered by R&H Music)
International Copyright Secured All Rights Reserved

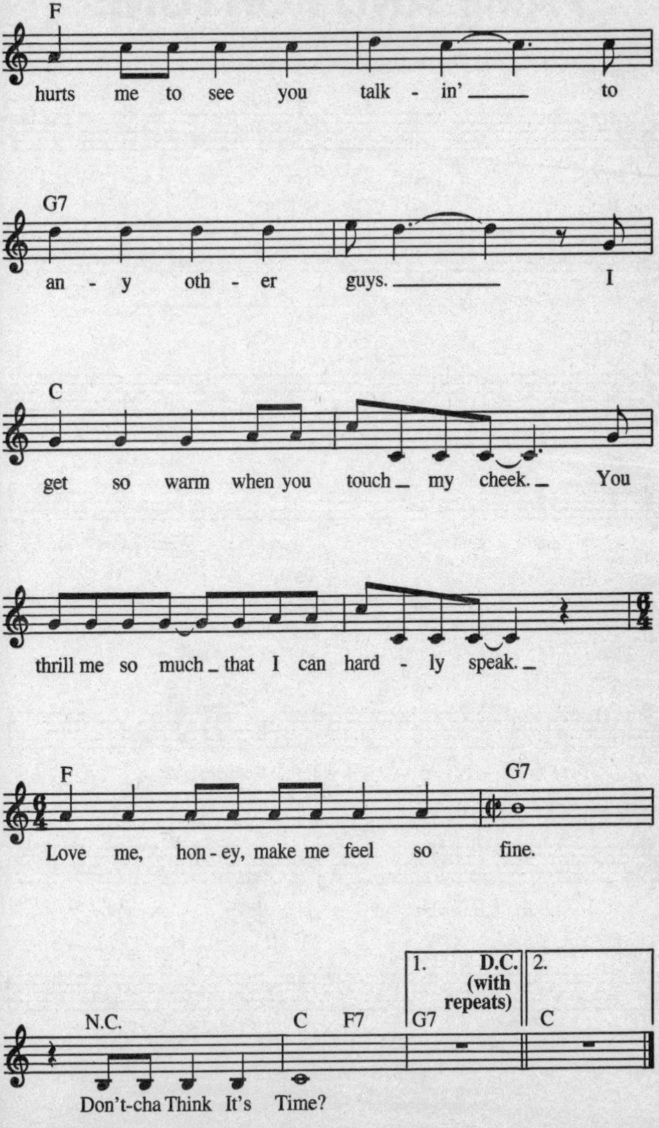
F
hurts me to see you talk - in' to
G7
an - y oth - er guys. I
C
get so warm when you touch my cheek. You
thrill me so much that I can hard - ly speak.
F
G7
Love me, hon - ey, make me feel so fine.
N.C.
C
F7
1.
D.C.
(with
repeats)
G7
2.
C
Don't-cha Think It's Time?

FAME AND FORTUNE

Words by FRED WISE
Music by BEN WEISMAN

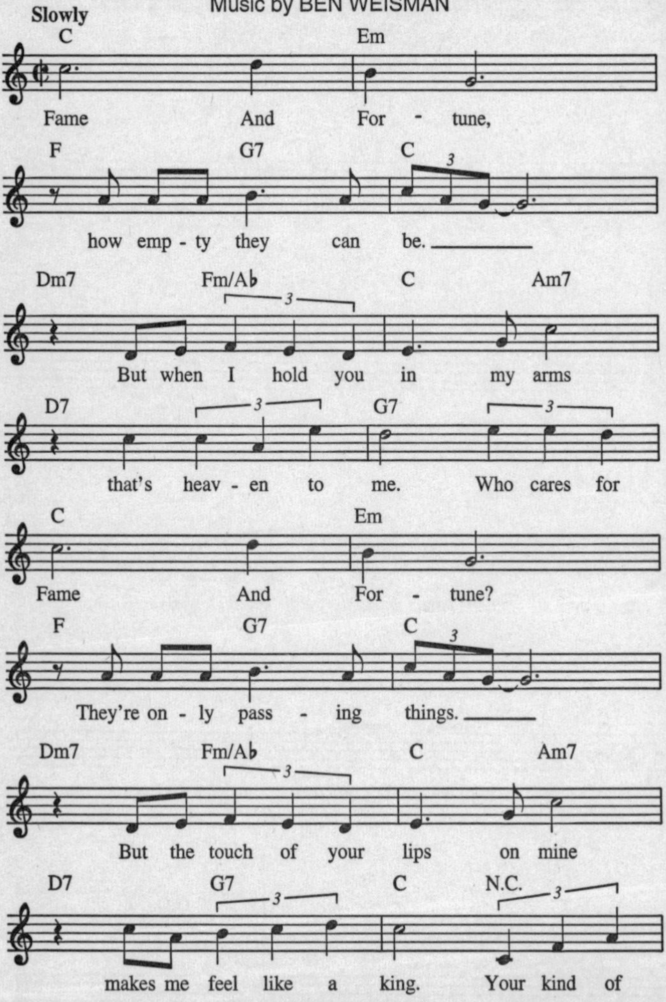
Slowly
C Em
Fame And For - tune,
F G7 C
how emp - ty they can be.
Dm7 Fm/A♭ C Am7
But when I hold you in my arms
D7 G7
that's heav - en to me. Who cares for
C Em
Fame And For - tune?
F G7 C
They're on - ly pass - ing things.
Dm7 Fm/A♭ C Am7
But the touch of your lips on mine
D7 G7 C N.C.
makes me feel like a king. Your kind of

Copyright © 1960 Gladys Music, Inc.
Copyright Renewed, Assigned to Chappell & Co. and Erika Publishing
International Copyright Secured All Rights Reserved

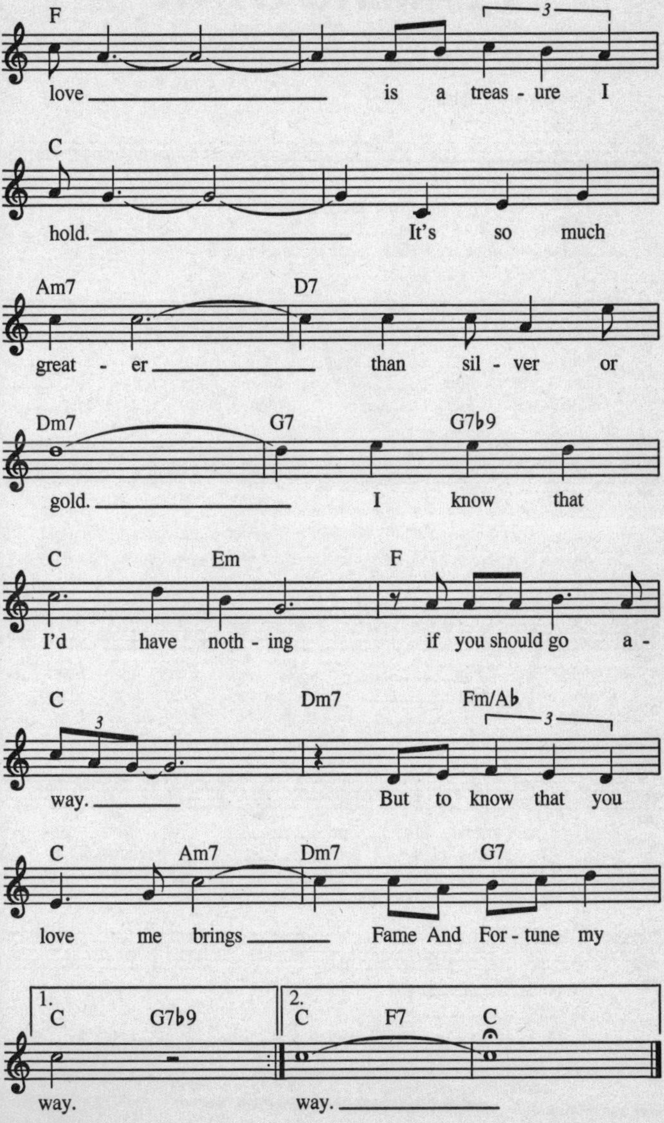
F
3
love ___ is a treas - ure I
C
hold. ___ It's so much
Am7 D7
great - er ___ than sil - ver or
Dm7 G7 G7♭9
gold. ___ I know that
C Em F
I'd have noth - ing if you should go a -
C Dm7 Fm/A♭
3
3
way. ___ But to know that you
C Am7 Dm7 G7
love me brings ___ Fame And For - tune my
1.
C G7♭9
way.
2.
C F7 C
way. ___

FLAMING STAR

Words by SID WAYNE
Music by SHERMAN EDWARDS

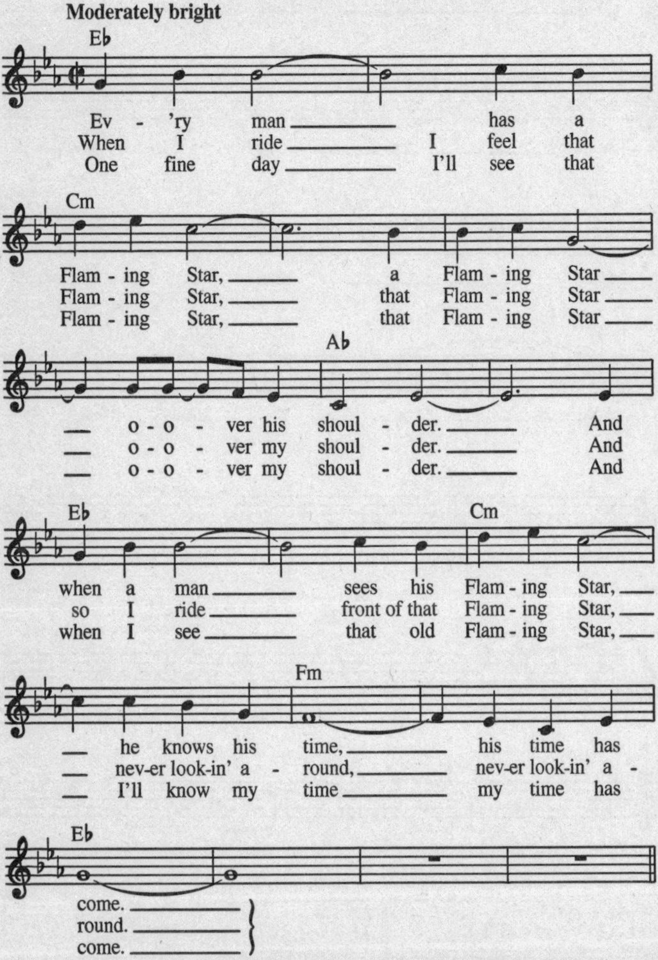
Moderately bright
Eb
Ev - 'ry man has a
When I ride I feel that
One fine day I'll see that
Cm
Flam - ing Star, a Flam - ing Star
Flam - ing Star, that Flam - ing Star
Flam - ing Star, that Flam - ing Star
Ab
o - o - ver his shoul - der. And
o - o - ver my shoul - der. And
o - o - ver my shoul - der. And
Eb
Cm
when a man sees his Flam - ing Star,
so I ride front of that Flam - ing Star,
when I see that old Flam - ing Star,
Fm
he knows his time, his time has
nev-er look-in' a - round, nev-er look-in' a -
I'll know my time my time has
Eb
come.
round.
come.

Copyright © 1961 by Gladys Music, Inc.
Copyright Renewed and Assigned to Holly Hill Music and Keith-Valerie Music
International Copyright Secured All Rights Reserved

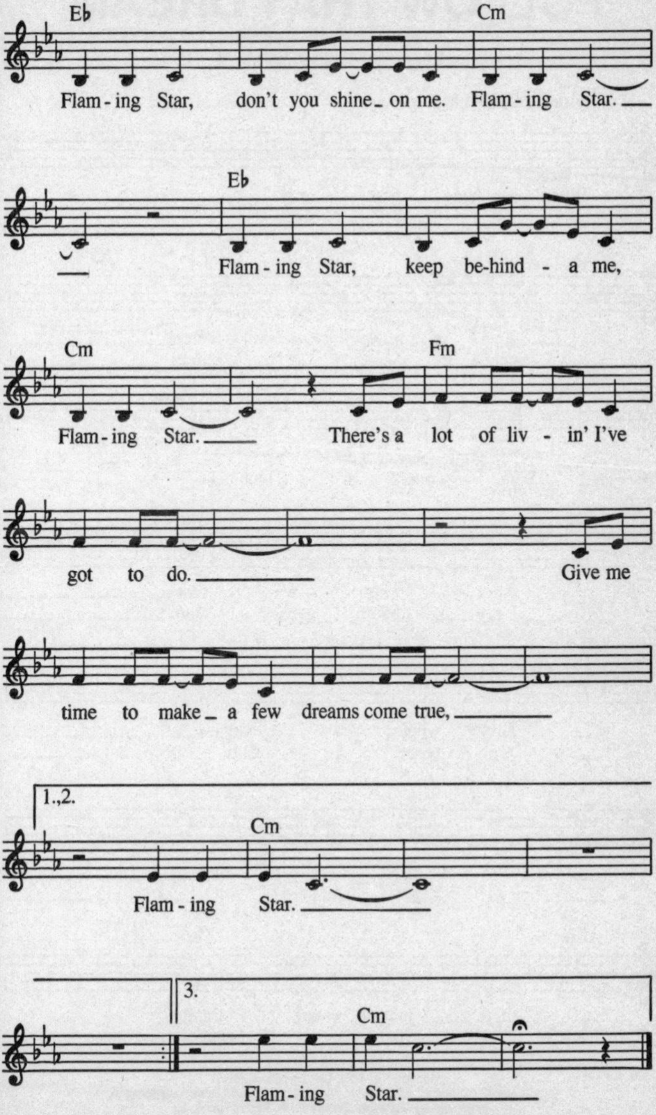
Eb
Cm
Flam - ing Star, don't you shine on me. Flam - ing Star.
Eb
Flam - ing Star, keep be-hind - a me,
Cm
Fm
Flam - ing Star. There's a lot of liv - in' I've
got to do. Give me
time to make a few dreams come true,
1.,2.
Cm
Flam - ing Star.
3.
Cm
Flam - ing Star.

FOLLOW THAT DREAM

Words by FRED WISE
Music by BEN WEISMAN

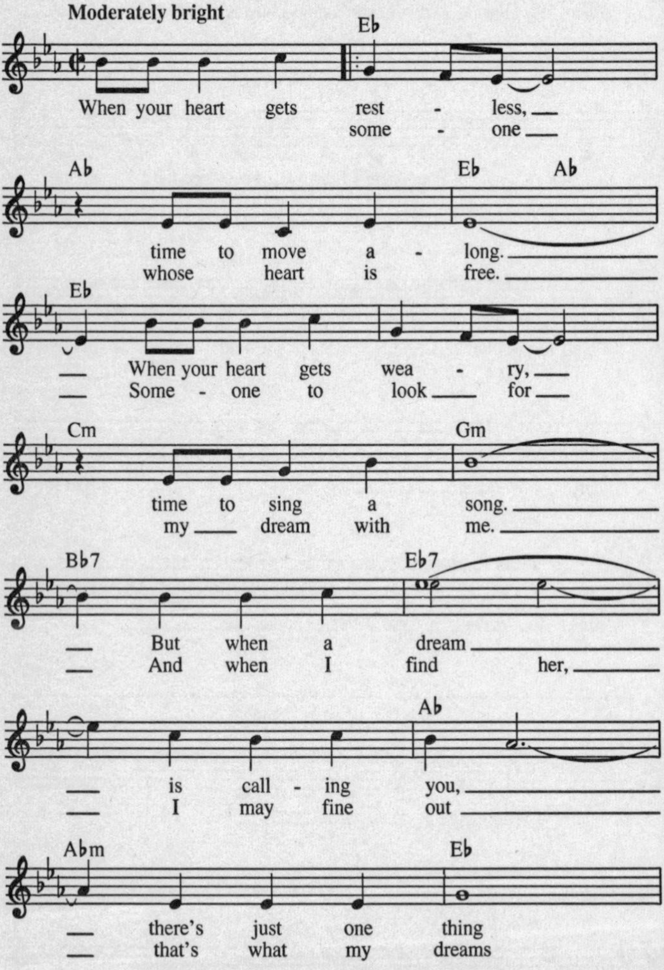
Moderately bright
Eb
When your heart gets rest - less,
some - one
Ab Eb Ab
time to move a - long.
whose heart is free.
Eb
When your heart gets wea - ry,
Some - one to look for
Cm Gm
time to sing a song.
my dream with me.
Bb7 Eb7
But when a dream
And when I find her,
Ab
is call - ing you,
I may fine out
Abm Eb
there's just one thing
that's what my dreams

Copyright © 1962 Gladys Music, Inc.
Copyright Renewed, Assigned to Chappell & Co. and Erika Publishing
International Copyright Secured All Rights Reserved

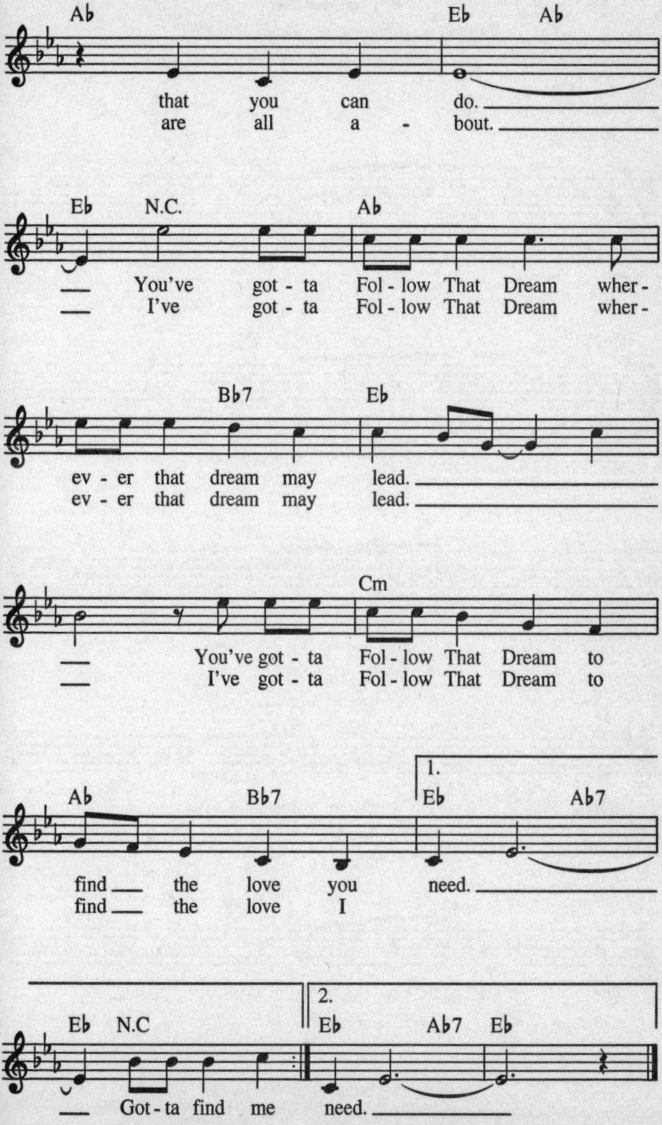
Ab Eb Ab
that you can do.
are all a - bout.
Eb N.C. Ab
You've got - ta Fol - low That Dream wher -
I've got - ta Fol - low That Dream wher -
Bb7 Eb
ev - er that dream may lead.
ev - er that dream may lead.
Cm
You've got - ta Fol - low That Dream to
I've got - ta Fol - low That Dream to
1.
Ab Bb7 Eb Ab7
find the love you need.
find the love I
2.
Eb N.C Eb Ab7 Eb
Got - ta find me need.

FOOL

Words and Music by JAMES LAST
and CARL SIGMAN

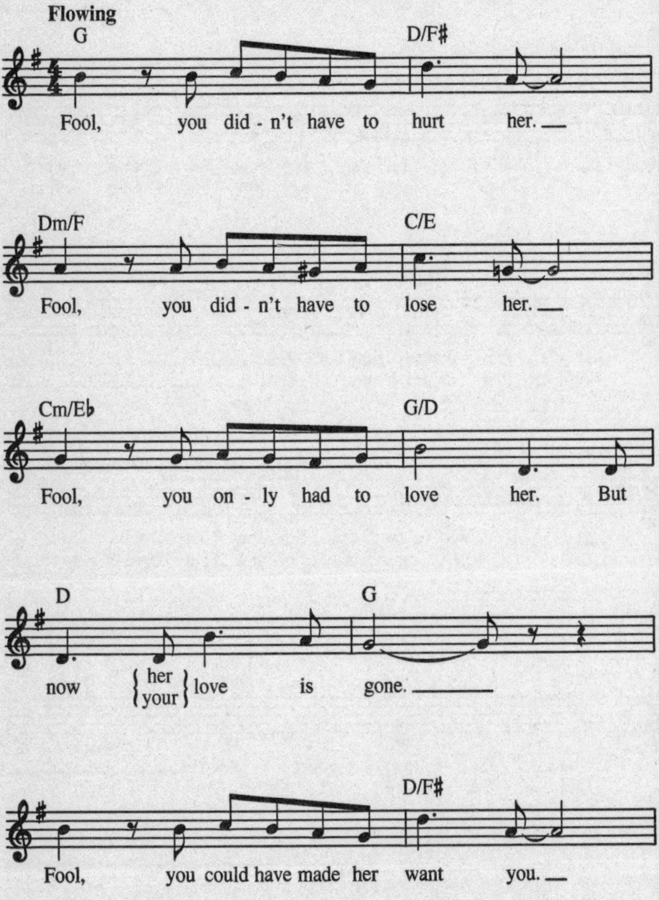
Flowing
G
D/F#
Fool, you did - n't have to hurt her.
Dm/F
C/E
Fool, you did - n't have to lose her.
Cm/Eb
G/D
Fool, you on - ly had to love her. But
D
G
now {her / your} love is gone.
D/F#
Fool, you could have made her want you.

Copyright © 1972 Happy Musikverlag GMBH
All Rights Administered by Chappell & Co.
International Copyright Secured All Rights Reserved

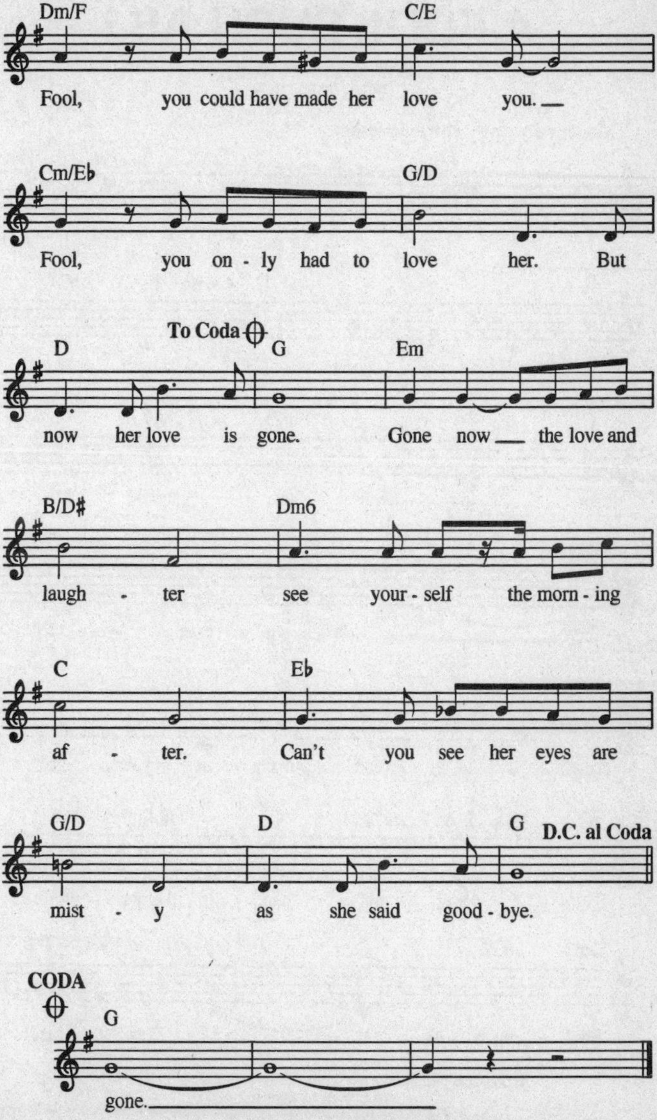
Dm/F
C/E
Fool, you could have made her love you.
Cm/E♭
G/D
Fool, you only had to love her. But
To Coda
D
G
Em
now her love is gone. Gone now the love and
B/D♯
Dm6
laughter see yourself the morning
C
E♭
after. Can't you see her eyes are
G/D
D
G
D.C. al Coda
misty as she said goodbye.
CODA
G
gone.

(Now and Then There's)

A FOOL SUCH AS I

Words and Music by
BILL TRADER

Moderately slow, with expression

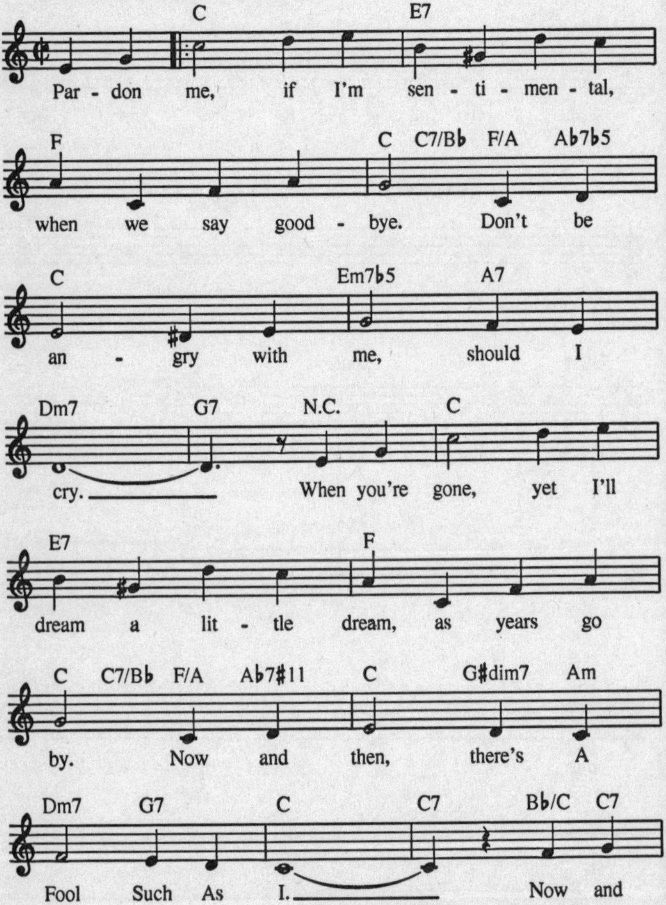
C E7
Par - don me, if I'm sen - ti - men - tal,
F C C7/Bb F/A Ab7b5
when we say good - bye. Don't be
C Em7b5 A7
an - gry with me, should I
Dm7 G7 N.C. C
cry. When you're gone, yet I'll
E7 F
dream a lit - tle dream, as years go
C C7/Bb F/A Ab7#11 C G#dim7 Am
by. Now and then, there's A
Dm7 G7 C C7 Bb/C C7
Fool Such As I. Now and

© Copyright 1952 by MCA MUSIC PUBLISHING, A Division of MCA INC.
Copyright Renewed
International Copyright Secured All Rights Reserved
MCA music publishing

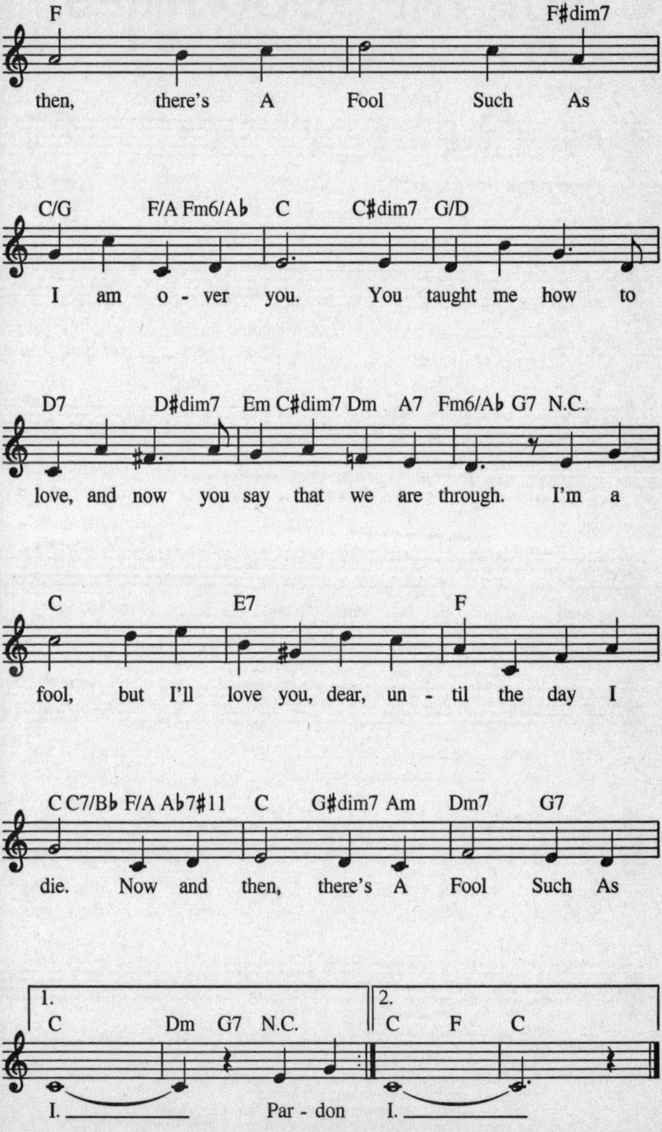
F F♯dim7
then, there's A Fool Such As
C/G F/A Fm6/A♭ C C♯dim7 G/D
I am o - ver you. You taught me how to
D7 D♯dim7 Em C♯dim7 Dm A7 Fm6/A♭ G7 N.C.
love, and now you say that we are through. I'm a
C E7 F
fool, but I'll love you, dear, un - til the day I
C C7/B♭ F/A A♭7♯11 C G♯dim7 Am Dm7 G7
die. Now and then, there's A Fool Such As
1. C Dm G7 N.C.
I. Par - don
2. C F C
I.

FOR THE GOOD TIMES

Words and Music by
KRIS KRISTOFFERSON

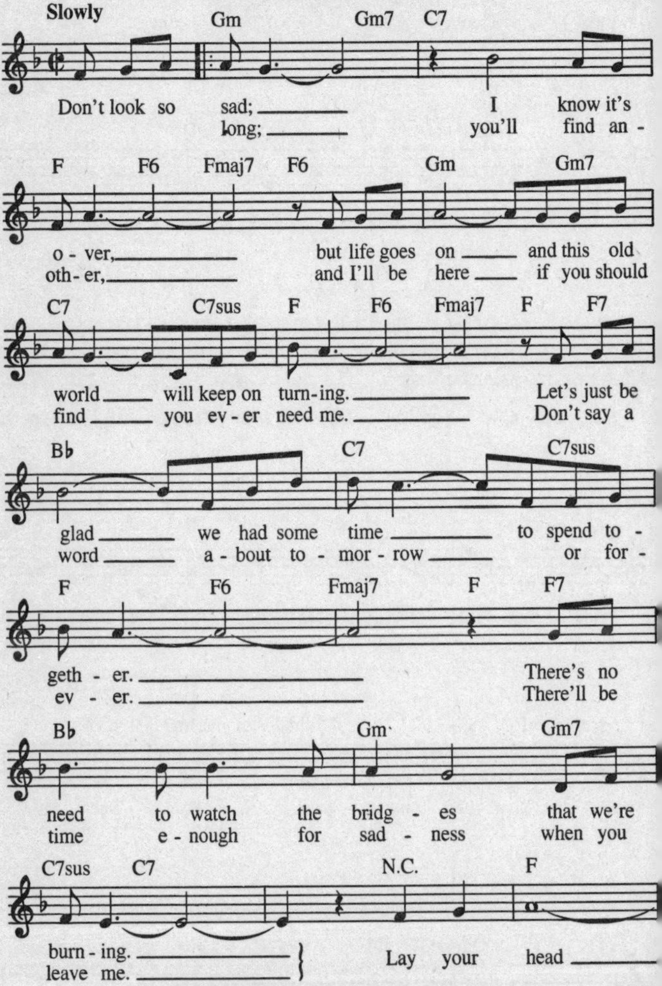
Slowly
Gm Gm7 C7
Don't look so sad; I know it's
long; you'll find an -
F F6 Fmaj7 F6 Gm Gm7
o - ver, but life goes on and this old
oth - er, and I'll be here if you should
C7 C7sus F F6 Fmaj7 F F7
world will keep on turn-ing. Let's just be
find you ev - er need me. Don't say a
B♭ C7 C7sus
glad we had some time to spend to -
word a - bout to - mor - row or for -
F F6 Fmaj7 F F7
geth - er. There's no
ev - er. There'll be
B♭ Gm Gm7
need to watch the bridg - es that we're
time e - nough for sad - ness when you
C7sus C7 N.C. F
burn - ing. Lay your head
leave me.

Copyright © 1968 by Careers-BMG Music Publishing, Inc.
Copyright Renewed
International Copyright Secured All Rights Reserved

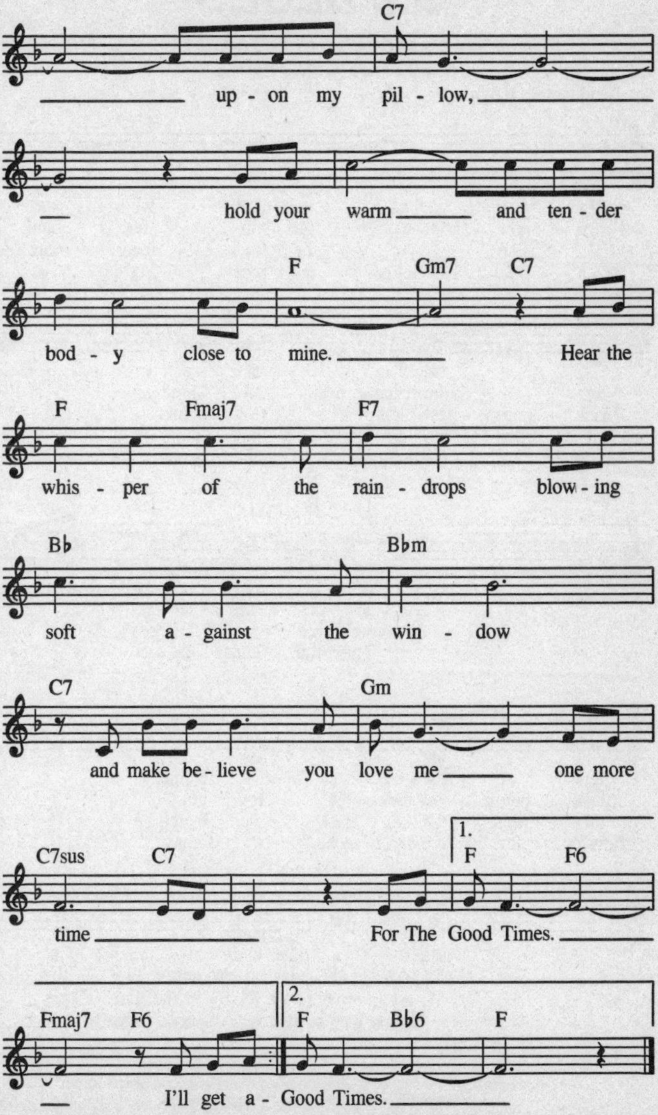
C7
up - on my pil - low,
hold your warm and ten - der
F Gm7 C7
bod - y close to mine. Hear the
F Fmaj7 F7
whis - per of the rain - drops blow - ing
B♭ B♭m
soft a - gainst the win - dow
C7 Gm
and make be - lieve you love me one more
1.
C7sus C7 F F6
time For The Good Times.
2.
Fmaj7 F6 F B♭6 F
I'll get a - Good Times.

G.I. BLUES

Words and Music by SID TEPPER
and ROY C. BENNETT

Moderately bright

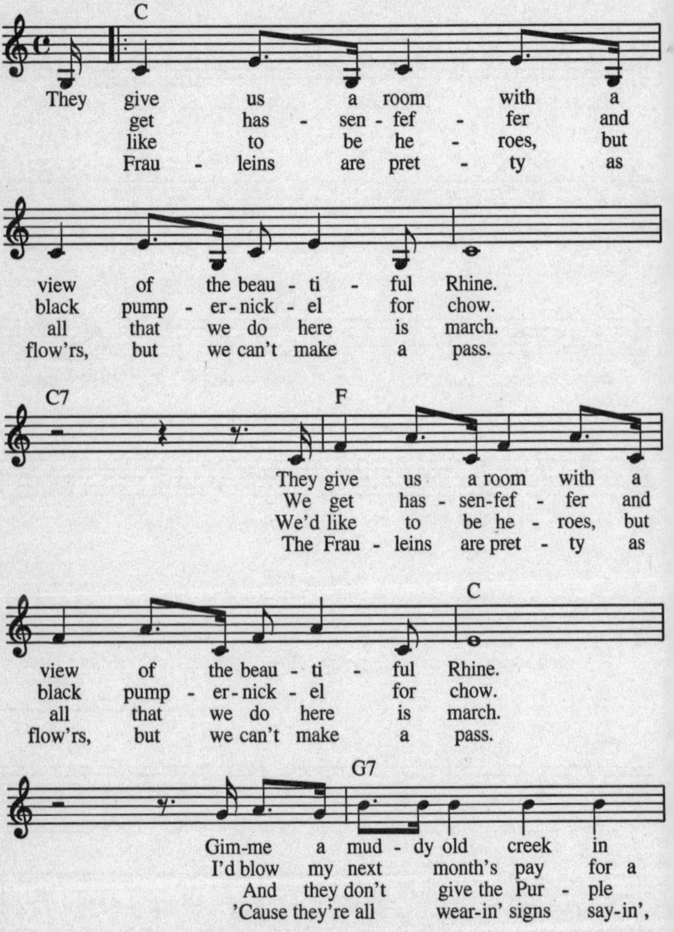
C
They give us a room with a
get has - sen - fef - fer and
like to be he - roes, but
Frau - leins are pret - ty as
view of the beau - ti - ful Rhine.
black pump - er - nick - el for chow.
all that we do here is march.
flow'rs, but we can't make a pass.
C7
F
They give us a room with a
We get has - sen-fef - fer and
We'd like to be he - roes, but
The Frau - leins are pret - ty as
C
view of the beau - ti - ful Rhine.
black pump - er - nick - el for chow.
all that we do here is march.
flow'rs, but we can't make a pass.
G7
Gim-me a mud - dy old creek in
I'd blow my next month's pay for a
And they don't give the Pur - ple
'Cause they're all wear-in' signs say-in',

Copyright © 1960 by Gladys Music, Inc.
Copyright Renewed and Assigned to Gladys Music (Administered by Williamson Music)
International Copyright Secured All Rights Reserved

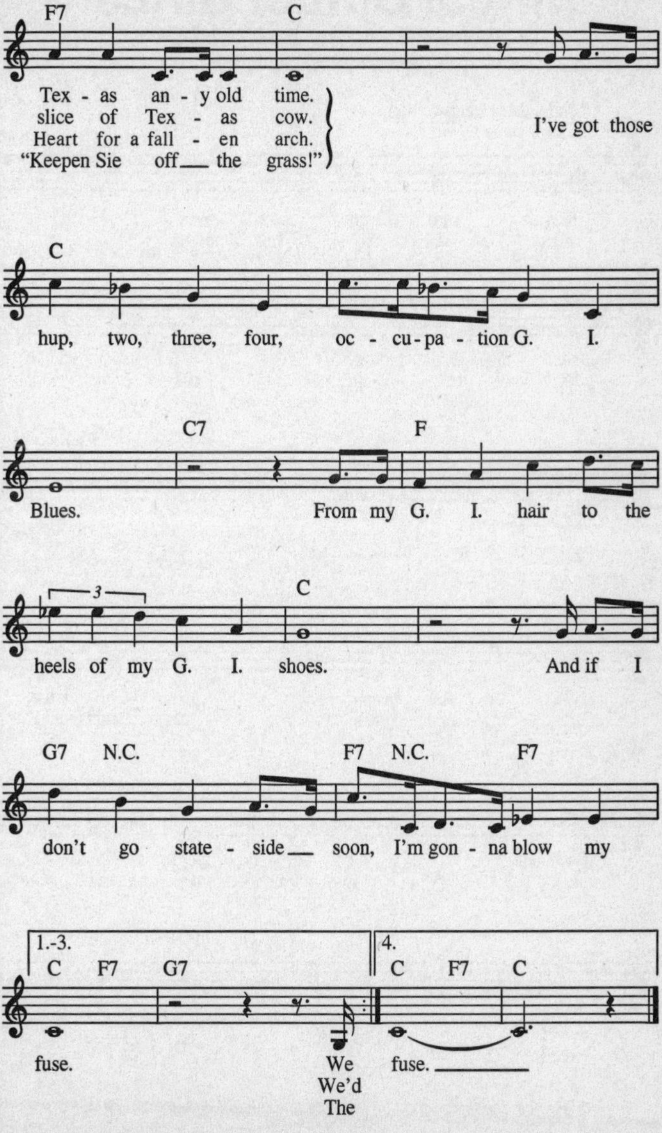
F7 C
Tex - as an - y old time.
slice of Tex - as cow.
Heart for a fall - en arch.
"Keepen Sie off the grass!"
I've got those
C
hup, two, three, four, oc - cu - pa - tion G. I.
C7 F
Blues. From my G. I. hair to the
3
C
heels of my G. I. shoes. And if I
G7 N.C. F7 N.C. F7
don't go state - side soon, I'm gon - na blow my
1.-3.
C F7 G7
4.
C F7 C
fuse. We
We'd
The
fuse.

GIRLS! GIRLS! GIRLS!

Words and Music by JERRY LEIBER
and MIKE STOLLER

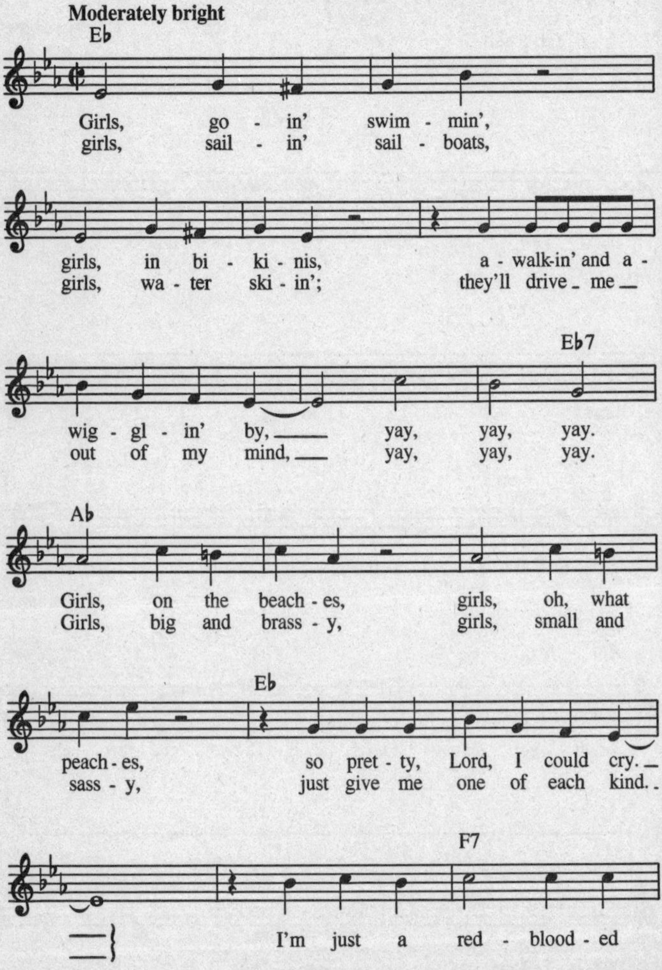
Moderately bright
E♭
Girls, go - in' swim - min',
girls, sail - in' sail - boats,
girls, in bi - ki - nis, a - walk-in' and a -
girls, wa - ter ski - in'; they'll drive me
E♭7
wig - gl - in' by, yay, yay, yay.
out of my mind, yay, yay, yay.
A♭
Girls, on the beach - es, girls, oh, what
Girls, big and brass - y, girls, small and
E♭
peach - es, so pret - ty, Lord, I could cry.
sass - y, just give me one of each kind.
F7
I'm just a red - blood - ed

© 1961, 1962 (Renewed 1990, 1991) JERRY LEIBER MUSIC and MIKE STOLLER MUSIC
All Rights Reserved

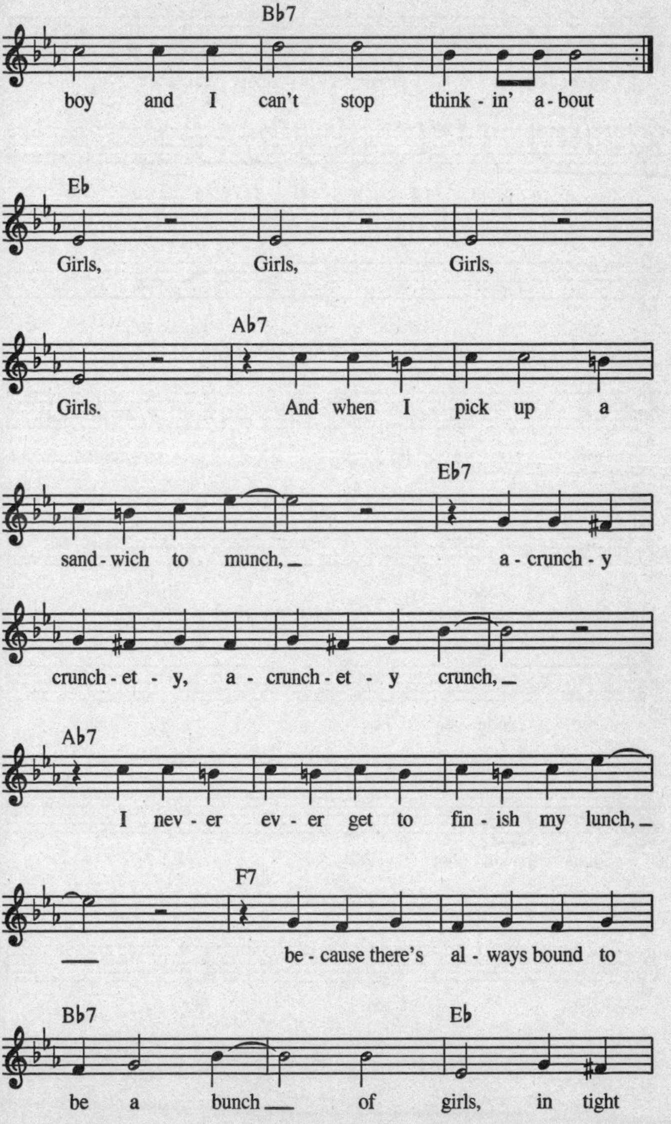
Bb7
boy and I can't stop think - in' a - bout
Eb
Girls, Girls, Girls,
Ab7
Girls. And when I pick up a
Eb7
sand - wich to munch, a - crunch - y
crunch - et - y, a - crunch - et - y crunch,
Ab7
I nev - er ev - er get to fin - ish my lunch,
F7
be - cause there's al - ways bound to
Bb7
Eb
be a bunch of girls, in tight

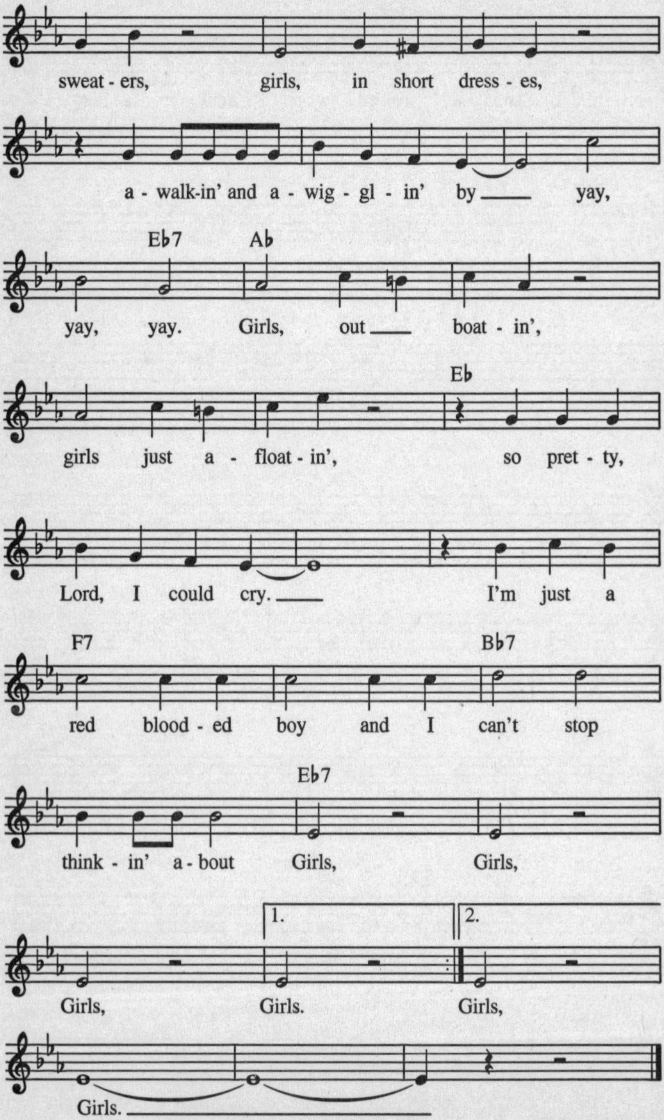
sweat - ers, girls, in short dress - es,
a - walk-in' and a - wig - gl - in' by yay,
Eb7 Ab
yay, yay. Girls, out boat - in',
Eb
girls just a - float - in', so pret - ty,
Lord, I could cry. I'm just a
F7 Bb7
red blood - ed boy and I can't stop
Eb7
think - in' a - bout Girls, Girls,
1. 2.
Girls, Girls. Girls,
Girls.

GOOD LUCK CHARM

Words and Music by AARON SCHROEDER
and WALLY GOLD

Moderately

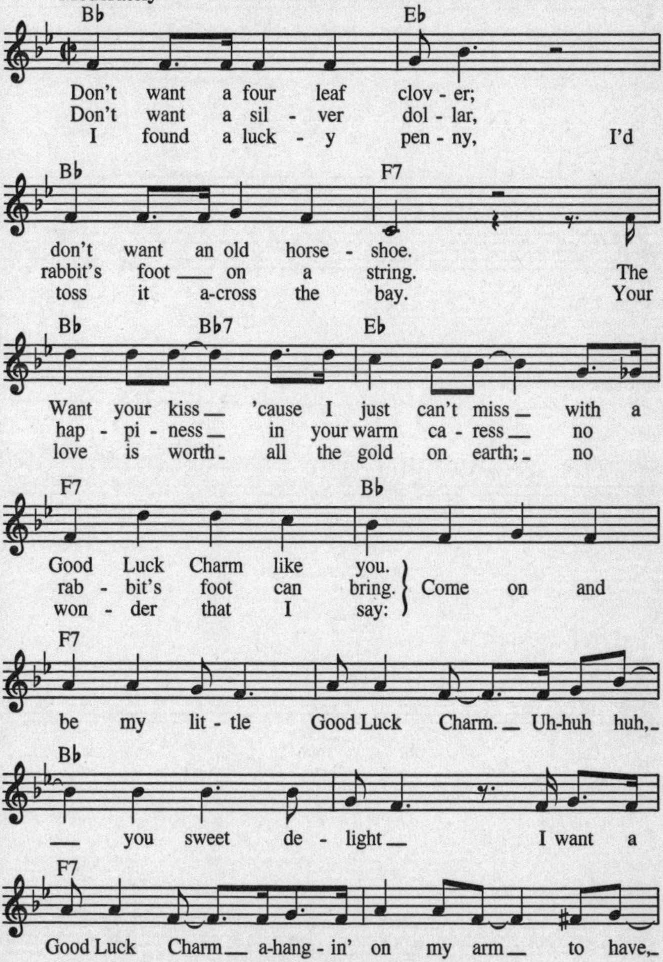
B♭ E♭
Don't want a four leaf clov - er;
Don't want a sil - ver dol - lar,
I found a luck - y pen - ny, I'd
B♭ F7
don't want an old horse - shoe.
rabbit's foot on a string. The
toss it a-cross the bay. Your
B♭ B♭7 E♭
Want your kiss 'cause I just can't miss with a
hap - pi - ness in your warm ca - ress no
love is worth all the gold on earth; no
F7 B♭
Good Luck Charm like you.
rab - bit's foot can bring. Come on and
won - der that I say:
F7
be my lit - tle Good Luck Charm. Uh-huh huh,
B♭
you sweet de - light I want a
F7
Good Luck Charm a-hang - in' on my arm to have,

Copyright © 1962 by Gladys Music, Inc.
Copyright Renewed and Assigned to Gladys Music (Administered by Williamson Music)
and Rachel's Own Music (Administered by A. Schroeder International Ltd.)
International Copyright Secured All Rights Reserved

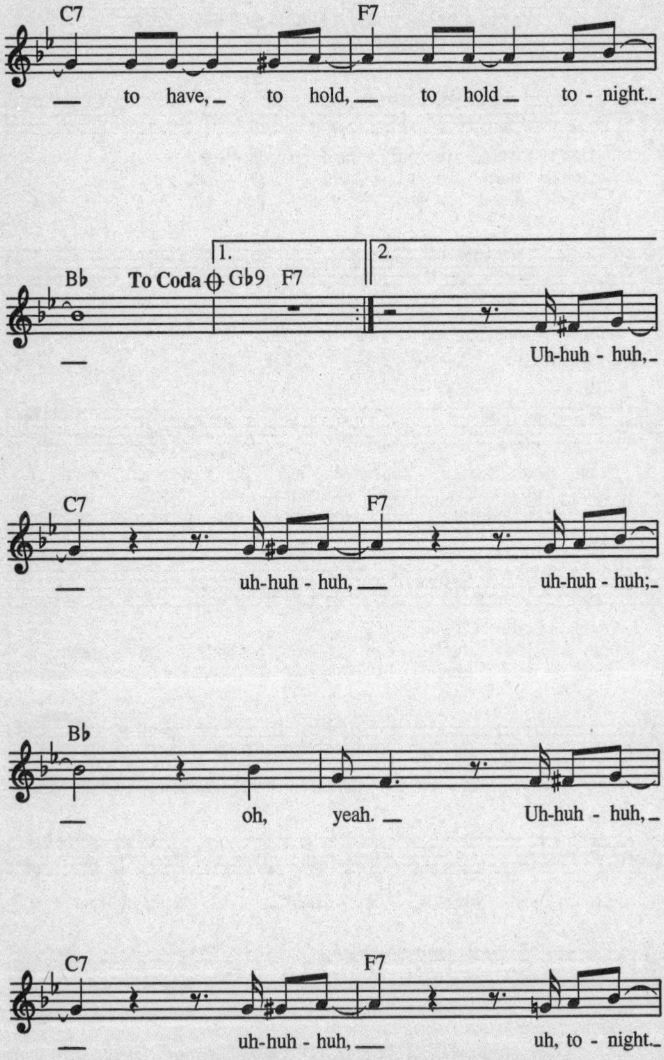
C7
F7
to have,
to hold,
to hold
to - night.
1.
2.
B♭
To Coda
G♭9
F7
Uh-huh - huh,
C7
F7
uh-huh - huh,
uh-huh - huh;
B♭
oh,
yeah.
Uh-huh - huh,
C7
F7
uh-huh - huh,
uh, to - night.

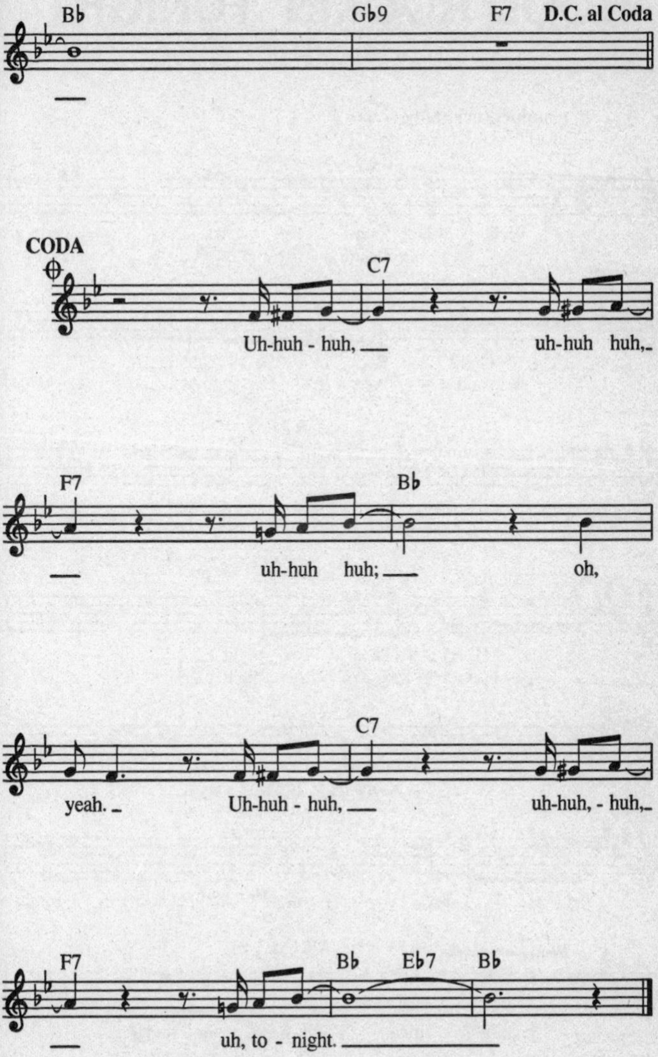
Bb Gb9 F7 D.C. al Coda
CODA
C7
Uh-huh - huh, uh-huh huh,
F7 Bb
uh-huh huh; oh,
C7
yeah. Uh-huh - huh, uh-huh, - huh,
F7 Bb Eb7 Bb
uh, to - night.

GOOD ROCKIN' TONIGHT

By ROY BROWN

In genuine Rockabilly

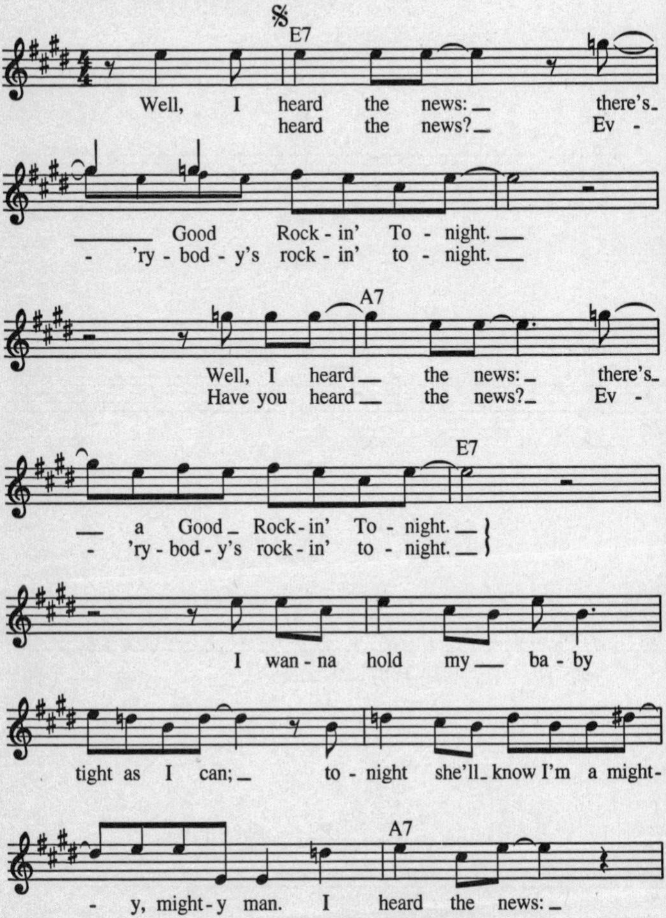
E7
Well, I heard the news: there's Good Rock-in' To-night.
heard the news? Ev-'ry-bod-y's rock-in' to-night.
A7
Well, I heard the news: there's
Have you heard the news? Ev-
E7
a Good Rock-in' To-night.
'ry-bod-y's rock-in' to-night.
I wan-na hold my ba-by
tight as I can; to-night she'll know I'm a might-
A7
y, might-y man. I heard the news:

Copyright © 1948 Blue Ridge Publishing Corporation
Copyright Renewed and Assigned to Fort Knox Music, Inc. and Trio Music Co., Inc.
International Copyright Secured All Rights Reserved
Used by Permission

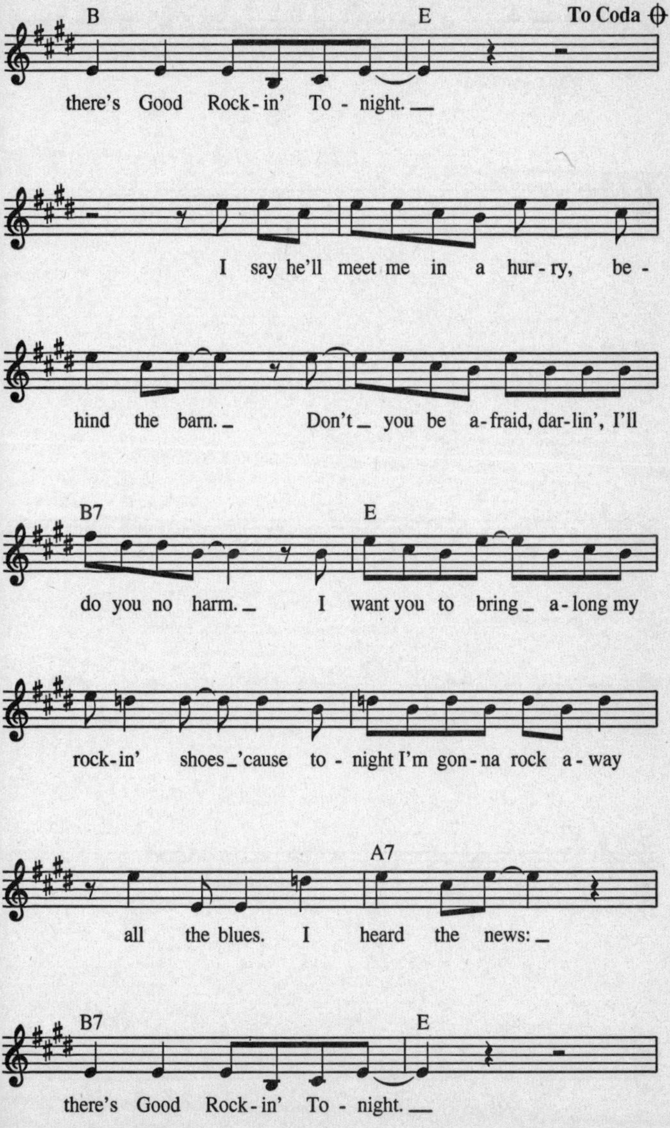
B
E
To Coda
there's Good Rock-in' To-night.
I say he'll meet me in a hur-ry, be-
hind the barn. Don't you be a-fraid, dar-lin', I'll
B7
E
do you no harm. I want you to bring a-long my
rock-in' shoes 'cause to-night I'm gon-na rock a-way
A7
all the blues. I heard the news:
B7
E
there's Good Rock-in' To-night.

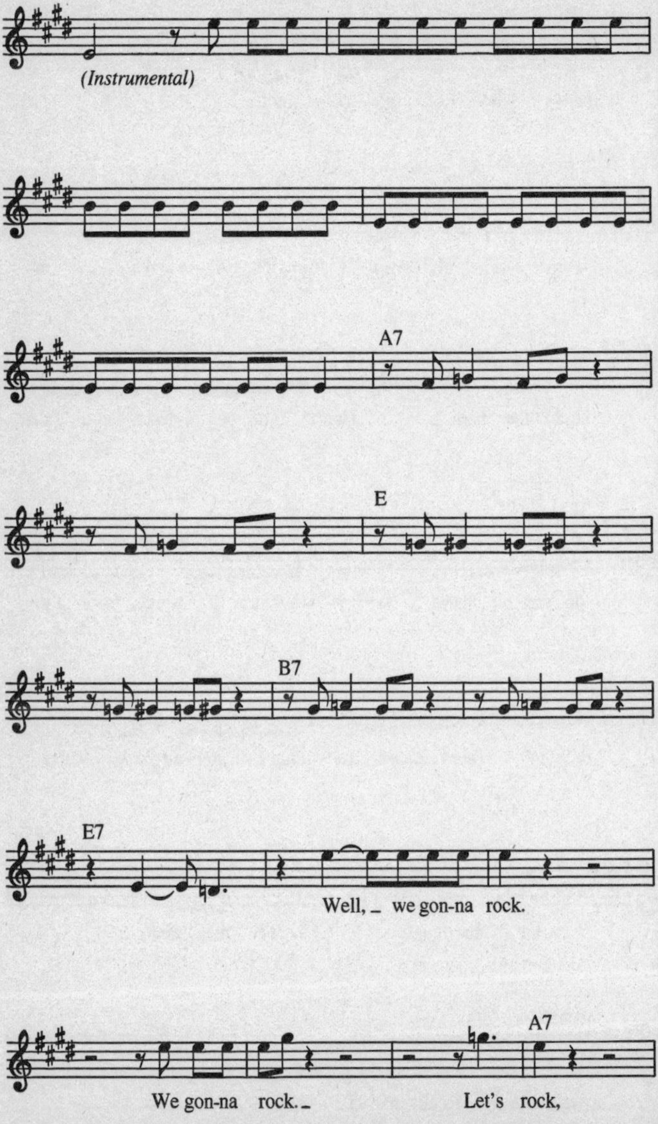
(Instrumental)
A7
E
B7
E7
Well, we gon-na rock.
We gon-na rock.
Let's rock,
A7

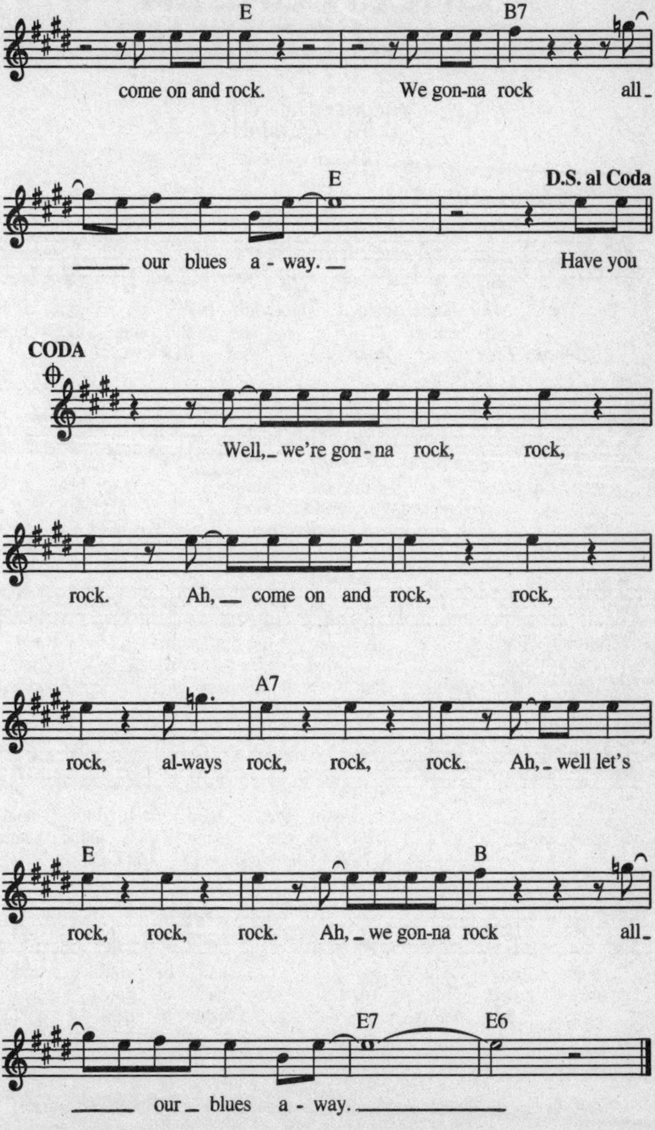
E
B7
come on and rock.
We gon-na rock
all
E
D.S. al Coda
our blues a - way.
Have you
CODA
Well, we're gon - na rock,
rock,
rock.
Ah, come on and rock,
rock,
A7
rock,
al-ways rock,
rock,
rock.
Ah, well let's
E
B
rock,
rock,
rock.
Ah, we gon-na rock
all
E7
E6
our blues a - way.

GREEN GREEN GRASS OF HOME

Words and Music by
CURLY PUTMAN

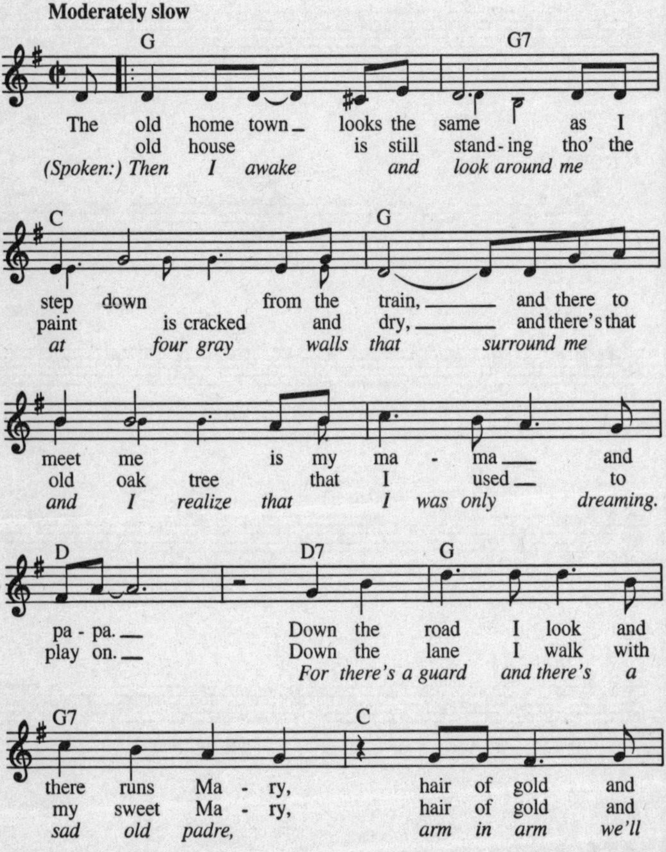
Moderately slow
G
G7
The old home town looks the same as I
old house is still stand-ing tho' the
(Spoken:) Then I awake and look around me
C
G
step down from the train, and there to
paint is cracked and dry, and there's that
at four gray walls that surround me
meet me is my ma - ma and
old oak tree that I used to
and I realize that I was only dreaming.
D
D7
G
pa - pa.
play on.
Down the road I look and
Down the lane I walk with
For there's a guard and there's a
G7
C
there runs Ma - ry, hair of gold and
my sweet Ma - ry, hair of gold and
sad old padre, arm in arm we'll

Copyright © 1965 Sony/ATV Songs LLC
Copyright Renewed
All Rights Administered by Sony/ATV Music Publishing, 8 Music Square West, Nashville, TN 37203
International Copyright Secured All Rights Reserved

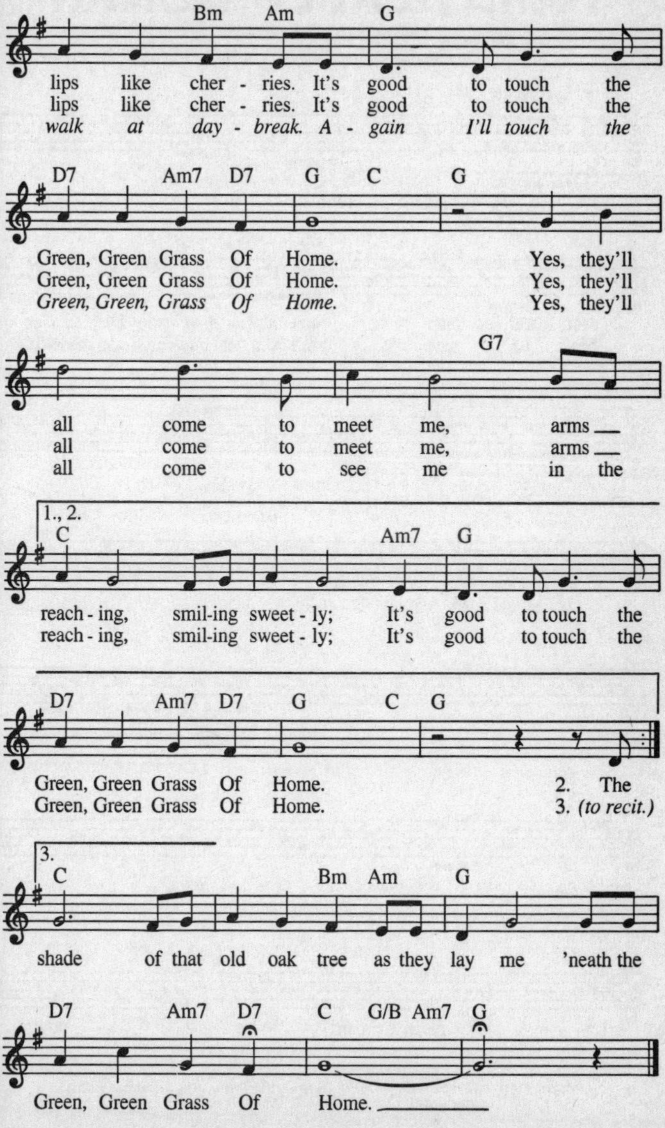
Bm Am G
lips like cher - ries. It's good to touch the
lips like cher - ries. It's good to touch the
walk at day - break. A - gain I'll touch the
D7 Am7 D7 G C G
Green, Green Grass Of Home. Yes, they'll
Green, Green Grass Of Home. Yes, they'll
Green, Green, Grass Of Home. Yes, they'll
G7
all come to meet me, arms
all come to meet me, arms
all come to see me in the
1., 2.
C Am7 G
reach - ing, smil-ing sweet - ly; It's good to touch the
reach - ing, smil-ing sweet - ly; It's good to touch the
D7 Am7 D7 G C G
Green, Green Grass Of Home. 2. The
Green, Green Grass Of Home. 3. (to recit.)
3.
C Bm Am G
shade of that old oak tree as they lay me 'neath the
D7 Am7 D7 C G/B Am7 G
Green, Green Grass Of Home.

HARD HEADED WOMAN

Words and Music by
CLAUDE DEMETRUIS

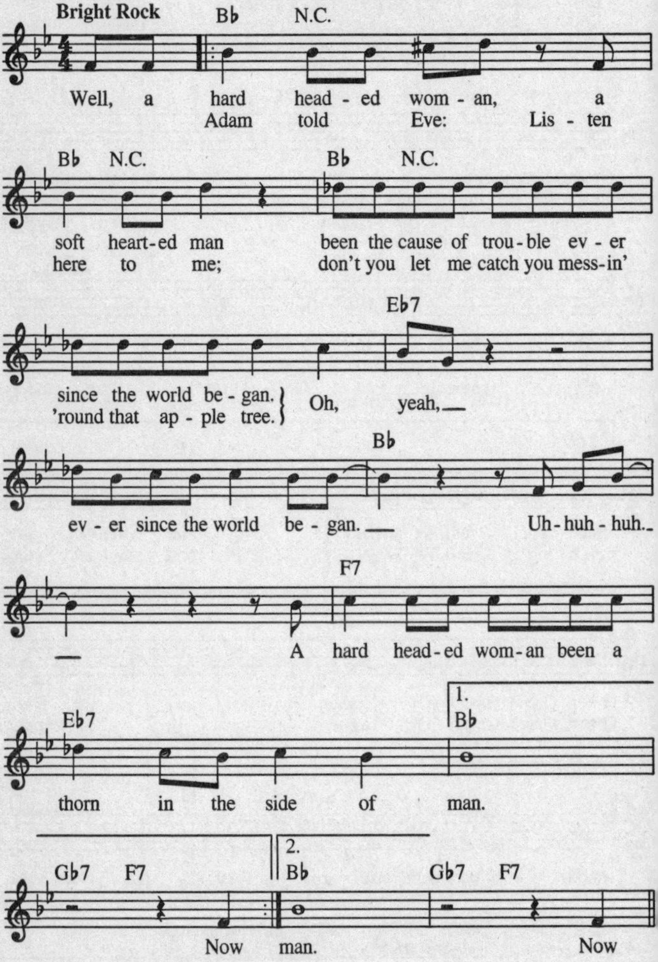
Bright Rock
Bb N.C.
Well, a hard head - ed wom - an, a
Adam told Eve: Lis - ten
Bb N.C. Bb N.C.
soft heart-ed man been the cause of trou - ble ev - er
here to me; don't you let me catch you mess-in'
Eb7
since the world be - gan. Oh, yeah,
'round that ap - ple tree.
Bb
ev - er since the world be - gan. Uh-huh - huh.
F7
A hard head-ed wom-an been a
Eb7
1.
Bb
thorn in the side of man.
Gb7 F7
2.
Bb
Gb7 F7
Now man. Now

Copyright © 1958 by Gladys Music, Inc.
Copyright Renewed and Assigned to Gladys Music (Administered by Williamson Music)
International Copyright Secured All Rights Reserved

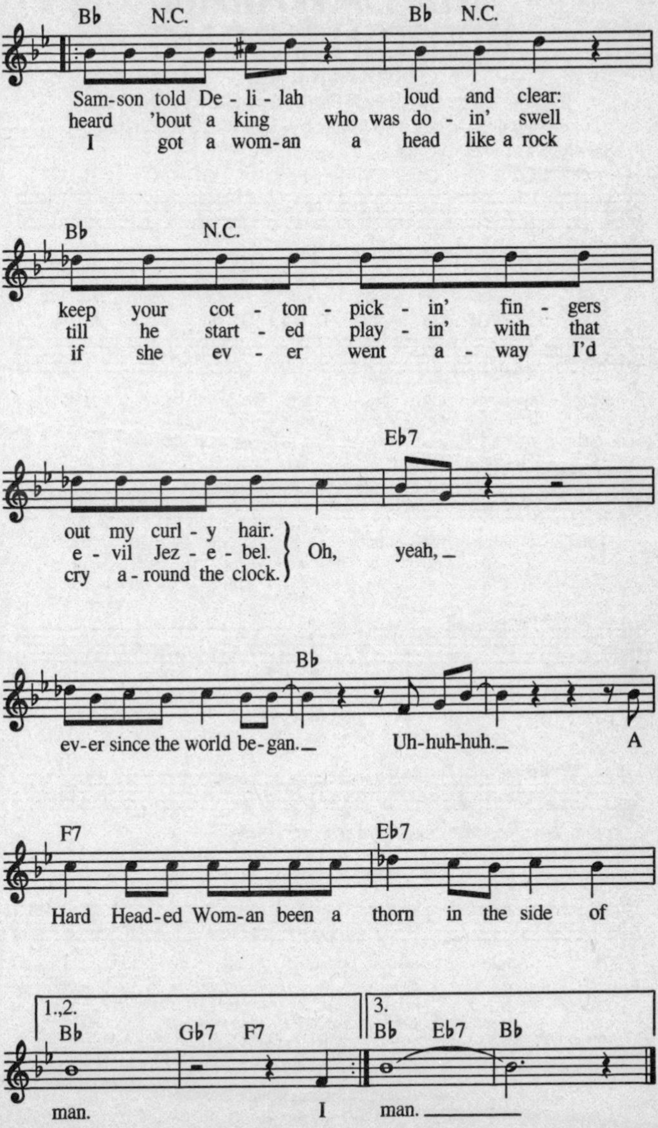
B♭ N.C. B♭ N.C.
Sam-son told De - li - lah loud and clear:
heard 'bout a king who was do - in' swell
I got a wom-an a head like a rock
B♭ N.C.
keep your cot - ton - pick - in' fin - gers
till he start - ed play - in' with that
if she ev - er went a - way I'd
E♭7
out my curl - y hair.
e - vil Jez - e - bel.
cry a - round the clock.
Oh, yeah,
B♭
ev-er since the world be-gan.
Uh-huh-huh.
A
F7 E♭7
Hard Head-ed Wom-an been a thorn in the side of
1.,2. 3.
B♭ G♭7 F7 B♭ E♭7 B♭
man. I man.

THE HAWAIIAN WEDDING SONG

(Ke Kali Nei Au)

English Lyrics by AL HOFFMAN and DICK MANNING
Hawaiian Lyrics and Music by CHARLES E. KING

Slowly, with much warmth

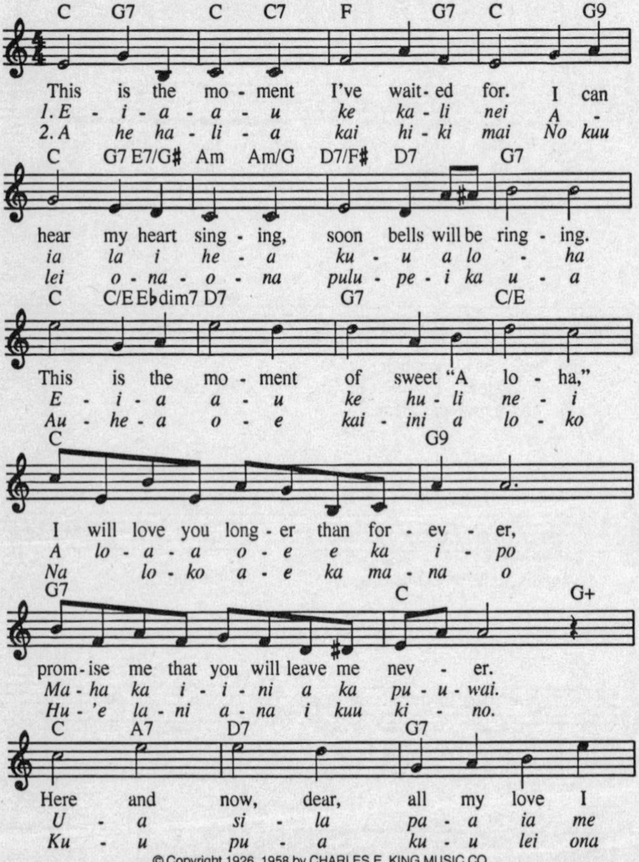
C G7 C C7 F G7 C G9
This is the mo - ment I've wait- ed for. I can
1. E - i - a - a - u ke ka - li nei A -
2. A he ha - li - a kai hi - ki mai No kuu
C G7 E7/G# Am Am/G D7/F# D7 G7
hear my heart sing - ing, soon bells will be ring - ing.
ia la i he - a ku - u a lo - ha
lei o - na - o - na pulu - pe - i ka u - a
C C/E Ebdim7 D7 G7 C/E
This is the mo - ment of sweet "A lo - ha,"
E - i - a a - u ke hu - li ne - i
Au - he - a o - e kai - ini a lo - ko
C G9
I will love you long - er than for - ev - er,
A lo - a - a o - e e ka i - po
Na lo - ko a - e ka ma - na o
G7 C G+
prom - ise me that you will leave me nev - er.
Ma - ha ka i - i - ni a ka pu - u - wai.
Hu - 'e la - ni a - na i kuu ki - no.
C A7 D7 G7
Here and now, dear, all my love I
U - a si - la pa - a ia me
Ku - u pu - a ku - u lei ona

© Copyright 1926, 1958 by CHARLES E. KING MUSIC CO.
Copyright Renewed 1986 and Assigned to CHARLES E. KING MUSIC CO., MCA MUSIC PUBLISHING, A Division of MCA INC. and AL HOFFMANN SONGS, INC.
All Rights for CHARLES E. KING MUSIC CO. Controlled and Administered by MCA MUSIC PUBLISHING, A Division of MCA INC.
International Copyright Secured All Rights Reserved
MCA music publishing

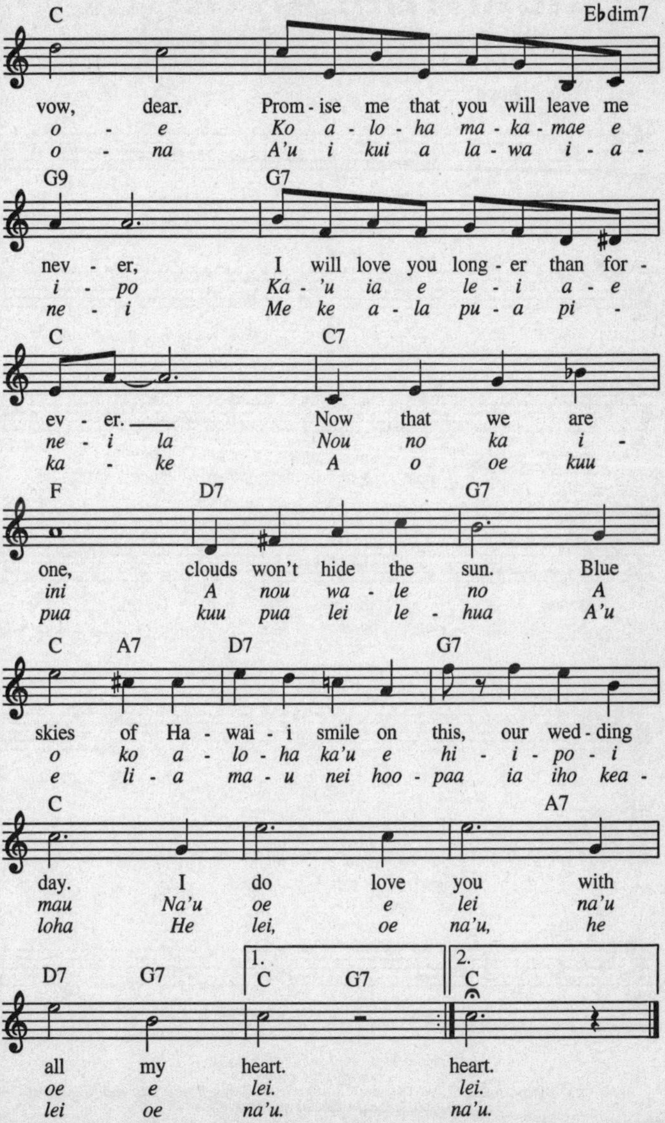
C Ebdim7
vow, dear. Prom - ise me that you will leave me
o - e Ko a - lo - ha ma - ka - mae e
o - na A'u i kui a la - wa i - a -
G9 G7
nev - er, I will love you long - er than for -
i - po Ka - 'u ia e le - i a - e
ne - i Me ke a - la pu - a pi -
C C7
ev - er. Now that we are
ne - i la Nou no ka i -
ka - ke A o oe kuu
F D7 G7
one, clouds won't hide the sun. Blue
ini A nou wa - le no A
pua kuu pua lei le - hua A'u
C A7 D7 G7
skies of Ha - wai - i smile on this, our wed - ding
o ko a - lo - ha ka'u e hi - i - po - i
e li - a ma - u nei hoo - paa ia iho kea -
C A7
day. I do love you with
mau Na'u oe e lei na'u
loha He lei, oe na'u, he
D7 G7 1. C G7 2. C
all my heart. heart.
oe e lei. lei.
lei oe na'u. na'u.

HEARTBREAK HOTEL

Words and Music by MAE BOREN AXTON,
TOMMY DURDEN and ELVIS PRESLEY

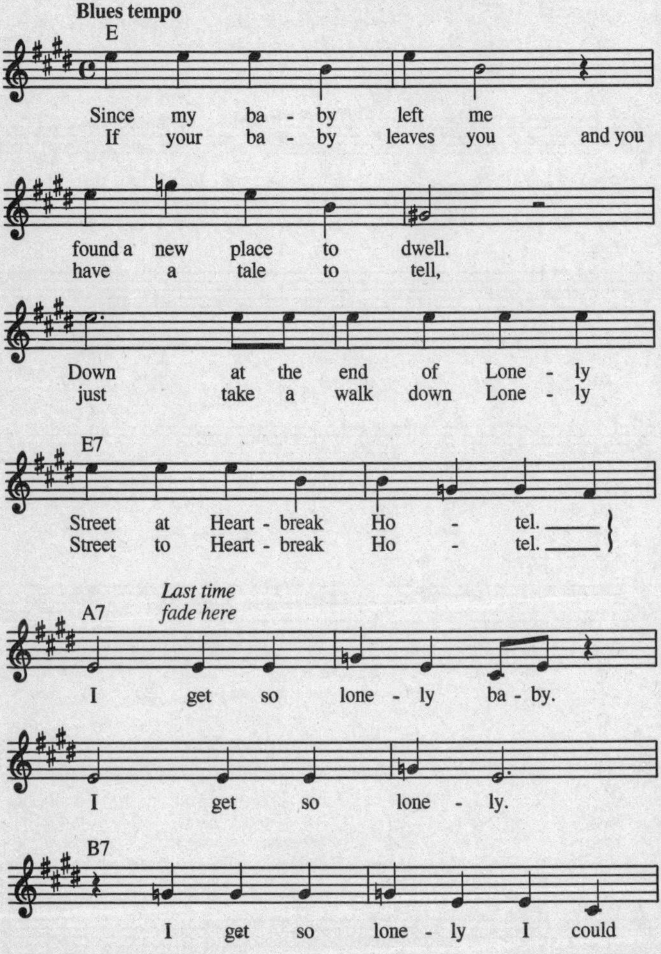
Blues tempo
E
Since my ba - by left me
If your ba - by leaves you and you
found a new place to dwell.
have a tale to tell,
Down at the end of Lone - ly
just take a walk down Lone - ly
E7
Street at Heart - break Ho - tel.
Street to Heart - break Ho - tel.
Last time
fade here
A7
I get so lone - ly ba - by.
I get so lone - ly.
B7
I get so lone - ly I could

Copyright © 1956 Sony/ATV Songs LLC
Copyright Renewed
All Rights Administered by Sony/ATV Music Publishing, 8 Music Square West, Nashville, TN 37203
International Copyright Secured All Rights Reserved

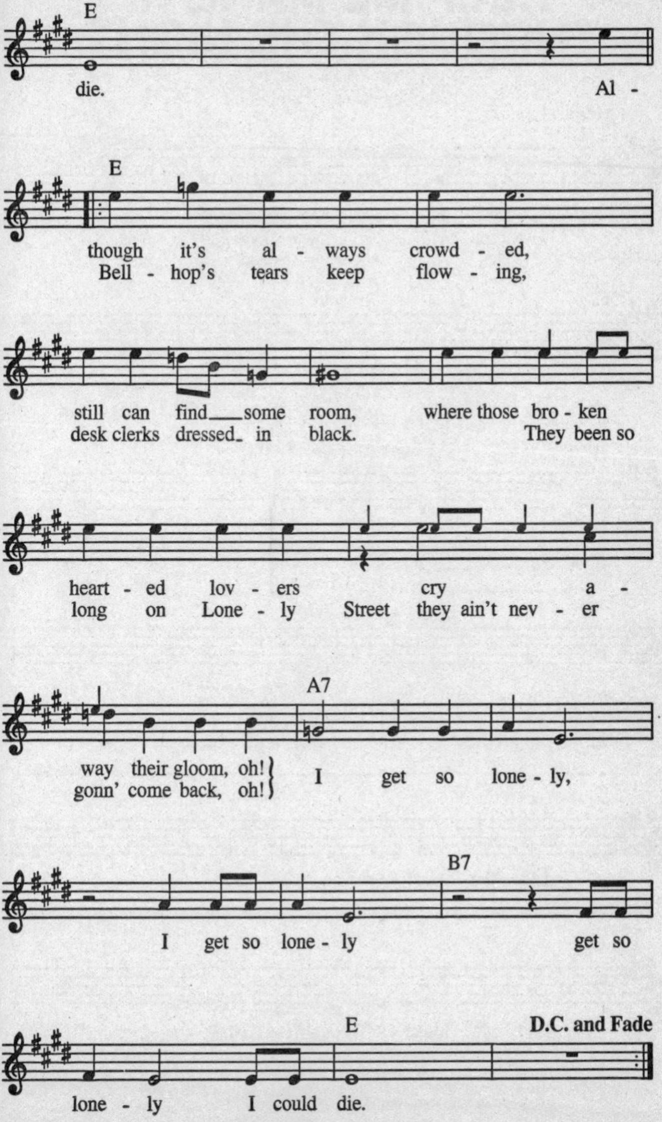
E
die. Al -
E
though it's al - ways crowd - ed,
Bell - hop's tears keep flow - ing,
still can find some room, where those bro - ken
desk clerks dressed in black. They been so
heart - ed lov - ers cry a -
long on Lone - ly Street they ain't nev - er
A7
way their gloom, oh!
gonn' come back, oh!
I get so lone - ly,
B7
I get so lone - ly get so
E
D.C. and Fade
lone - ly I could die.

HELP ME MAKE IT THROUGH THE NIGHT

Words and Music by
KRIS KRISTOFFERSON

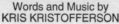

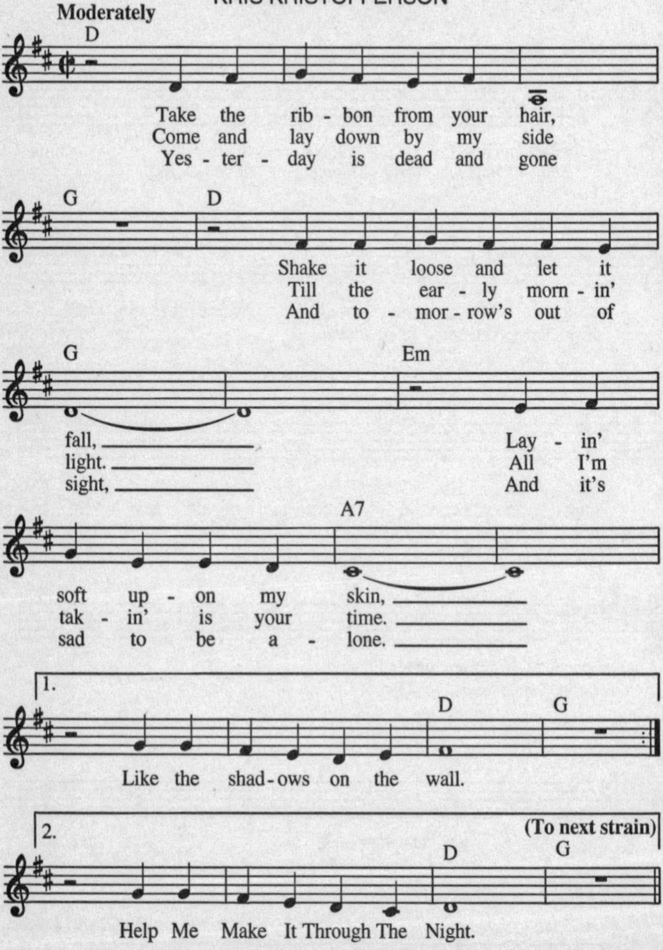
Moderately
D
Take the rib - bon from your hair,
Come and lay down by my side
Yes - ter - day is dead and gone
G D
Shake it loose and let it
Till the ear - ly morn - in'
And to - mor - row's out of
G Em
fall,
light.
sight,
Lay - in'
All I'm
And it's
A7
soft up - on my skin,
tak - in' is your time.
sad to be a - lone.
1.
D G
Like the shad - ows on the wall.
2.
(To next strain)
D G
Help Me Make It Through The Night.

© 1970 TEMI COMBINE INC.
All Rights Controlled by COMBINE MUSIC CORP. and Administered by EMI BLACKWOOD MUSIC INC.
All Rights Reserved International Copyright Secured Used by Permission

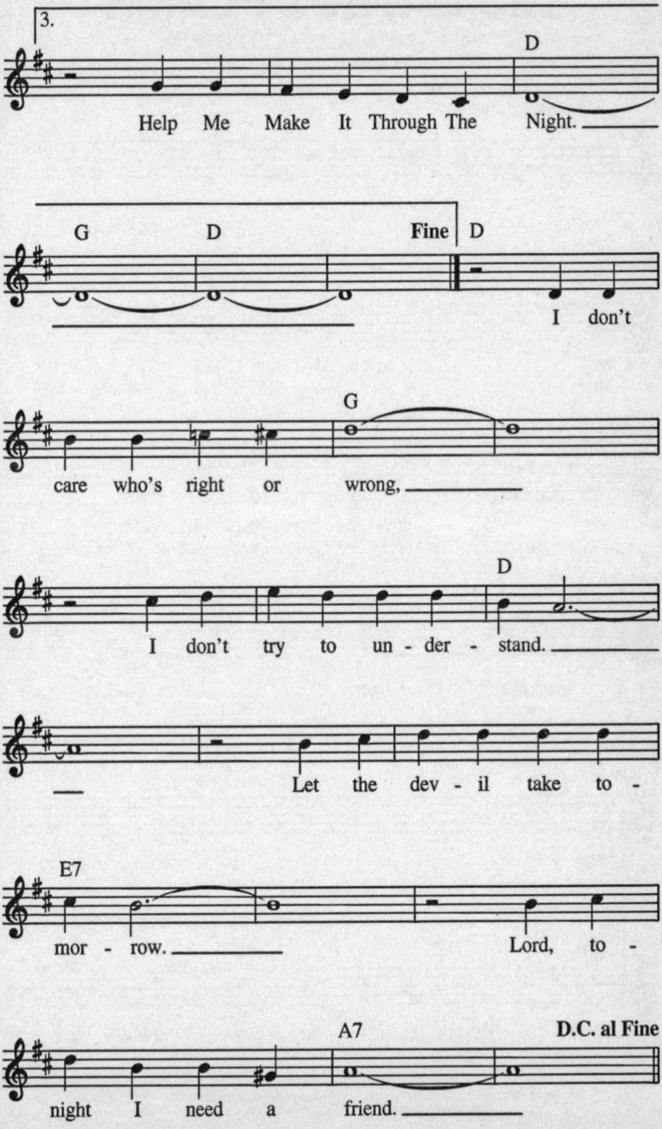
3.
D
Help Me Make It Through The Night.
G D Fine D
I don't
G
care who's right or wrong,
D
I don't try to un - der - stand.
Let the dev - il take to -
E7
mor - row.
Lord, to -
A7 D.C. al Fine
night I need a friend.

HIS LATEST FLAME

Words and Music by DOC POMUS
and MORT SHUMAN

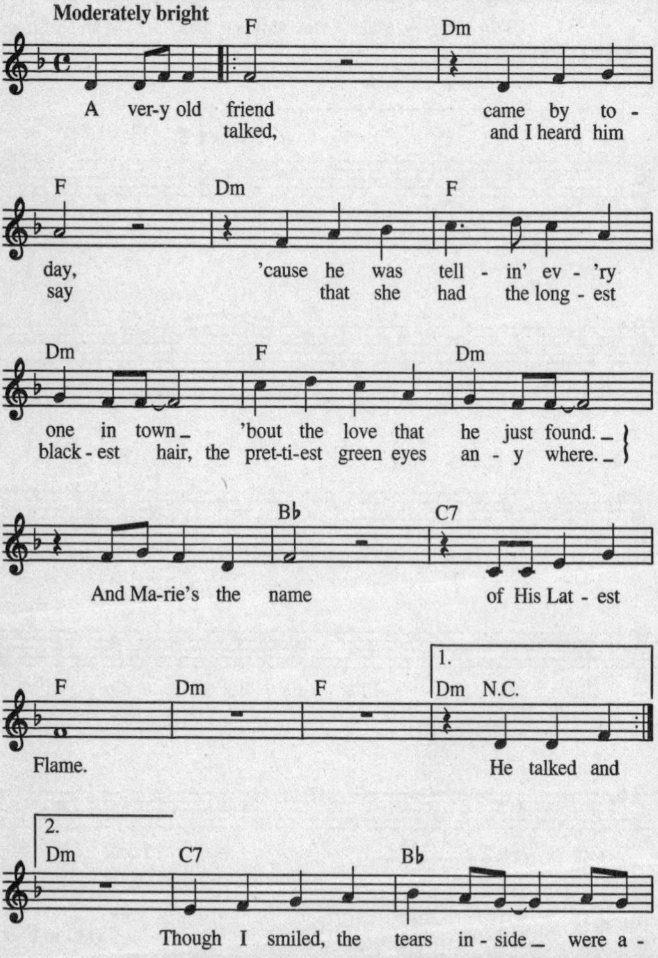
Moderately bright
F Dm
A ver-y old friend came by to -
talked, and I heard him
F Dm F
day, 'cause he was tell - in' ev - 'ry
say that she had the long - est
Dm F Dm
one in town _ 'bout the love that he just found. _
black - est hair, the pret-ti-est green eyes an - y where. _
B♭ C7
And Ma-rie's the name of His Lat - est
F Dm F
1.
Dm N.C.
Flame. He talked and
2.
Dm C7 B♭
Though I smiled, the tears in - side _ were a -

Copyright © 1961 by Valley Publishers, Inc.
Copyright Renewed and Assigned to Elvis Presley Music (Administered by R&H Music)
International Copyright Secured All Rights Reserved

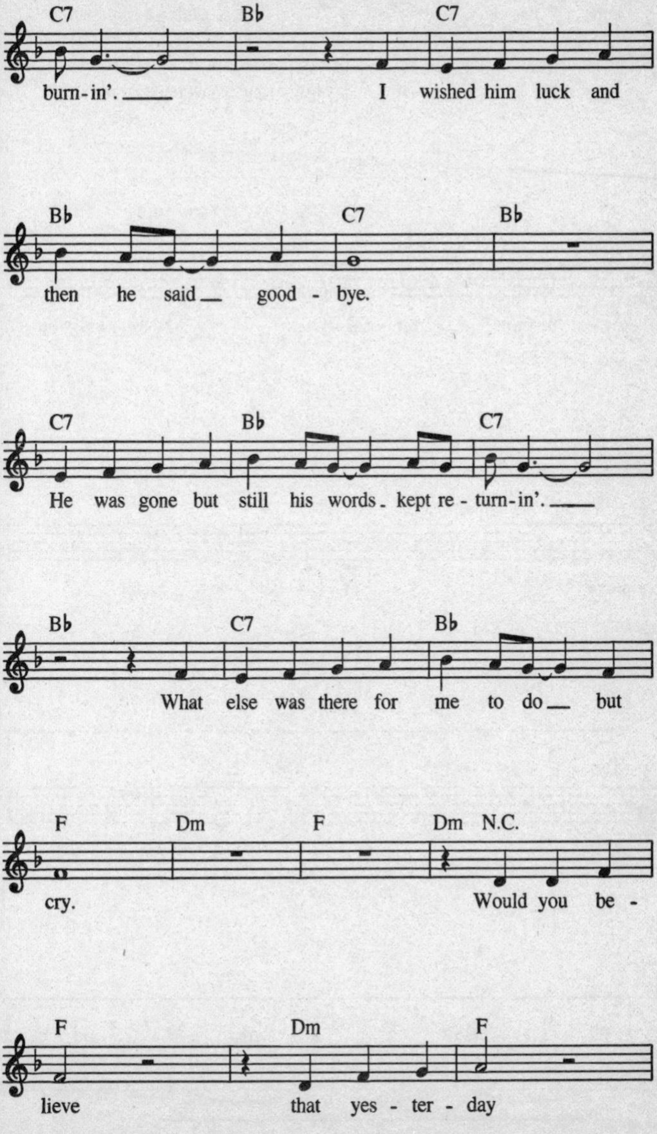
C7 Bb C7
burn-in'. I wished him luck and
Bb C7 Bb
then he said good - bye.
C7 Bb C7
He was gone but still his words kept re - turn-in'.
Bb C7 Bb
What else was there for me to do but
F Dm F Dm N.C.
cry. Would you be -
F Dm F
lieve that yes - ter - day

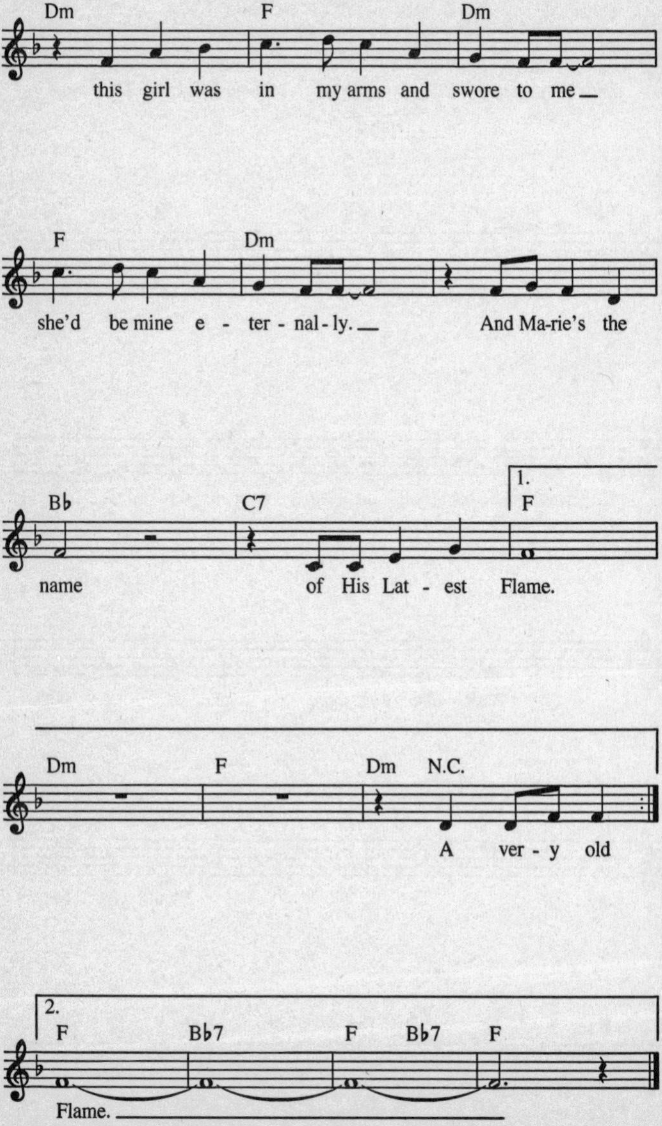
Dm F Dm
this girl was in my arms and swore to me
F Dm
she'd be mine e - ter - nal - ly.
And Ma-rie's the
B♭ C7
1.
F
name of His Lat - est Flame.
Dm F Dm N.C.
A ver - y old
2.
F B♭7 F B♭7 F
Flame.

I FEEL SO BAD

Words and Music by
CHUCK WILLIS

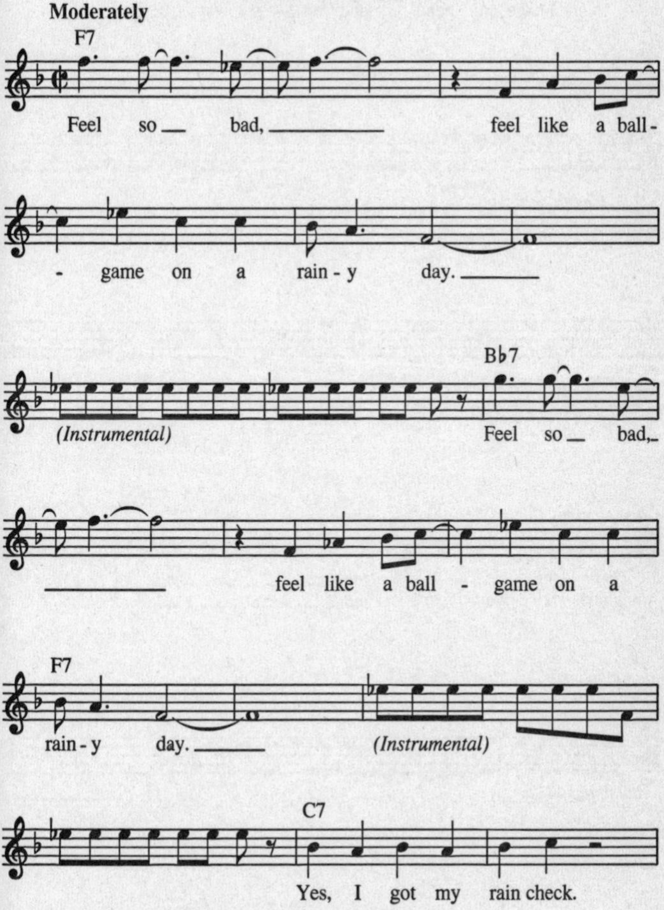
Moderately
F7
Feel so bad, feel like a ball-
- game on a rain - y day.
Bb7
(Instrumental)
Feel so bad,
feel like a ball - game on a
F7
rain - y day.
(Instrumental)
C7
Yes, I got my rain check.

Copyright © 1961 Tideland Music and Chuck Willis Music
Copyright Renewed 1989 Tideland Music and Chuck Willis Music
International Copyright Secured All Rights Reserved
Used by Permission

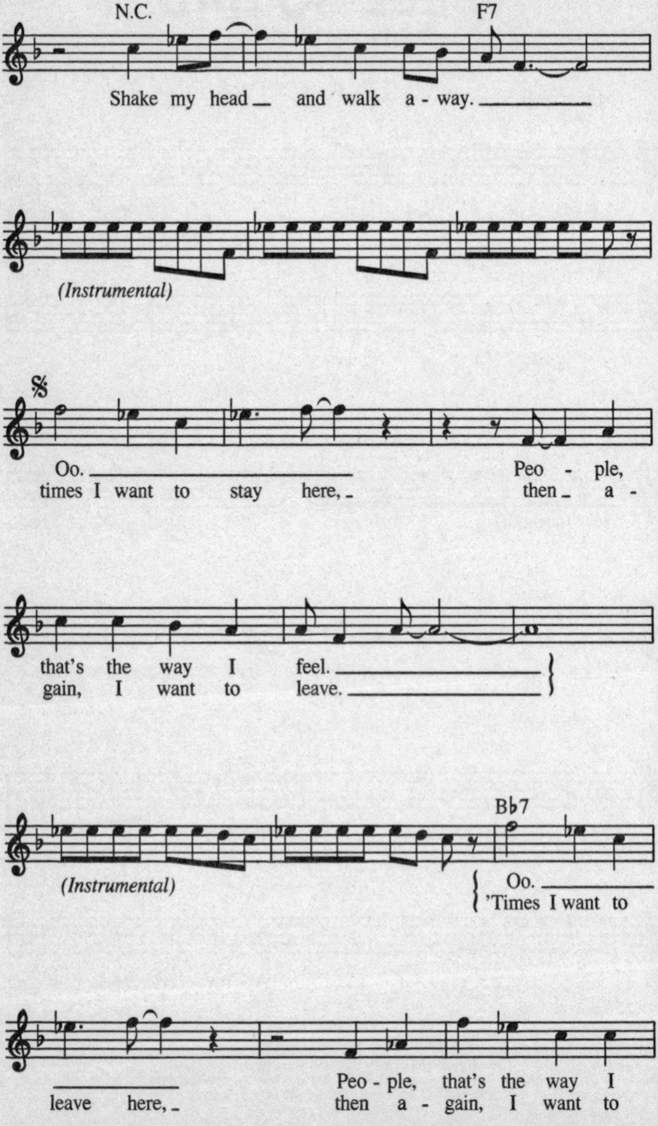
N.C.
F7
Shake my head and walk a - way.
(Instrumental)
Oo.
times I want to stay here,
Peo - ple,
then a -
that's the way I feel.
gain, I want to leave.
Bb7
(Instrumental)
Oo.
'Times I want to
leave here,
Peo - ple, that's the way I
then a - gain, I want to

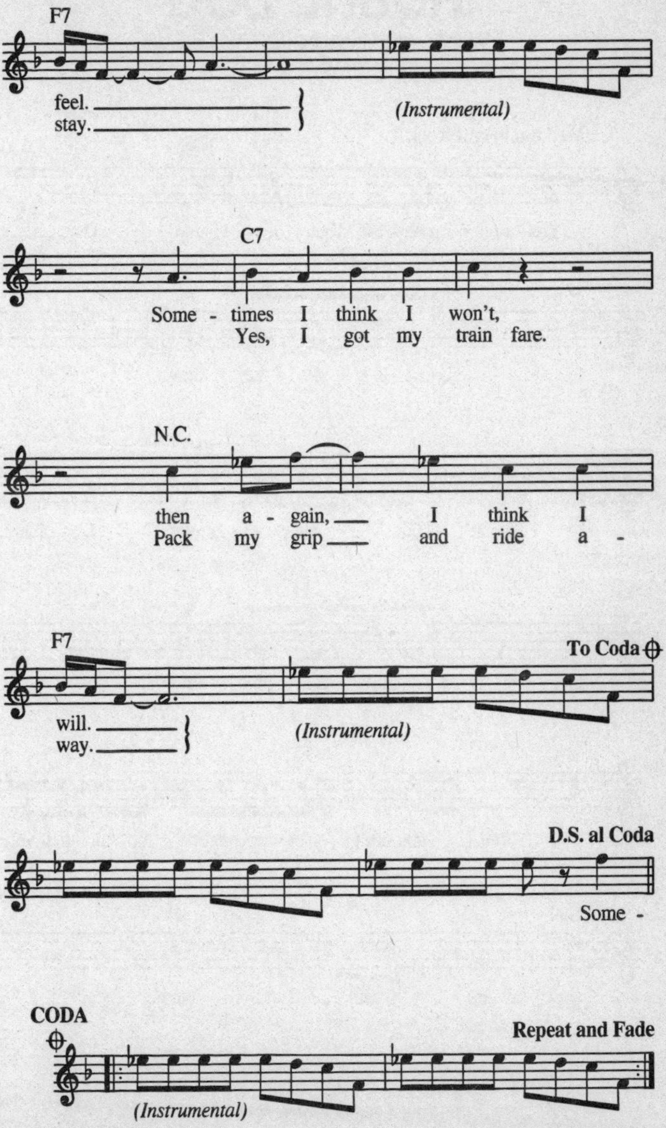
F7
feel.
stay.
(Instrumental)
C7
Some - times I think I won't,
Yes, I got my train fare.
N.C.
then a - gain, I think I
Pack my grip and ride a -
F7
To Coda
will.
way.
(Instrumental)
D.S. al Coda
Some -
CODA
Repeat and Fade
(Instrumental)

HOUND DOG

Words and Music by JERRY LEIBER
and MIKE STOLLER

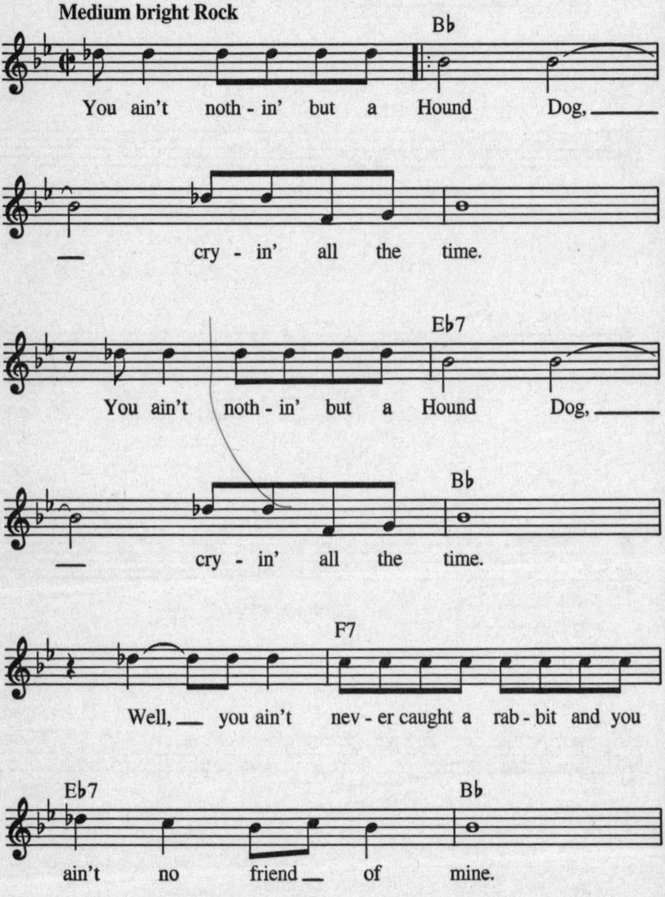
Medium bright Rock
B♭
You ain't noth - in' but a Hound Dog,
cry - in' all the time.
E♭7
You ain't noth - in' but a Hound Dog,
B♭
cry - in' all the time.
F7
Well, you ain't nev - er caught a rab - bit and you
E♭7
B♭
ain't no friend of mine.

Copyright © 1956 by Elvis Presley Music, Inc. and Lion Publishing Co., Inc.
Copyright Renewed, Assigned to Gladys Music (Administered by Williamson Music)
and MCA Music Publishing, a Division of MCA Inc.
International Copyright Secured All Rights Reserved

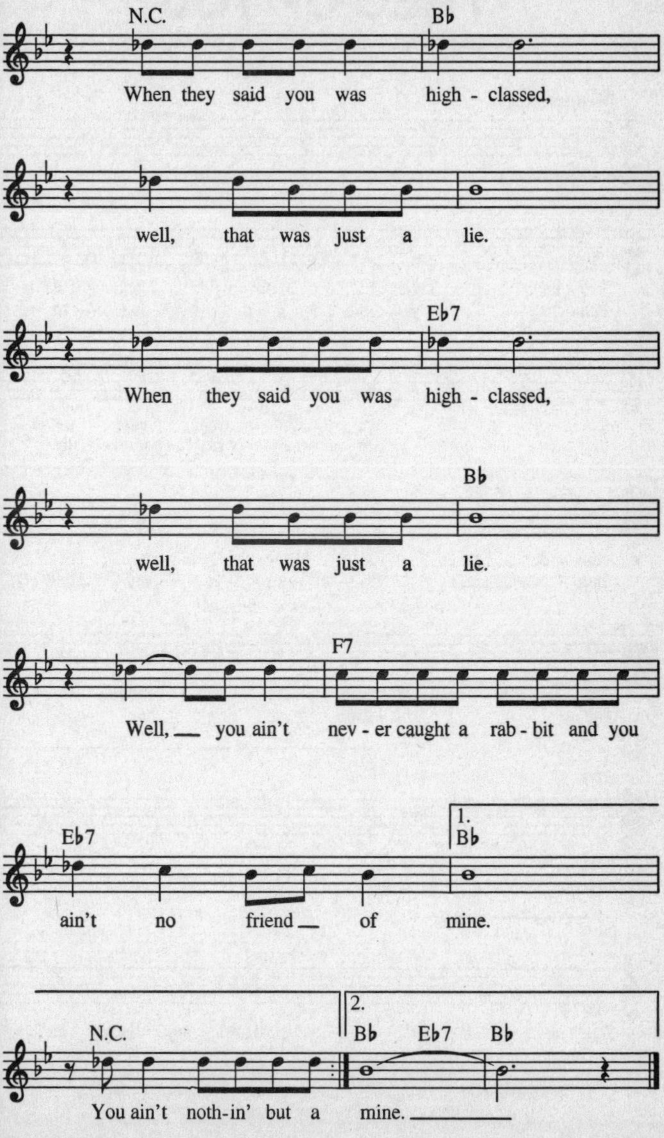
N.C.
Bb
When they said you was high - classed,
well, that was just a lie.
Eb7
When they said you was high - classed,
Bb
well, that was just a lie.
F7
Well, you ain't nev - er caught a rab - bit and you
Eb7
1.
Bb
ain't no friend of mine.
N.C.
2.
Bb Eb7 Bb
You ain't noth-in' but a mine.

I BEG OF YOU

Words and Music by ROSE MARIE McCOY
and KELLY OWENS

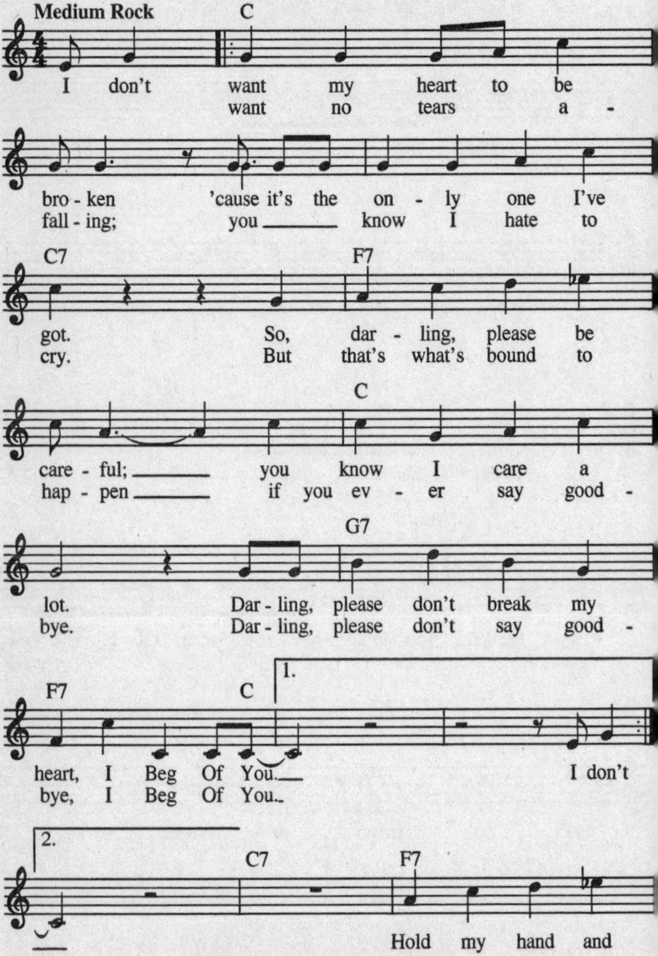
Medium Rock
C
I don't want my heart to be
want no tears a -
bro - ken 'cause it's the on - ly one I've
fall - ing; you know I hate to
C7
F7
got. So, dar - ling, please be
cry. But that's what's bound to
C
care - ful; you know I care a
hap - pen if you ev - er say good -
G7
lot. Dar - ling, please don't break my
bye. Dar - ling, please don't say good -
F7
C
1.
heart, I Beg Of You. I don't
bye, I Beg Of You.
2.
C7
F7
Hold my hand and

Copyright © 1957 by Rio Grande Music, Inc.
Copyright Assigned to Elvis Presley Music, Inc.
Copyright Renewed and Assigned to Elvis Presley Music (Administered by R&H Music)
International Copyright Secured All Rights Reserved

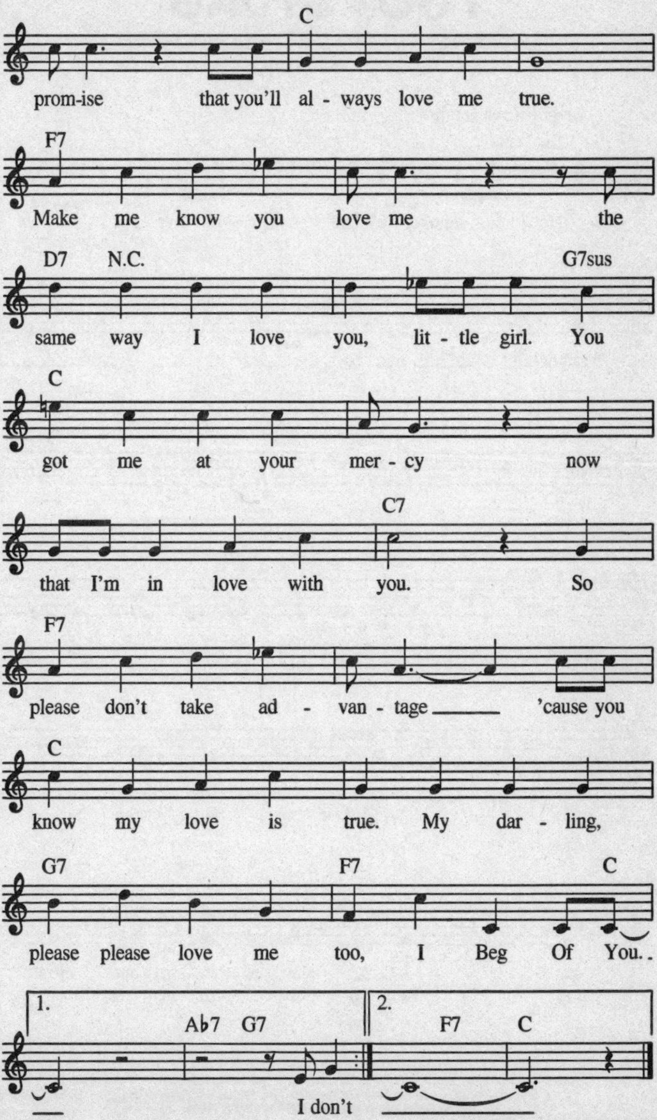
C
prom-ise that you'll al - ways love me true.
F7
Make me know you love me the
D7 N.C. G7sus
same way I love you, lit - tle girl. You
C
got me at your mer - cy now
C7
that I'm in love with you. So
F7
please don't take ad - van - tage ’cause you
C
know my love is true. My dar - ling,
G7 F7 C
please please love me too, I Beg Of You.
1. A♭7 G7
I don't
2. F7 C

I GOT STUNG

Words and Music by AARON SCHROEDER
and DAVID HILL

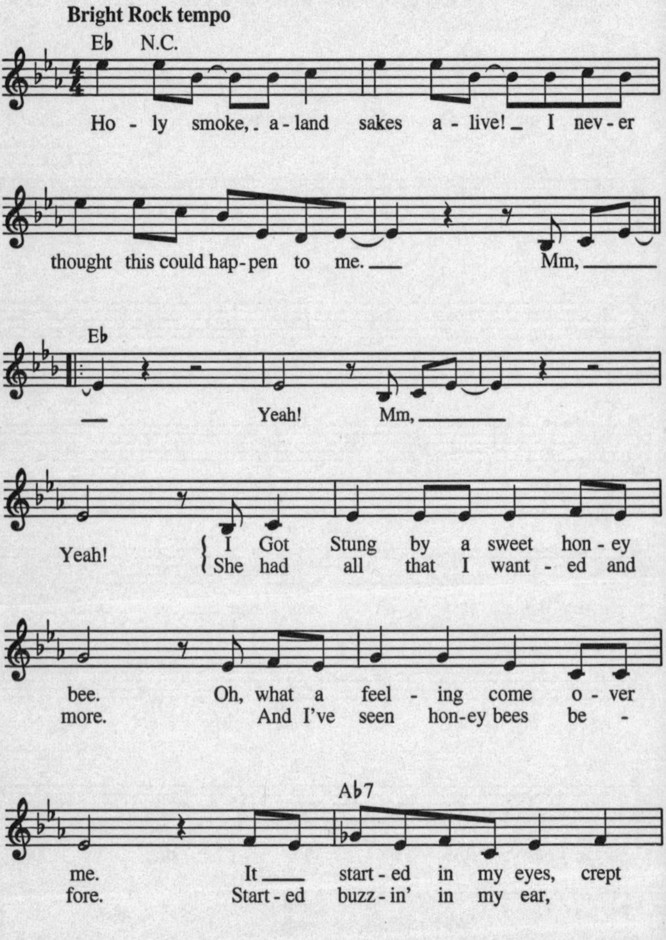
Bright Rock tempo
E♭ N.C.
Ho - ly smoke, a - land sakes a - live! I nev - er
thought this could hap - pen to me. Mm,
E♭
Yeah! Mm,
Yeah!
I Got Stung by a sweet hon - ey
She had all that I want - ed and
bee. Oh, what a feel - ing come o - ver
more. And I've seen hon - ey bees be -
A♭7
me. It start - ed in my eyes, crept
fore. Start - ed buzz - in' in my ear,

Copyright © 1958 by Gladys Music, Inc.
Copyright Renewed and Assigned to Gladys Music (Administered by Williamson Music)
and Rachel's Own Music (Administered by A. Schroeder International Ltd.)
International Copyright Secured All Rights Reserved

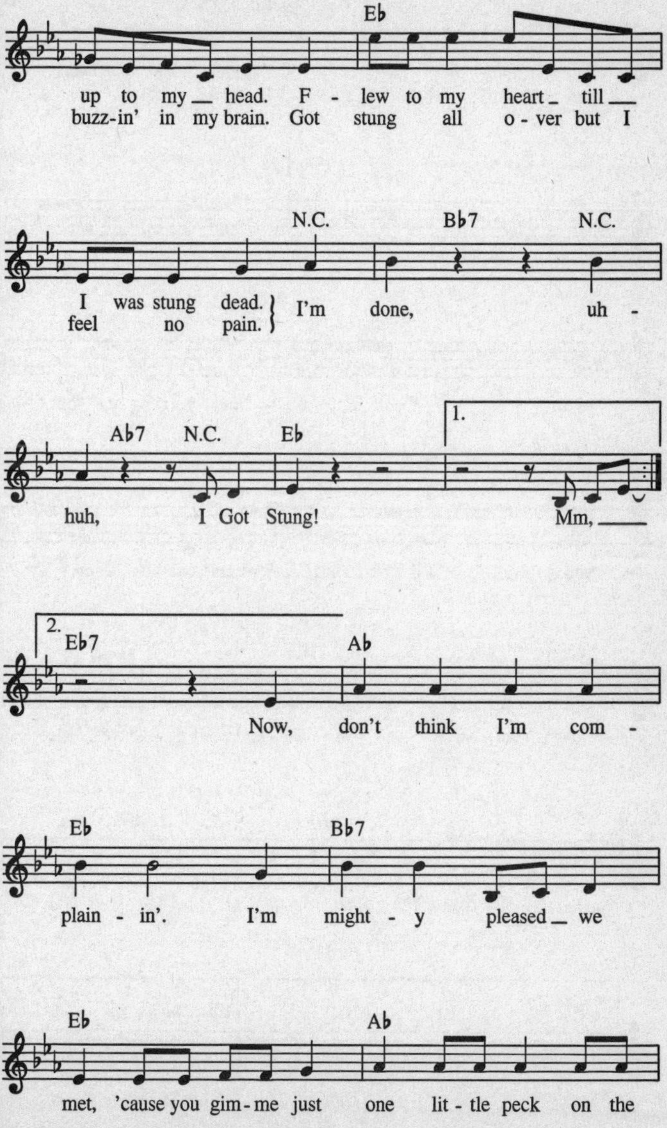
E♭
up to my __ head. F - lew to my heart __ till __
buzz-in' in my brain. Got stung all o - ver but I
N.C. B♭7 N.C.
I was stung dead.
feel no pain.
I'm done, uh -
A♭7 N.C. E♭
1.
huh, I Got Stung! Mm, __
2.
E♭7 A♭
Now, don't think I'm com -
E♭ B♭7
plain - in'. I'm might - y pleased __ we
E♭ A♭
met, 'cause you gim - me just one lit - tle peck on the

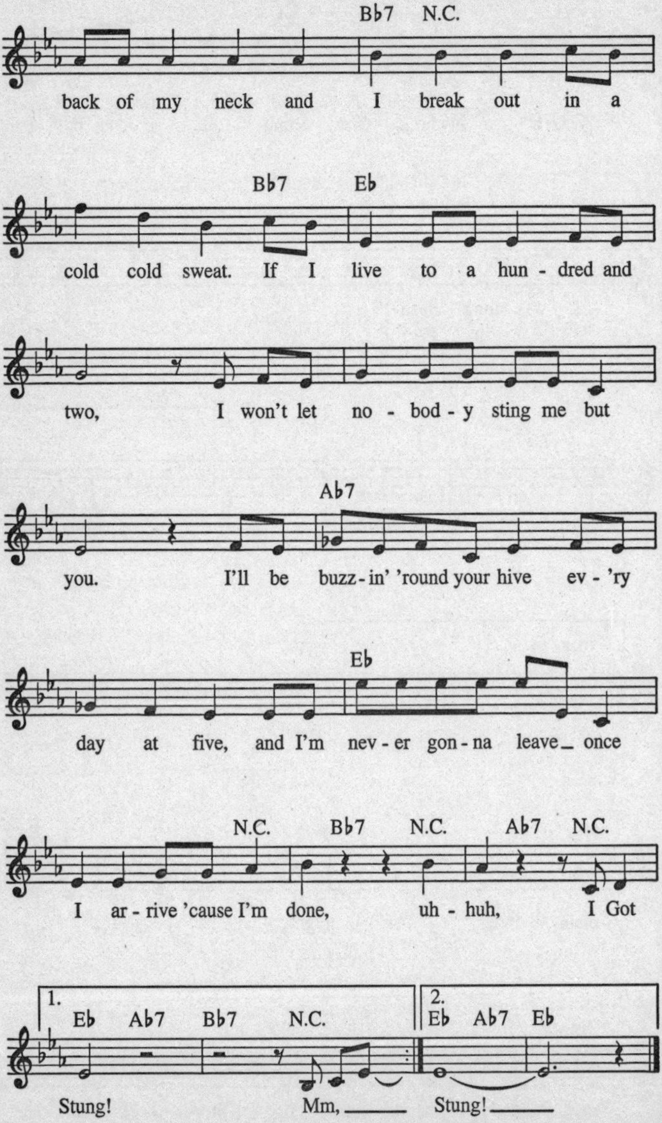
Bb7 N.C.
back of my neck and I break out in a
Bb7 Eb
cold cold sweat. If I live to a hun - dred and
two, I won't let no - bod - y sting me but
Ab7
you. I'll be buzz - in' 'round your hive ev - 'ry
Eb
day at five, and I'm nev - er gon - na leave once
N.C. Bb7 N.C. Ab7 N.C.
I ar - rive 'cause I'm done, uh - huh, I Got
1. Eb Ab7 Bb7 N.C.
Stung! Mm,
2. Eb Ab7 Eb
Stung!

IF I CAN DREAM

Words and Music by
W. EARL BROWN

Very slow, with much drive

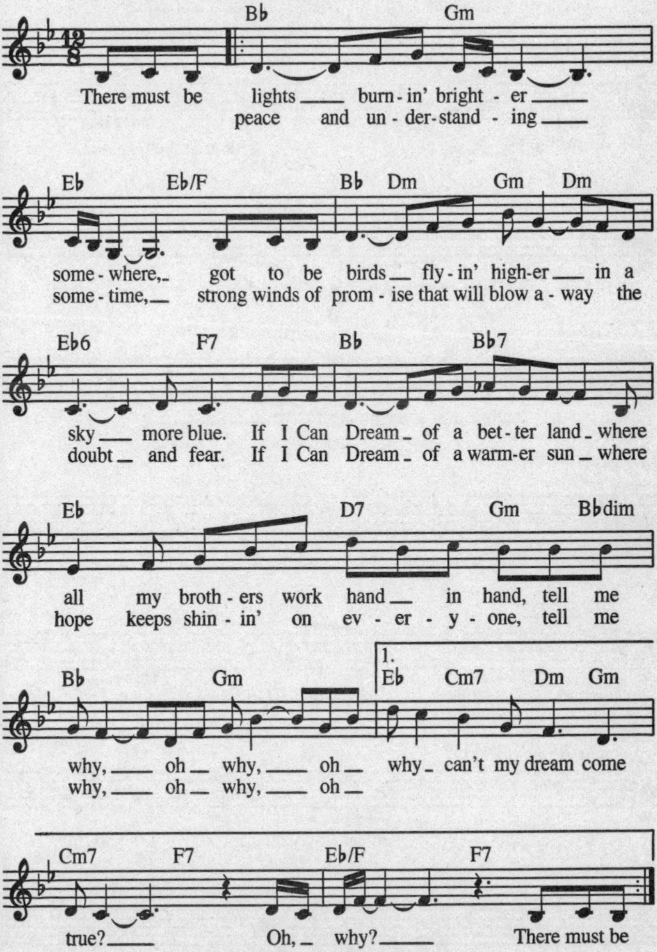
Bb Gm
There must be lights burn-in' bright - er
peace and un - der-stand - ing
Eb Eb/F Bb Dm Gm Dm
some - where, got to be birds fly - in' high-er in a
some - time, strong winds of prom - ise that will blow a - way the
Eb6 F7 Bb Bb7
sky more blue. If I Can Dream of a bet - ter land where
doubt and fear. If I Can Dream of a warm-er sun where
Eb D7 Gm Bbdim
all my broth - ers work hand in hand, tell me
hope keeps shin - in' on ev - er - y - one, tell me
Bb Gm
why, oh why, oh
why, oh why, oh
1.
Eb Cm7 Dm Gm
why can't my dream come
Cm7 F7 Eb/F F7
true? Oh, why? There must be

Copyright © 1968 by Gladys Music, Inc.
Copyright Renewed and Assigned to Gladys Music (Administered by Williamson Music)
International Copyright Secured All Rights Reserved

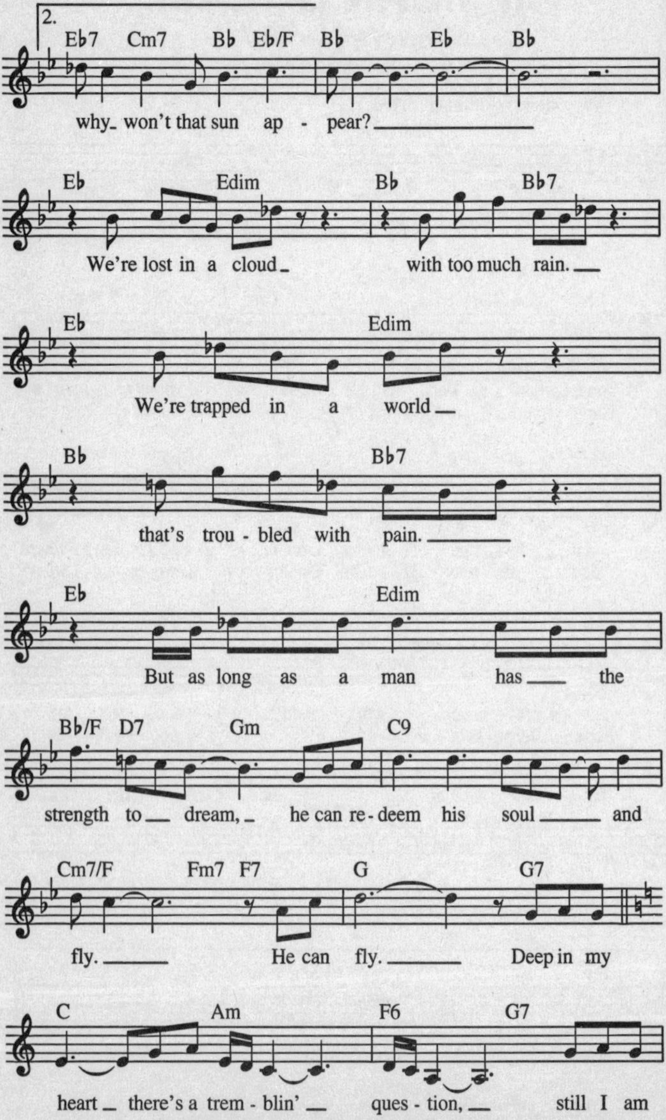
2.
Eb7 Cm7 Bb Eb/F Bb Eb Bb
why_ won't that sun ap - pear?
Eb Edim Bb Bb7
We're lost in a cloud_ with too much rain._
Eb Edim
We're trapped in a world_
Bb Bb7
that's trou - bled with pain.
Eb Edim
But as long as a man has_ the
Bb/F D7 Gm C9
strength to_ dream,_ he can re - deem his soul_ and
Cm7/F Fm7 F7 G G7
fly._ He can fly._ Deep in my
C Am F6 G7
heart_ there's a trem - blin'_ ques - tion,_ still I am

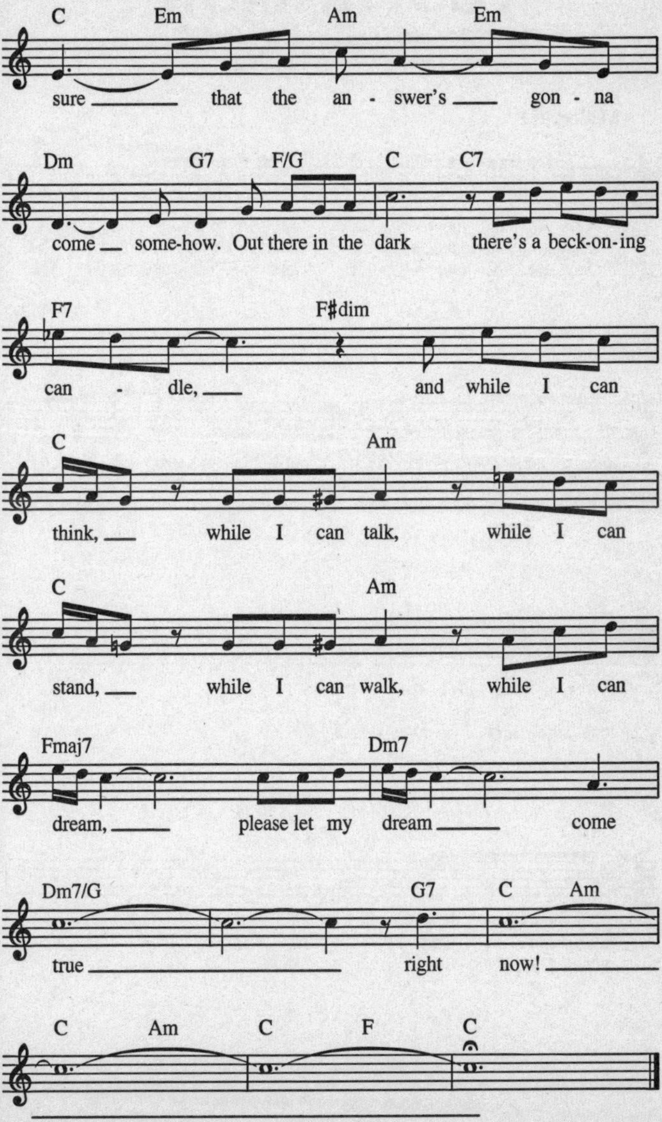
C Em Am Em
sure that the an - swer's gon - na
Dm G7 F/G C C7
come some-how. Out there in the dark there's a beck-on-ing
F7 F♯dim
can - dle, and while I can
C Am
think, while I can talk, while I can
C Am
stand, while I can walk, while I can
Fmaj7 Dm7
dream, please let my dream come
Dm7/G G7 C Am
true right now!
C Am C F C

I GOTTA KNOW

Words and Music by PAUL EVANS
and MATT WILLIAMS

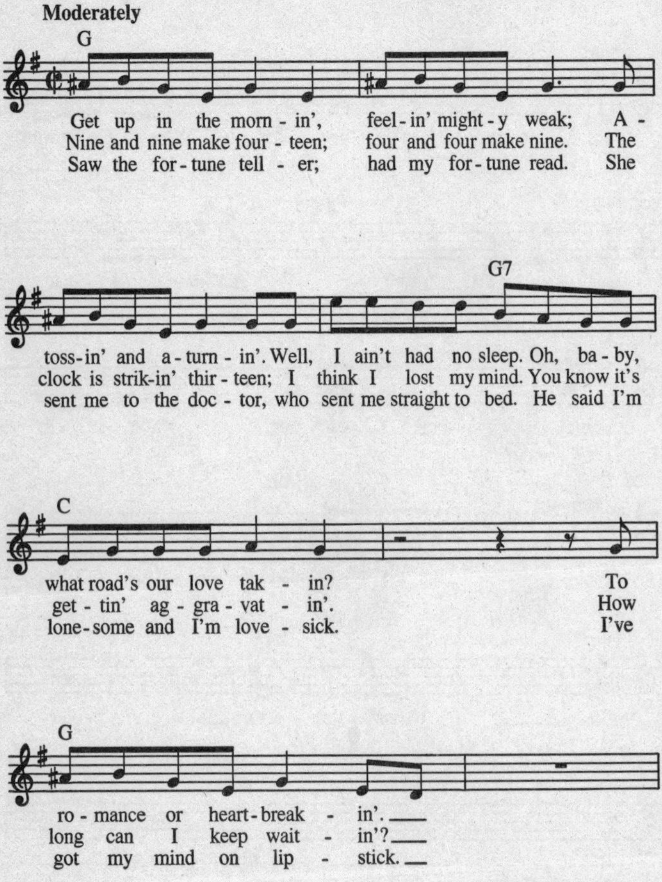
Moderately
G
Get up in the morn - in', feel - in' might - y weak; A -
Nine and nine make four - teen; four and four make nine. The
Saw the for - tune tell - er; had my for - tune read. She
G7
toss-in' and a - turn - in'. Well, I ain't had no sleep. Oh, ba - by,
clock is strik-in' thir - teen; I think I lost my mind. You know it's
sent me to the doc - tor, who sent me straight to bed. He said I'm
C
what road's our love tak - in? To
get - tin' ag - gra - vat - in'. How
lone-some and I'm love - sick. I've
G
ro - mance or heart-break - in'.
long can I keep wait - in'?
got my mind on lip - stick.

Copyright © 1959 by Gladys Music, Inc.
Copyright Renewed and Assigned to Gladys Music (Administered by Williamson Music) and Port Music, Inc.
International Copyright Secured All Rights Reserved

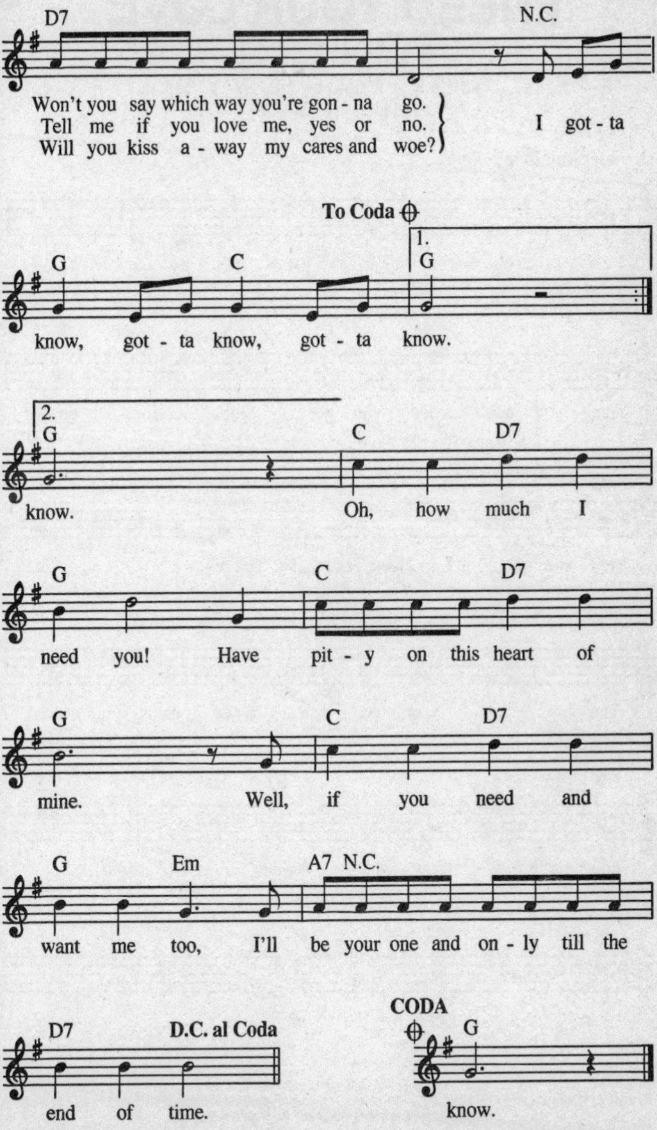
D7
N.C.
Won't you say which way you're gon - na go.
Tell me if you love me, yes or no.
Will you kiss a - way my cares and woe?
I got - ta
To Coda
1.
G C G
know, got - ta know, got - ta know.
2.
G C D7
know. Oh, how much I
G C D7
need you! Have pit - y on this heart of
G C D7
mine. Well, if you need and
G Em A7 N.C.
want me too, I'll be your one and on - ly till the
D7 D.C. al Coda
end of time.
CODA
G
know.

I NEED YOUR LOVE TONIGHT

Words and Music by SID WAYNE
and BIX REICHNER

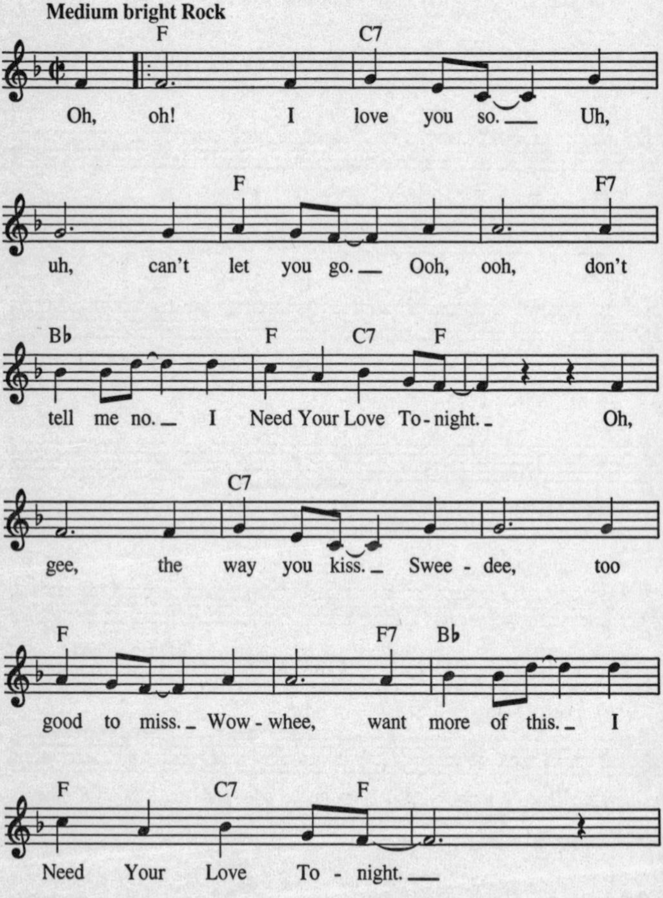
Medium bright Rock
F
C7
Oh, oh! I love you so. Uh,
F
F7
uh, can't let you go. Ooh, ooh, don't
B♭
F
C7
F
tell me no. I Need Your Love To-night. Oh,
C7
gee, the way you kiss. Swee - dee, too
F
F7
B♭
good to miss. Wow - whee, want more of this. I
F
C7
F
Need Your Love To - night.

Copyright © 1959 by Gladys Music, Inc.
Copyright Renewed and Assigned to Gladys Music (Administered by Williamson Music) and Holly Hill Music
International Copyright Secured All Rights Reserved

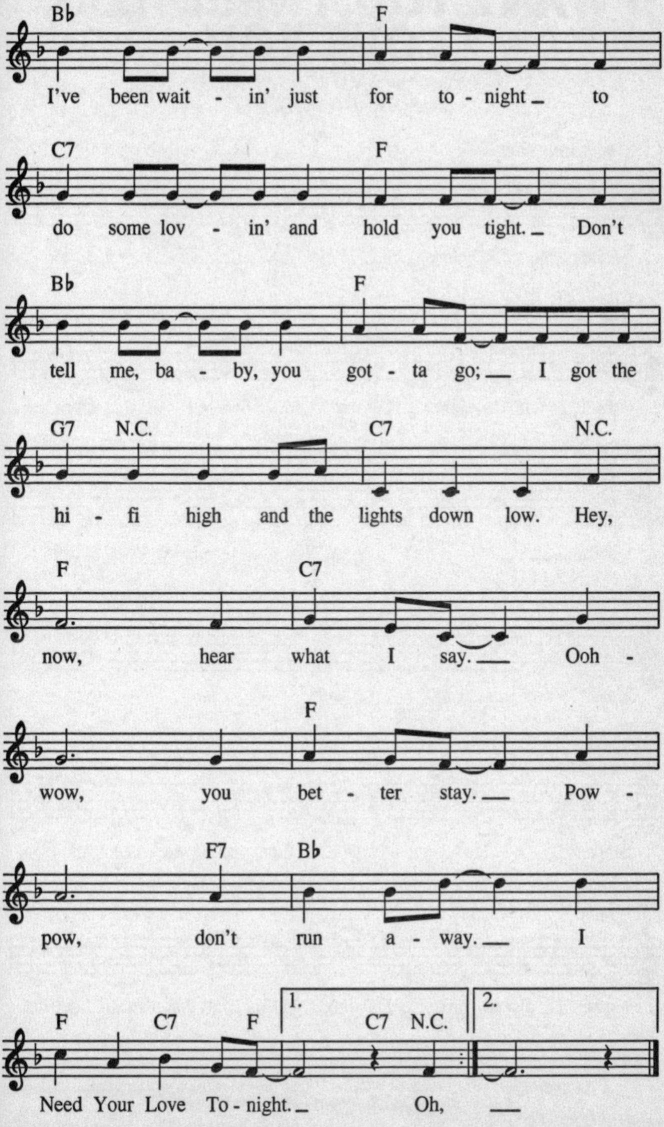
Bb F
I've been wait - in' just for to - night _ to
C7 F
do some lov - in' and hold you tight. _ Don't
Bb F
tell me, ba - by, you got - ta go; _ I got the
G7 N.C. C7 N.C.
hi - fi high and the lights down low. Hey,
F C7
now, hear what I say. _ Ooh -
F
wow, you bet - ter stay. _ Pow -
F7 Bb
pow, don't run a - way. _ I
1. 2.
F C7 F C7 N.C.
Need Your Love To - night. _ Oh, _

I WANT YOU, I NEED YOU, I LOVE YOU

Words by MAURICE MYSELS
Music by IRA KOSLOFF

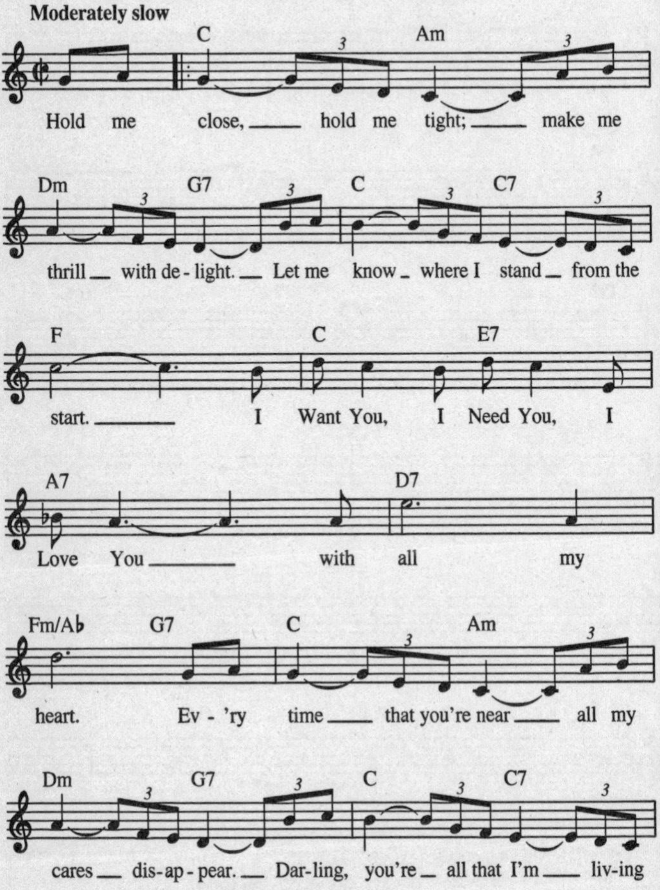
Moderately slow
C Am
Hold me close, hold me tight; make me
Dm G7 C C7
thrill with de-light. Let me know where I stand from the
F C E7
start. I Want You, I Need You, I
A7 D7
Love You with all my
Fm/Ab G7 C Am
heart. Ev - 'ry time that you're near all my
Dm G7 C C7
cares dis-ap-pear. Dar-ling, you're all that I'm liv-ing

Copyright © 1956 by Elvis Presley Music, Inc.
Copyright Renewed and Assigned to Gladys Music (Administered by Williamson Music)
International Copyright Secured All Rights Reserved

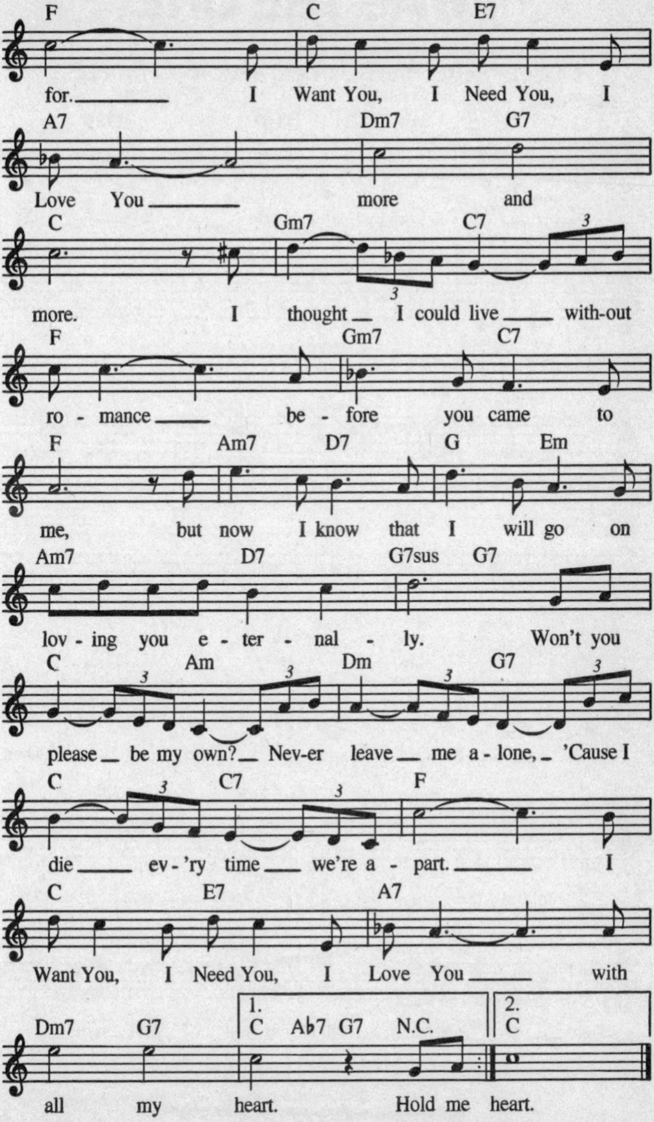
F C E7
for.___ I Want You, I Need You, I
A7 Dm7 G7
Love You___ more and
C Gm7 C7
more. I thought_ I could live___ with-out
F Gm7 C7
ro - mance___ be - fore you came to
F Am7 D7 G Em
me, but now I know that I will go on
Am7 D7 G7sus G7
lov - ing you e - ter - nal - ly. Won't you
C Am Dm G7
please_ be my own?_ Nev-er leave_ me a - lone,_ 'Cause I
C C7 F
die___ ev - 'ry time___ we're a - part.___ I
C E7 A7
Want You, I Need You, I Love You___ with
Dm7 G7 1. C Ab7 G7 N.C. 2. C
all my heart. Hold me heart.

I WAS THE ONE

Words and Music by CLAUDE DEMETRUIS,
BILL PEPPERS, HAL BLAIR and AARON SCHROEDER

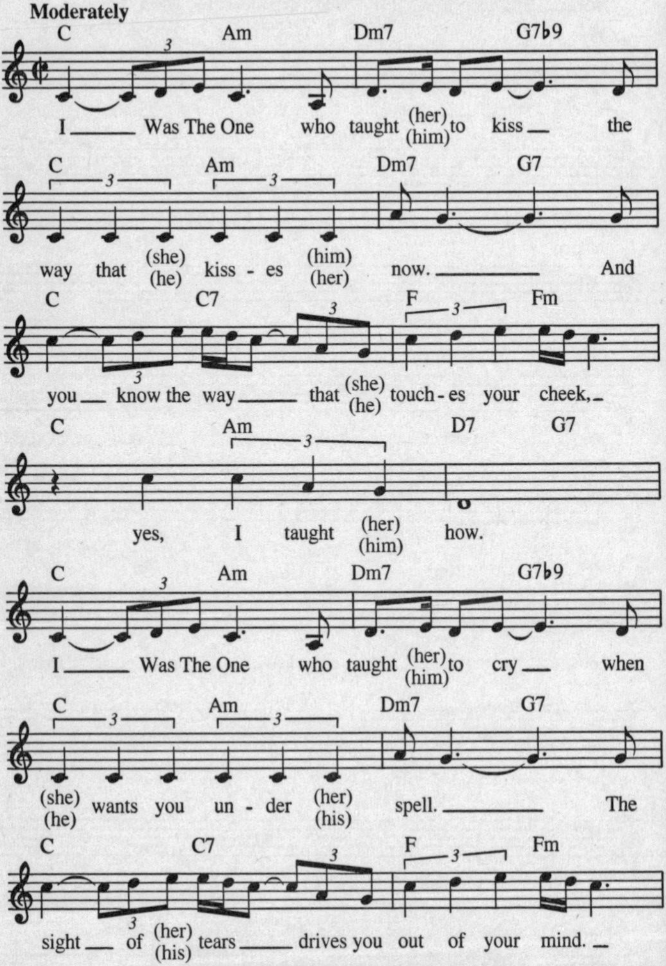
Moderately
C Am Dm7 G7♭9
I ___ Was The One who taught (her) (him) to kiss ___ the
C Am Dm7 G7
way that (she) (he) kiss - es (him) (her) now. ___ And
C C7 F Fm
you ___ know the way ___ that (she) (he) touch - es your cheek, ___
C Am D7 G7
yes, I taught (her) (him) how.
C Am Dm7 G7♭9
I ___ Was The One who taught (her) (him) to cry ___ when
C Am Dm7 G7
(she) (he) wants you un - der (her) (his) spell. ___ The
C C7 F Fm
sight ___ of (her) (his) tears ___ drives you out of your mind. ___

Copyright © 1956 by Chappell & Co., and Rachel's Own Music
(Administered by A. Schroeder International Ltd.)
Copyright Renewed
International Copyright Secured All Rights Reserved

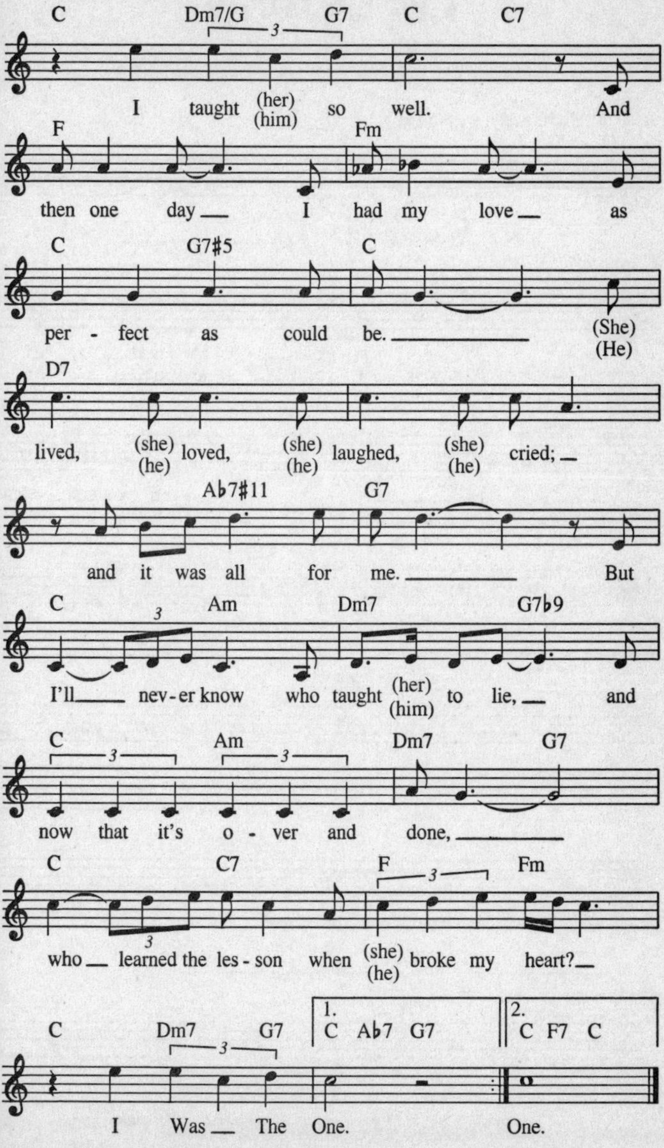
C Dm7/G G7 C C7
I taught (her) (him) so well. And
F Fm
then one day I had my love as
C G7#5 C
per - fect as could be. (She) (He)
D7
lived, (she) (he) loved, (she) (he) laughed, (she) (he) cried;
Ab7#11 G7
and it was all for me. But
C Am Dm7 G7b9
I'll nev - er know who taught (her) (him) to lie, and
C Am Dm7 G7
now that it's o - ver and done,
C C7 F Fm
who learned the les - son when (she) (he) broke my heart?
C Dm7 G7
1. C Ab7 G7
2. C F7 C
I Was The One.
One.

I'M LEAVIN'

Words and Music by
MICHAEL JARRETT and SONNY CHARLES

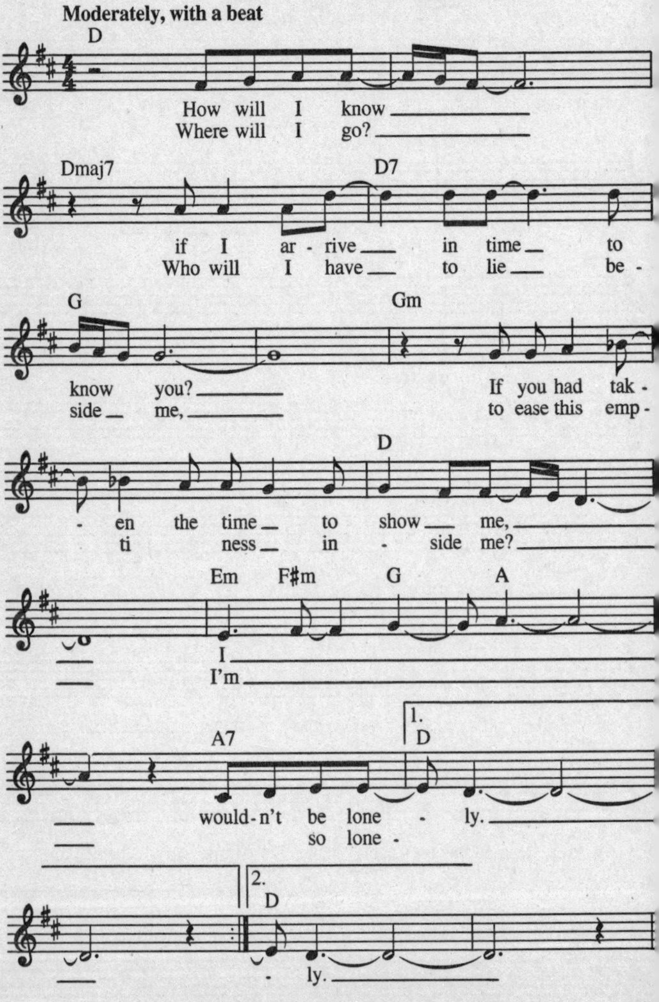
Moderately, with a beat
D
How will I know
Where will I go?
Dmaj7
D7
if I ar - rive in time to
Who will I have to lie be -
G
Gm
know you? If you had tak -
side me, to ease this emp -
D
- en the time to show me,
ti ness in - side me?
Em F#m G A
I
I'm
A7
1.
D
would-n't be lone - ly.
so lone -
2.
D
- ly.

Copyright © 1971 by Elvis Presley Music (Administered by R&H Music)
International Copyright Secured All Rights Reserved

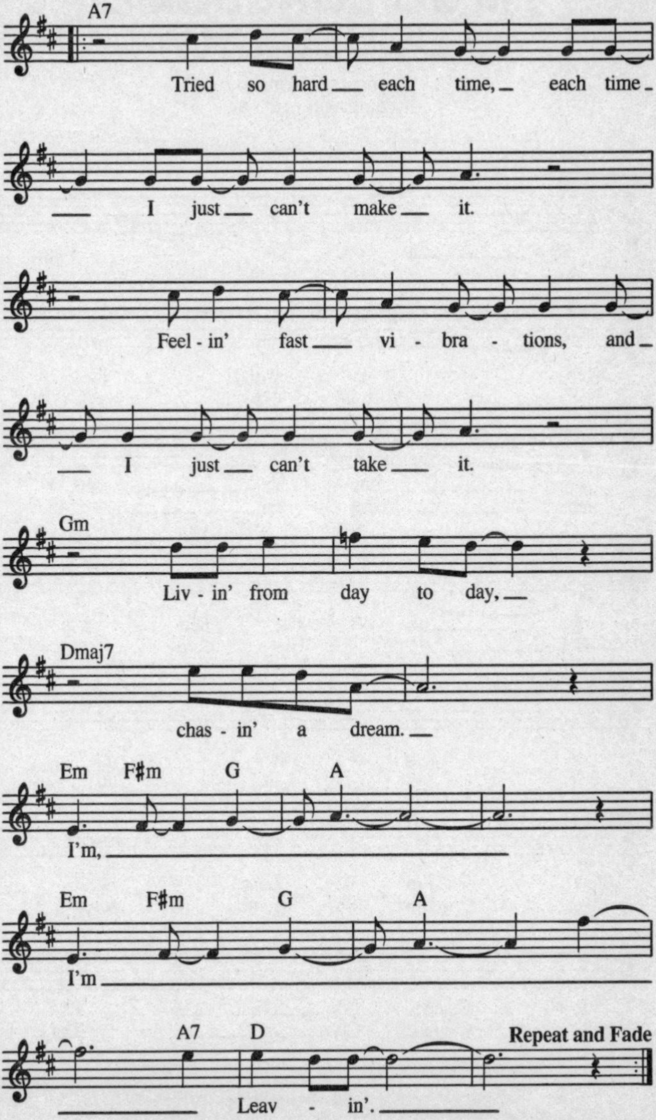
A7
Tried so hard each time, each time
I just can't make it.
Feel - in' fast vi - bra - tions, and
I just can't take it.
Gm
Liv - in' from day to day,
Dmaj7
chas - in' a dream.
Em F♯m G A
I'm,
Em F♯m G A
I'm
A7 D
Repeat and Fade
Leav - in'.

I'M SO LONESOME I COULD CRY

Words and Music by
HANK WILLIAMS

Moderately

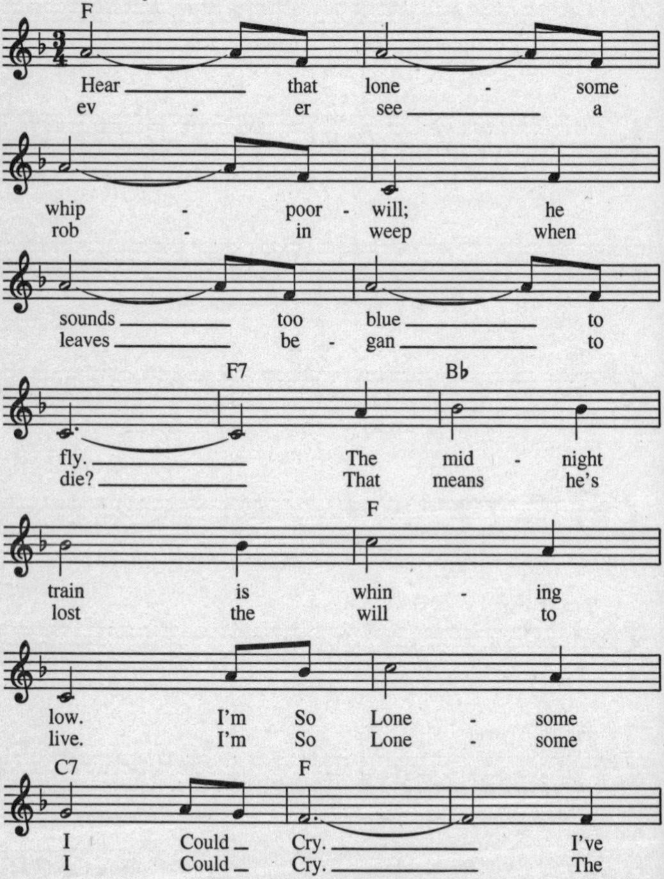
F
Hear ___ that lone - some
ev - er see ___ a
whip - poor - will; he
rob - in weep when
sounds ___ too blue ___ to
leaves ___ be - gan ___ to
F7
Bb
fly. ___ The mid - night
die? ___ That means he's
F
train is whin - ing
lost the will to
low. I'm So Lone - some
live. I'm So Lone - some
C7
F
I Could _ Cry. ___ I've
I Could _ Cry. ___ The

Copyright © 1949 by Hiriam Music and Acuff-Rose Music, Inc. in the U.S.A.
Copyright Renewed
All Rights for Hiriam Music Administered by Rightsong Music Inc.
All Rights outside the U.S.A. Controlled by Acuff-Rose Music, Inc.
International Copyright Secured All Rights Reserved

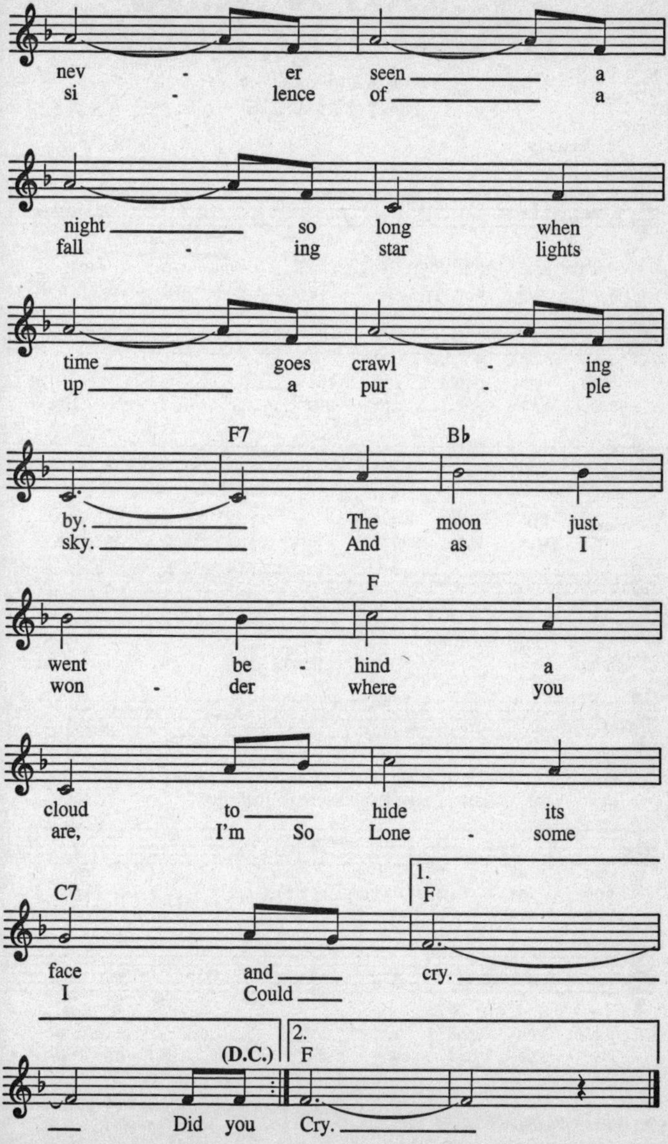
nev - er seen a
si - lence of a
night so long when
fall - ing star lights
time goes crawl - ing
up a pur - ple
F7
B♭
by. The moon just
sky. And as I
F
went be - hind a
won - der where you
cloud to hide its
are, I'm So Lone - some
C7
1.
F
face and cry.
I Could
(D.C.)
2.
F
Did you Cry.

I'VE GOT A THING ABOUT YOU, BABY

Words and Music by
TONY JOE WHITE

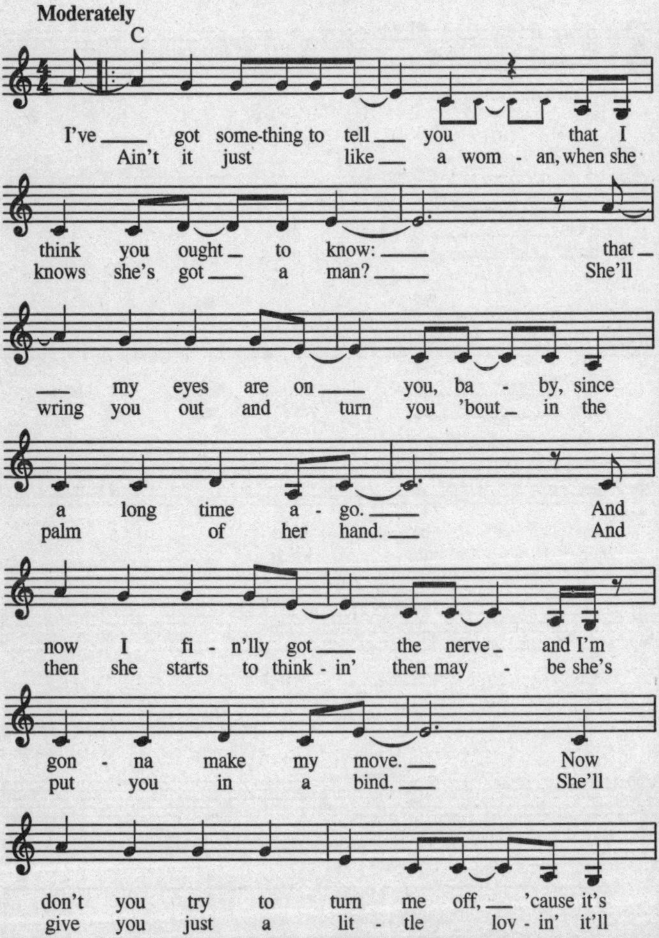
Moderately
C
I've got some-thing to tell you that I
Ain't it just like a wom - an, when she
think you ought to know: that
knows she's got a man? She'll
my eyes are on you, ba - by, since
wring you out and turn you 'bout in the
a long time a - go. And
palm of her hand. And
now I fi - n'lly got the nerve and I'm
then she starts to think - in' then may - be she's
gon - na make my move. Now
put you in a bind. She'll
don't you try to turn me off, 'cause it's
give you just a lit - tle lov - in' it'll

© 1972, 1974 TENNESSEE SWAMP FOX MUSIC CO.
All Rights Controlled and Administered by EMI APRIL MUSIC INC.
All Rights Reserved International Copyright Secured Used by Permission

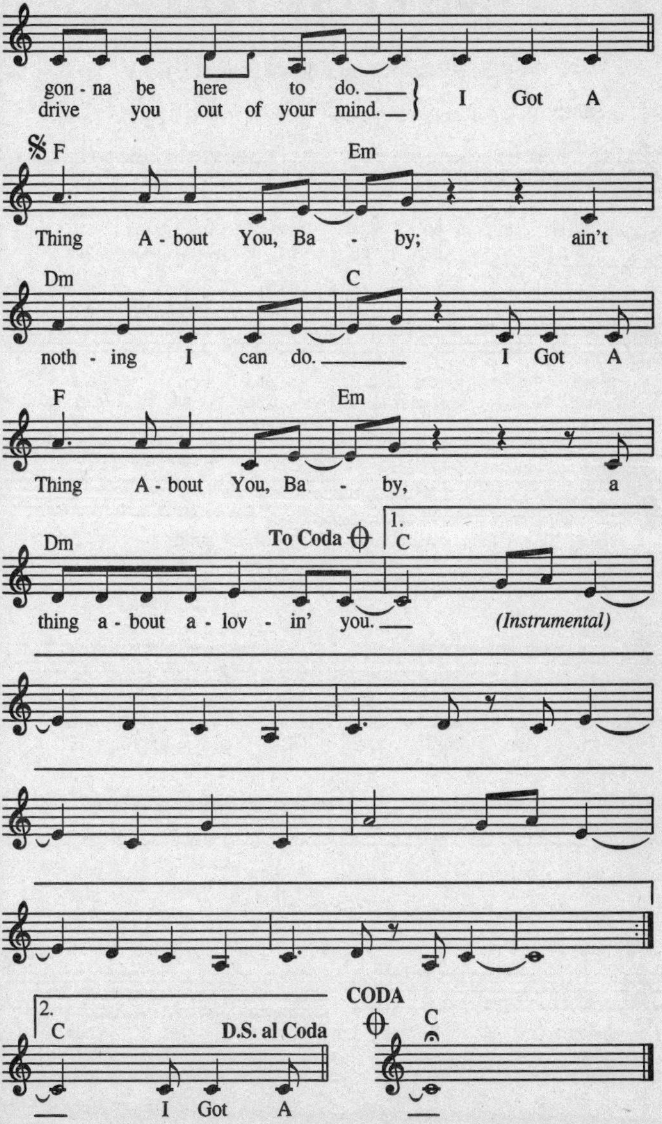
gon - na be here to do.
drive you out of your mind.
I Got A
F
Em
Thing A - bout You, Ba - by; ain't
Dm
C
noth - ing I can do.
I Got A
F
Em
Thing A - bout You, Ba - by, a
Dm
To Coda
1.
C
thing a - bout a - lov - in' you.
(Instrumental)
2.
C
D.S. al Coda
I Got A
CODA
C

I'VE LOST YOU

Words and Music by
KEN HOWARD and ALAN BLAIKLEY

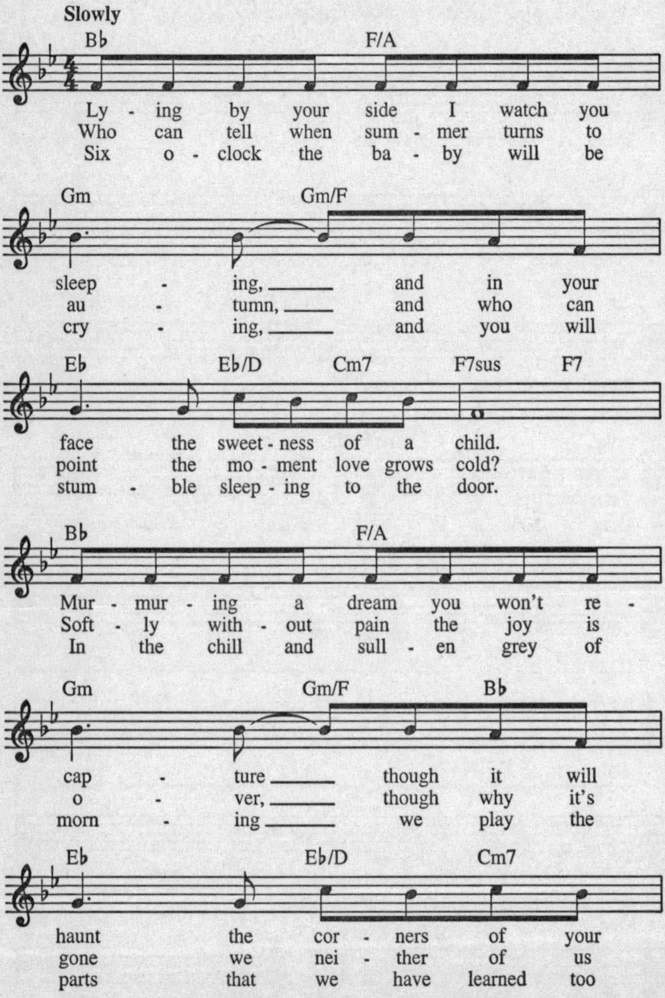
Slowly
B♭ F/A
Ly - ing by your side I watch you
Who can tell when sum - mer turns to
Six o - clock the ba - by will be
Gm Gm/F
sleep - ing, and in your
au - tumn, and who can
cry - ing, and you will
E♭ E♭/D Cm7 F7sus F7
face the sweet - ness of a child.
point the mo - ment love grows cold?
stum - ble sleep - ing to the door.
B♭ F/A
Mur - mur - ing a dream you won't re -
Soft - ly with - out pain the joy is
In the chill and sull - en grey of
Gm Gm/F B♭
cap - ture though it will
o - ver, though why it's
morn - ing we play the
E♭ E♭/D Cm7
haunt the cor - ners of your
gone we nei - ther of us
parts that we have learned too

Copyright © 1970 by Carlin Music Corp. (Administered by Gladys Music c/o Williamson Music)
International Copyright Secured All Rights Reserved

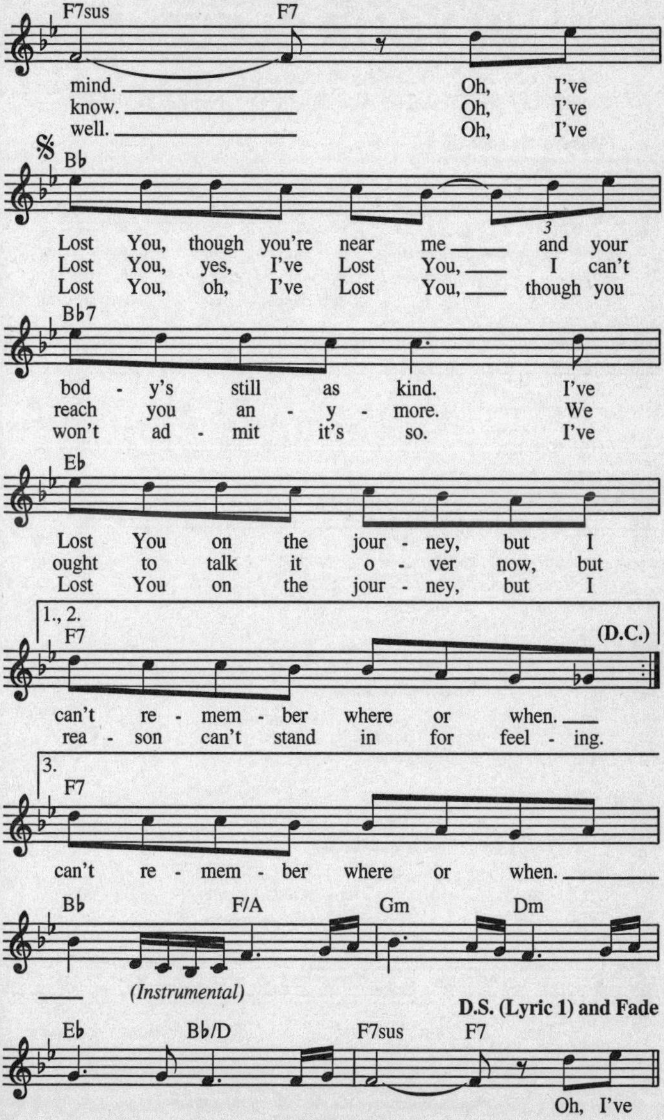
F7sus
F7
mind. Oh, I've
know. Oh, I've
well. Oh, I've
B♭
Lost You, though you're near me and your
Lost You, yes, I've Lost You, I can't
Lost You, oh, I've Lost You, though you
3
B♭7
bod - y's still as kind. I've
reach you an - y - more. We
won't ad - mit it's so. I've
E♭
Lost You on the jour - ney, but I
ought to talk it o - ver now, but
Lost You on the jour - ney, but I
1., 2.
F7
(D.C.)
can't re - mem - ber where or when.
rea - son can't stand in for feel - ing.
3.
F7
can't re - mem - ber where or when.
B♭
F/A
Gm
Dm
(Instrumental)
D.S. (Lyric 1) and Fade
E♭
B♭/D
F7sus
F7
Oh, I've

IF YOU TALK IN YOUR SLEEP

Words and Music by
BOBBY "RED" WEST and JOHNNY CHRISTOPHER

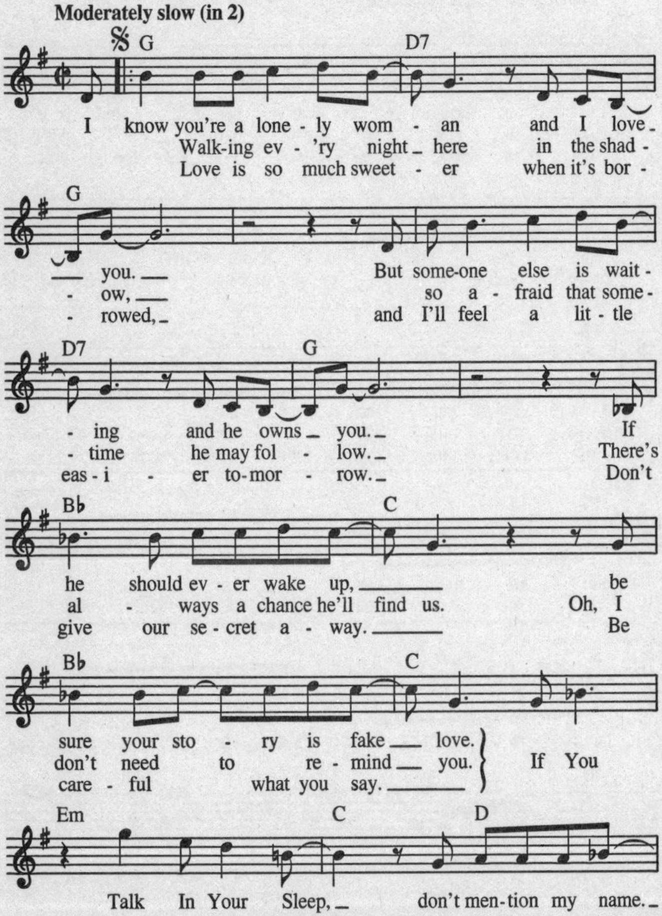
Moderately slow (in 2)
G
D7
I know you're a lone - ly wom - an and I love
Walk-ing ev - 'ry night here in the shad -
Love is so much sweet - er when it's bor -
G
you. But some-one else is wait -
- ow, so a - fraid that some -
- rowed, and I'll feel a lit - tle
D7
G
- ing and he owns you. If
- time he may fol - low. There's
eas - i - er to-mor - row. Don't
B♭
C
he should ev - er wake up, be
al - ways a chance he'll find us. Oh, I
give our se - cret a - way. Be
B♭
C
sure your sto - ry is fake love.
don't need to re - mind you.
care - ful what you say.
If You
Em
C
D
Talk In Your Sleep, don't men-tion my name.

Copyright © 1974 Easy Nine Music (administered by Copyright Management, Inc.),
Elvis Presley Music and Herb O'Mell Music
International Copyright Secured All Rights Reserved
Used by Permission

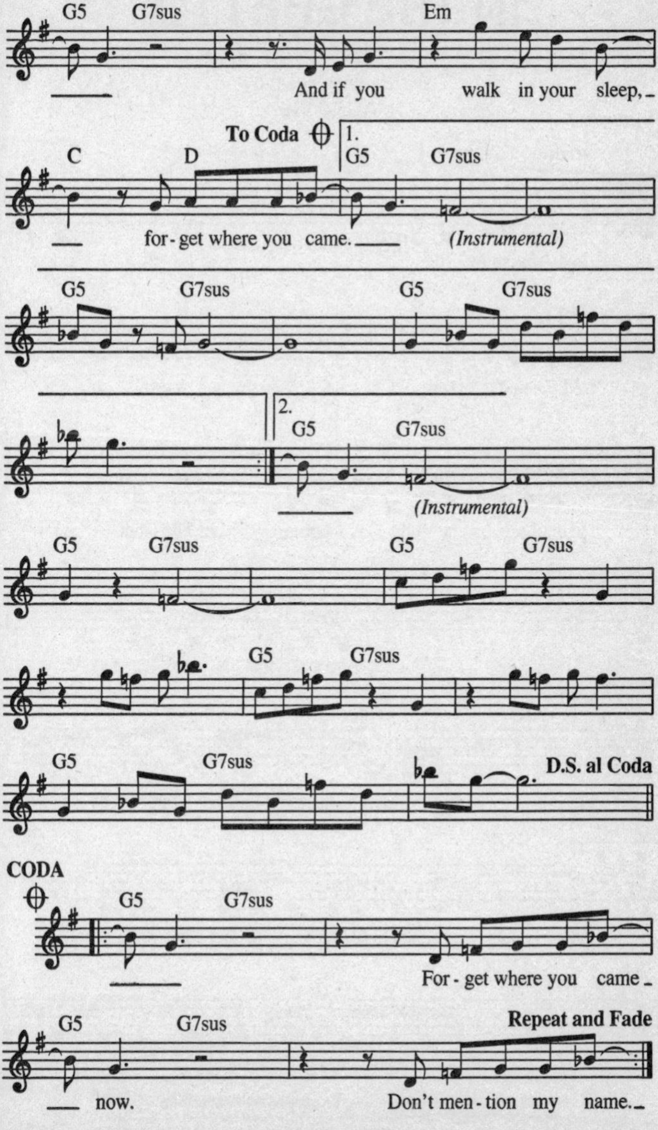
G5 G7sus Em
And if you walk in your sleep,
To Coda
1.
C D G5 G7sus
for - get where you came.
(Instrumental)
G5 G7sus G5 G7sus
2.
G5 G7sus
(Instrumental)
G5 G7sus G5 G7sus
G5 G7sus
G5 G7sus
D.S. al Coda
CODA
G5 G7sus
For - get where you came
G5 G7sus
Repeat and Fade
now.
Don't men - tion my name.

IN THE GHETTO
(The Vicious Circle)

Words and Music by
MAC DAVIS

Medium Folk beat

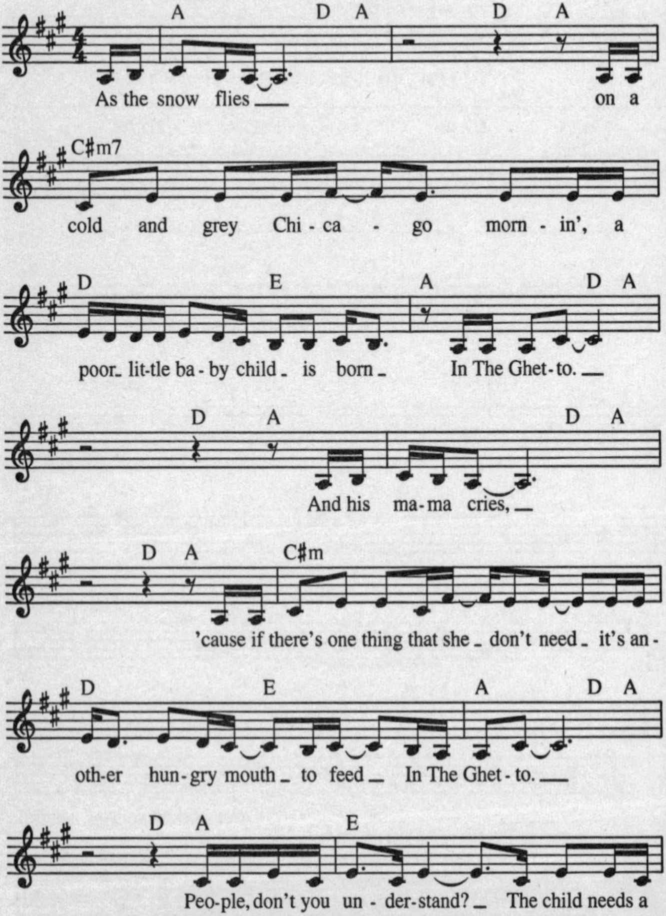
A D A D A
As the snow flies on a
C#m7
cold and grey Chi - ca - go morn - in', a
D E A D A
poor lit-tle ba - by child is born In The Ghet - to.
D A D A
And his ma - ma cries,
D A C#m
'cause if there's one thing that she don't need it's an -
D E A D A
oth-er hun - gry mouth to feed In The Ghet - to.
D A E
Peo-ple, don't you un - der - stand? The child needs a

© 1969 SCREEN GEMS-EMI MUSIC INC. and ELVIS PRESLEY MUSIC, INC.
All Rights Controlled and Administered by SCREEN GEMS-EMI MUSIC INC.
All Rights Reserved International Copyright Secured Used by Permission

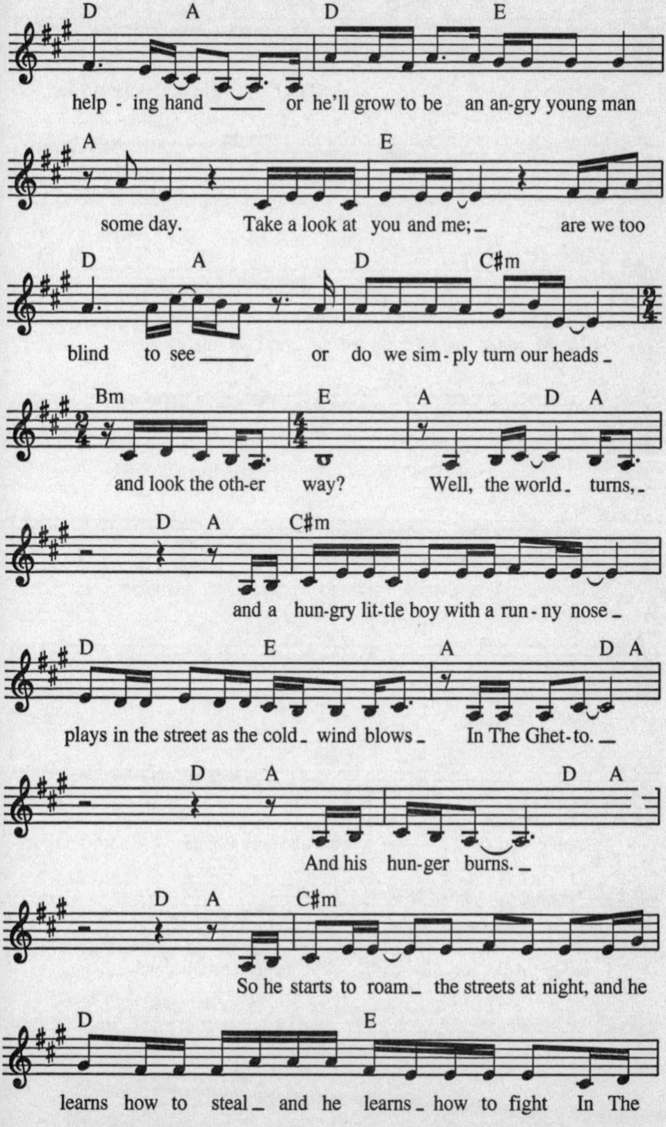
D A D E
help - ing hand or he'll grow to be an an-gry young man
A E
some day. Take a look at you and me; are we too
D A D C#m
blind to see or do we sim - ply turn our heads
Bm E A D A
and look the oth-er way? Well, the world turns,
D A C#m
and a hun-gry lit-tle boy with a run - ny nose
D E A D A
plays in the street as the cold wind blows In The Ghet-to.
D A D A
And his hun-ger burns.
D A C#m
So he starts to roam the streets at night, and he
D E
learns how to steal and he learns how to fight In The

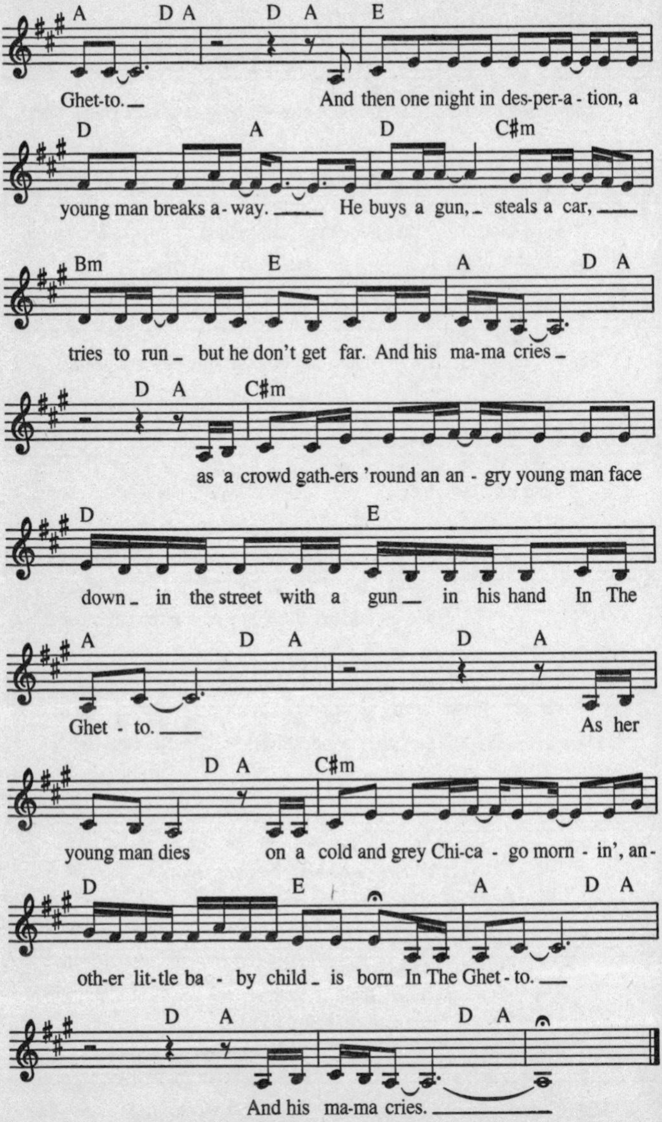
A D A D A E
Ghet-to. And then one night in des-per-a - tion, a
D A D C#m
young man breaks a - way. He buys a gun, steals a car,
Bm E A D A
tries to run but he don't get far. And his ma-ma cries
D A C#m
as a crowd gath-ers 'round an an - gry young man face
D E
down in the street with a gun in his hand In The
A D A D A
Ghet - to. As her
D A C#m
young man dies on a cold and grey Chi-ca - go morn - in', an-
D E A D A
oth-er lit-tle ba - by child is born In The Ghet - to.
D A D A
And his ma-ma cries.

KENTUCKY RAIN

Words and Music by
EDDIE RABBITT and DICK HEARD

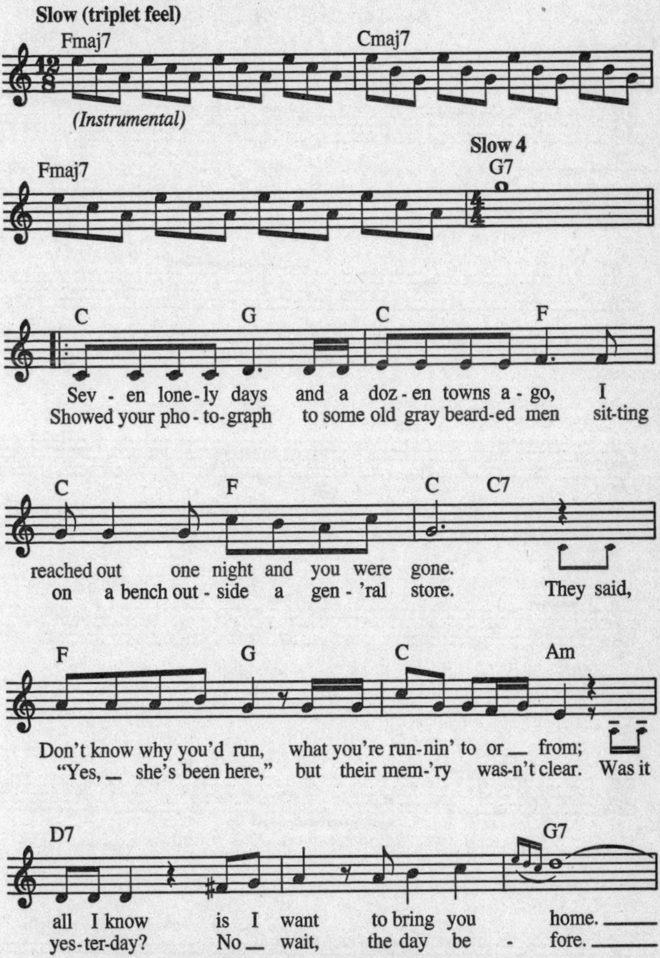
Slow (triplet feel)
Fmaj7
Cmaj7
(Instrumental)
Fmaj7
Slow 4
G7
C G C F
Sev - en lone - ly days and a doz - en towns a - go, I
Showed your pho - to - graph to some old gray beard - ed men sit - ting
C F C C7
reached out one night and you were gone.
on a bench out - side a gen - 'ral store. They said,
F G C Am
Don't know why you'd run, what you're run - nin' to or ___ from;
"Yes, ___ she's been here," but their mem - 'ry was - n't clear. Was it
D7 G7
all I know is I want to bring you home. ___
yes - ter - day? No ___ wait, the day be - fore. ___

Copyright © 1970 by Elvis Presley Music, Inc. and S-P-R Music Corp.
Copyright Assigned to Elvis Presley Music and Careers-BMG Music Publishing, Inc.
All Rights Administered by R&H Music
International Copyright Secured All Rights Reserved

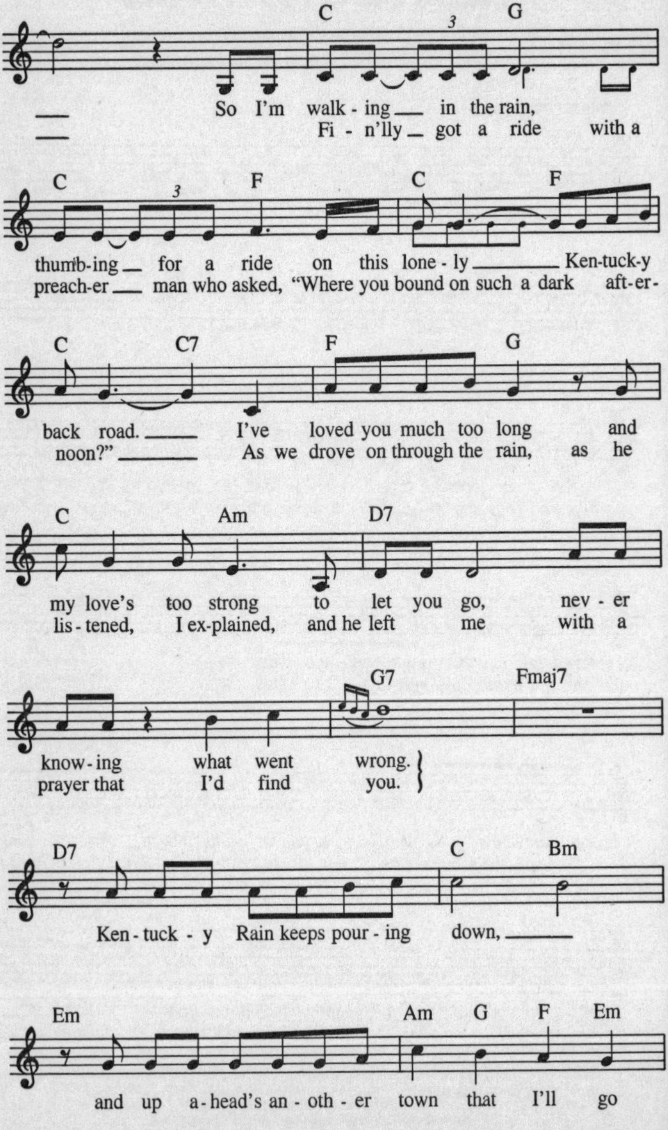
C
3
G
So I'm walk - ing in the rain,
Fi - n'lly got a ride with a
C
3
F
C
F
thumb-ing for a ride on this lone - ly Ken-tuck-y
preach-er man who asked, "Where you bound on such a dark aft-er-
C
C7
F
G
back road. I've loved you much too long and
noon?" As we drove on through the rain, as he
C
Am
D7
my love's too strong to let you go, nev - er
lis - tened, I ex-plained, and he left me with a
G7
Fmaj7
know - ing what went wrong.
prayer that I'd find you.
D7
C
Bm
Ken - tuck - y Rain keeps pour - ing down,
Em
Am
G
F
Em
and up a - head's an - oth - er town that I'll go

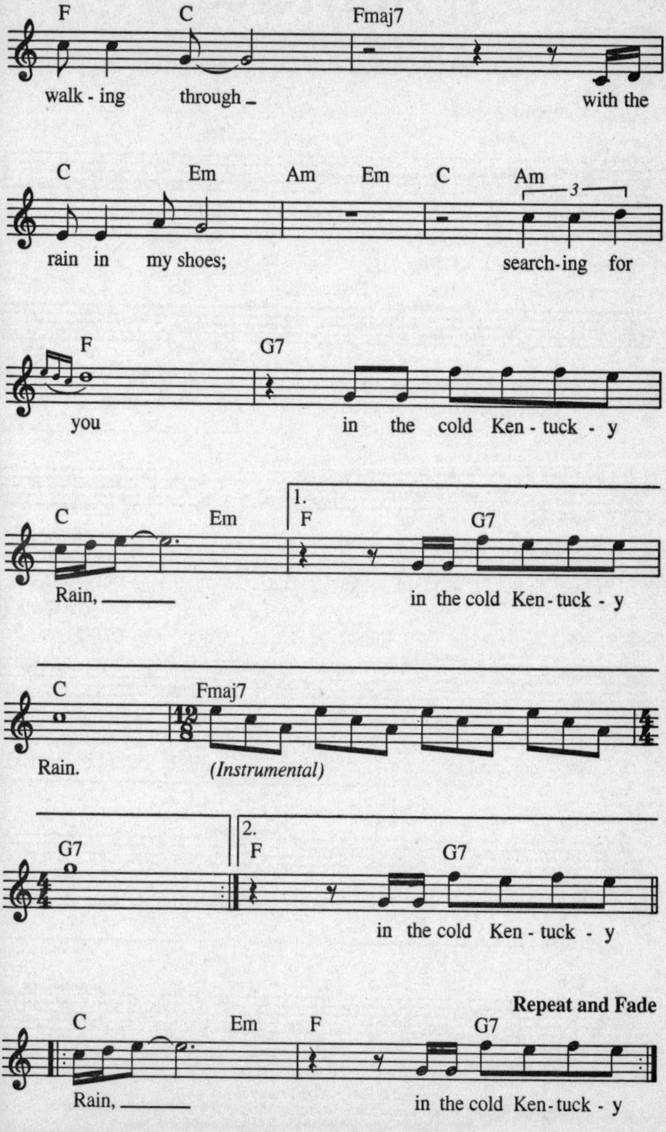
F C Fmaj7
walk - ing through _ with the
C Em Am Em C Am
3
rain in my shoes; search-ing for
F G7
you in the cold Ken - tuck - y
1.
C Em F G7
Rain, ___ in the cold Ken - tuck - y
C Fmaj7
Rain. (Instrumental)
2.
G7 F G7
in the cold Ken - tuck - y
Repeat and Fade
C Em F G7
Rain, ___ in the cold Ken - tuck - y

IT HURTS ME

Words and Music by
JOY BYERS and CHARLES E. DANIELS

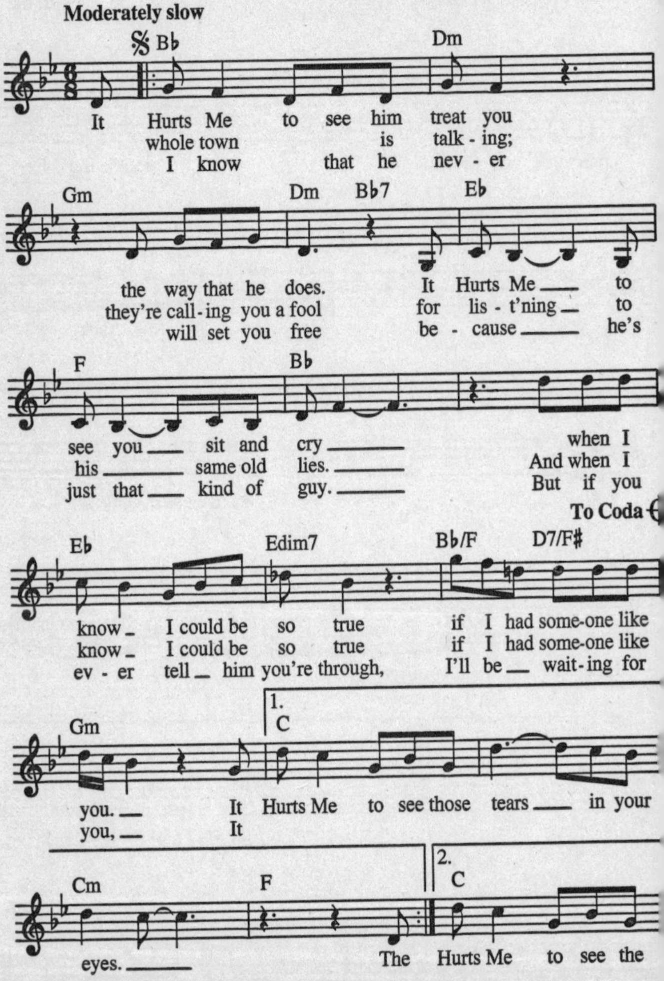
Moderately slow
Bb Dm
It Hurts Me to see him treat you
whole town is talk - ing;
I know that he nev - er
Gm Dm Bb7 Eb
the way that he does. It Hurts Me to
they're call-ing you a fool for lis - t'ning to
will set you free be - cause he's
F Bb
see you sit and cry when I
his same old lies. And when I
just that kind of guy. But if you
To Coda
Eb Edim7 Bb/F D7/F#
know I could be so true if I had some-one like
know I could be so true if I had some-one like
ev - er tell him you're through, I'll be wait-ing for
Gm 1. C
you. It Hurts Me to see those tears in your
you, It
Cm F 2. C
eyes. The Hurts Me to see the

Copyright © 1964 by Elvis Presley Music, Inc.
Copyright Renewed and Assigned to Elvis Presley Music (Administered by R&H Music)
International Copyright Secured All Rights Reserved

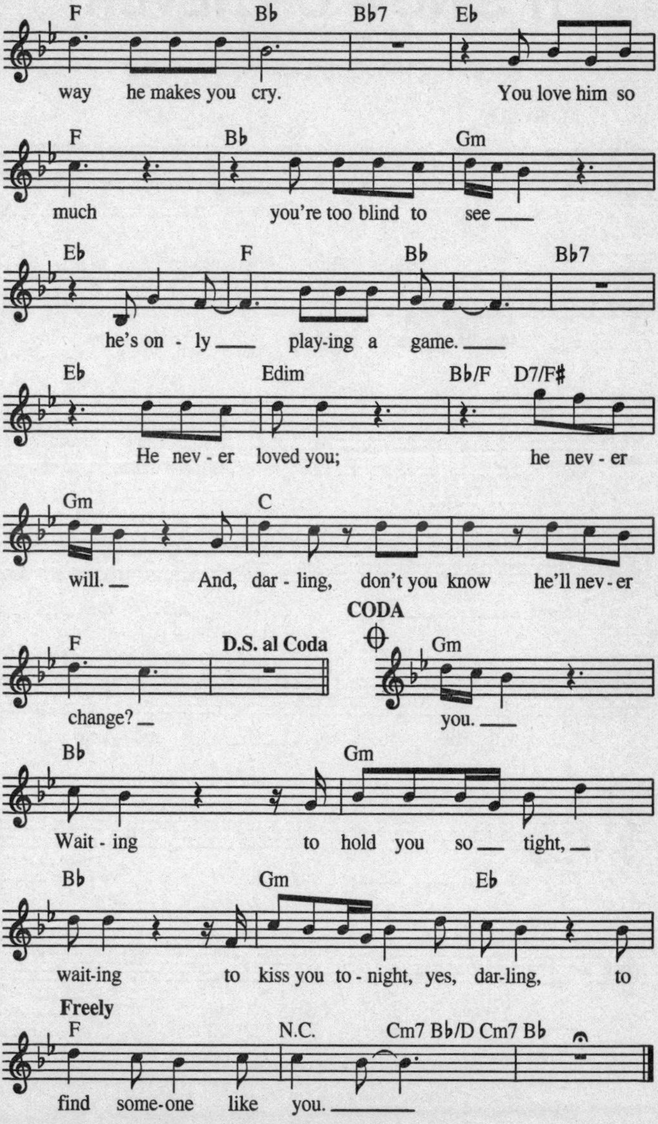
F Bb Bb7 Eb
way he makes you cry. You love him so
F Bb Gm
much you're too blind to see
Eb F Bb Bb7
he's on - ly playing a game.
Eb Edim Bb/F D7/F#
He nev - er loved you; he nev - er
Gm C
will. And, dar - ling, don't you know he'll nev - er
CODA
F D.S. al Coda Gm
change? you.
Bb Gm
Wait - ing to hold you so tight,
Bb Gm Eb
wait-ing to kiss you to - night, yes, dar-ling, to
Freely
F N.C. Cm7 Bb/D Cm7 Bb
find some-one like you.

IT'S NOW OR NEVER

Words and Music by
AARON SCHROEDER and WALLY GOLD

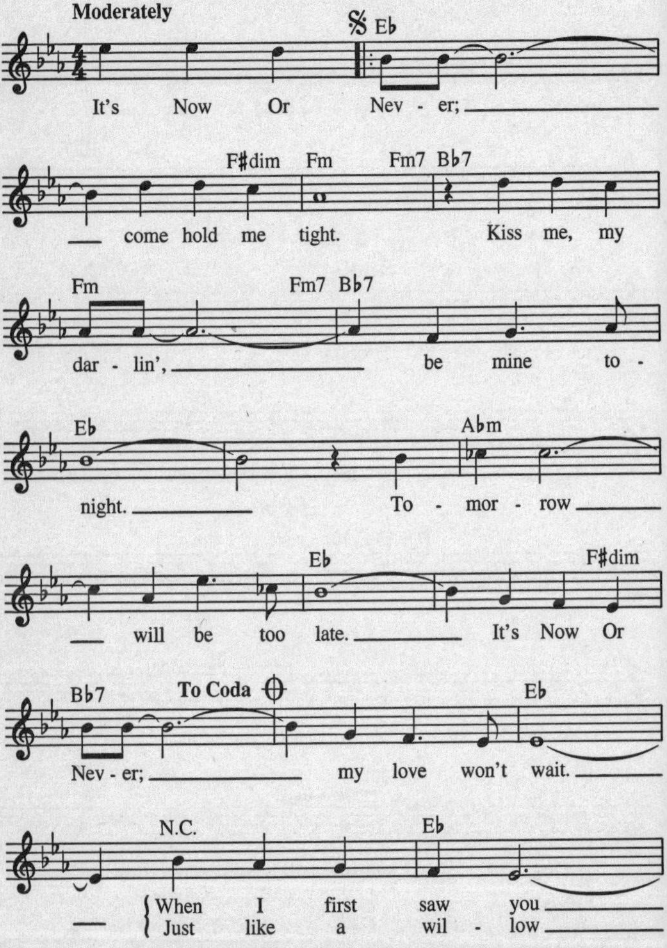
Moderately
Eb
It's Now Or Nev - er;
F#dim Fm Fm7 Bb7
come hold me tight. Kiss me, my
Fm Fm7 Bb7
dar - lin', be mine to -
Eb Abm
night. To - mor - row
Eb F#dim
will be too late. It's Now Or
Bb7 To Coda Eb
Nev - er; my love won't wait.
N.C. Eb
When I first saw you
Just like a wil - low

Copyright (for the U.S.A.) © 1960 by Gladys Music, Inc.
U.S.A. Copyright Renewed and Assigned to Gladys Music (Administered by Williamson Music) and Rachel's Own Music (Administered by A.Schroeder International Ltd.);
rights for all countries in the world (except U.S.A.) owned by Edizioni Bideri S.p.A, Naples
International Copyright Secured All Rights Reserved

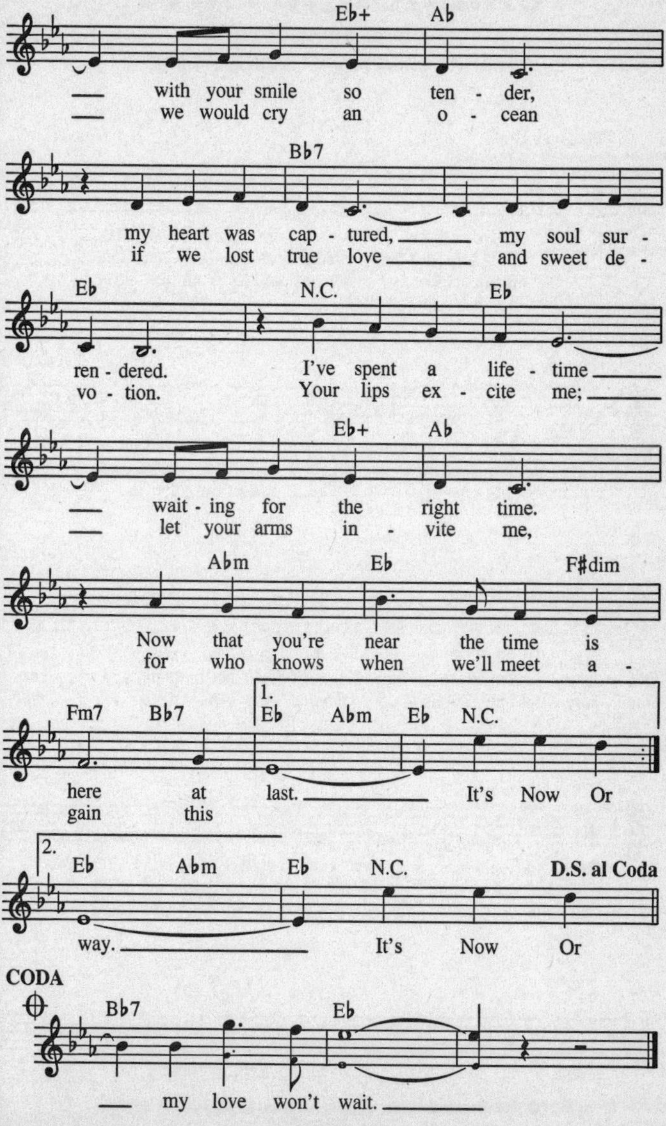
Eb+ Ab
— with your smile so ten - der,
— we would cry an o - cean
Bb7
my heart was cap - tured, — my soul sur -
if we lost true love — and sweet de -
Eb N.C. Eb
ren - dered. I've spent a life - time —
vo - tion. Your lips ex - cite me; —
Eb+ Ab
— wait - ing for the right time.
— let your arms in - vite me,
Abm Eb F#dim
Now that you're near the time is
for who knows when we'll meet a -
1.
Fm7 Bb7 Eb Abm Eb N.C.
here at last. — It's Now Or
gain this
2.
Eb Abm Eb N.C. D.S. al Coda
way. — It's Now Or
CODA
Bb7 Eb
— my love won't wait. —

JAILHOUSE ROCK

Words and Music by
JERRY LEIBER and MIKE STOLLER

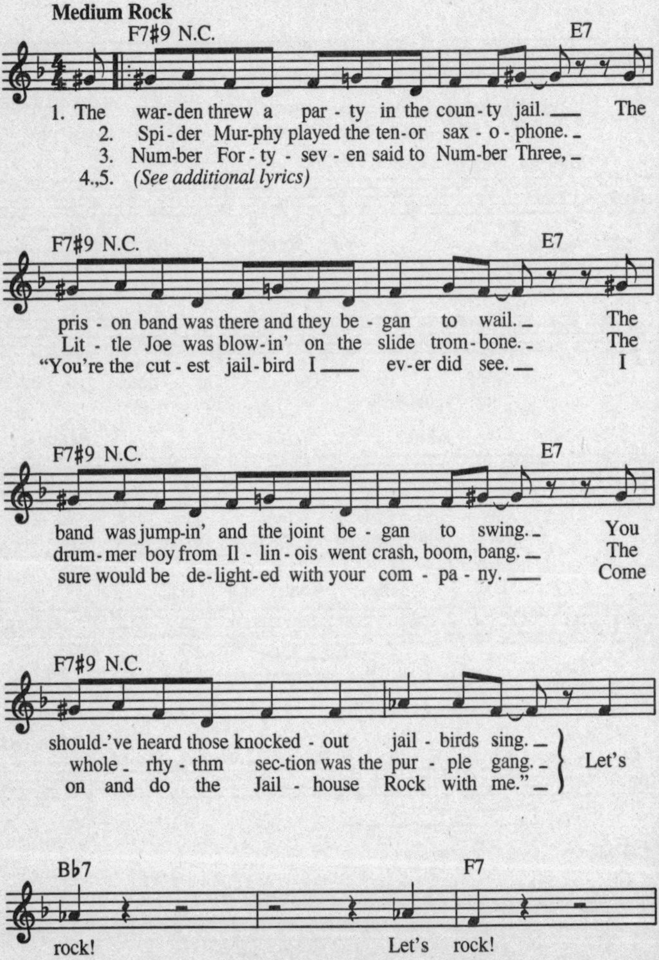
Medium Rock
F7#9 N.C.
E7
1. The war-den threw a par - ty in the coun - ty jail. The
2. Spi - der Mur-phy played the ten - or sax - o - phone.
3. Num-ber For - ty - sev - en said to Num-ber Three,
4.,5. (See additional lyrics)
F7#9 N.C.
E7
pris - on band was there and they be - gan to wail. The
Lit - tle Joe was blow - in' on the slide trom - bone. The
"You're the cut - est jail - bird I ev - er did see. I
F7#9 N.C.
E7
band was jump-in' and the joint be - gan to swing. You
drum - mer boy from Il - lin - ois went crash, boom, bang. The
sure would be de - light - ed with your com - pa - ny. Come
F7#9 N.C.
should-'ve heard those knocked - out jail - birds sing.
whole rhy - thm sec-tion was the pur - ple gang.
on and do the Jail - house Rock with me."
Let's
Bb7
F7
rock!
Let's rock!

© 1957 (Renewed) JERRY LEIBER MUSIC and MIKE STOLLER MUSIC
All Rights Reserved

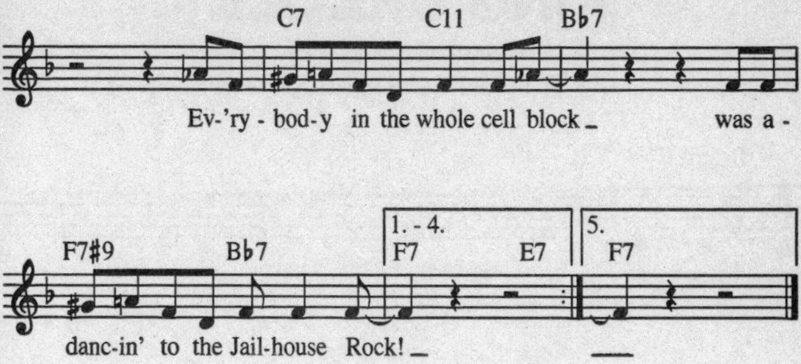

C7 C11 B♭7
Ev-'ry - bod-y in the whole cell block _ was a -
F7♯9 B♭7
1. - 4.
F7 E7
5.
F7
danc-in' to the Jail-house Rock! _

Additional Lyrics

4. The sad sack was a-sittin' on a block of stone,
   Way over in the corner weeping all alone.
   The warden said, "Hey, buddy, don't you be no square.
   If you can't find a partner, use a wooden chair!"
   Let's rock, *etc.*

5. Shifty Henry said to Bugs, "For Heaven's sake,
   No one's lookin'; now's our chance to make a break."
   Bugsy turned to Shifty and he said, "Nix, nix;
   I wanna stick around a while and get my kicks."
   Let's rock, *etc.*

KING CREOLE

Words and Music by
JERRY LEIBER and MIKE STOLLER

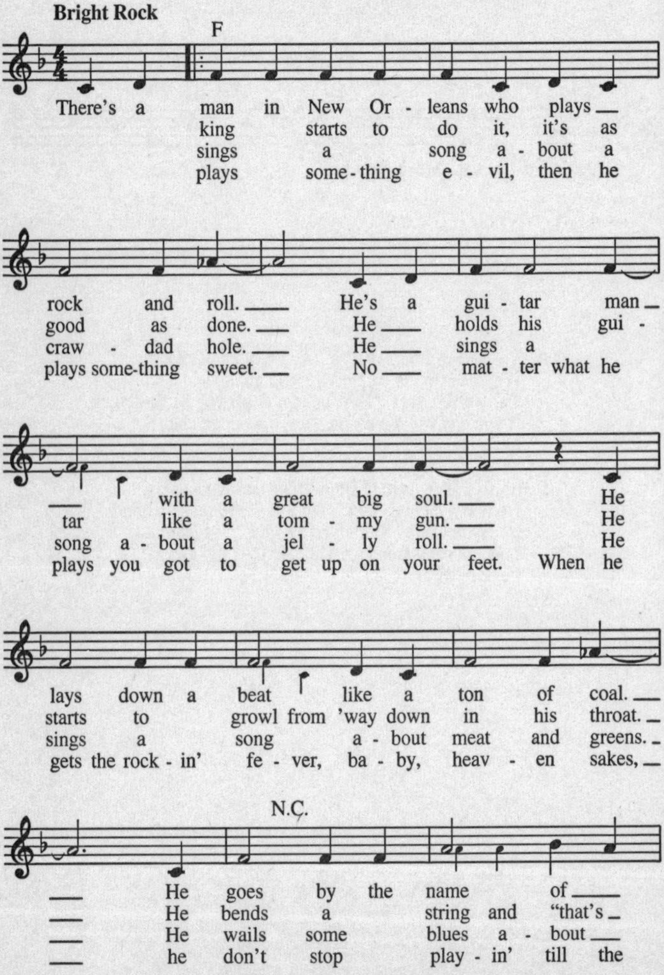
Bright Rock
F
There's a man in New Or - leans who plays
king starts to do it, it's as
sings a song a - bout a
plays some - thing e - vil, then he
rock and roll. He's a gui - tar man
good as done. He holds his gui -
craw - dad hole. He sings a
plays some-thing sweet. No mat - ter what he
with a great big soul. He
tar like a tom - my gun. He
song a - bout a jel - ly roll. He
plays you got to get up on your feet. When he
lays down a beat like a ton of coal.
starts to growl from 'way down in his throat.
sings a song a - bout meat and greens.
gets the rock - in' fe - ver, ba - by, heav - en sakes,
N.C.
He goes by the name of
He bends a string and "that's
He wails some blues a - bout
he don't stop play - in' till the

© 1958 (Renewed) JERRY LEIBER MUSIC and MIKE STOLLER MUSIC
All Rights Reserved

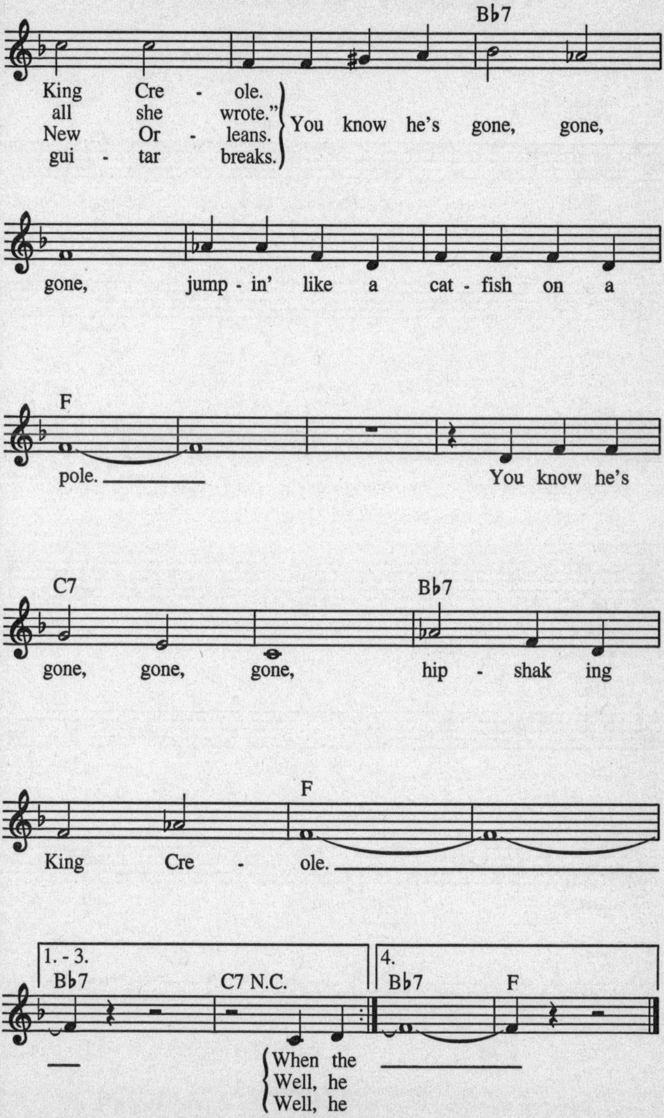
Bb7
King Cre - ole.
all she wrote."
New Or - leans.
gui - tar breaks.
You know he's gone, gone,
gone, jump - in' like a cat - fish on a
F
pole.
You know he's
C7
Bb7
gone, gone, gone, hip - shak ing
King Cre - ole.
F
1. - 3.
Bb7
C7 N.C.
When the
Well, he
Well, he
4.
Bb7
F

KISSIN' COUSINS

Words and Music by
FRED WISE and RANDY STARR

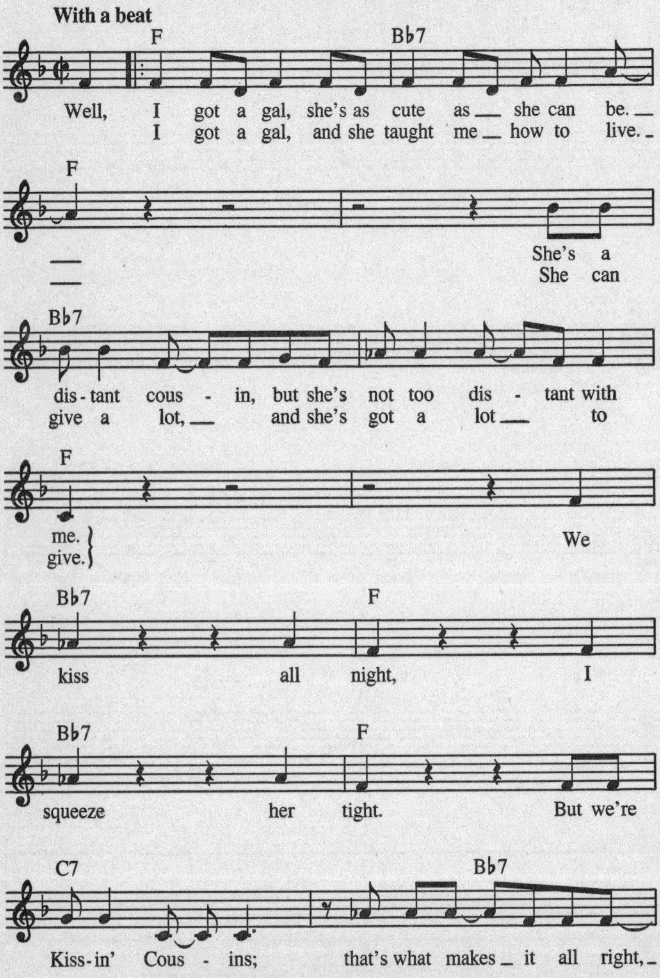
With a beat
F
Bb7
Well, I got a gal, she's as cute as she can be.
I got a gal, and she taught me how to live.
F
She's a
She can
Bb7
dis-tant cous - in, but she's not too dis - tant with
give a lot, and she's got a lot to
F
me.
give.
We
Bb7
F
kiss all night,
I
Bb7
F
squeeze her tight.
But we're
C7
Bb7
Kiss-in' Cous - ins; that's what makes it all right,

Copyright © 1964 by Gladys Music
Copyright Renewed, Assigned to Erika Publishing and Nadel Music for the United States
International Copyright Secured All Rights Reserved

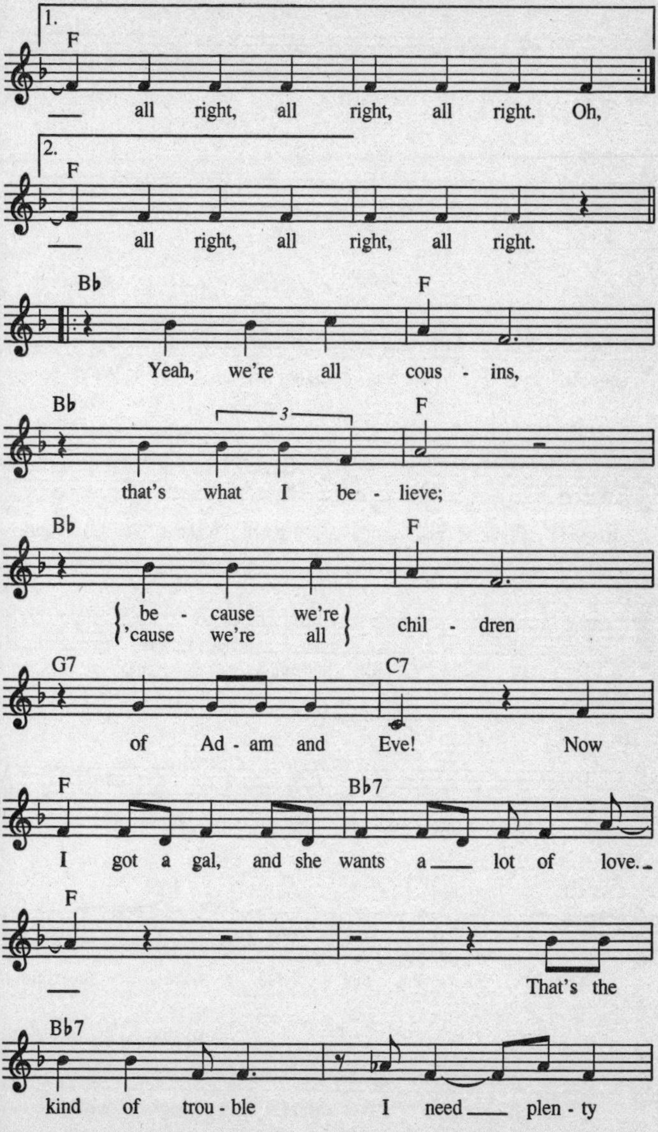
1.
F
— all right, all right, all right. Oh,
2.
F
— all right, all right, all right.
B♭ F
Yeah, we're all cous - ins,
B♭ F
3
that's what I be - lieve;
B♭ F
be - cause we're
'cause we're all
chil - dren
G7 C7
of Ad - am and Eve! Now
F B♭7
I got a gal, and she wants a — lot of love. —
F
— That's the
B♭7
kind of trou - ble I need — plen - ty

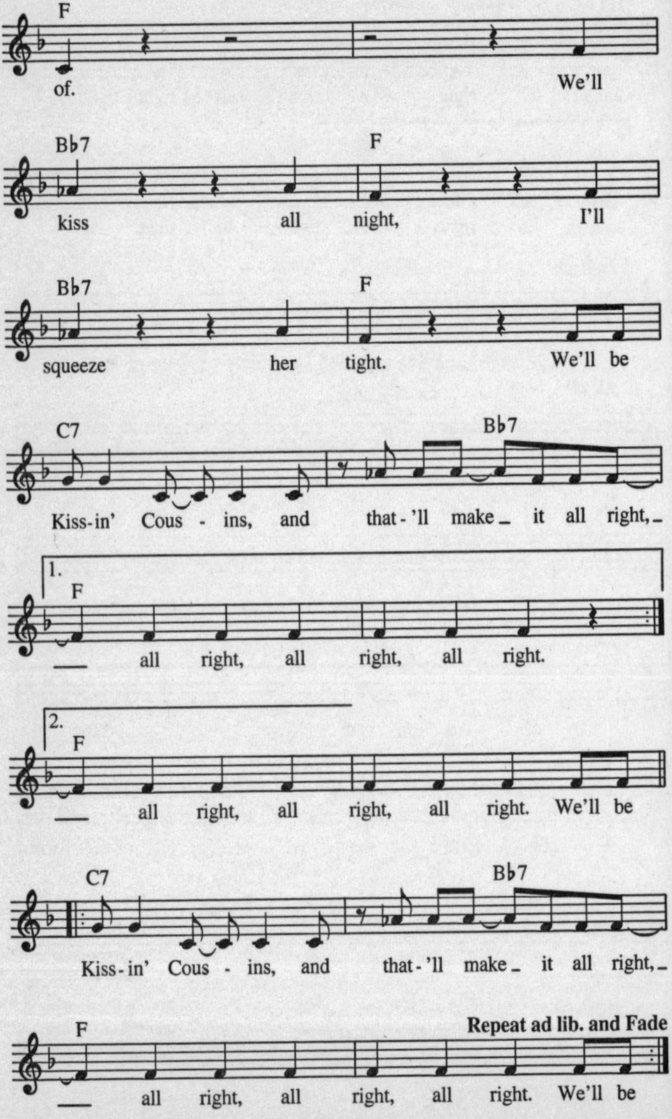
F
of.
We'll
Bb7
F
kiss all night, I'll
Bb7
F
squeeze her tight. We'll be
C7
Bb7
Kiss-in' Cous - ins, and that-'ll make it all right,
1.
F
all right, all right, all right.
2.
F
all right, all right, all right. We'll be
C7
Bb7
Kiss-in' Cous - ins, and that-'ll make it all right,
F
Repeat ad lib. and Fade
all right, all right, all right. We'll be

LITTLE SISTER

Words and Music by
DOC POMUS and MORT SHUMAN

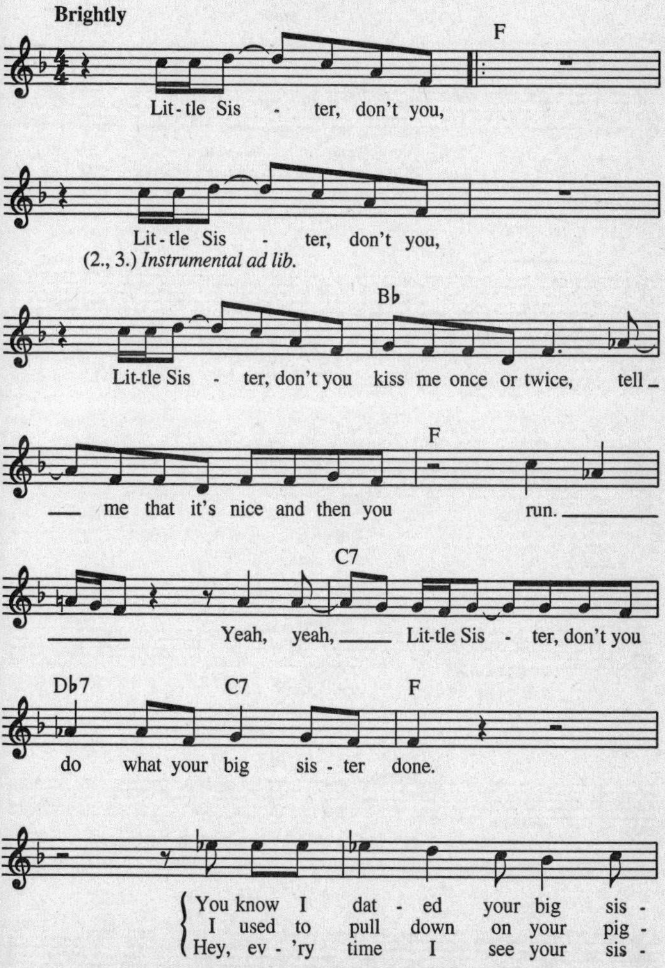
Brightly
F
Lit-tle Sis - ter, don't you,
Lit-tle Sis - ter, don't you,
(2., 3.) Instrumental ad lib.
B♭
Lit-tle Sis - ter, don't you kiss me once or twice, tell
me that it's nice and then you
F
run.
C7
Yeah, yeah, Lit-tle Sis - ter, don't you
D♭7
C7
F
do what your big sis - ter done.
You know I dat - ed your big sis -
I used to pull down on your pig -
Hey, ev - 'ry time I see your sis -

Copyright © 1961 by Elvis Presley Music, Inc.
Copyright Renewed and Assigned to Elvis Presley Music (Administered by R&H Music)
International Copyright Secured All Rights Reserved

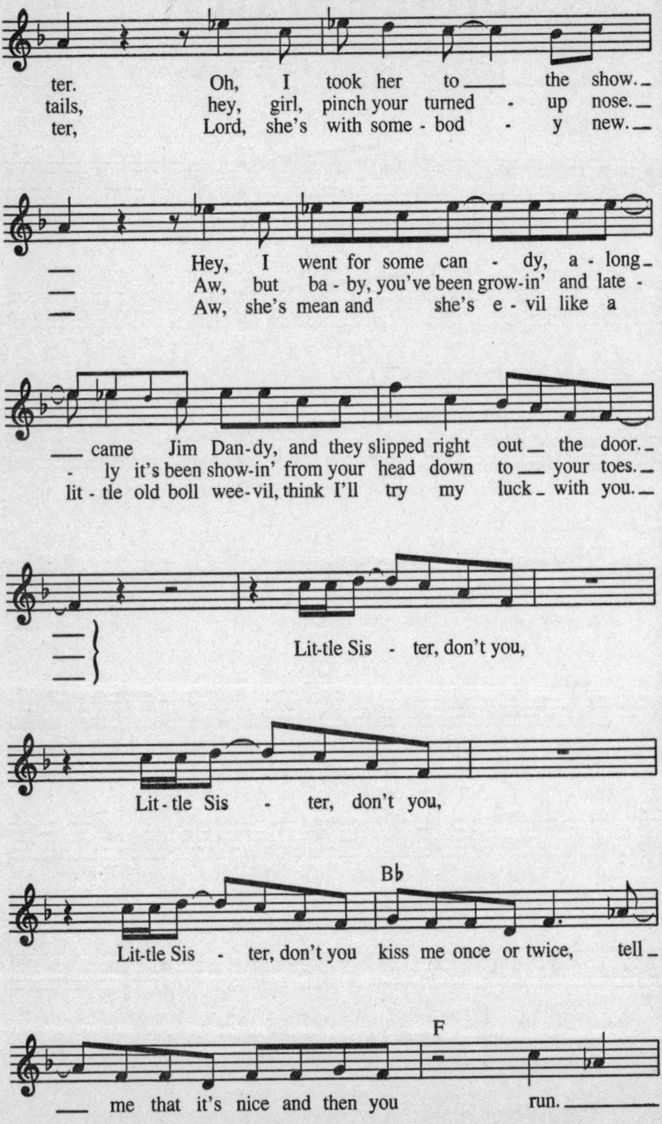
ter. Oh, I took her to the show.
tails, hey, girl, pinch your turned - up nose.
ter, Lord, she's with some - bod - y new.
Hey, I went for some can - dy, a - long
Aw, but ba - by, you've been grow-in' and late -
Aw, she's mean and she's e - vil like a
came Jim Dan-dy, and they slipped right out the door.
- ly it's been show-in' from your head down to your toes.
lit - tle old boll wee-vil, think I'll try my luck with you.
Lit-tle Sis - ter, don't you,
Lit - tle Sis - ter, don't you,
B♭
Lit-tle Sis - ter, don't you kiss me once or twice, tell
F
me that it's nice and then you run.

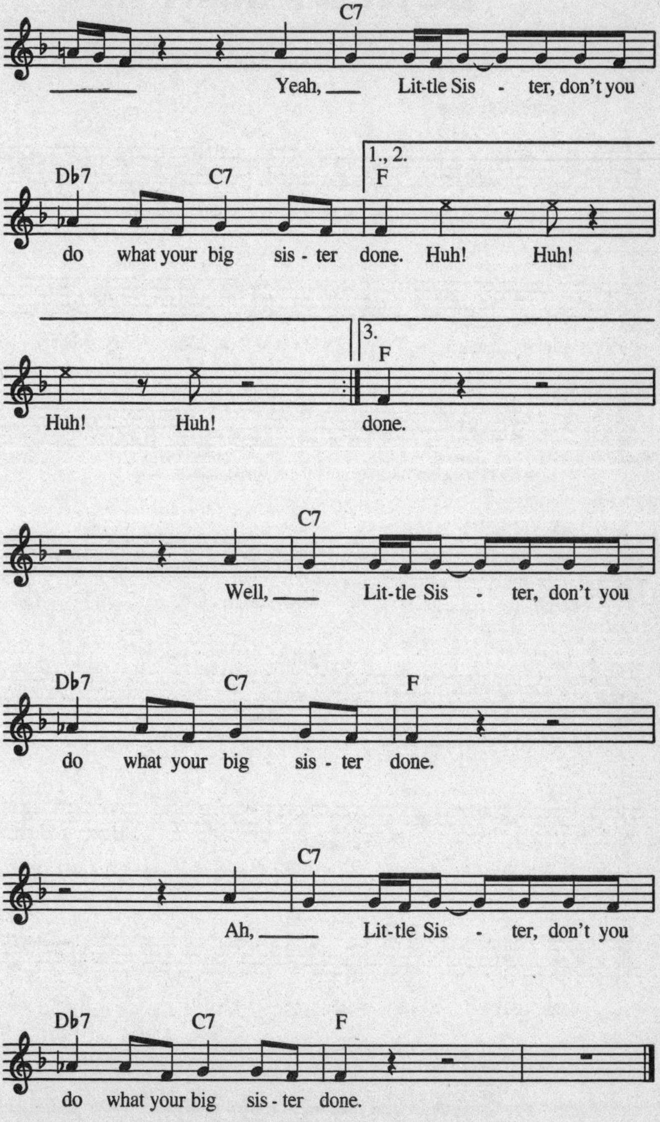
C7
Yeah, Lit-tle Sis - ter, don't you
Db7 C7 1., 2. F
do what your big sis - ter done. Huh! Huh!
Huh! Huh!
3. F
done.
C7
Well, Lit-tle Sis - ter, don't you
Db7 C7 F
do what your big sis - ter done.
C7
Ah, Lit-tle Sis - ter, don't you
Db7 C7 F
do what your big sis - ter done.

LONELY MAN

Words and Music by
BENNIE BENJAMIN and SOL MARCUS

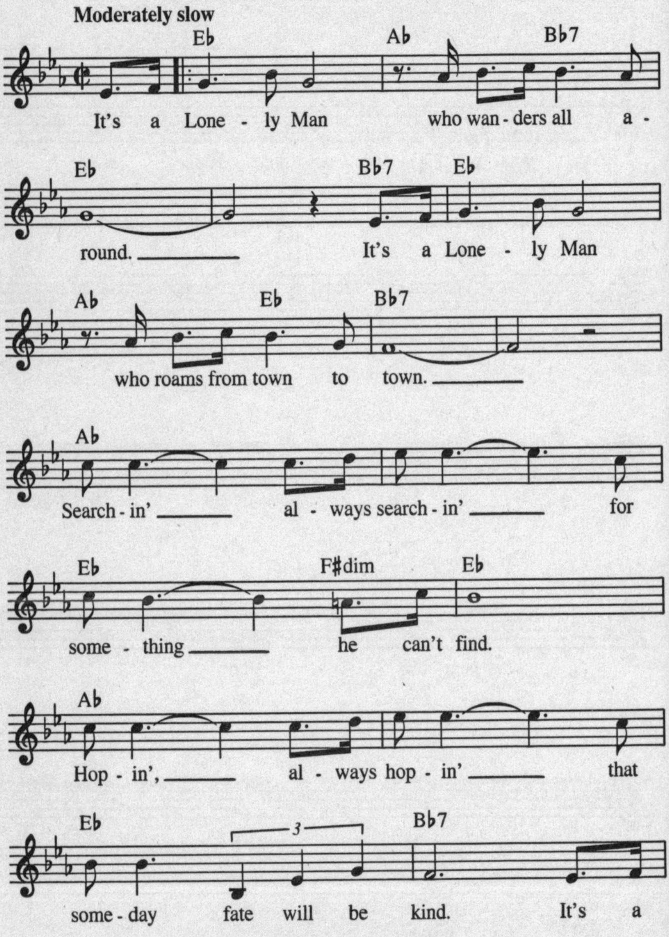
Moderately slow
Eb Ab Bb7
It's a Lone - ly Man who wan - ders all a -
Eb Bb7 Eb
round. It's a Lone - ly Man
Ab Eb Bb7
who roams from town to town.
Ab
Search - in' al - ways search - in' for
Eb F#dim Eb
some - thing he can't find.
Ab
Hop - in', al - ways hop - in' that
Eb 3 Bb7
some - day fate will be kind. It's a

Copyright © 1961 by Gladys Music
Copyright Renewed and Assigned to Bennie Benjamin Music, Inc. and WB Music Corp.
All Rights for Bennie Benjamin Music, Inc. Administered by Chappell & Co.
All Rights for the world excluding the United States Controlled
by Gladys Music (Administered by Williamson Music)
International Copyright Secured All Rights Reserved

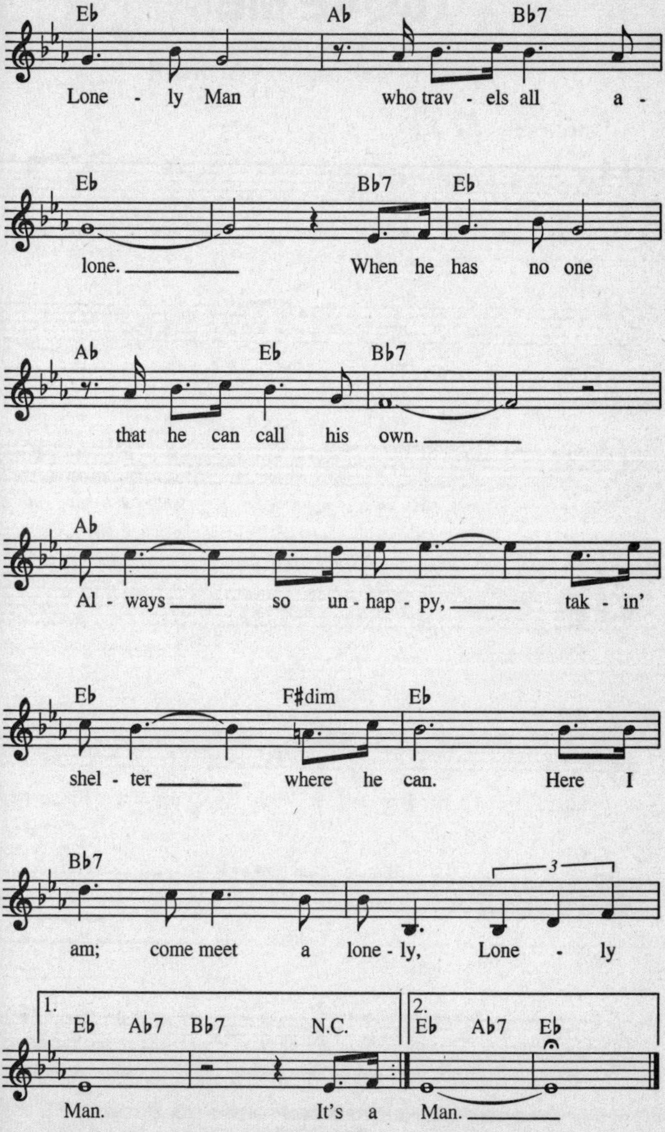
Eb Ab Bb7
Lone - ly Man who trav - els all a -
Eb Bb7 Eb
lone. When he has no one
Ab Eb Bb7
that he can call his own.
Ab
Al - ways so un - hap - py, tak - in'
Eb F#dim Eb
shel - ter where he can. Here I
Bb7
3
am; come meet a lone - ly, Lone - ly
1.
Eb Ab7 Bb7 N.C.
Man. It's a
2.
Eb Ab7 Eb
Man.

LOVE ME

Words and Music by
JERRY LEIBER and MIKE STOLLER

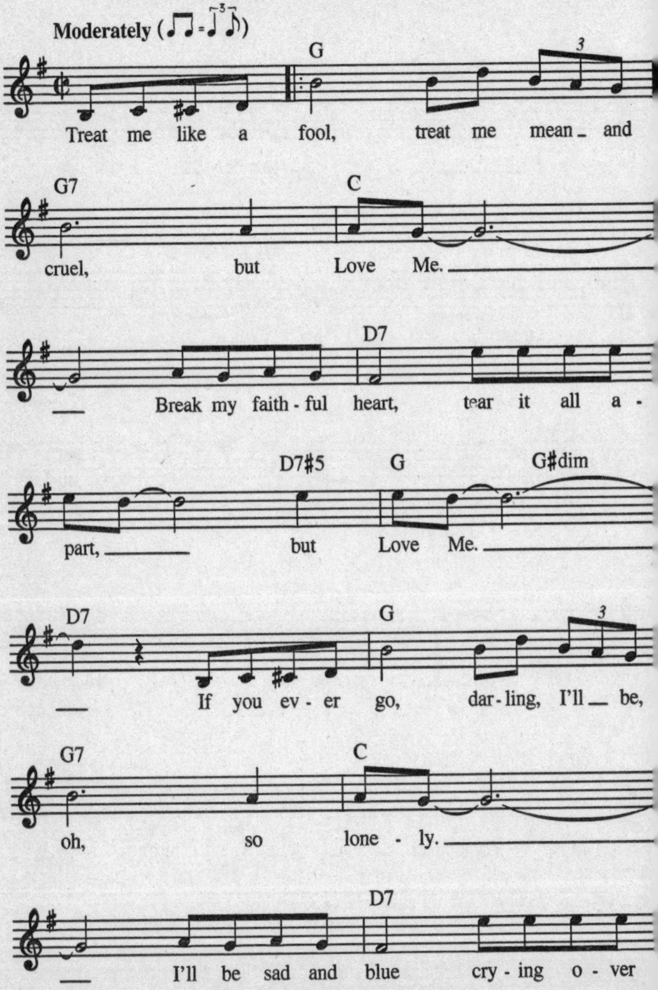
Moderately
G
Treat me like a fool, treat me mean _ and
G7 C
cruel, but Love Me. ___
D7
___ Break my faith - ful heart, tear it all a -
D7#5 G G#dim
part, ___ but Love Me. ___
D7 G
___ If you ev - er go, dar - ling, I'll _ be,
G7 C
oh, so lone - ly. ___
D7
___ I'll be sad and blue cry - ing o - ver

© 1954 (Renewed) JERRY LEIBER MUSIC and MIKE STOLLER MUSIC
All Rights Reserved

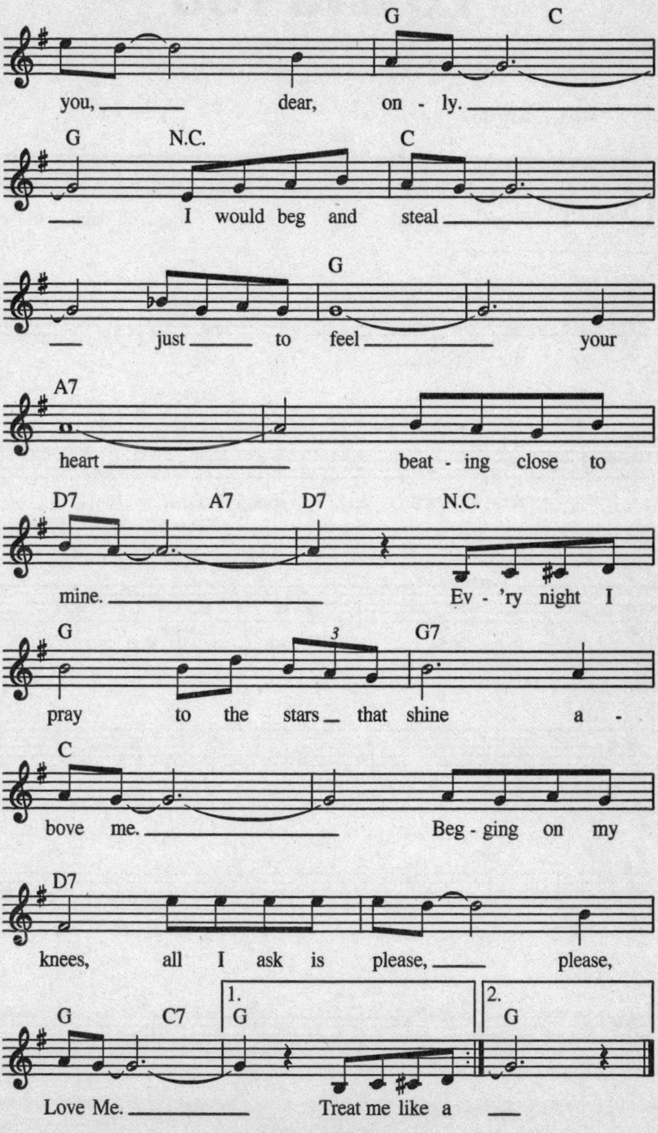
G C
you, dear, on - ly.
G N.C. C
I would beg and steal
G
just to feel your
A7
heart beat - ing close to
D7 A7 D7 N.C.
mine. Ev - 'ry night I
G 3 G7
pray to the stars that shine a -
C
bove me. Beg - ging on my
D7
knees, all I ask is please, please,
1. 2.
G C7 G G
Love Me. Treat me like a

LOVING YOU

Words and Music by
JERRY LEIBER and MIKE STOLLER

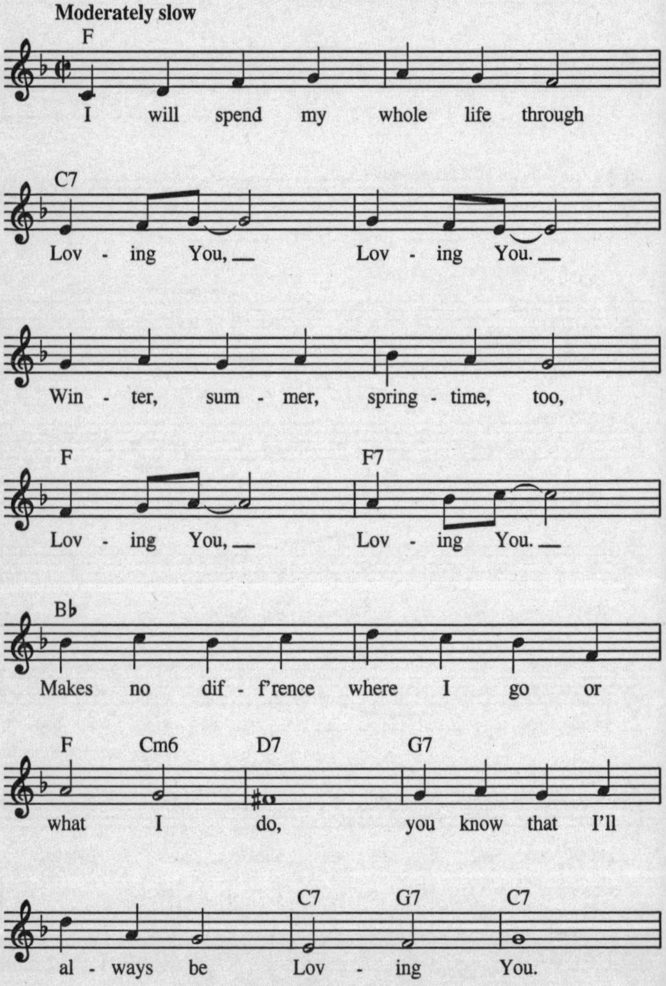
Moderately slow
F
I will spend my whole life through
C7
Lov - ing You, Lov - ing You.
Win - ter, sum - mer, spring - time, too,
F F7
Lov - ing You, Lov - ing You.
B♭
Makes no dif - f'rence where I go or
F Cm6 D7 G7
what I do, you know that I'll
C7 G7 C7
al - ways be Lov - ing You.

© 1957 (Renewed) JERRY LEIBER MUSIC and MIKE STOLLER MUSIC
All Rights Reserved

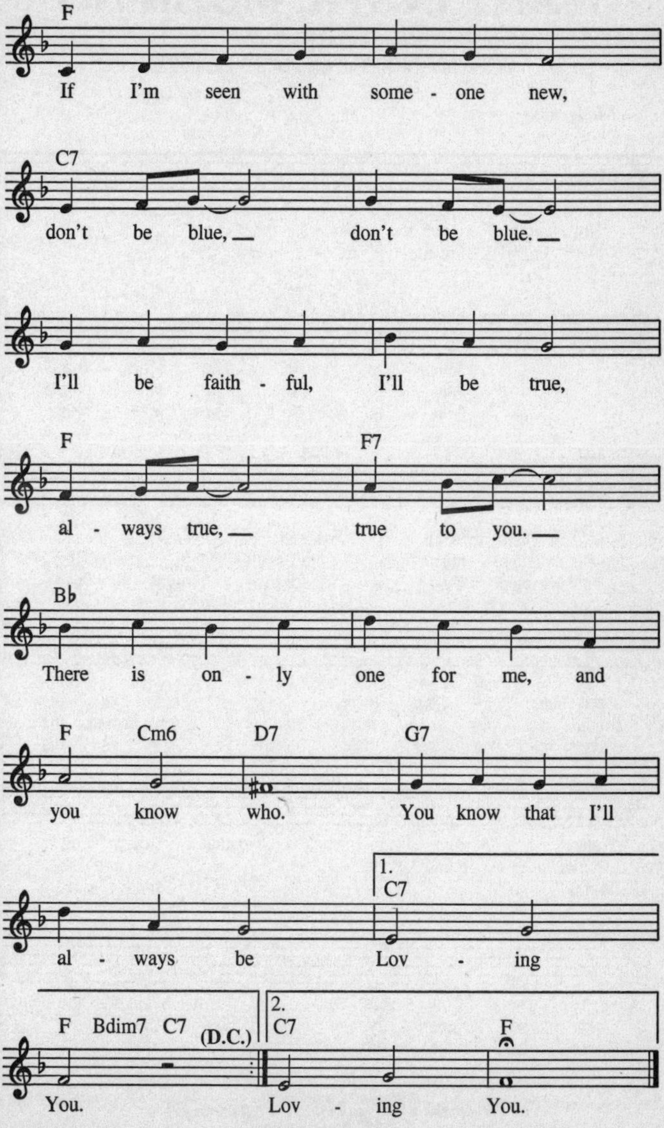
F
If I'm seen with some - one new,
C7
don't be blue, don't be blue.
I'll be faith - ful, I'll be true,
F F7
al - ways true, true to you.
B♭
There is on - ly one for me, and
F Cm6 D7 G7
you know who. You know that I'll
1. C7
al - ways be Lov - ing
F Bdim7 C7 (D.C.) 2. C7 F
You. Lov - ing You.

MARY IN THE MORNING

Words and Music by
JOHNNY CYMBAL and MIKE LENDELL

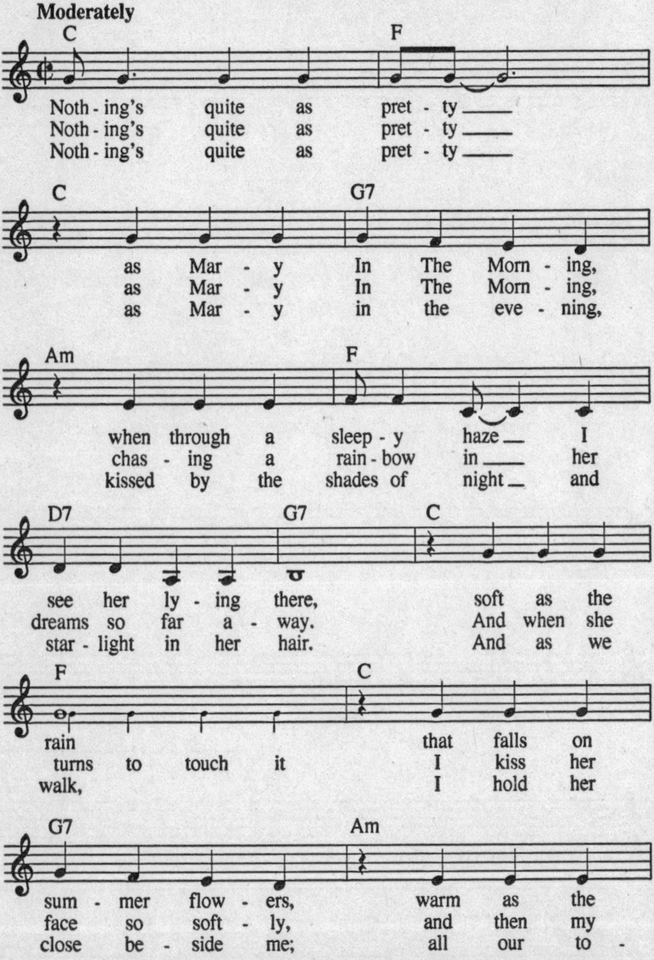
Moderately
C F
Noth - ing's quite as pret - ty
Noth - ing's quite as pret - ty
Noth - ing's quite as pret - ty
C G7
as Mar - y In The Morn - ing,
as Mar - y In The Morn - ing,
as Mar - y in the eve - ning,
Am F
when through a sleep - y haze I
chas - ing a rain - bow in her
kissed by the shades of night and
D7 G7 C
see her ly - ing there, soft as the
dreams so far a - way. And when she
star - light in her hair. And as we
F C
rain that falls on
turns to touch it I kiss her
walk, I hold her
G7 Am
sum - mer flow - ers, warm as the
face so soft - ly, and then my
close be - side me; all our to -

© Copyright 1967 by DUCHESS MUSIC CORPORATION, an MCA company
Copyright Renewed
International Copyright Secured All Rights Reserved
MCA music publishing

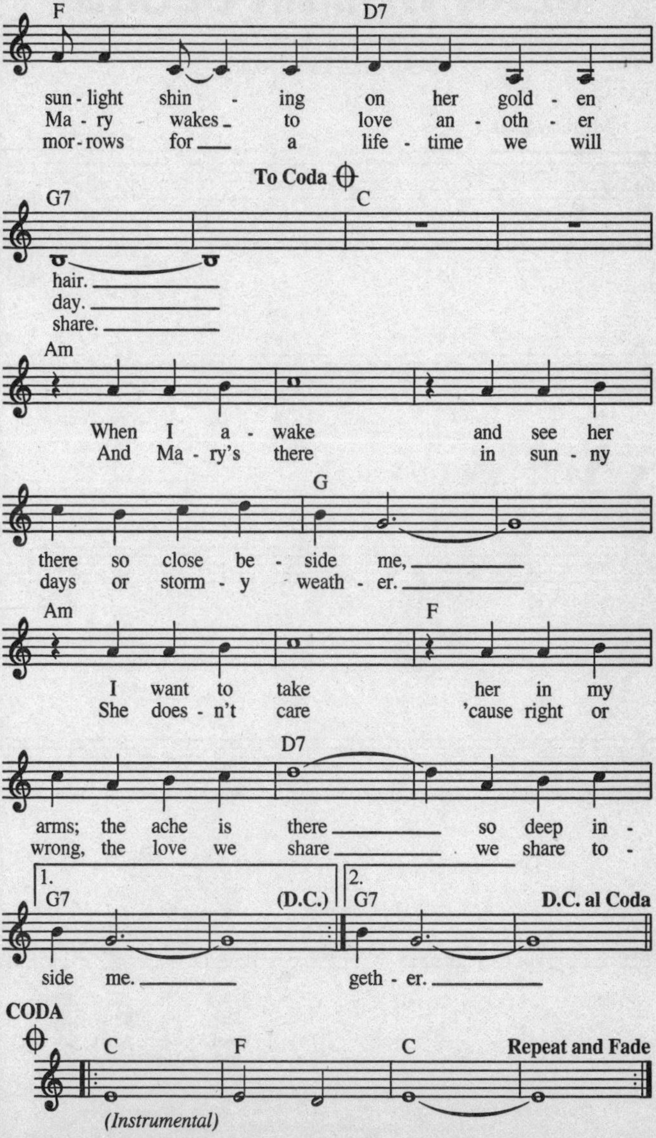
F D7
sun - light shin - ing on her gold - en
Ma - ry wakes to love an - oth - er
mor - rows for a life - time we will
To Coda
G7 C
hair.
day.
share.
Am
When I a - wake and see her
And Ma - ry's there in sun - ny
G
there so close be - side me,
days or storm - y weath - er.
Am F
I want to take her in my
She does - n't care 'cause right or
D7
arms; the ache is there so deep in -
wrong, the love we share we share to -
1. G7 (D.C.)
side me.
2. G7 D.C. al Coda
geth - er.
CODA
C F C Repeat and Fade
(Instrumental)

MEAN WOMAN BLUES

Words and Music by
CLAUDE DEMETRUIS

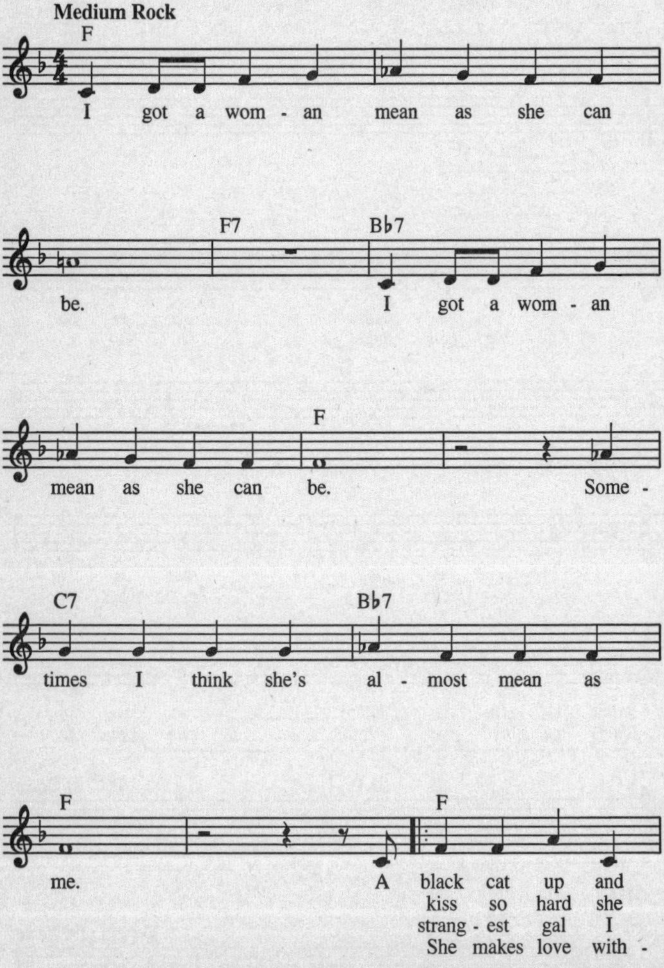
Medium Rock
F
I got a wom - an mean as she can
F7
Bb7
be. I got a wom - an
F
mean as she can be. Some -
C7
Bb7
times I think she's al - most mean as
F
F
me. A black cat up and
kiss so hard she
strang - est gal I
She makes love with -

Copyright © 1957 by Gladys Music, Inc.
Copyright Renewed and Assigned to Gladys Music (Administered by Williamson Music)
International Copyright Secured All Rights Reserved

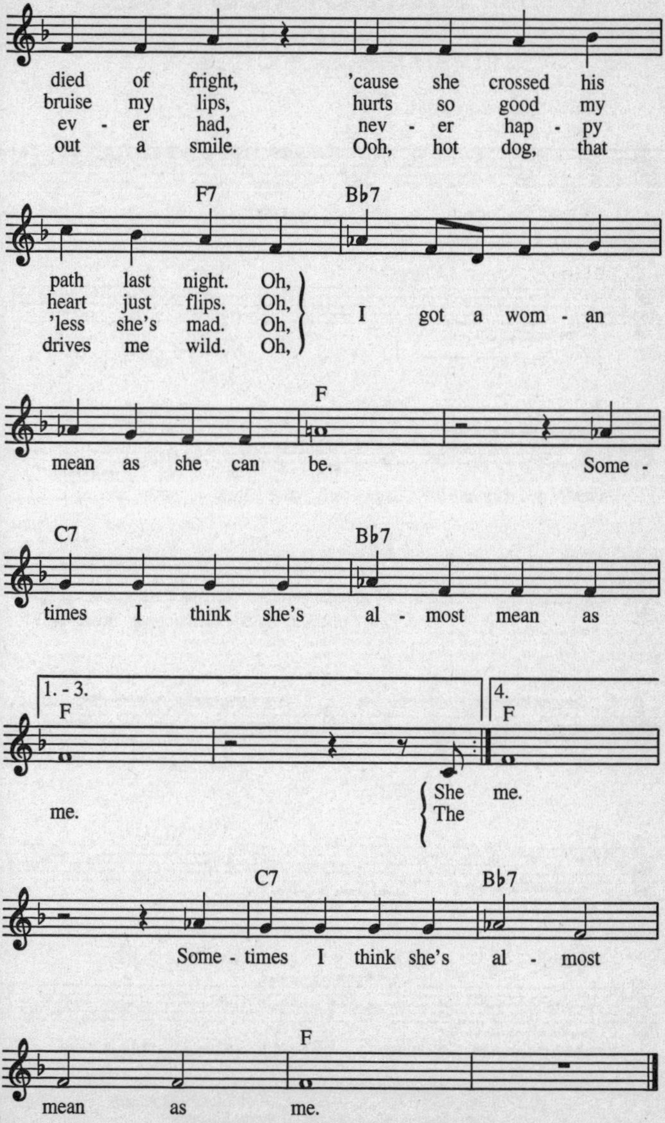
died of fright, 'cause she crossed his
bruise my lips, hurts so good my
ev - er had, nev - er hap - py
out a smile. Ooh, hot dog, that
F7
B♭7
path last night. Oh,
heart just flips. Oh,
'less she's mad. Oh,
drives me wild. Oh,
I got a wom - an
mean as she can be.
F
Some -
C7
B♭7
times I think she's al - most mean as
1. - 3.
F
me.
She
The
4.
F
me.
C7
B♭7
Some - times I think she's al - most
F
mean as me.

MEMORIES

Words and Music by
BILLY STRANGE and SCOTT DAVIS

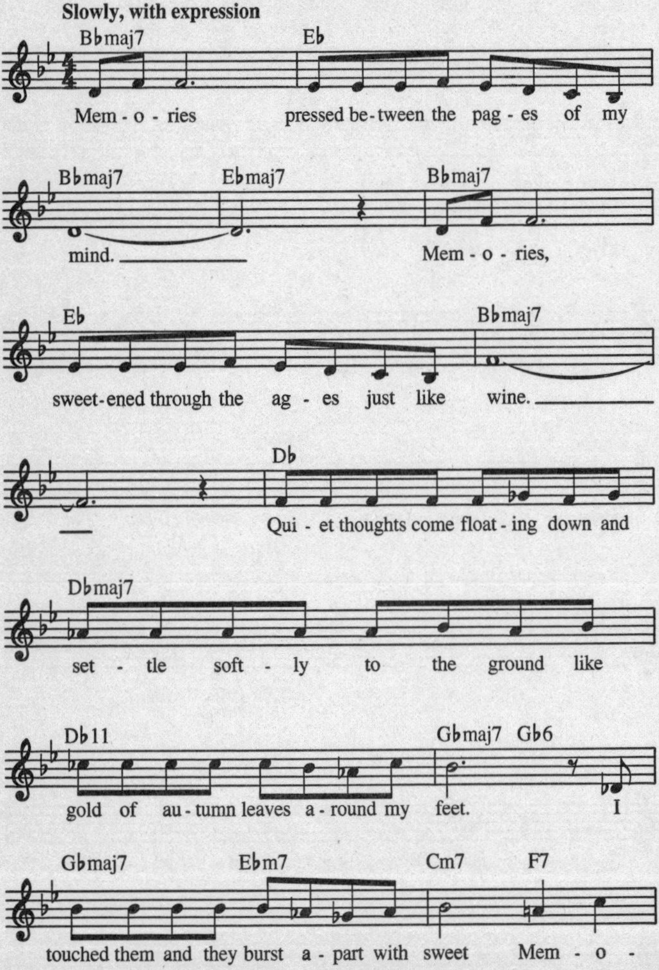
Slowly, with expression
Bbmaj7 Eb
Mem - o - ries pressed be - tween the pag - es of my
Bbmaj7 Ebmaj7 Bbmaj7
mind. Mem - o - ries,
Eb Bbmaj7
sweet - ened through the ag - es just like wine.
Db
Qui - et thoughts come float - ing down and
Dbmaj7
set - tle soft - ly to the ground like
Db11 Gbmaj7 Gb6
gold of au - tumn leaves a - round my feet. I
Gbmaj7 Ebm7 Cm7 F7
touched them and they burst a - part with sweet Mem - o -

Copyright © 1969 by Gladys Music, Inc.
Copyright Assigned to Gladys Music (Administered by Williamson Music)
International Copyright Secured All Rights Reserved

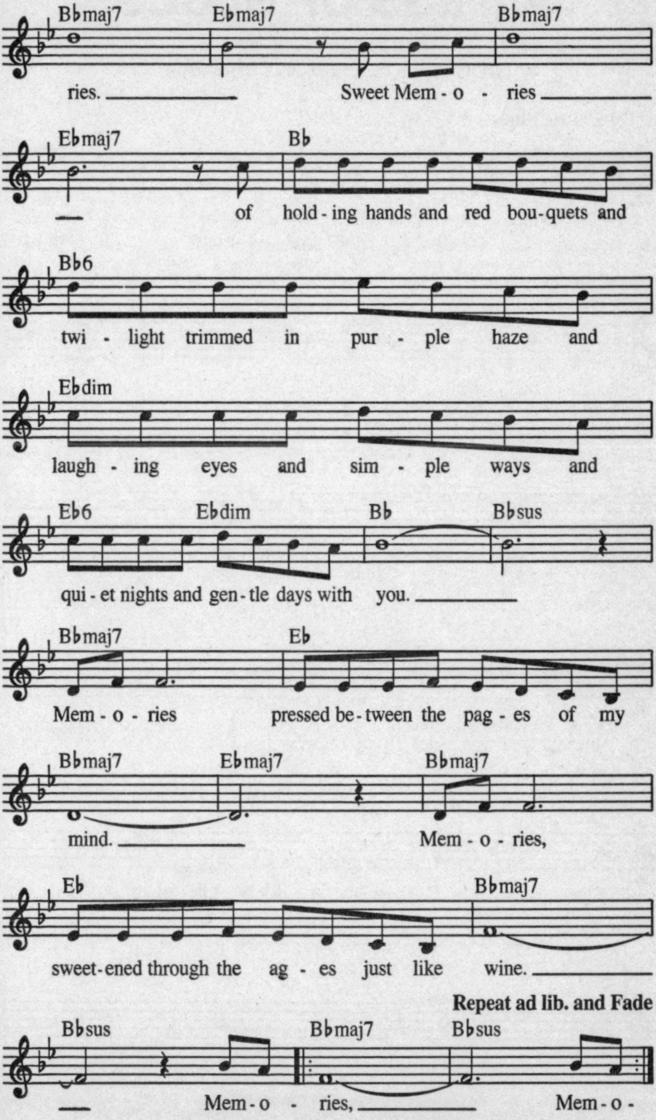
Bbmaj7
Ebmaj7
Bbmaj7
ries. Sweet Mem - o - ries
Ebmaj7
Bb
of hold - ing hands and red bou - quets and
Bb6
twi - light trimmed in pur - ple haze and
Ebdim
laugh - ing eyes and sim - ple ways and
Eb6
Ebdim
Bb
Bbsus
qui - et nights and gen - tle days with you.
Bbmaj7
Eb
Mem - o - ries pressed be - tween the pag - es of my
Bbmaj7
Ebmaj7
Bbmaj7
mind. Mem - o - ries,
Eb
Bbmaj7
sweet - ened through the ag - es just like wine.
Repeat ad lib. and Fade
Bbsus
Bbmaj7
Bbsus
Mem - o - ries, Mem - o -

A MESS OF BLUES

Words and Music by
DOC POMUS and MORT SHUMAN

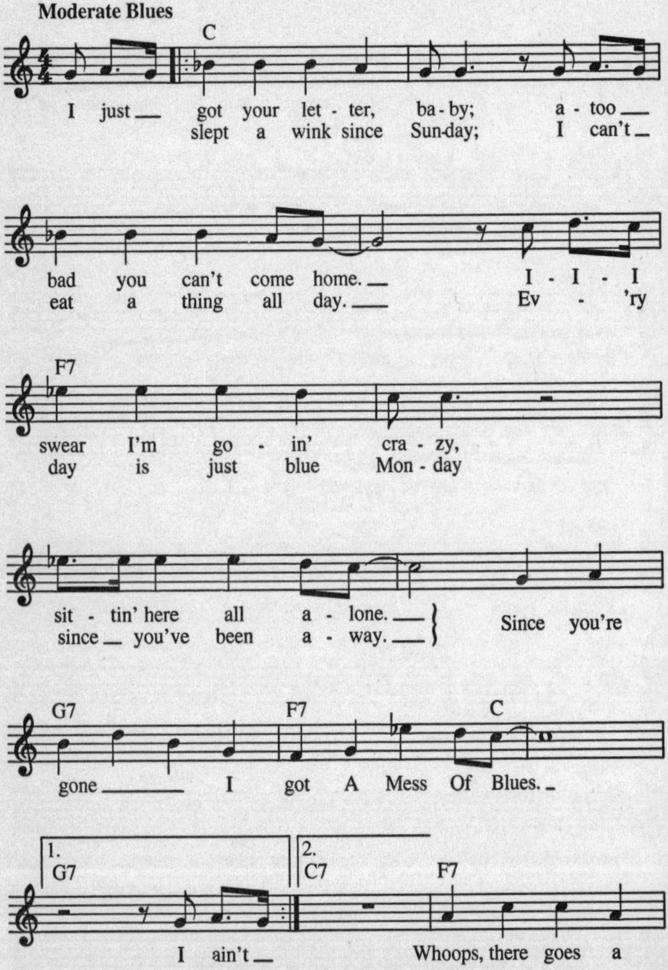
Moderate Blues
C
I just got your let - ter, ba - by; a - too
slept a wink since Sun-day; I can't
bad you can't come home. I - I - I
eat a thing all day. Ev - 'ry
F7
swear I'm go - in' cra - zy,
day is just blue Mon - day
sit - tin' here all a - lone.
since you've been a - way.
Since you're
G7 F7 C
gone I got A Mess Of Blues.
1. G7
I ain't
2. C7 F7
Whoops, there goes a

Copyright © 1960 by Elvis Presley Music, Inc.
Copyright Renewed and Assigned to Elvis Presley Music (Administered by R&H Music)
International Copyright Secured All Rights Reserved

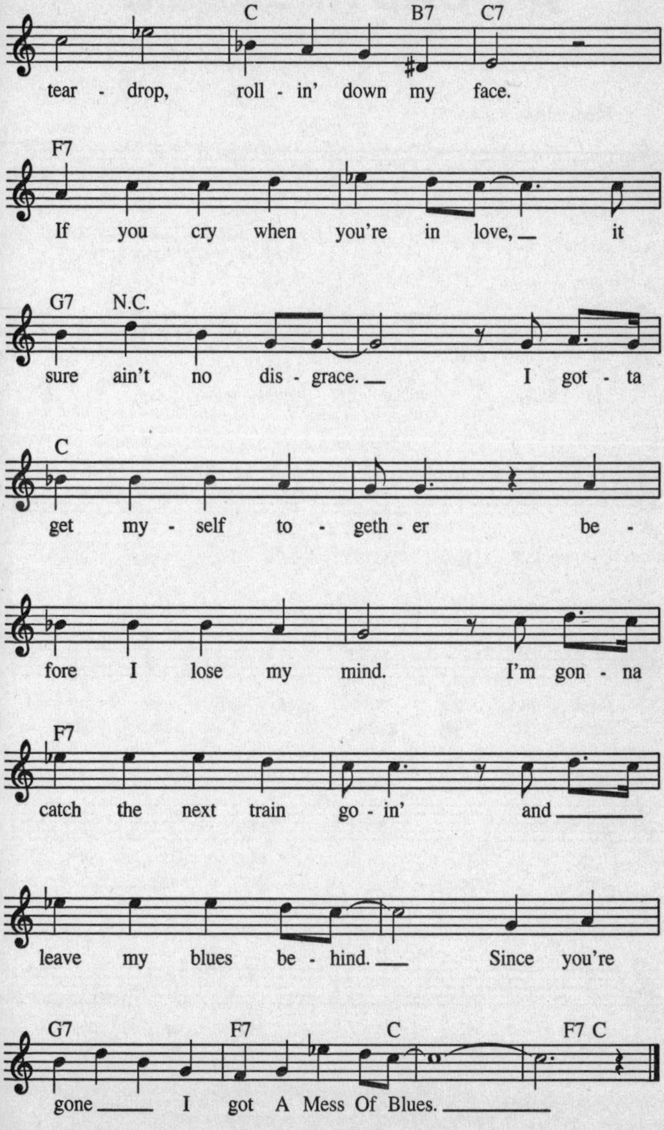
C B7 C7
tear - drop, roll - in' down my face.
F7
If you cry when you're in love, it
G7 N.C.
sure ain't no dis - grace. I got - ta
C
get my - self to - geth - er be -
fore I lose my mind. I'm gon - na
F7
catch the next train go - in' and
leave my blues be - hind. Since you're
G7 F7 C F7 C
gone I got A Mess Of Blues.

MY BABY LEFT ME

Words and Music by
ARTHUR CRUDUP

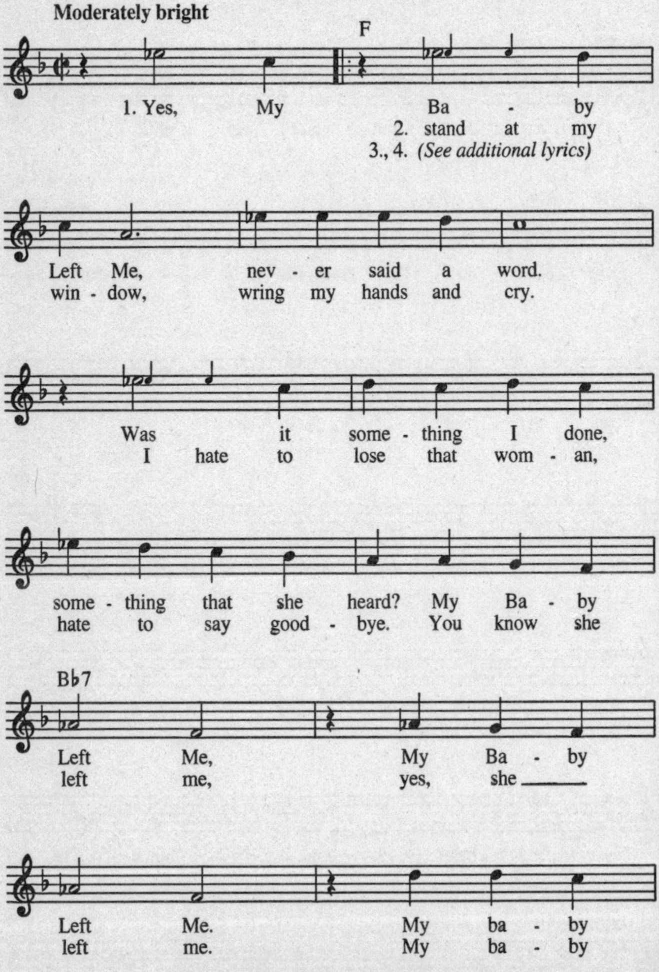
Moderately bright
F
1. Yes, My Ba - by
2. stand at my
3., 4. (See additional lyrics)
Left Me, nev - er said a word.
win - dow, wring my hands and cry.
Was it some - thing I done,
I hate to lose that wom - an,
some - thing that she heard? My Ba - by
hate to say good - bye. You know she
Bb7
Left Me, My Ba - by
left me, yes, she ___
Left Me. My ba - by
left me. My ba - by

Copyright © 1956 by Elvis Presley Music, Inc.
Copyright Renewed and Assigned to Elvis Presley Music (Administered by R&H Music)
International Copyright Secured All Rights Reserved

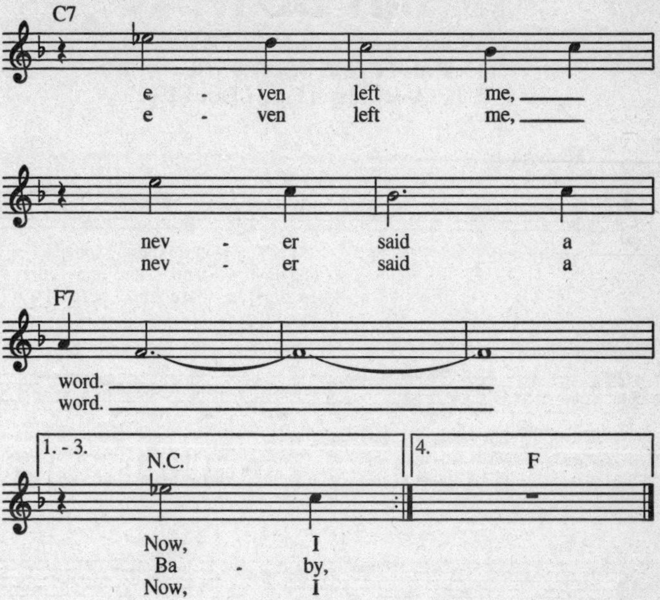
C7
e - ven left me, ___
e - ven left me, ___
nev - er said a
nev - er said a
F7
word. ___
word. ___
1. - 3.
N.C.
Now, I
Ba - by,
Now, I
4.
F

Additional Lyrics

3. Baby, one of these mornings, Lord, it won't be long,
You'll look for me and, baby, and Daddy he'll be gone.
You know you left me, you know you left me.
My baby even left me, never said goodbye.

4. Now, I stand at my window, wring my hands and moan.
All I know is that the one I love is gone.
My Baby Left Me, you know she left me.
My baby even left me, never said a word.

MY BOY

Words and Music by CLAUDE FRANCOIS,
JEAN-PIERRE BOURTAYRE,
BILL MARTIN and PHIL COULTER

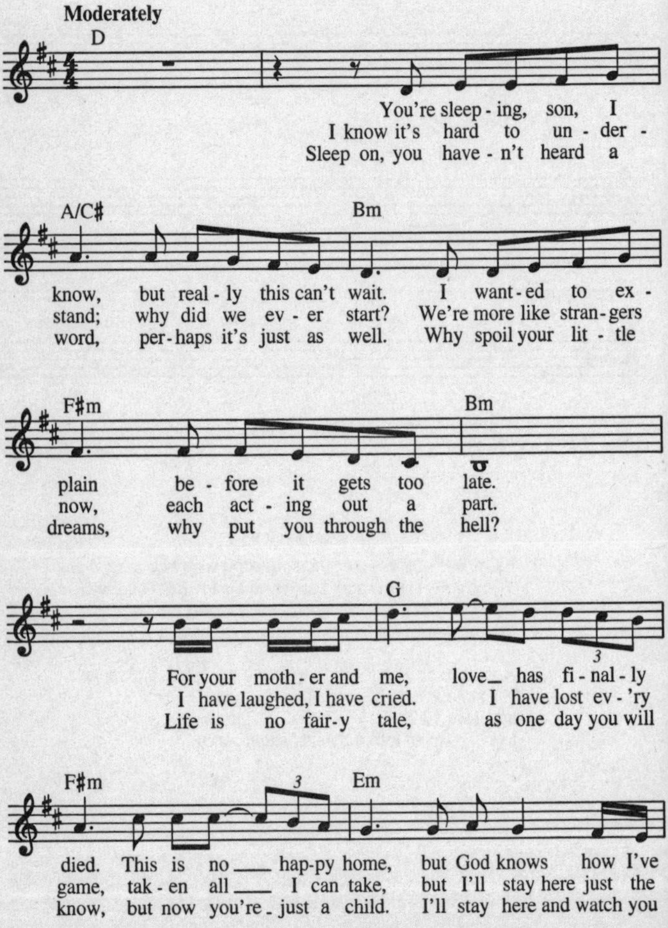
Moderately
D
You're sleep - ing, son, I
I know it's hard to un - der -
Sleep on, you have - n't heard a
A/C#
Bm
know, but real - ly this can't wait. I want - ed to ex -
stand; why did we ev - er start? We're more like stran - gers
word, per - haps it's just as well. Why spoil your lit - tle
F#m
Bm
plain be - fore it gets too late.
now, each act - ing out a part.
dreams, why put you through the hell?
G
For your moth - er and me, love has fi - nal - ly
I have laughed, I have cried. I have lost ev - 'ry
Life is no fair - y tale, as one day you will
F#m
Em
died. This is no hap - py home, but God knows how I've
game, tak - en all I can take, but I'll stay here just the
know, but now you're just a child. I'll stay here and watch you

© 1971, 1972 EMI MUSIC PUBLISHING LTD.
All Rights for the U.S.A. and Canada Controlled and Administered by COLGEMS-EMI MUSIC INC.
All Rights Reserved International Copyright Secured Used by Permission

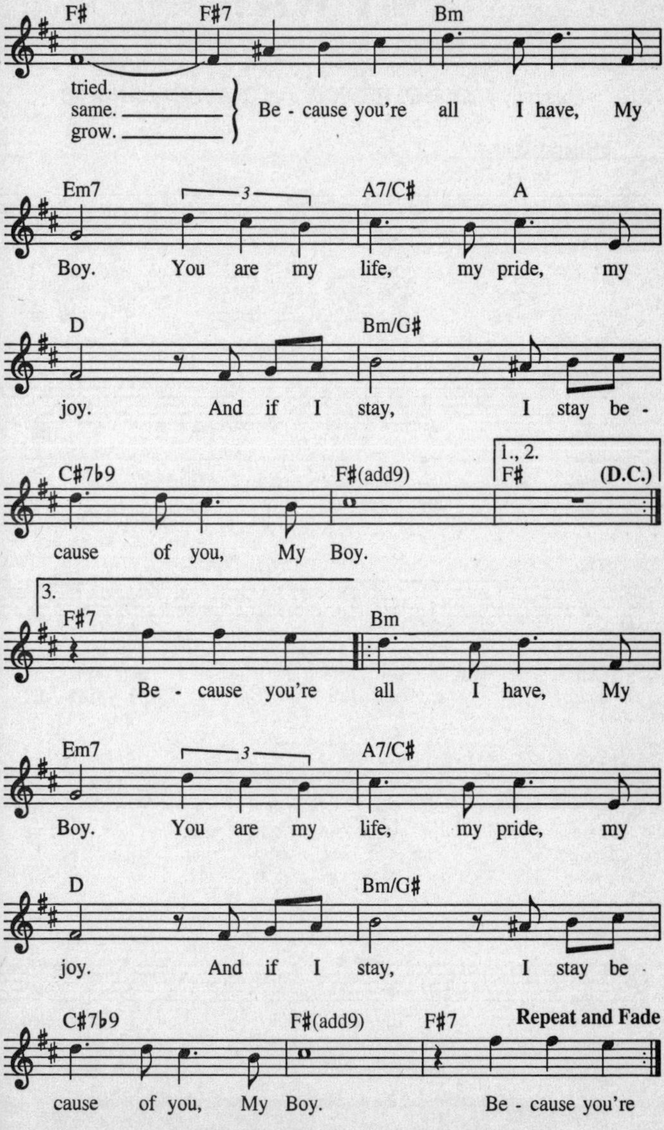
F# F#7 Bm
tried.
same.
grow.
Be - cause you're all I have, My
Em7 3 A7/C# A
Boy. You are my life, my pride, my
D Bm/G#
joy. And if I stay, I stay be -
C#7b9 F#(add9) 1., 2. F# (D.C.)
cause of you, My Boy.
3. F#7 Bm
Be - cause you're all I have, My
Em7 3 A7/C#
Boy. You are my life, my pride, my
D Bm/G#
joy. And if I stay, I stay be -
C#7b9 F#(add9) F#7 Repeat and Fade
cause of you, My Boy. Be - cause you're

MY WAY

English Words by PAUL ANKA
Original French Words by GILES THIBAULT
Music by JACQUES REVAUX and CLAUDE FRANCOIS

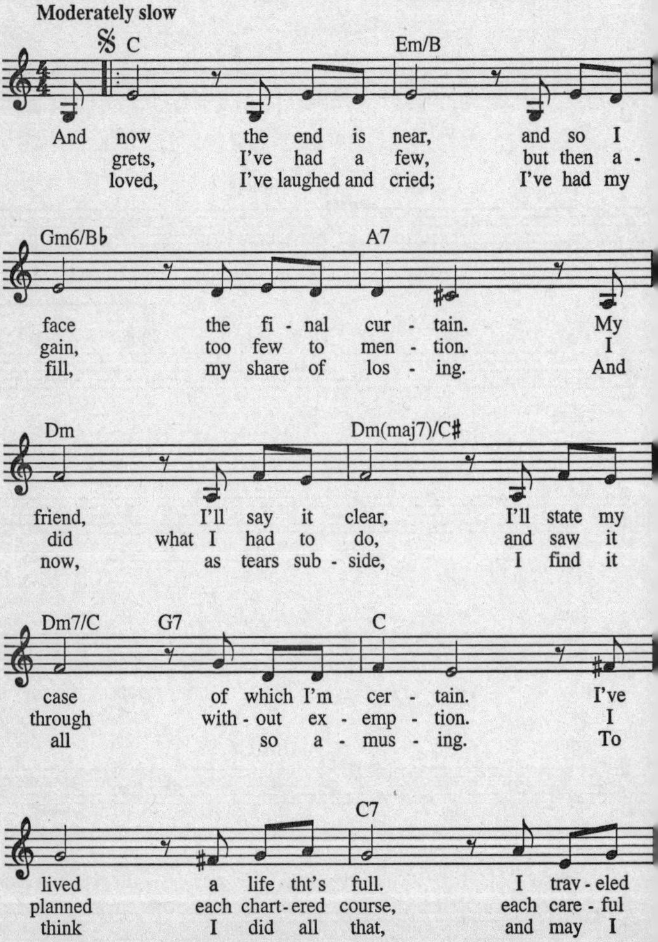
Moderately slow
C
Em/B
And now the end is near, and so I
grets, I've had a few, but then a -
loved, I've laughed and cried; I've had my
Gm6/B♭
A7
face the fi - nal cur - tain. My
gain, too few to men - tion. I
fill, my share of los - ing. And
Dm
Dm(maj7)/C♯
friend, I'll say it clear, I'll state my
did what I had to do, and saw it
now, as tears sub - side, I find it
Dm7/C
G7
C
case of which I'm cer - tain. I've
through with - out ex - emp - tion. I
all so a - mus - ing. To
C7
lived a life tht's full. I trav - eled
planned each chart - ered course, each care - ful
think I did all that, and may I

Copyright © 1967 Societe des Nouvelles Editions Eddie Barclay, Paris, France
Copyright for the U.S.A. and Canada © 1969 Management Agency & Music Publishing, Inc. (BMI)
All Rights Reserved Used by Permission

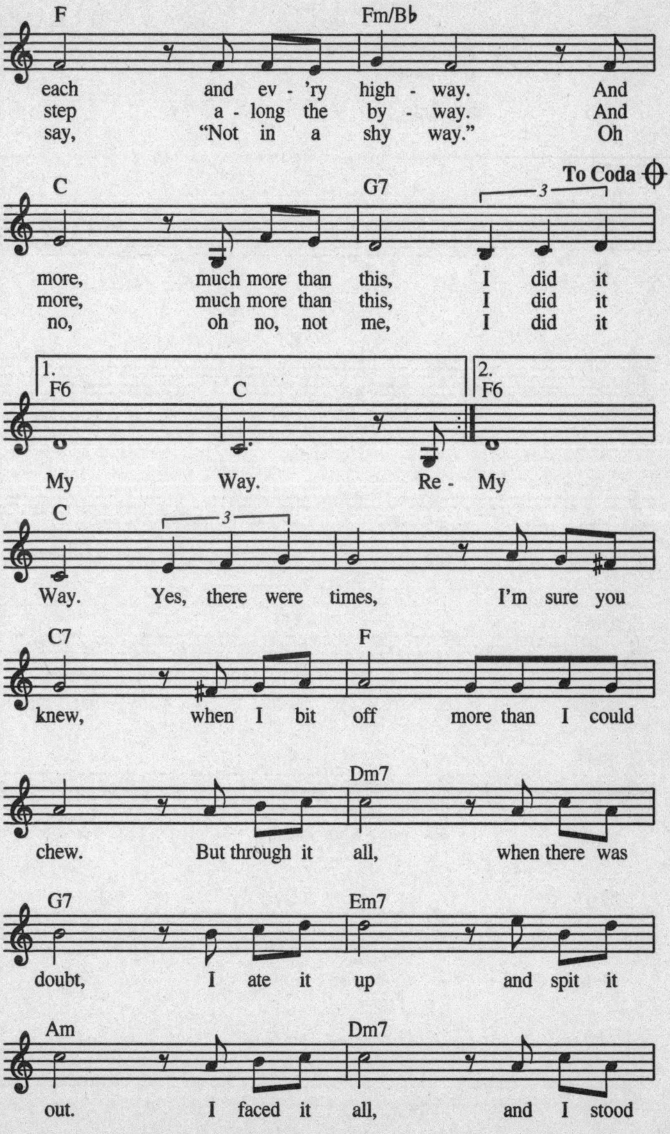
F
Fm/B♭
each and ev - 'ry high - way. And
step a - long the by - way. And
say, "Not in a shy way." Oh
To Coda
C
G7
more, much more than this, I did it
more, much more than this, I did it
no, oh no, not me, I did it
1.
F6
C
2.
F6
My Way. Re - My
C
Way. Yes, there were times, I'm sure you
C7
F
knew, when I bit off more than I could
Dm7
chew. But through it all, when there was
G7
Em7
doubt, I ate it up and spit it
Am
Dm7
out. I faced it all, and I stood

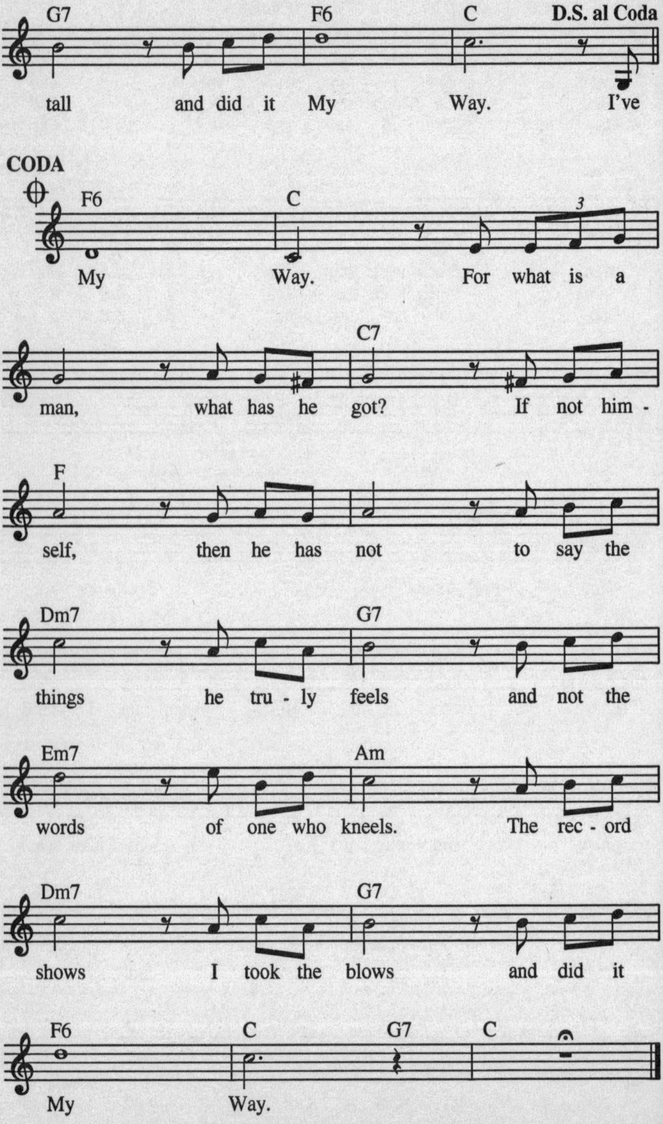
G7 F6 C D.S. al Coda
tall and did it My Way. I've
CODA
F6 C
My Way. For what is a
C7
man, what has he got? If not him -
F
self, then he has not to say the
Dm7 G7
things he tru - ly feels and not the
Em7 Am
words of one who kneels. The rec - ord
Dm7 G7
shows I took the blows and did it
F6 C G7 C
My Way.

LOVE ME TENDER

Words and Music by
ELVIS PRESLEY and VERA MATSON

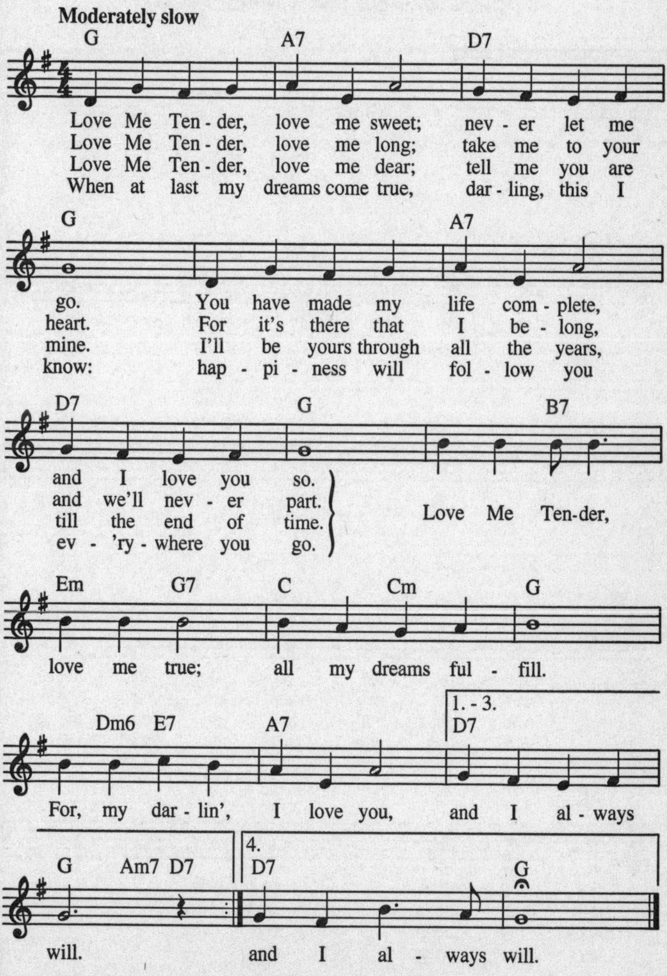
Moderately slow
G
A7
D7
Love Me Ten - der, love me sweet; nev - er let me
Love Me Ten - der, love me long; take me to your
Love Me Ten - der, love me dear; tell me you are
When at last my dreams come true, dar - ling, this I
G
A7
go. You have made my life com - plete,
heart. For it's there that I be - long,
mine. I'll be yours through all the years,
know: hap - pi - ness will fol - low you
D7
G
B7
and I love you so.
and we'll nev - er part.
till the end of time.
ev - 'ry - where you go.
Love Me Ten-der,
Em
G7
C
Cm
G
love me true; all my dreams ful - fill.
1. - 3.
Dm6
E7
A7
D7
For, my dar - lin', I love you, and I al - ways
G
Am7
D7
4.
D7
G
will. and I al - ways will.

Copyright © 1956 by Elvis Presley Music, Inc.
Copyright Renewed and Assigned to Elvis Presley Music (Administered by R&H Music)
International Copyright Secured All Rights Reserved

ONE BROKEN HEART FOR SALE

Words and Music by
OTIS BLACKWELL and WINFIELD SCOTT

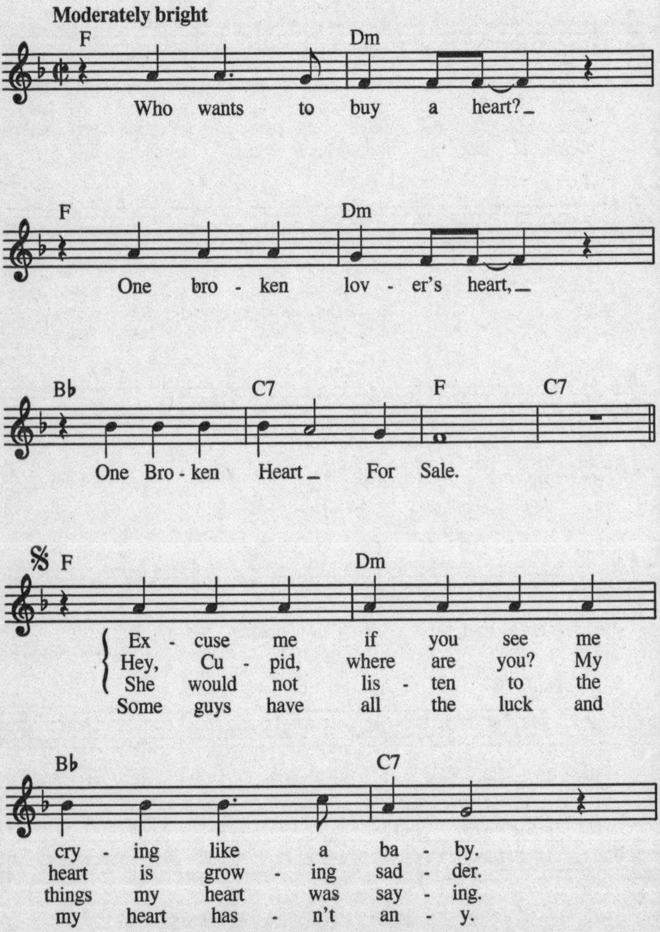
Moderately bright
F Dm
Who wants to buy a heart?
F Dm
One bro - ken lov - er's heart,
B♭ C7 F C7
One Bro - ken Heart For Sale.
F Dm
Ex - cuse me if you see me
Hey, Cu - pid, where are you? My
She would not lis - ten to the
Some guys have all the luck and
B♭ C7
cry - ing like a ba - by.
heart is grow - ing sad - der.
things my heart was say - ing.
my heart has - n't an - y.

Copyright © 1963 by Elvis Presley Music, Inc.
Copyright Renewed and Assigned to Elvis Presley Music (Administered by R&H Music)
International Copyright Secured All Rights Reserved

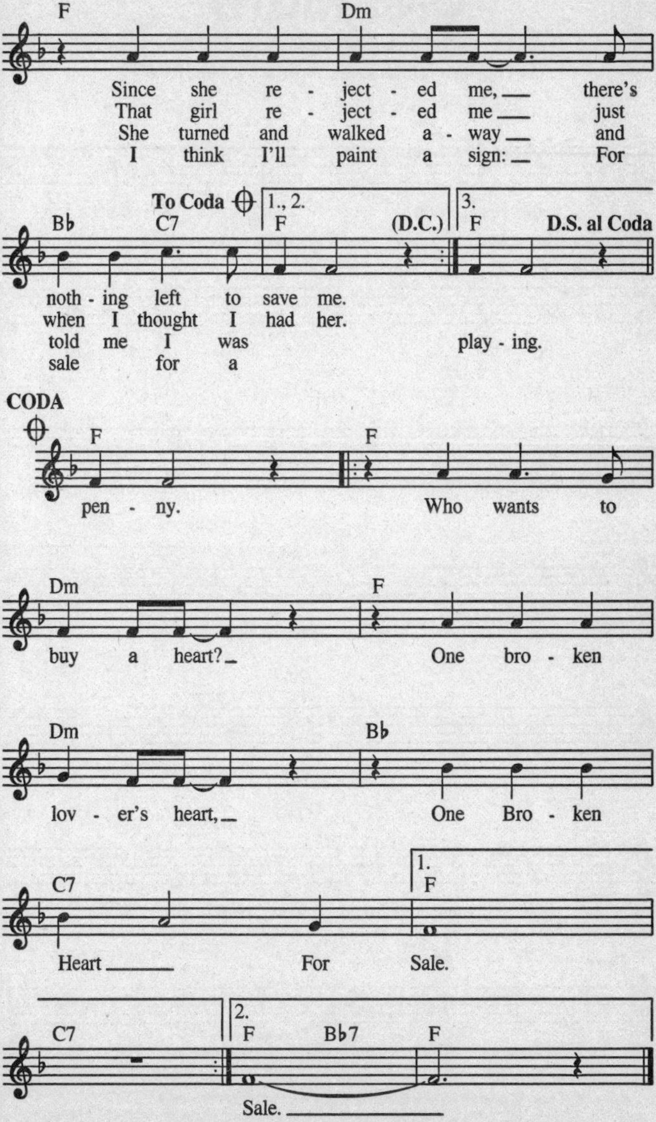
F Dm
Since she re - ject - ed me, there's
That girl re - ject - ed me just
She turned and walked a - way and
I think I'll paint a sign: For
To Coda
1., 2.
3.
B♭ C7 F (D.C.) F D.S. al Coda
noth - ing left to save me.
when I thought I had her.
told me I was play - ing.
sale for a
CODA
F F
pen - ny. Who wants to
Dm F
buy a heart? One bro - ken
Dm B♭
lov - er's heart, One Bro - ken
C7 1. F
Heart For Sale.
C7 2. F B♭7 F
Sale.

ONE NIGHT

Words and Music by
DAVE BARTHOLOMEW and PEARL KING

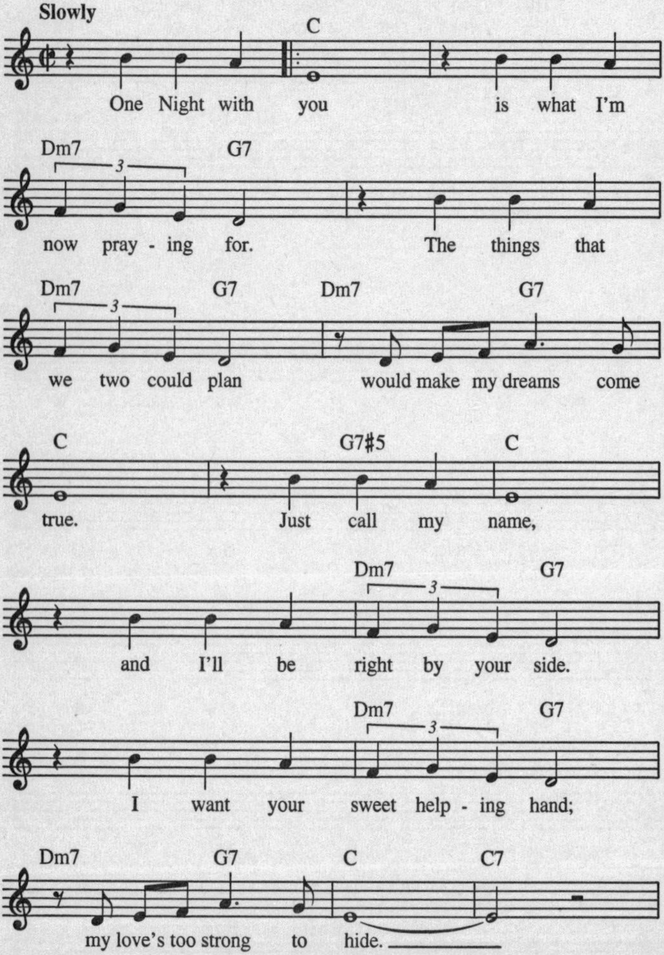
Slowly
C
One Night with you is what I'm
Dm7 G7
now pray - ing for. The things that
Dm7 G7 Dm7 G7
we two could plan would make my dreams come
C G7#5 C
true. Just call my name,
Dm7 G7
and I'll be right by your side.
Dm7 G7
I want your sweet help - ing hand;
Dm7 G7 C C7
my love's too strong to hide.

Copyright © 1957 Travis Music, Inc.
Copyright Renewed and Assigned to Unart Music Corporation
All Rights for the U.S.A. and Canada Assigned to Elvis Presley Music (Administered by R&H Music)
International Copyright Secured All Rights Reserved

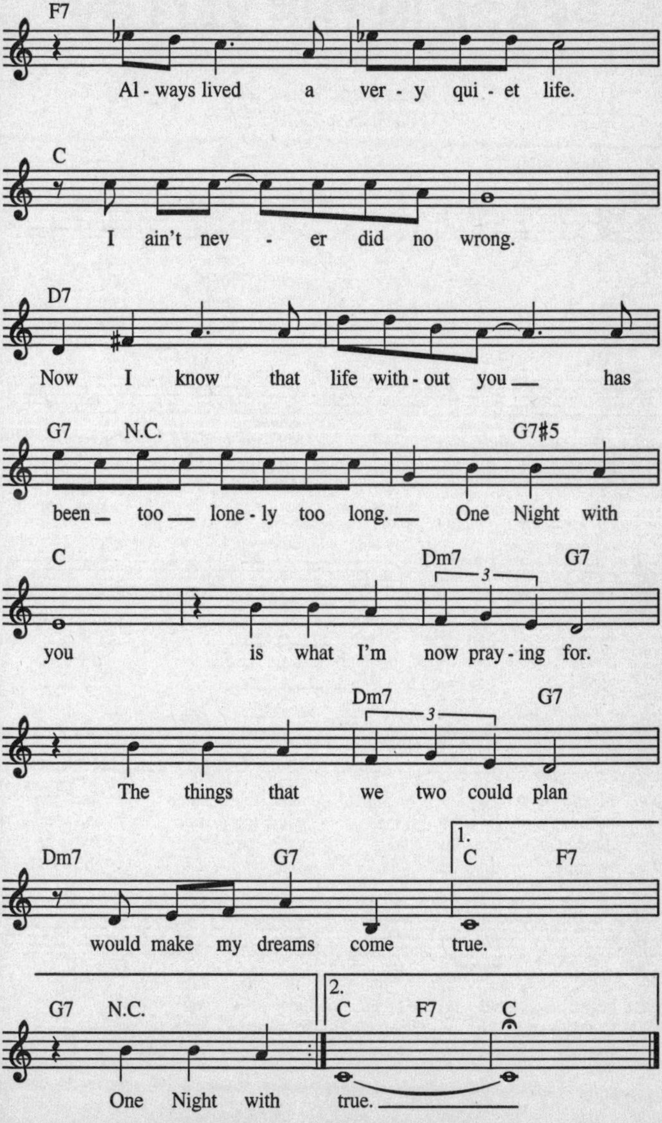
F7
Al - ways lived a ver - y qui - et life.
C
I ain't nev - er did no wrong.
D7
Now I know that life with - out you has
G7 N.C. G7#5
been too lone - ly too long. One Night with
C Dm7 G7
you is what I'm now pray - ing for.
Dm7 G7
The things that we two could plan
Dm7 G7
would make my dreams come
1.
C F7
true.
G7 N.C.
One Night with
2.
C F7 C
true.
3

(There'll Be)
PEACE IN THE VALLEY
(For Me)

Words and Music by
THOMAS A. DORSEY

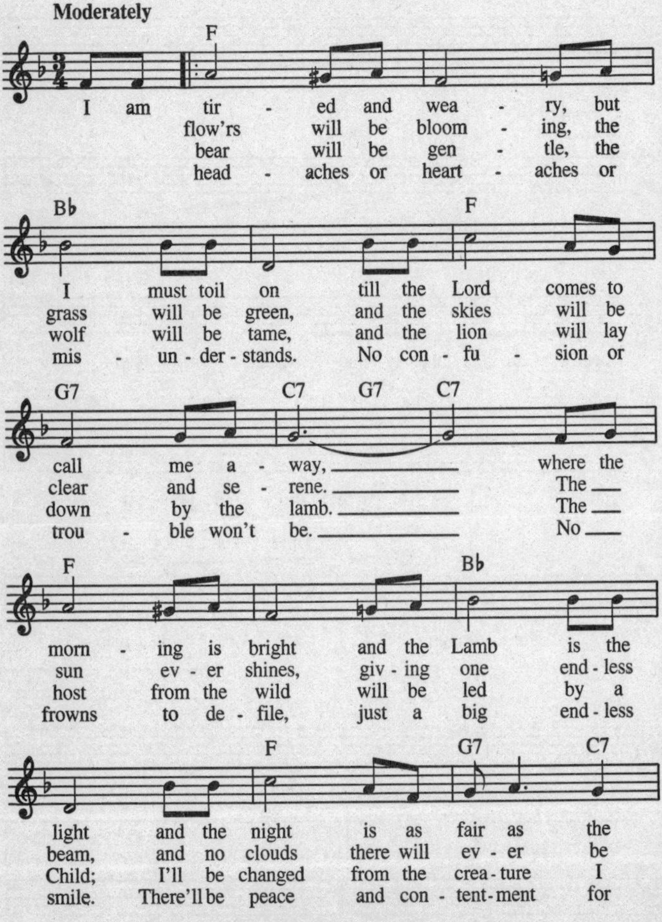
Moderately
F
I am tir - ed and wea - ry, but
flow'rs will be bloom - ing, the
bear will be gen - tle, the
head - aches or heart - aches or
Bb F
I must toil on till the Lord comes to
grass will be green, and the skies will be
wolf will be tame, and the lion will lay
mis - un - der - stands. No con - fu - sion or
G7 C7 G7 C7
call me a - way, where the
clear and se - rene. The
down by the lamb. The
trou - ble won't be. No
F Bb
morn - ing is bright and the Lamb is the
sun ev - er shines, giv - ing one end - less
host from the wild will be led by a
frowns to de - file, just a big end - less
F G7 C7
light and the night is as fair as the
beam, and no clouds there will ev - er be
Child; I'll be changed from the crea - ture I
smile. There'll be peace and con - tent - ment for

Copyright © 1939 by Thomas A. Dorsey
Copyright Renewed, Assigned to Unichappell Music Inc.
International Copyright Secured All Rights Reserved

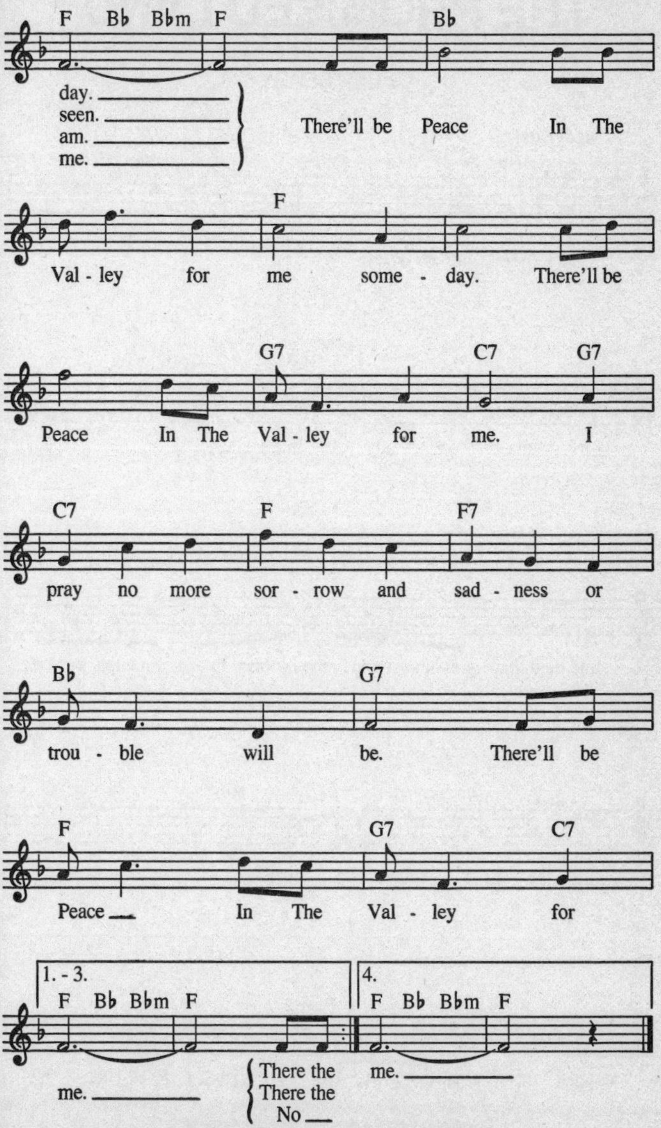
F Bb Bbm F Bb
day.
seen.
am.
me.
There'll be Peace In The
F
Val - ley for me some - day. There'll be
G7 C7 G7
Peace In The Val - ley for me. I
C7 F F7
pray no more sor - row and sad - ness or
Bb G7
trou - ble will be. There'll be
F G7 C7
Peace In The Val - ley for
1. - 3.
F Bb Bbm F
me.
There the
There the
No
4.
F Bb Bbm F
me.

THE PROMISED LAND

Words and Music by
CHUCK BERRY

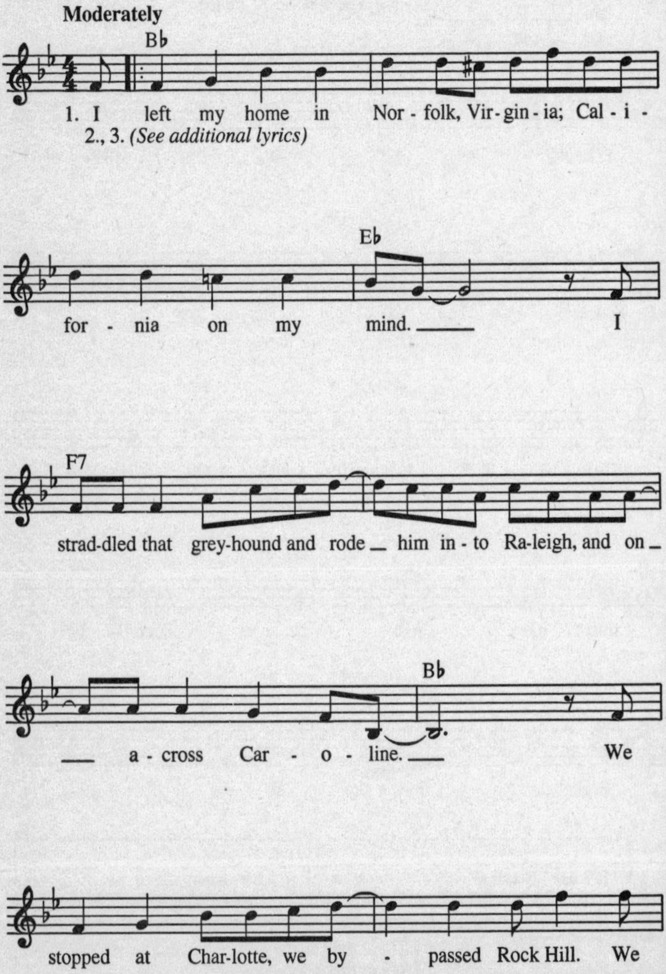
Moderately
B♭
1. I left my home in Nor - folk, Vir - gin - ia; Cal - i -
2., 3. (See additional lyrics)
E♭
for - nia on my mind. ___ I
F7
strad-dled that grey-hound and rode _ him in - to Ra-leigh, and on _
B♭
___ a - cross Car - o - line. ___ We
stopped at Char-lotte, we by - passed Rock Hill. We

Copyright © 1964 (Renewed) by Arc Music Corporation
International Copyright Secured All Rights Reserved

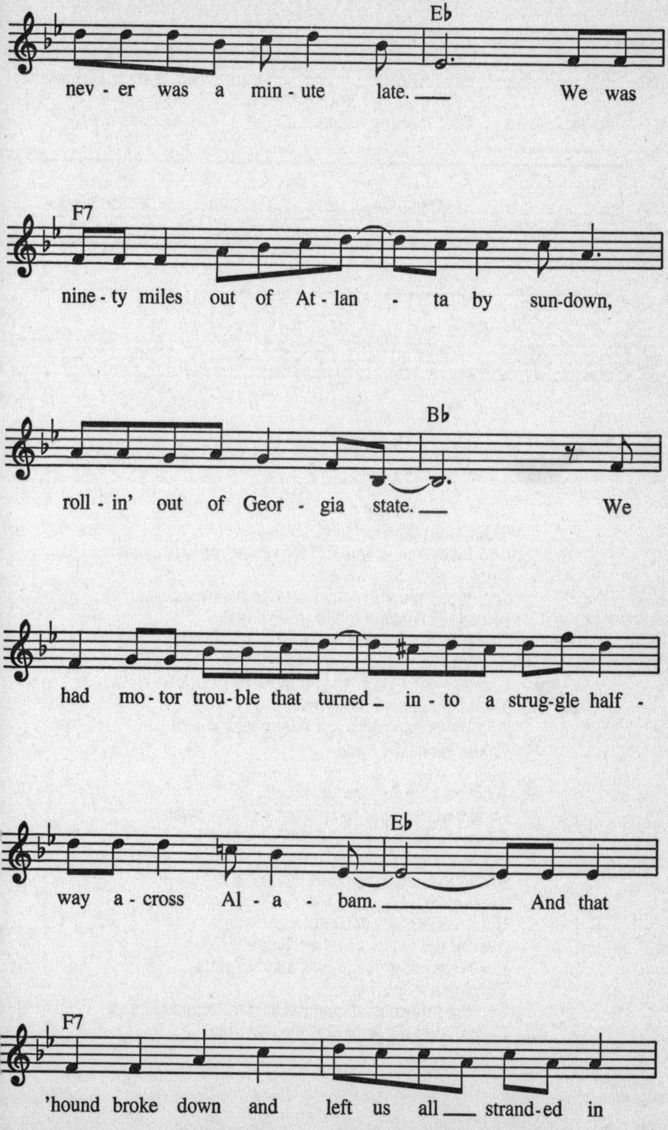
Eb
nev - er was a min - ute late. We was
F7
nine - ty miles out of At - lan - ta by sun-down,
Bb
roll - in' out of Geor - gia state. We
had mo - tor trou - ble that turned in - to a strug-gle half -
Eb
way a - cross Al - a - bam. And that
F7
'hound broke down and left us all strand-ed in

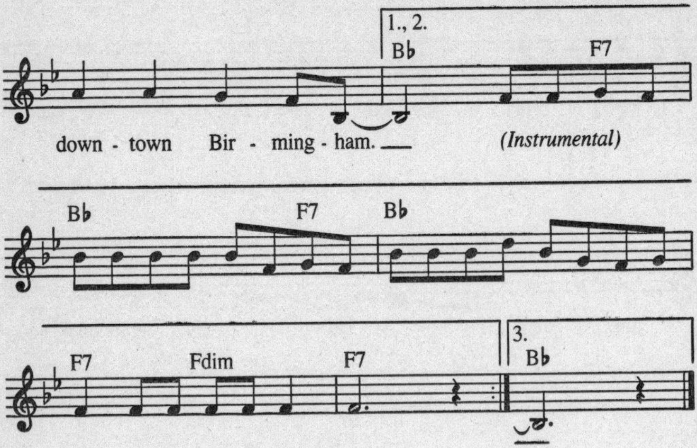
1., 2.
B♭
F7
down - town Bir - ming - ham.
(Instrumental)
B♭
F7
B♭
F7
Fdim
F7
3.
B♭

Additional Lyrics

2. Right away I bought me a through train ticket,
Ridin' across Mississippi clean.
And I was on the Midnight Flyer out of Birmingham,
Smokin' into New Orleans.
Somebody helped me get out of Louisiana,
Just to help me get to Houston Town.
There are people there who care a little about me,
And they won't let a poor boy down.
Sure as you're born, they bought me a silk suit,
They put luggage in my hand.
And I woke up high over Albuquerque on a jet
To the Promised Land.

3. Workin' on a T-bone steak,
I had a party flyin' over to the Golden State,
When the pilot told us in thirteen minutes
He would get us at the Terminal Gate.
Swing low, chariot, come down easy,
Taxi to the Terminal Line.
Cut your engines and cool your wings,
And let me make it to the telephone.
Los Angeles, give me Norfolk, Virginia,
Tidewater 4-10-0-0.
Tell the folks back home this is the Promised Land
Callin', and the poor boy's on the line.

SEPARATE WAYS

Words and Music by
RED WEST and RICHARD MAINEGRA

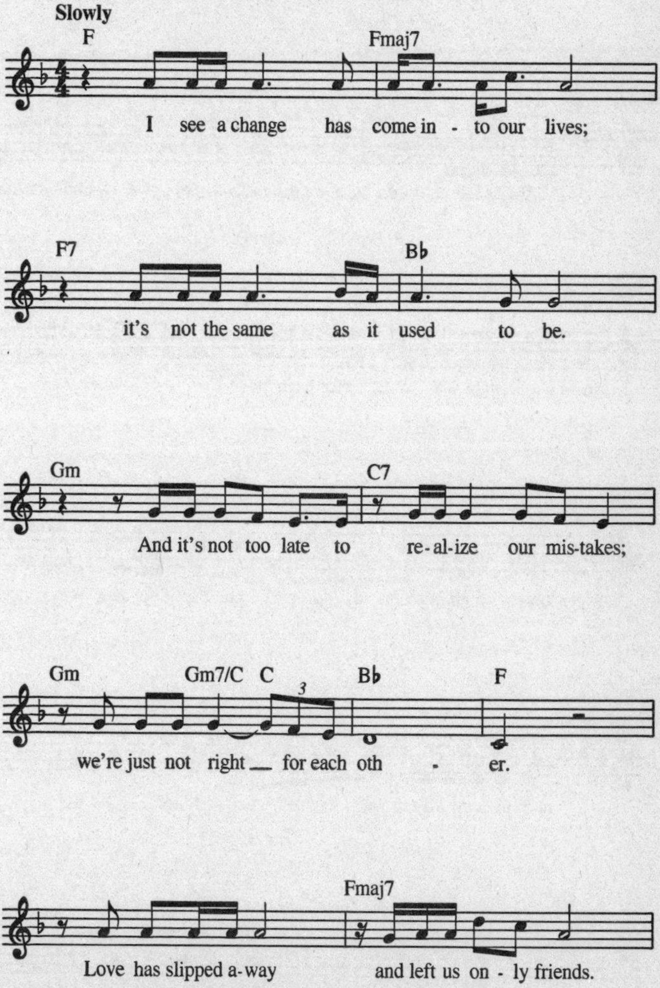
Slowly
F
Fmaj7
I see a change has come in - to our lives;
F7
B♭
it's not the same as it used to be.
Gm
C7
And it's not too late to re-al-ize our mis-takes;
Gm
Gm7/C C
3
B♭
F
we're just not right ___ for each oth - er.
Fmaj7
Love has slipped a-way and left us on - ly friends.

© 1970 SCREEN GEMS-EMI MUSIC INC.
All Rights Reserved International Copyright Secured Used by Permission

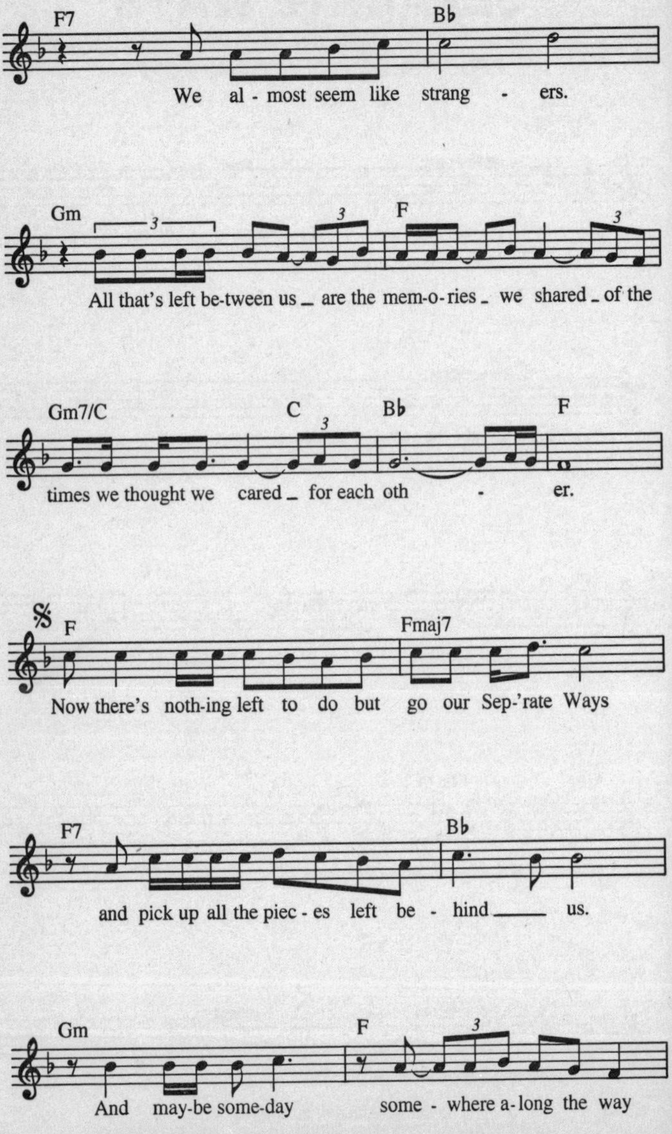
F7
Bb
We al - most seem like strang - ers.
Gm
F
All that's left be-tween us _ are the mem-o-ries _ we shared _ of the
Gm7/C
C
Bb
F
times we thought we cared _ for each oth - er.
F
Fmaj7
Now there's noth-ing left to do but go our Sep-'rate Ways
F7
Bb
and pick up all the piec - es left be - hind ___ us.
Gm
F
And may-be some-day some - where a-long the way

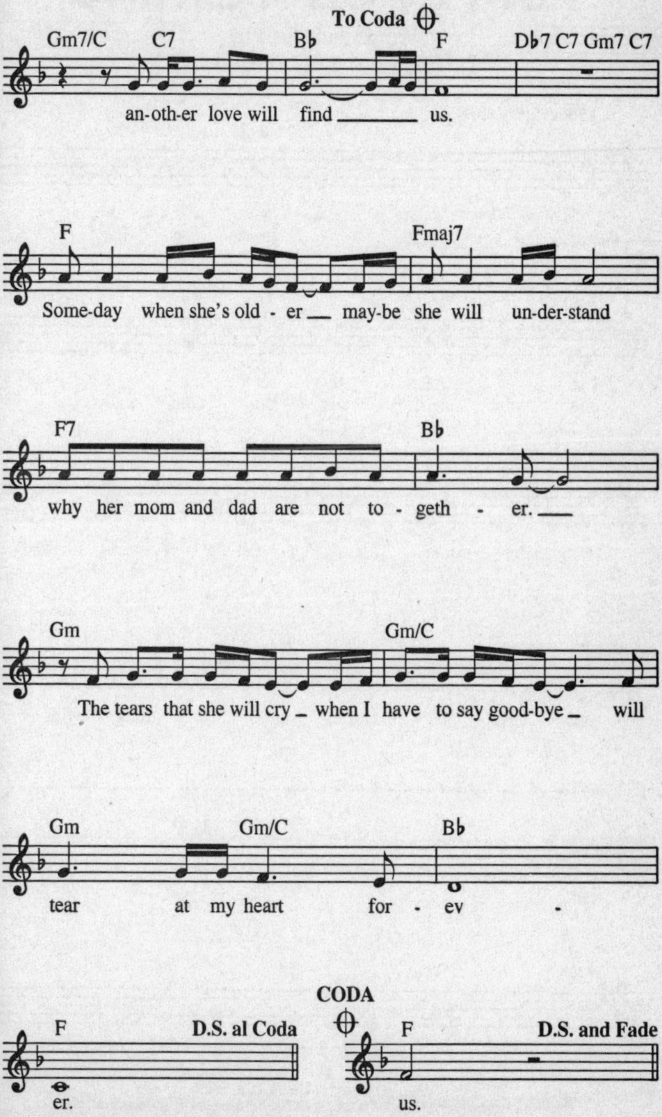
To Coda
Gm7/C C7 B♭ F D♭7 C7 Gm7 C7
an-oth-er love will find us.
F Fmaj7
Some-day when she's old - er may-be she will un-der-stand
F7 B♭
why her mom and dad are not to - geth - er.
Gm Gm/C
The tears that she will cry when I have to say good-bye will
Gm Gm/C B♭
tear at my heart for - ev -
CODA
F D.S. al Coda
er.
F D.S. and Fade
us.

PUPPET ON A STRING

Words and Music by
SID TEPPER and ROY C. BENNETT

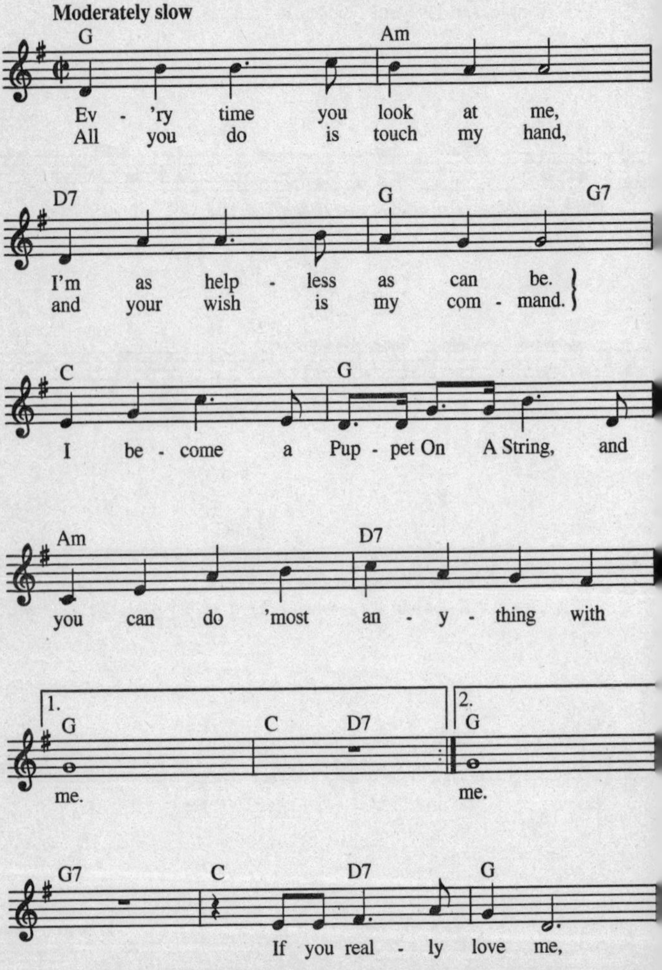
Moderately slow
G
Am
Ev - 'ry time you look at me,
All you do is touch my hand,
D7
G
G7
I'm as help - less as can be.
and your wish is my com - mand.
C
G
I be - come a Pup - pet On A String, and
Am
D7
you can do 'most an - y - thing with
1.
G
C
D7
me.
2.
G
me.
G7
C
D7
G
If you real - ly love me,

Copyright © 1965 by Gladys Music, Inc.
Copyright Renewed and Assigned to Gladys Music (Administered by Williamson Music)
International Copyright Secured All Rights Reserved

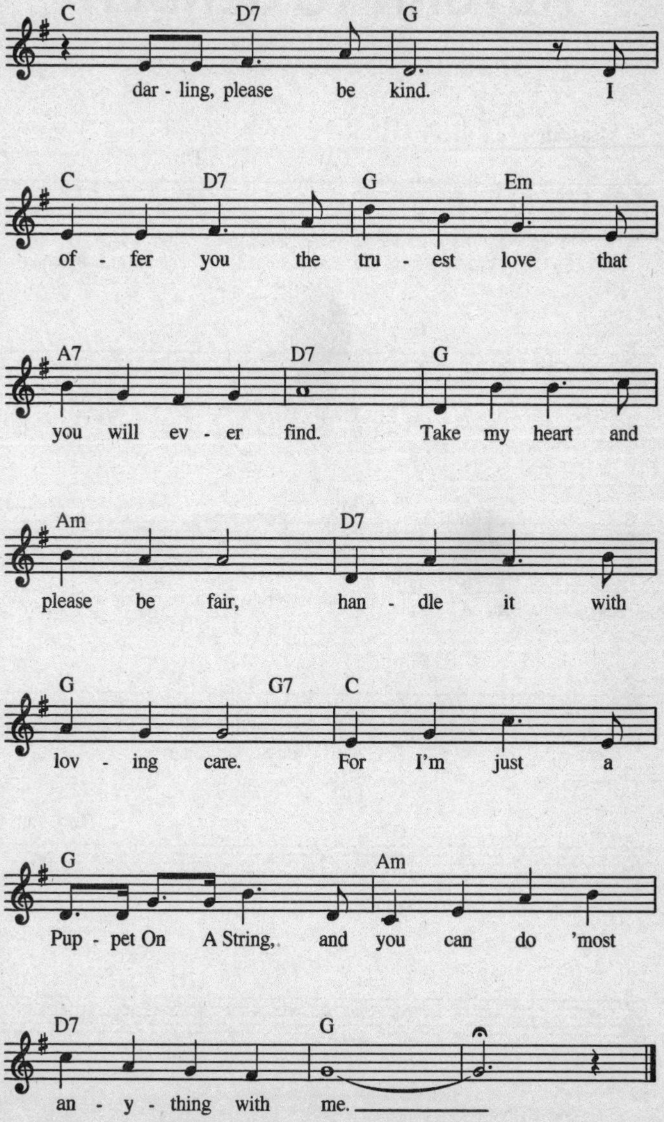
C D7 G
dar - ling, please be kind. I
C D7 G Em
of - fer you the tru - est love that
A7 D7 G
you will ev - er find. Take my heart and
Am D7
please be fair, han - dle it with
G G7 C
lov - ing care. For I'm just a
G Am
Pup - pet On A String, and you can do 'most
D7 G
an - y - thing with me.

RETURN TO SENDER

Words and Music by
OTIS BLACKWELL and WINFIELD SCOTT

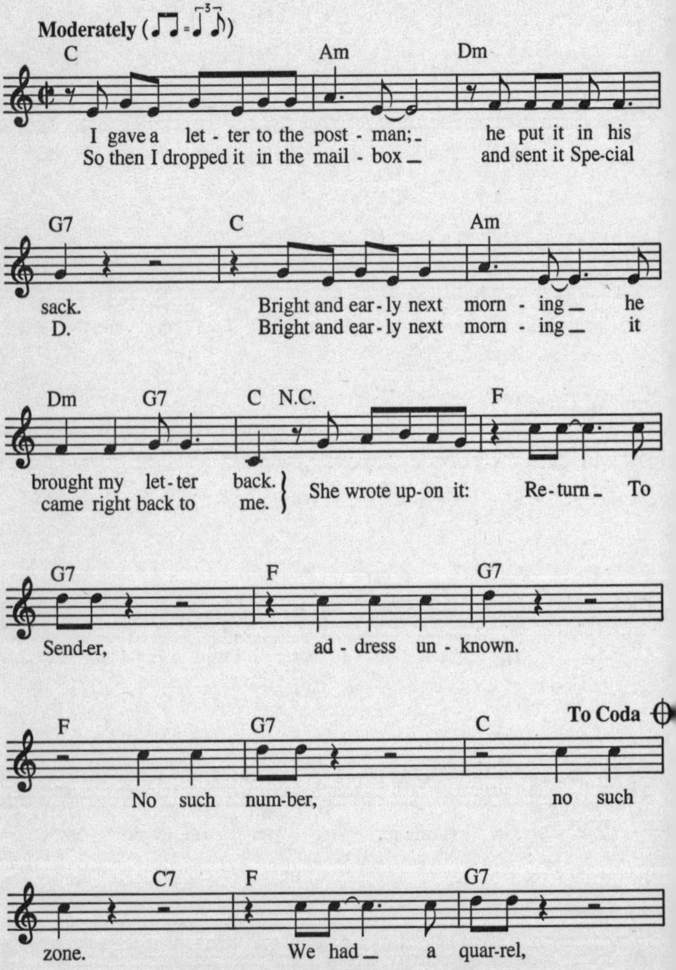
Moderately
C
Am
Dm
I gave a let - ter to the post - man;
he put it in his
So then I dropped it in the mail - box
and sent it Spe-cial
G7
C
Am
sack.
Bright and ear - ly next morn - ing
he
D.
Bright and ear - ly next morn - ing
it
Dm
G7
C N.C.
F
brought my let - ter back.
came right back to me.
She wrote up-on it:
Re - turn To
G7
F
G7
Send-er,
ad - dress un - known.
F
G7
C
To Coda
No such num-ber,
no such
C7
F
G7
zone.
We had a quar-rel,

Copyright © 1962 by Elvis Presley Music, Inc.
Copyright Renewed and Assigned to Elvis Presley Music (Administered by R&H Music)
International Copyright Secured All Rights Reserved

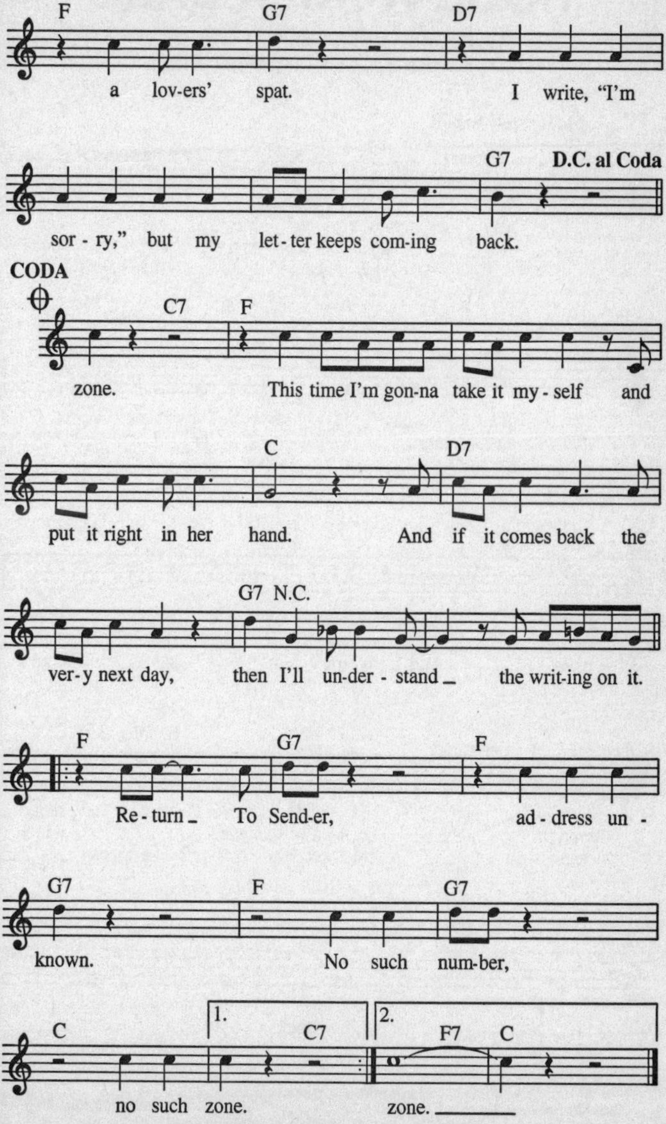
F G7 D7
a lov-ers' spat. I write, "I'm
G7 D.C. al Coda
sor - ry," but my let - ter keeps com-ing back.
CODA
C7 F
zone. This time I'm gon-na take it my - self and
C D7
put it right in her hand. And if it comes back the
G7 N.C.
ver - y next day, then I'll un-der - stand the writ-ing on it.
F G7 F
Re - turn To Send-er, ad - dress un -
G7 F G7
known. No such num-ber,
C 1. C7 2. F7 C
no such zone. zone.

ROCK-A-HULA BABY

Words and Music by BEN WEISMAN,
DOLORES FULLER and FRED WISE

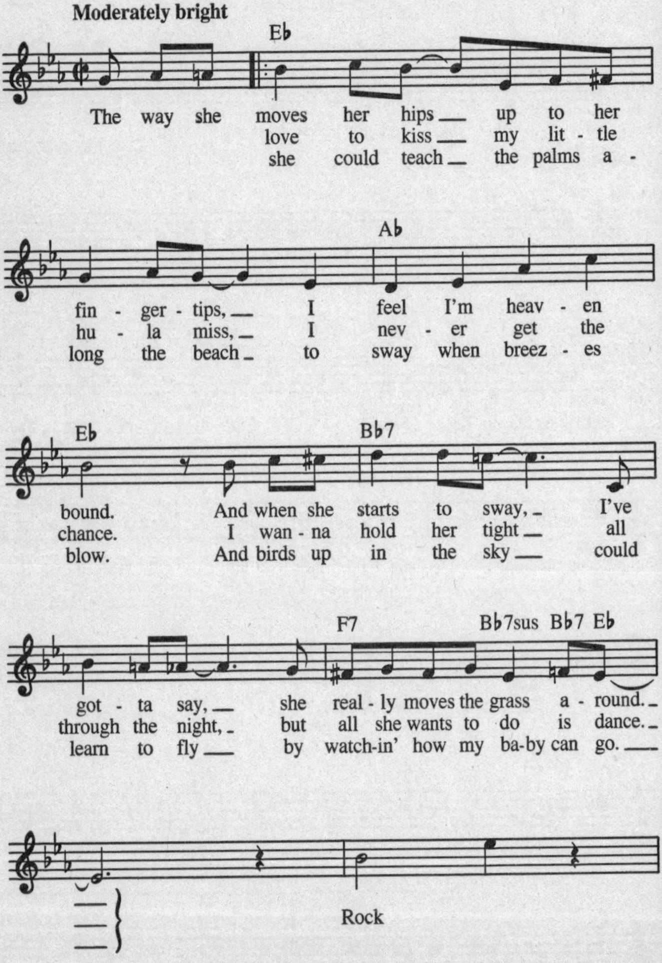
Moderately bright
Eb
The way she moves her hips up to her
love to kiss my lit - tle
she could teach the palms a -
Ab
fin - ger - tips, I feel I'm heav - en
hu - la miss, I nev - er get the
long the beach to sway when breez - es
Eb
Bb7
bound. And when she starts to sway, I've
chance. I wan - na hold her tight all
blow. And birds up in the sky could
F7
Bb7sus Bb7 Eb
got - ta say, she real - ly moves the grass a - round.
through the night, but all she wants to do is dance.
learn to fly by watch-in' how my ba-by can go.
Rock

Copyright © 1961 Gladys Music, Inc.
Copyright Renewed, Assigned to Chappell & Co., Bienstock Publishing Company and Erika Publishing
International Copyright Secured All Rights Reserved

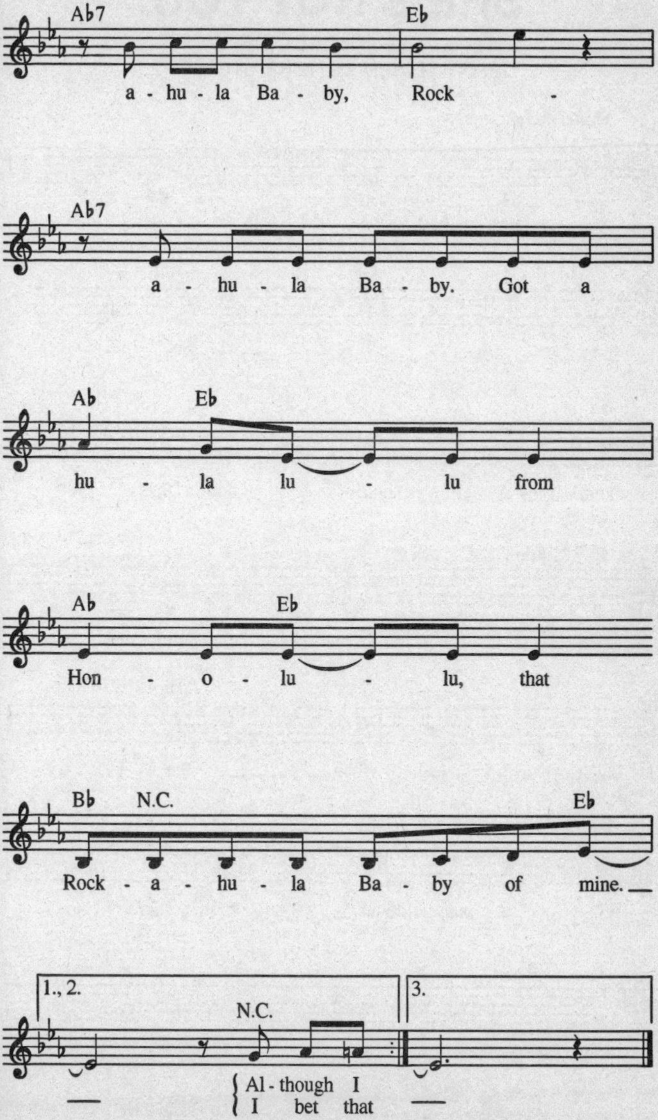
Ab7
Eb
a - hu - la Ba - by, Rock -
Ab7
a - hu - la Ba - by. Got a
Ab
Eb
hu - la lu - lu from
Ab
Eb
Hon - o - lu - lu, that
Bb
N.C.
Eb
Rock - a - hu - la Ba - by of mine.
1., 2.
N.C.
Al - though I
I bet that
3.

SHE'S NOT YOU

Words and Music by DOC POMUS,
JERRY LEIBER and MIKE STOLLER

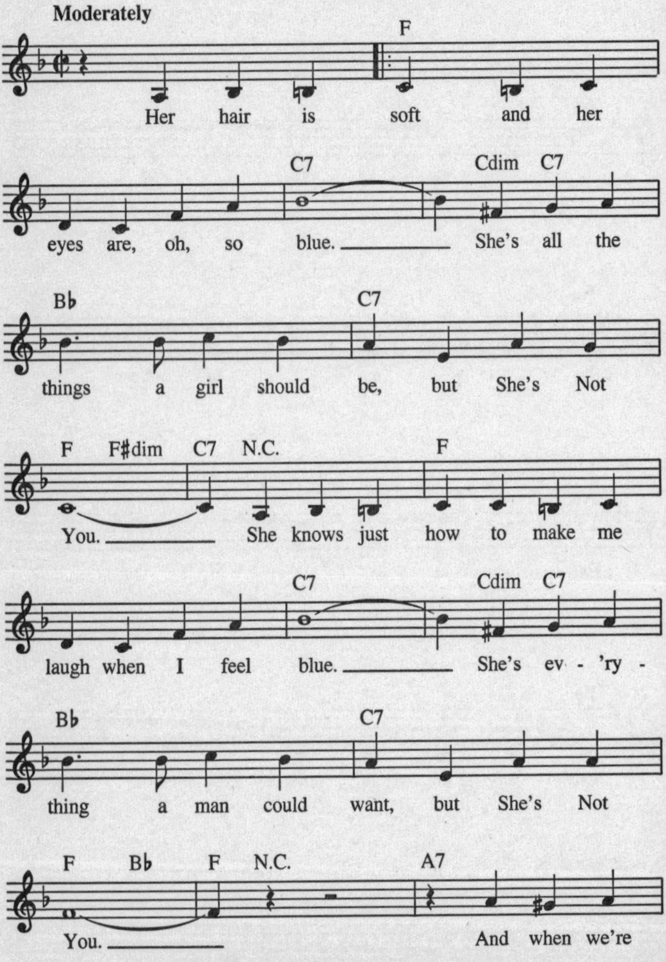
Moderately
F
Her hair is soft and her
C7 Cdim C7
eyes are, oh, so blue. She's all the
Bb C7
things a girl should be, but She's Not
F F#dim C7 N.C. F
You. She knows just how to make me
C7 Cdim C7
laugh when I feel blue. She's ev - 'ry -
Bb C7
thing a man could want, but She's Not
F Bb F N.C. A7
You. And when we're

Copyright © 1962 by Elvis Presley Music, Inc.
Copyright Renewed and Assigned to Elvis Presley Music
(Administered by R&H Music), Jerry Leiber Music and Mike Stoller Music
International Copyright Secured All Rights Reserved

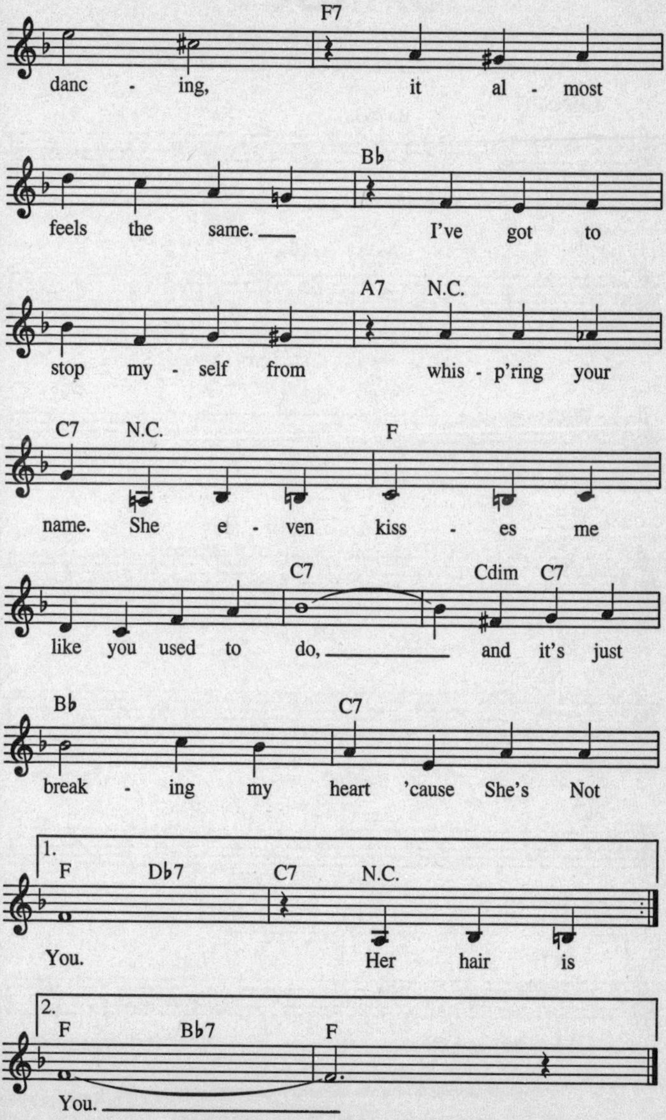
F7
danc - ing, it al - most
B♭
feels the same. I've got to
A7 N.C.
stop my - self from whis - p'ring your
C7 N.C. F
name. She e - ven kiss - es me
C7 Cdim C7
like you used to do, and it's just
B♭ C7
break - ing my heart 'cause She's Not
1.
F D♭7 C7 N.C.
You. Her hair is
2.
F B♭7 F
You.

SPINOUT

Words and Music by SID WAYNE,
BEN WEISMAN and DARRELL FULLER

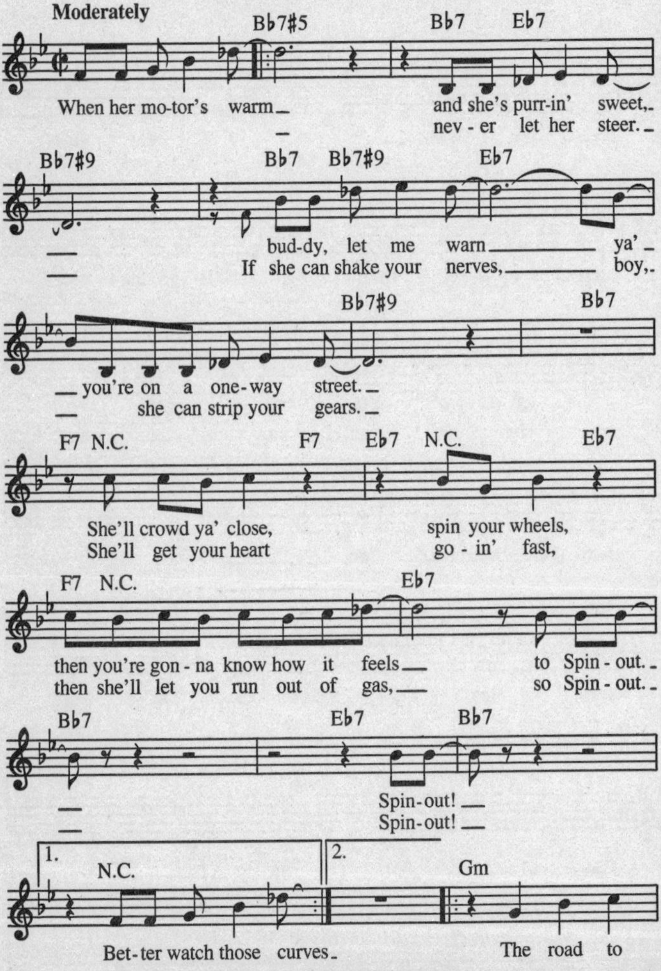
Moderately
Bb7#5
Bb7
Eb7
When her mo-tor's warm _ and she's purr-in' sweet, _
_ nev - er let her steer. _
Bb7#9
Bb7
Bb7#9
Eb7
_ bud-dy, let me warn _ ya' _
_ If she can shake your nerves, _ boy, _
Bb7#9
Bb7
_ you're on a one-way street. _
_ she can strip your gears. _
F7 N.C.
F7
Eb7 N.C.
Eb7
She'll crowd ya' close, spin your wheels,
She'll get your heart go - in' fast,
F7 N.C.
Eb7
then you're gon - na know how it feels _ to Spin - out. _
then she'll let you run out of gas, _ so Spin - out. _
Bb7
Eb7
Bb7
_ Spin-out! _
_ Spin-out! _
1.
N.C.
2.
Gm
Bet-ter watch those curves _ The road to

Copyright © 1966 by Gladys Music, Inc.
Copyright Assigned to Gladys Music (Administered by Williamson Music)
Copyright Renewed
International Copyright Secured All Rights Reserved

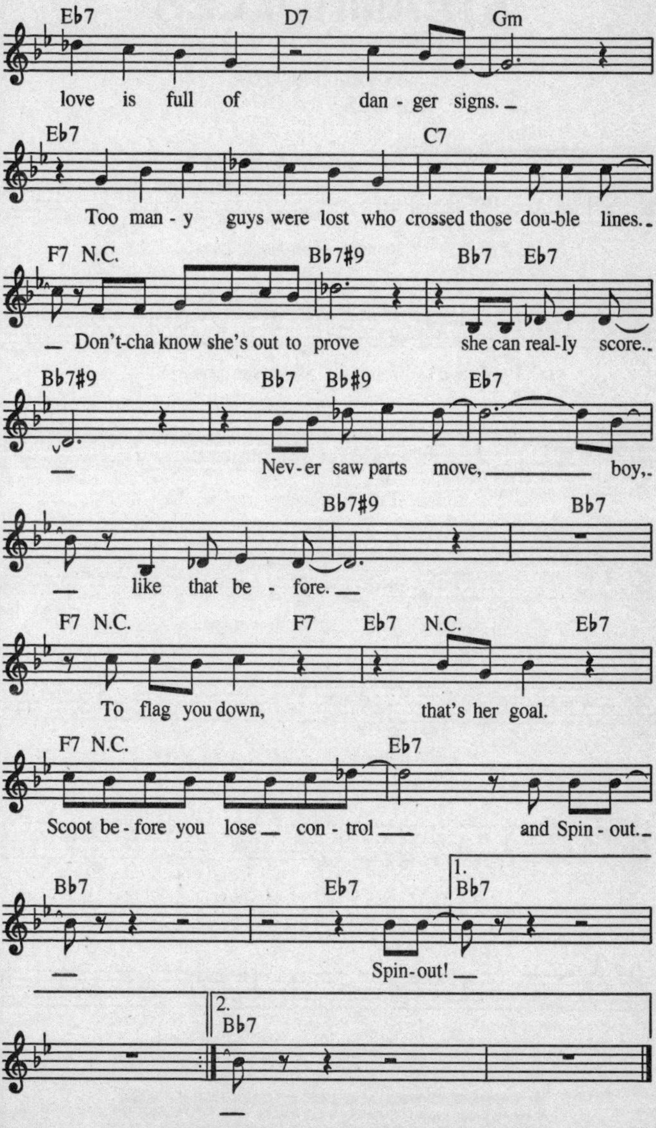
Eb7 D7 Gm
love is full of dan - ger signs.
Eb7 C7
Too man - y guys were lost who crossed those dou-ble lines.
F7 N.C. Bb7#9 Bb7 Eb7
Don't-cha know she's out to prove she can real-ly score.
Bb7#9 Bb7 Bb#9 Eb7
Nev-er saw parts move, boy,
Bb7#9 Bb7
like that be - fore.
F7 N.C. F7 Eb7 N.C. Eb7
To flag you down, that's her goal.
F7 N.C. Eb7
Scoot be - fore you lose con - trol and Spin - out.
Bb7 Eb7 1. Bb7
Spin-out!
2. Bb7

STEAMROLLER
(Steamroller Blues)

Words and Music by
JAMES TAYLOR

Moderate Blues (in 4)

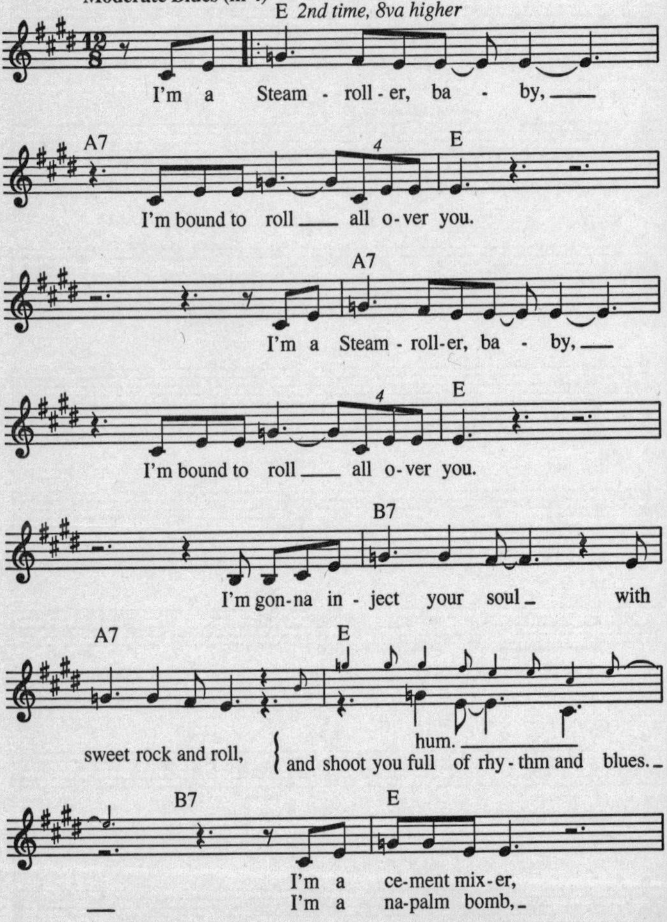
E 2nd time, 8va higher
I'm a Steam - roll - er, ba - by,
A7
4
E
I'm bound to roll all o - ver you.
A7
I'm a Steam - roll - er, ba - by,
4
E
I'm bound to roll all o - ver you.
B7
I'm gon - na in - ject your soul with
A7
E
sweet rock and roll,
hum.
and shoot you full of rhy - thm and blues.
B7
E
I'm a ce - ment mix - er,
I'm a na - palm bomb,

© 1970 EMI BLACKWOOD MUSIC INC. and COUNTRY ROAD MUSIC
All Rights Controlled and Administered by EMI BLACKWOOD MUSIC INC.
All Rights Reserved International Copyright Secured Used by Permission

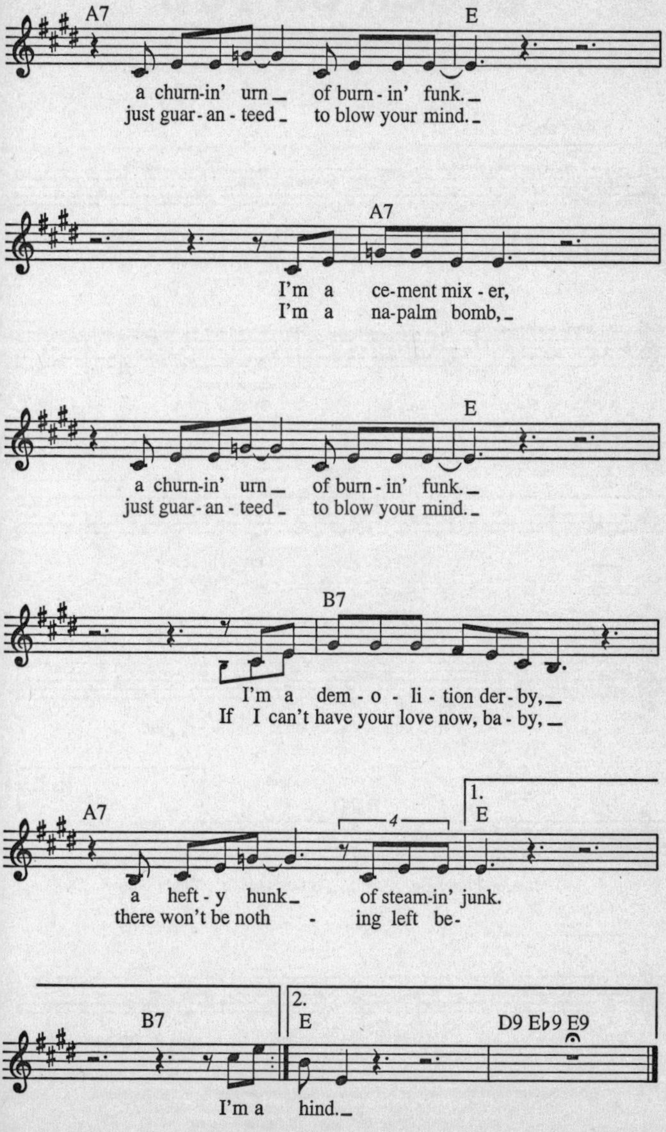
A7
E
a churn-in' urn _ of burn - in' funk. _
just guar - an - teed _ to blow your mind. _
A7
I'm a cement mix - er,
I'm a na-palm bomb, _
E
a churn-in' urn _ of burn - in' funk. _
just guar - an - teed _ to blow your mind. _
B7
I'm a dem - o - li - tion der - by, _
If I can't have your love now, ba - by, _
A7
4
1.
E
a heft - y hunk _ of steam-in' junk.
there won't be noth - ing left be-
B7
2.
E
D9 E♭9 E9
I'm a hind. _

STUCK ON YOU

Words and Music by
AARON SCHROEDER and J. LESLIE McFARLAND

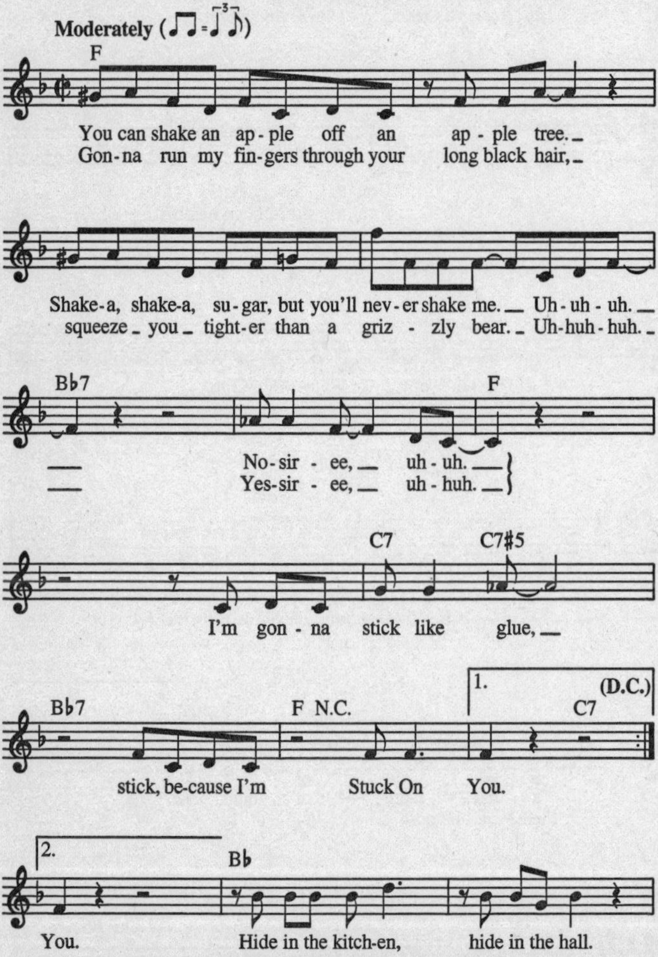
Moderately
F
You can shake an ap - ple off an ap - ple tree.
Gon - na run my fin - gers through your long black hair,
Shake-a, shake-a, su - gar, but you'll nev - er shake me. Uh - uh - uh.
squeeze you tight - er than a griz - zly bear. Uh-huh - huh.
Bb7
F
No - sir - ee, uh - uh.
Yes - sir - ee, uh - huh.
C7
C7#5
I'm gon - na stick like glue,
Bb7
F N.C.
1.
(D.C.)
C7
stick, be-cause I'm Stuck On You.
2.
Bb
You. Hide in the kitch-en, hide in the hall.

Copyright © 1960 by Gladys Music, Inc.
Copyright Renewed and Assigned to Gladys Music (Administered by Williamson Music)
and Rachel's Own Music (Administered by A. Schroeder International Ltd.)
International Copyright Secured All Rights Reserved

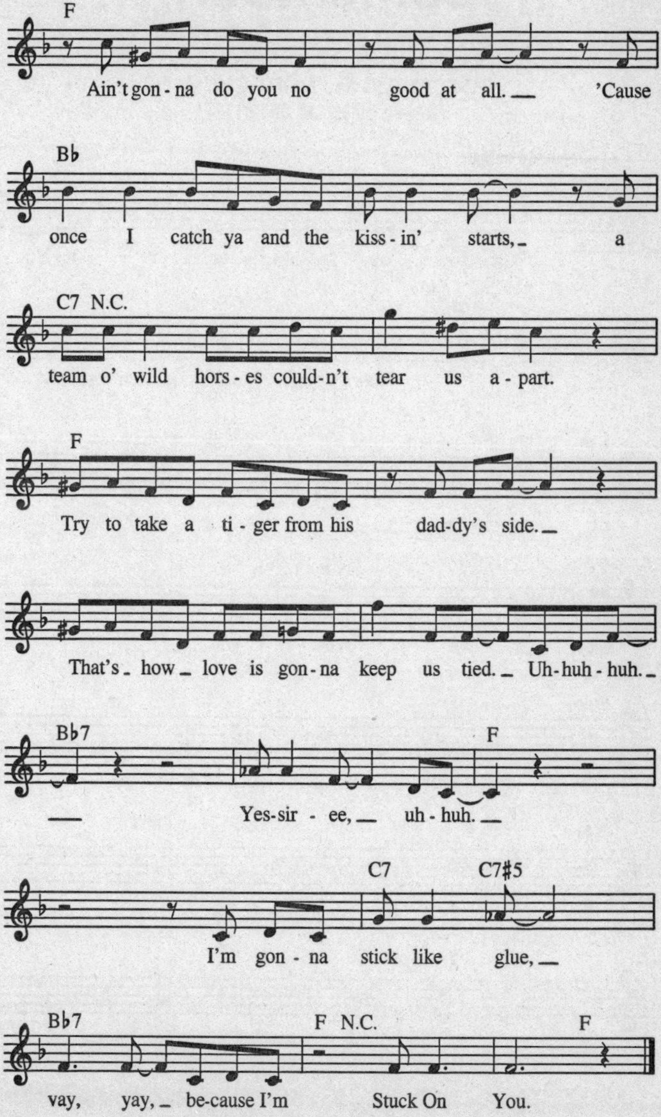
F
Ain't gon - na do you no good at all. 'Cause
B♭
once I catch ya and the kiss - in' starts, a
C7 N.C.
team o' wild hors - es could - n't tear us a - part.
F
Try to take a ti - ger from his dad - dy's side.
That's how love is gon - na keep us tied. Uh - huh - huh.
B♭7
F
Yes - sir - ee, uh - huh.
C7
C7♯5
I'm gon - na stick like glue,
B♭7
F N.C.
F
yay, yay, be - cause I'm Stuck On You.

SURRENDER

Original Italian Lyrics by G.B. De CURTIS
English Words and Adaptation by
DOC POMUS and MORT SHUMAN
Music by E. De CURTIS

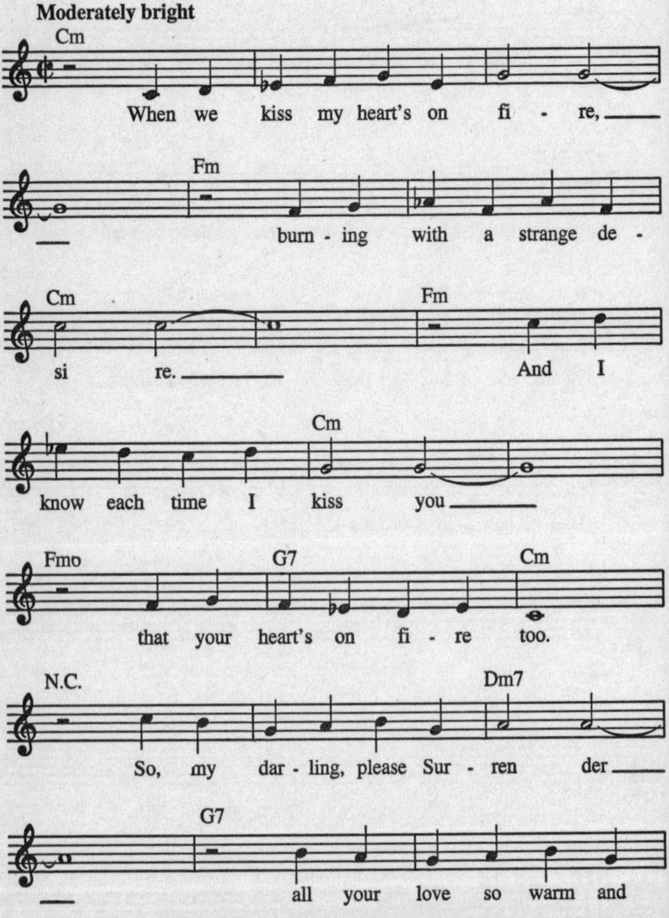
Moderately bright
Cm
When we kiss my heart's on fi - re,
Fm
burn - ing with a strange de -
Cm
si re.
Fm
And I
know each time I kiss
Cm
you
Fmo
that your
G7
heart's on fi - re
Cm
too.
N.C.
So, my dar - ling, please Sur - ren
Dm7
der
G7
all your love so warm and

Copyright (for the U.S.A.) © 1960 by Elvis Presley Music, Inc.
Copyright (for the U.S.A.) Renewed and Assigned to Elvis Presley Music (Administered by R&H Music);
rights for all countries in the world (except U.S.A.) owned by Edizioni Bideri S.p.A, Naples
International Copyright Secured All Rights Reserved

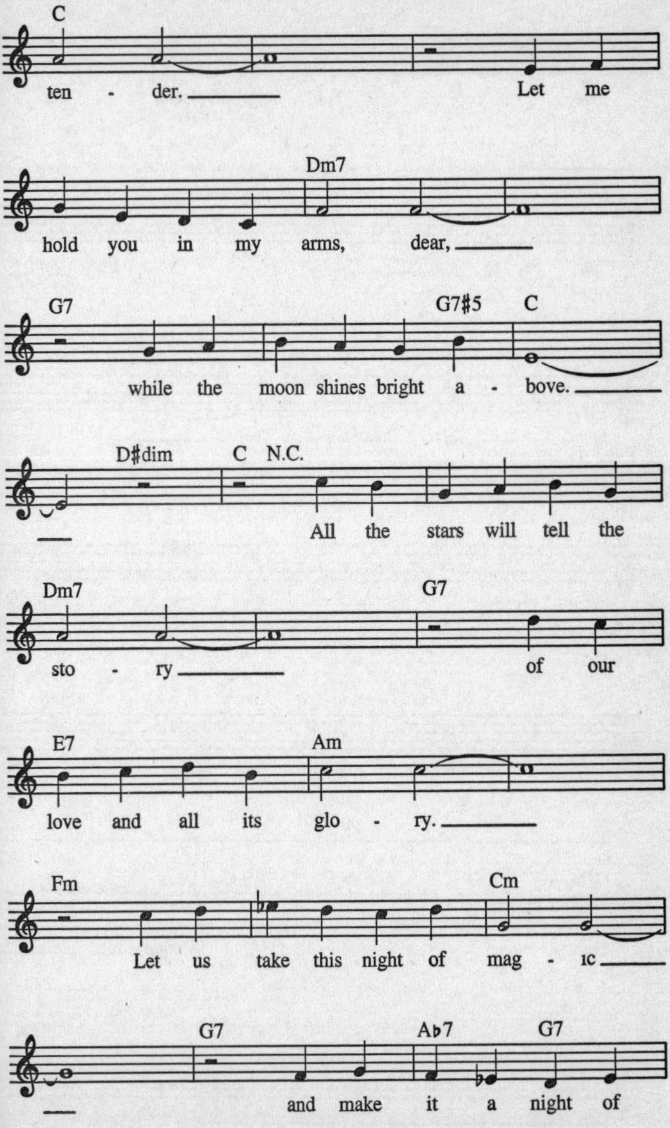
C
ten - der. Let me
Dm7
hold you in my arms, dear,
G7 G7♯5 C
while the moon shines bright a - bove.
D♯dim C N.C.
All the stars will tell the
Dm7 G7
sto - ry of our
E7 Am
love and all its glo - ry.
Fm Cm
Let us take this night of mag - ic
G7 A♭7 G7
and make it a night of

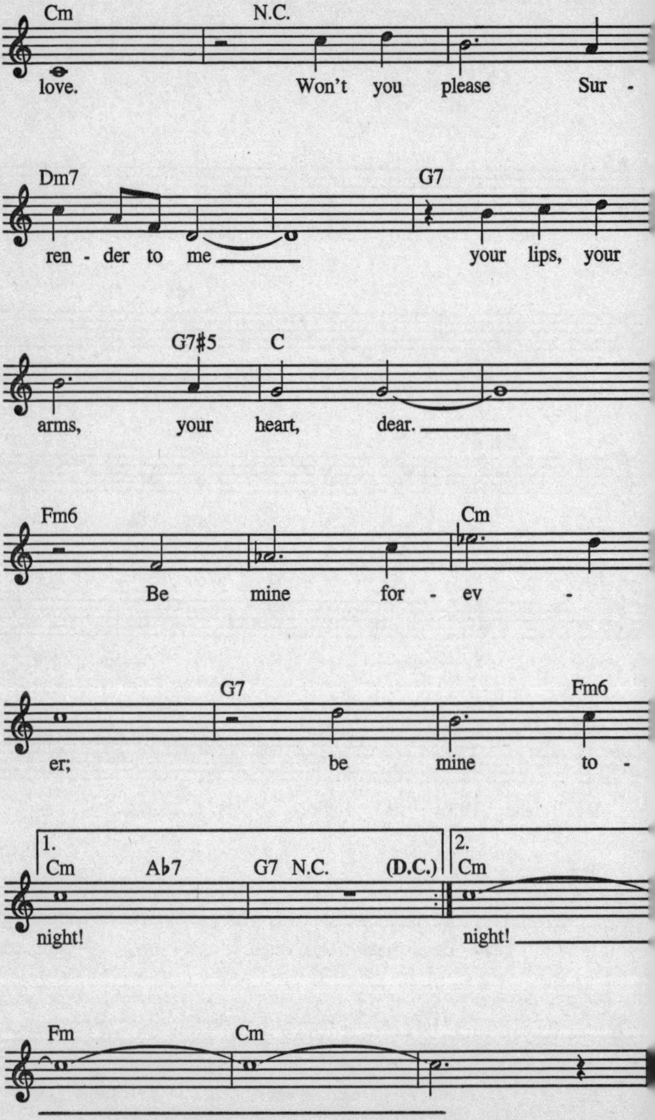
Cm N.C.
love. Won't you please Sur -
Dm7 G7
ren - der to me your lips, your
G7#5 C
arms, your heart, dear.
Fm6 Cm
Be mine for - ev -
G7 Fm6
er; be mine to -
1. Cm Ab7 G7 N.C. (D.C.) 2. Cm
night! night!
Fm Cm

TREAT ME NICE

Words and Music by
JERRY LEIBER and MIKE STOLLER

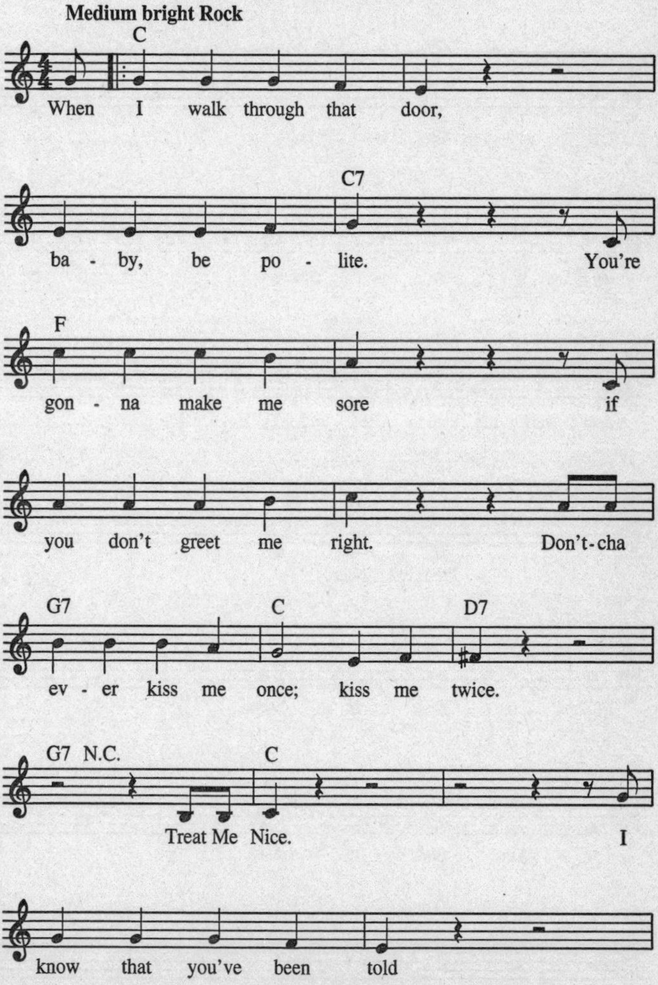
Medium bright Rock
C
When I walk through that door,
C7
ba - by, be po - lite. You're
F
gon - na make me sore if
you don't greet me right. Don't-cha
G7 C D7
ev - er kiss me once; kiss me twice.
G7 N.C. C
Treat Me Nice. I
know that you've been told

© 1957 (Renewed) JERRY LEIBER MUSIC and MIKE STOLLER MUSIC
All Rights Reserved

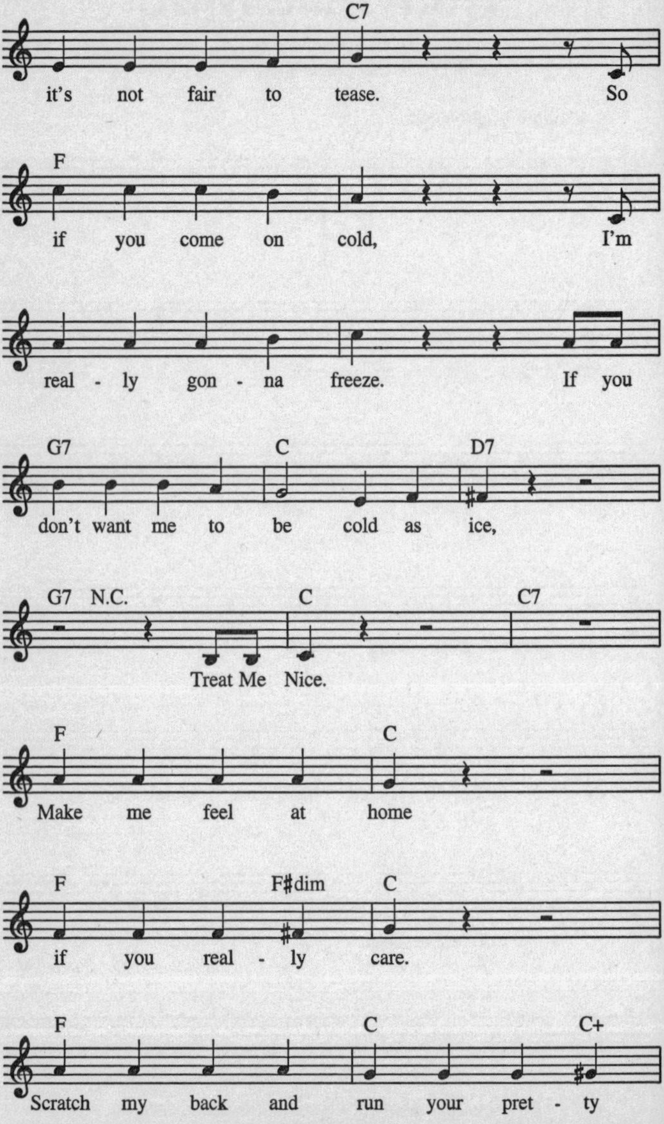
C7
it's not fair to tease. So
F
if you come on cold, I'm
real - ly gon - na freeze. If you
G7 C D7
don't want me to be cold as ice,
G7 N.C. C C7
Treat Me Nice.
F C
Make me feel at home
F F♯dim C
if you real - ly care.
F C C+
Scratch my back and run your pret - ty

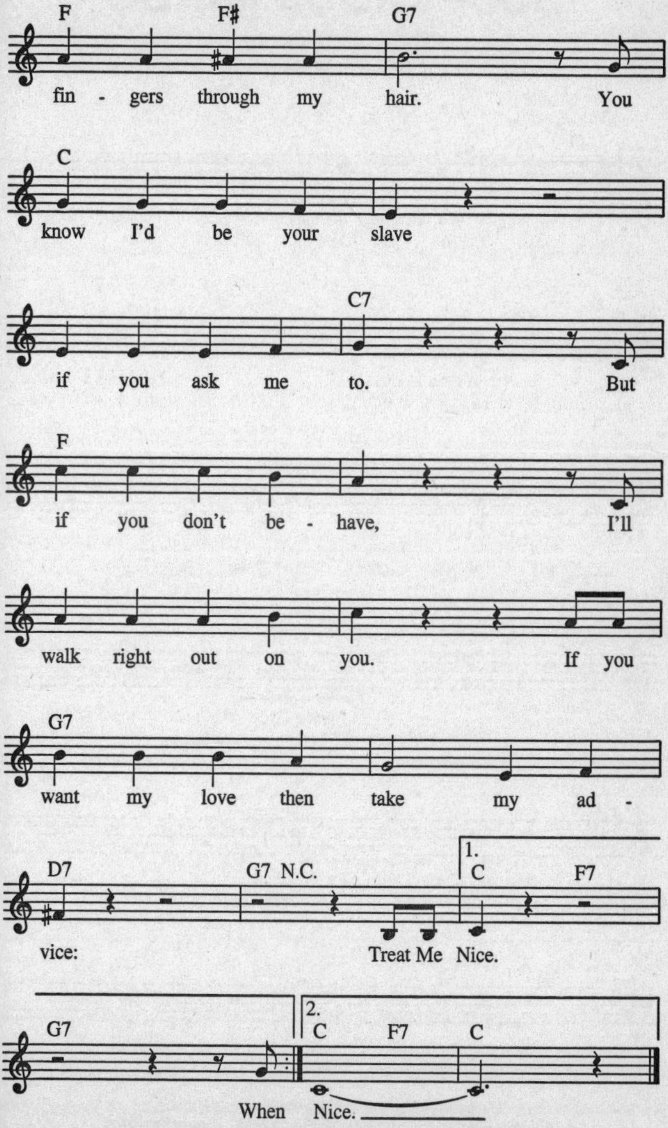
F F# G7
fin - gers through my hair. You
C
know I'd be your slave
C7
if you ask me to. But
F
if you don't be - have, I'll
walk right out on you. If you
G7
want my love then take my ad -
1.
D7 G7 N.C. C F7
vice: Treat Me Nice.
2.
G7 C F7 C
When Nice.

SUSPICIOUS MINDS

Words and Music by
MARK JAMES

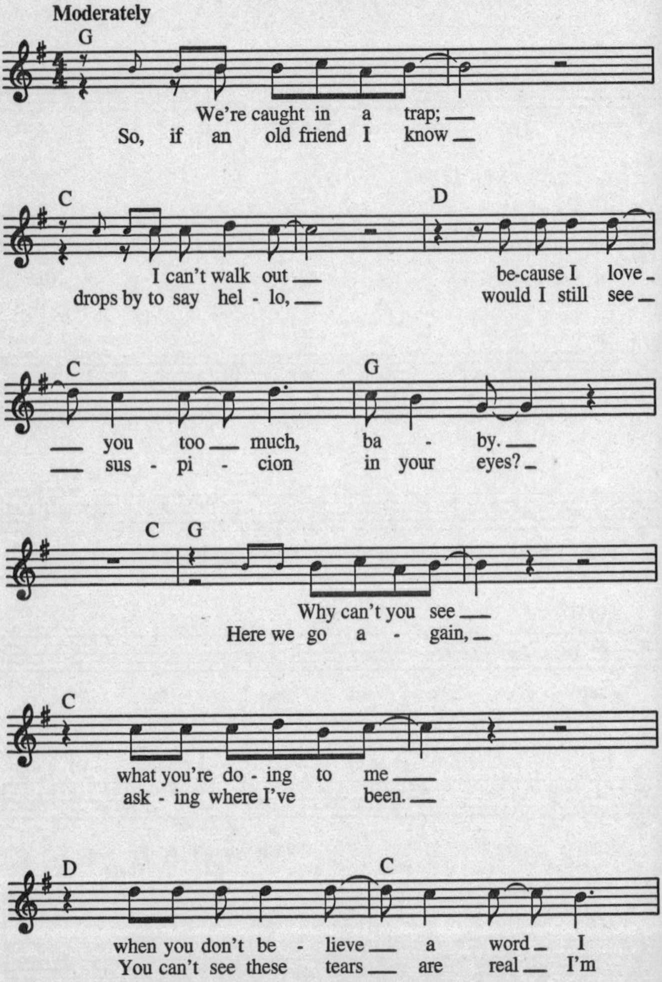
Moderately
G
We're caught in a trap;
So, if an old friend I know
C
I can't walk out
drops by to say hel - lo,
D
be-cause I love
would I still see
C
you too much,
sus - pi - cion
G
ba - by.
in your eyes?
C G
Why can't you see
Here we go a - gain,
C
what you're do - ing to me
ask - ing where I've been.
D
when you don't be - lieve
You can't see these tears
C
a word I
are real I'm

© 1968 (Renewed 1996) SCREEN GEMS-EMI MUSIC INC.
All Rights Reserved International Copyright Secured Used by Permission

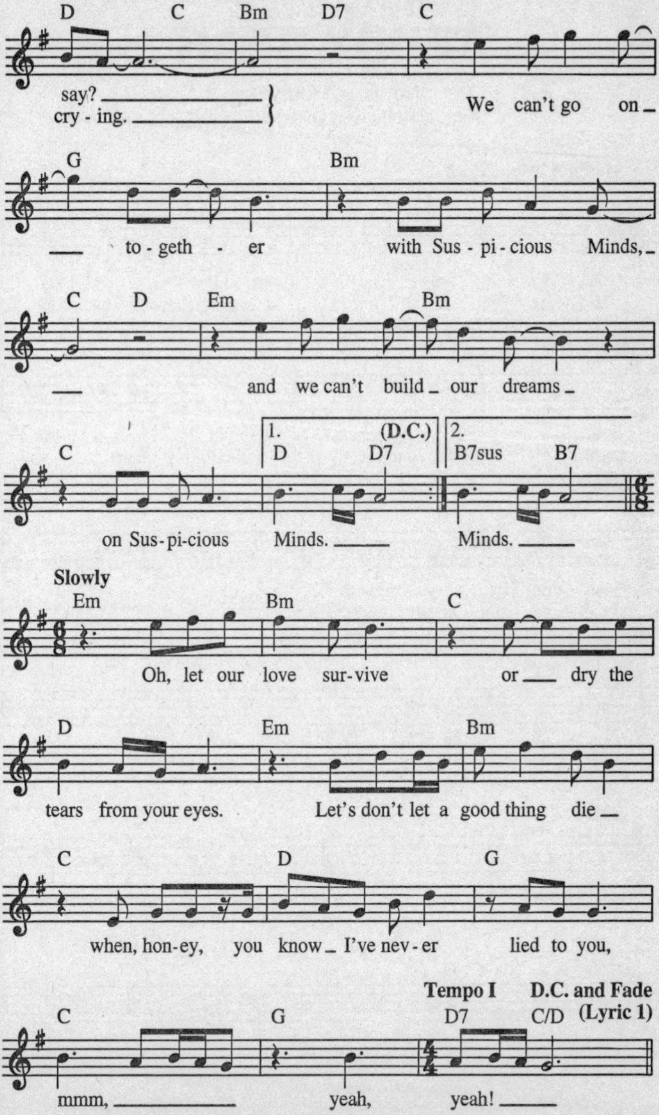
D C Bm D7 C
say? ______
cry - ing. ______
We can't go on_
G Bm
__ to - geth - er with Sus - pi - cious Minds, _
C D Em Bm
__ and we can't build_ our dreams_
1. (D.C.) 2.
C D D7 B7sus B7
on Sus - pi - cious Minds. ____ Minds. ____
Slowly
Em Bm C
Oh, let our love sur - vive or __ dry the
D Em Bm
tears from your eyes. Let's don't let a good thing die __
C D G
when, hon - ey, you know_ I've nev - er lied to you,
Tempo I D.C. and Fade
C G D7 C/D (Lyric 1)
mmm, ______ yeah, yeah! ____

(Let Me Be Your)
TEDDY BEAR

Words and Music by
KAL MANN and BERNIE LOWE

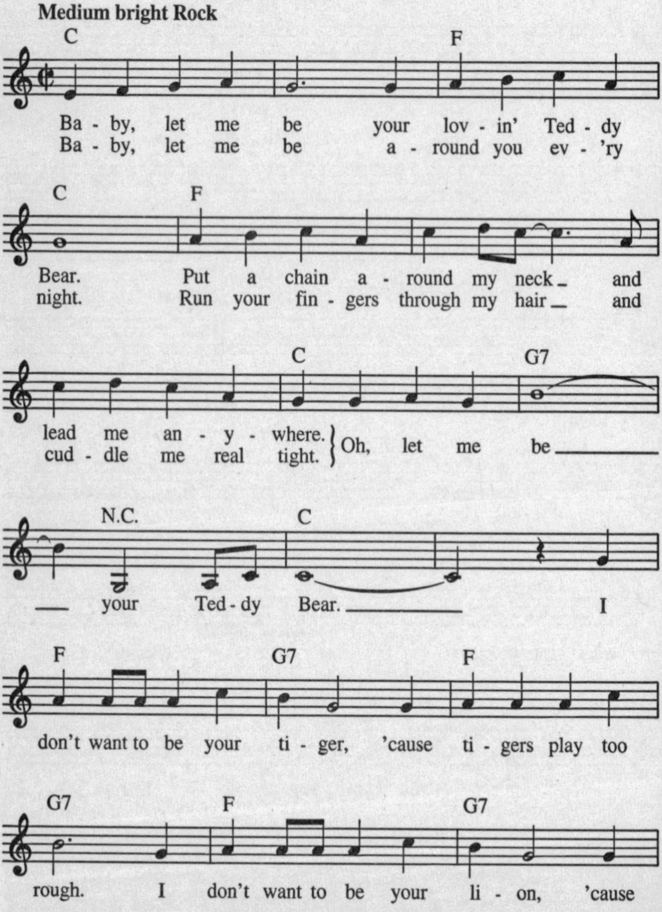
Medium bright Rock
C
F
Ba - by, let me be your lov - in' Ted - dy
Ba - by, let me be a - round you ev - 'ry
C
F
Bear. Put a chain a - round my neck and
night. Run your fin - gers through my hair and
C
G7
lead me an - y - where.
cud - dle me real tight.
Oh, let me be
N.C.
C
your Ted - dy Bear. I
F
G7
F
don't want to be your ti - ger, 'cause ti - gers play too
G7
F
G7
rough. I don't want to be your li - on, 'cause

Copyright © 1957 by Gladys Music, Inc.
Copyright Renewed and Assigned to Gladys Music (Administered by Williamson Music)
International Copyright Secured All Rights Reserved

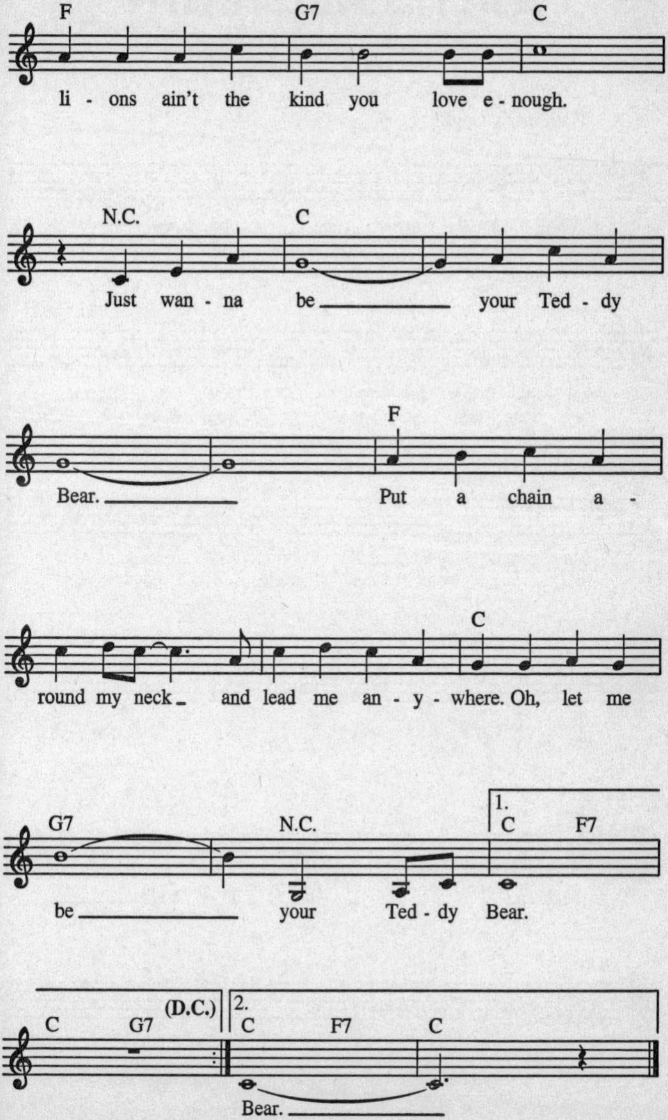
F G7 C
li - ons ain't the kind you love e - nough.
N.C. C
Just wan - na be your Ted - dy
F
Bear. Put a chain a -
C
round my neck and lead me an - y - where. Oh, let me
G7 N.C. 1. C F7
be your Ted - dy Bear.
C G7 (D.C.) 2. C F7 C
Bear.

THAT'S ALL RIGHT

Words and Music by
ARTHUR CRUDUP

Moderately bright

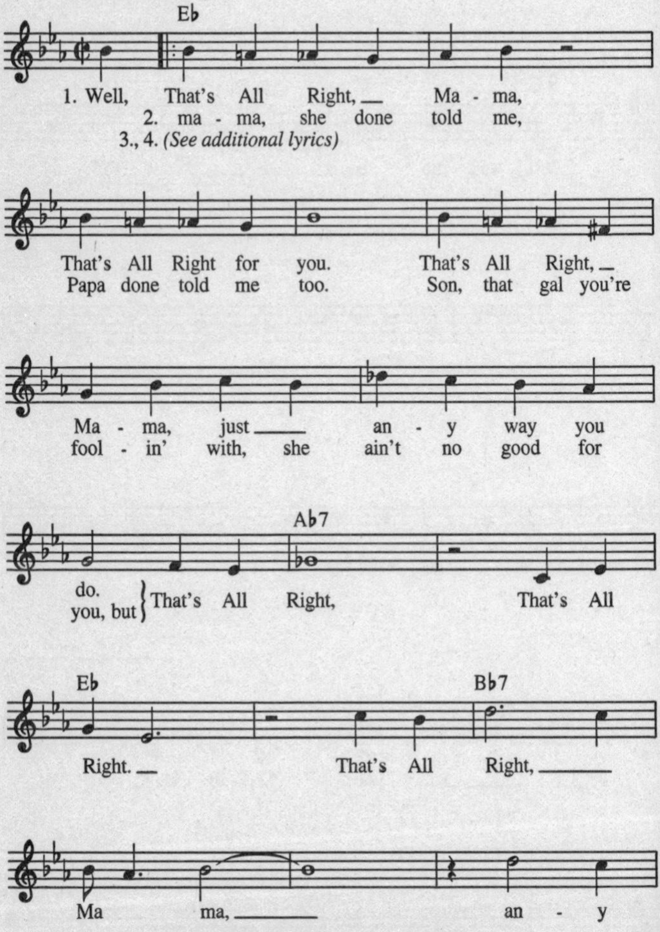
Eb
1. Well, That's All Right, Ma - ma,
2. ma - ma, she done told me,
3., 4. (See additional lyrics)
That's All Right for you. That's All Right,
Papa done told me too. Son, that gal you're
Ma - ma, just an - y way you
fool - in' with, she ain't no good for
Ab7
do.
you, but
That's All Right, That's All
Eb
Bb7
Right. That's All Right,
Ma ma, an - y

Copyright © 1947 by Unichappell Music Inc. and Crudup Music
Copyright Renewed
All Rights Administered by Unichappell Music Inc.
International Copyright Secured All Rights Reserved

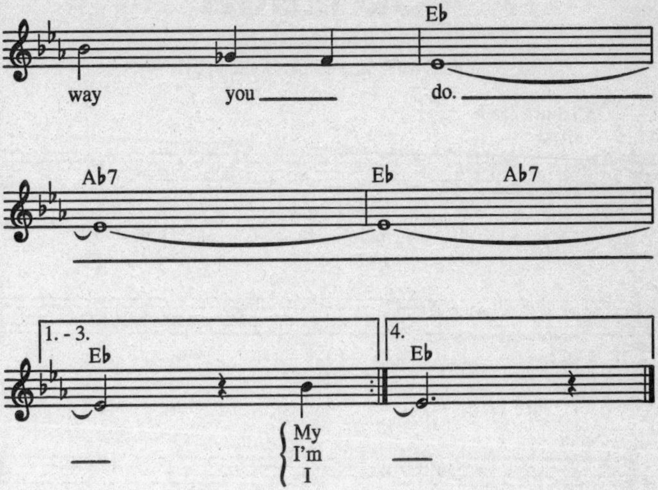
Eb
way
you
do.
Ab7
Eb
Ab7
1. - 3.
Eb
4.
Eb
My
I'm
I

Additional Lyrics

3. I'm leavin' town tomorrow, leavin' town for sure.
   Then you won't be bothered with me hangin' 'round your door.
   But That's All Right, That's All Right.
   That's All Right, Mama, any way you do.

4. I oughta mind my papa; guess I'm not too smart.
   If I was I'd leave you, go before you break my heart.
   But That's All Right, That's All Right.
   That's All Right, Mama, any way you do.

TOO MUCH

Words and Music by
LEE ROSENBERG and BERNIE WEINMAN

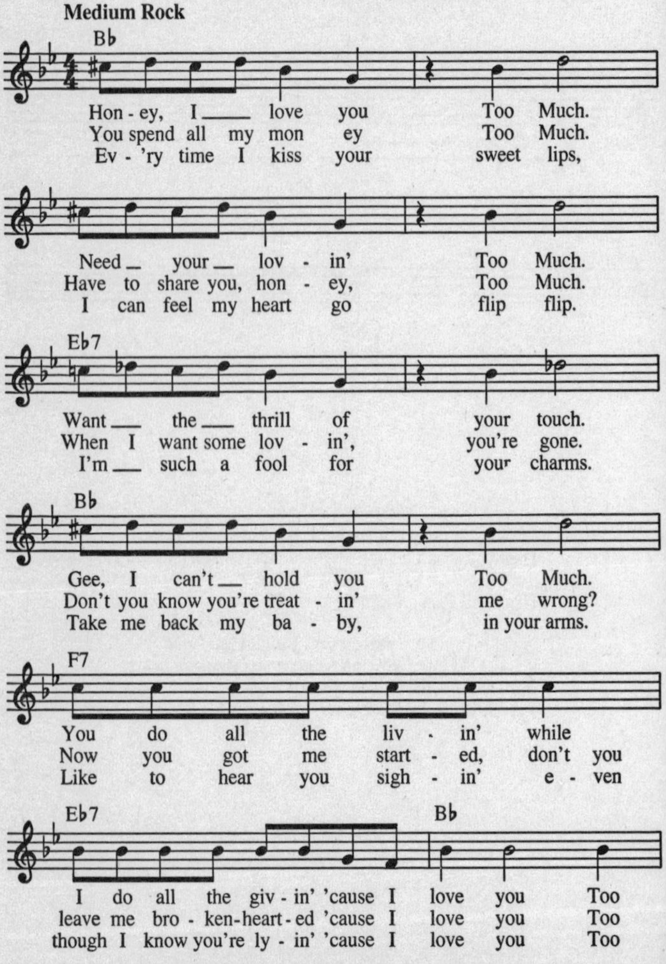
Medium Rock
B♭
Hon - ey, I ___ love you Too Much.
You spend all my mon ey Too Much.
Ev - 'ry time I kiss your sweet lips,
Need ___ your ___ lov - in' Too Much.
Have to share you, hon - ey, Too Much.
I can feel my heart go flip flip.
E♭7
Want ___ the ___ thrill of your touch.
When I want some lov - in', you're gone.
I'm ___ such a fool for your charms.
B♭
Gee, I can't ___ hold you Too Much.
Don't you know you're treat - in' me wrong?
Take me back my ba - by, in your arms.
F7
You do all the liv - in' while
Now you got me start - ed, don't you
Like to hear you sigh - in' e - ven
E♭7
B♭
I do all the giv - in' 'cause I love you Too
leave me bro - ken-heart - ed 'cause I love you Too
though I know you're ly - in' 'cause I love you Too

Copyright © 1956 by Elvis Presley Music, Inc. and Southern Belle Music
Copyright Renewed and Assigned to Elvis Presley Music
(Administered by R&H Music) and Southern Belle Music
International Copyright Secured All Rights Reserved

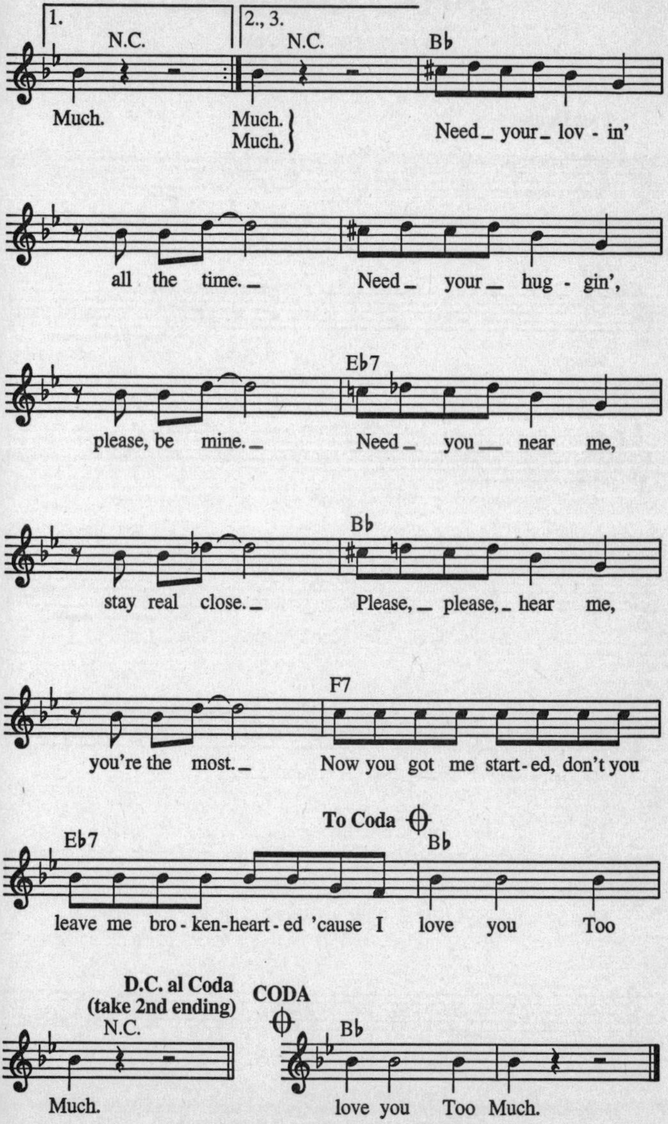
1.
N.C.
Much.
2., 3.
N.C.
Much.
Much.
B♭
Need your lov - in'
all the time.
Need your hug - gin',
please, be mine.
E♭7
Need you near me,
stay real close.
B♭
Please, please, hear me,
you're the most.
F7
Now you got me start - ed, don't you
E♭7
leave me bro - ken - heart - ed 'cause I
To Coda
B♭
love you Too
D.C. al Coda
(take 2nd ending)
N.C.
Much.
CODA
B♭
love you Too Much.

T-R-O-U-B-L-E

Words and Music by
JERRY CHESNUT

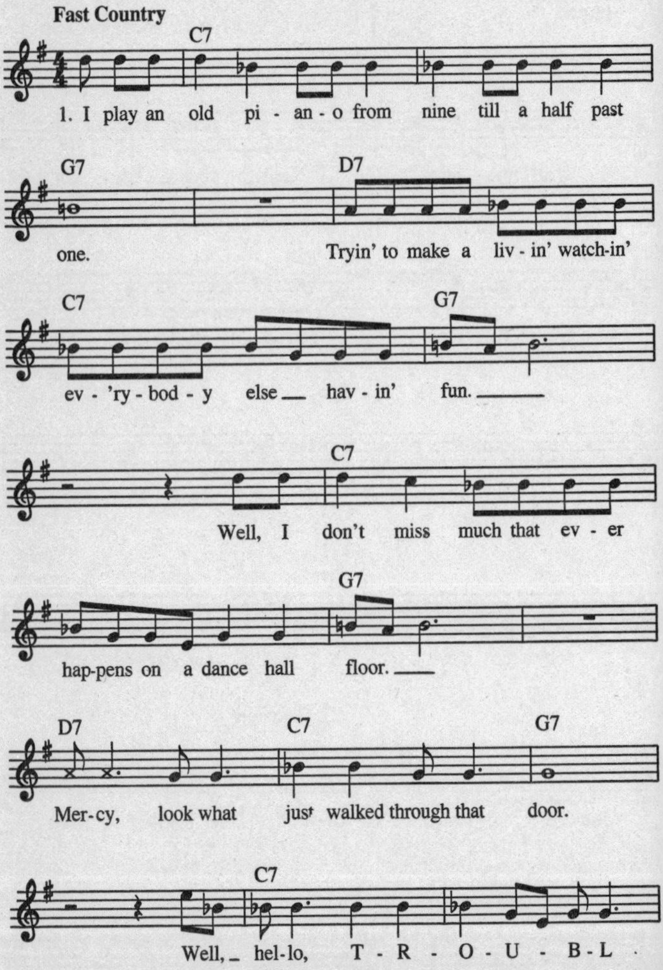
Fast Country
C7
1. I play an old pi - an - o from nine till a half past
G7
D7
one. Tryin' to make a liv - in' watch-in'
C7
G7
ev - 'ry - bod - y else hav - in' fun.
C7
Well, I don't miss much that ev - er
G7
hap-pens on a dance hall floor.
D7
C7
G7
Mer-cy, look what just walked through that door.
C7
Well, hel-lo, T - R - O - U - B - L -

Copyright © 1975 Sony/ATV Songs LLC
All Rights Administered by Sony/ATV Music Publishing, 8 Music Square West, Nashville, TN 37203
International Copyright Secured All Rights Reserved

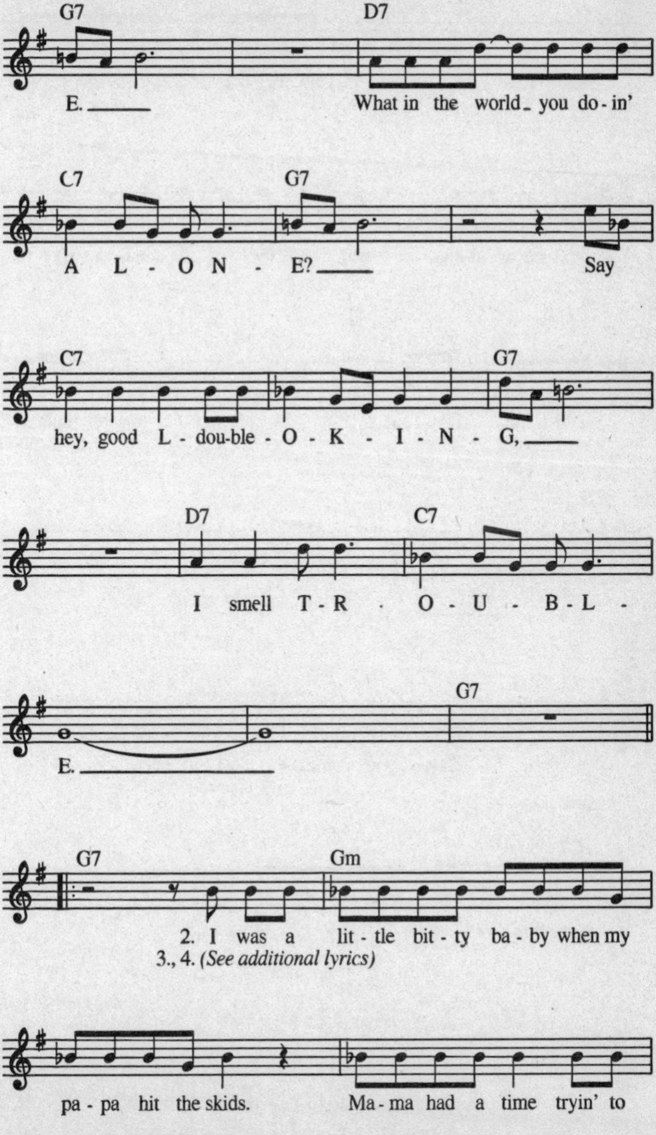
G7
D7
E.
What in the world you do-in'
C7
G7
A L - O N - E?
Say
C7
G7
hey, good L - dou-ble - O - K - I - N - G,
D7
C7
I smell T - R - O - U - B - L -
G7
E.
G7
Gm
2. I was a lit - tle bit - ty ba - by when my
3., 4. (See additional lyrics)
pa - pa hit the skids.
Ma - ma had a time tryin' to

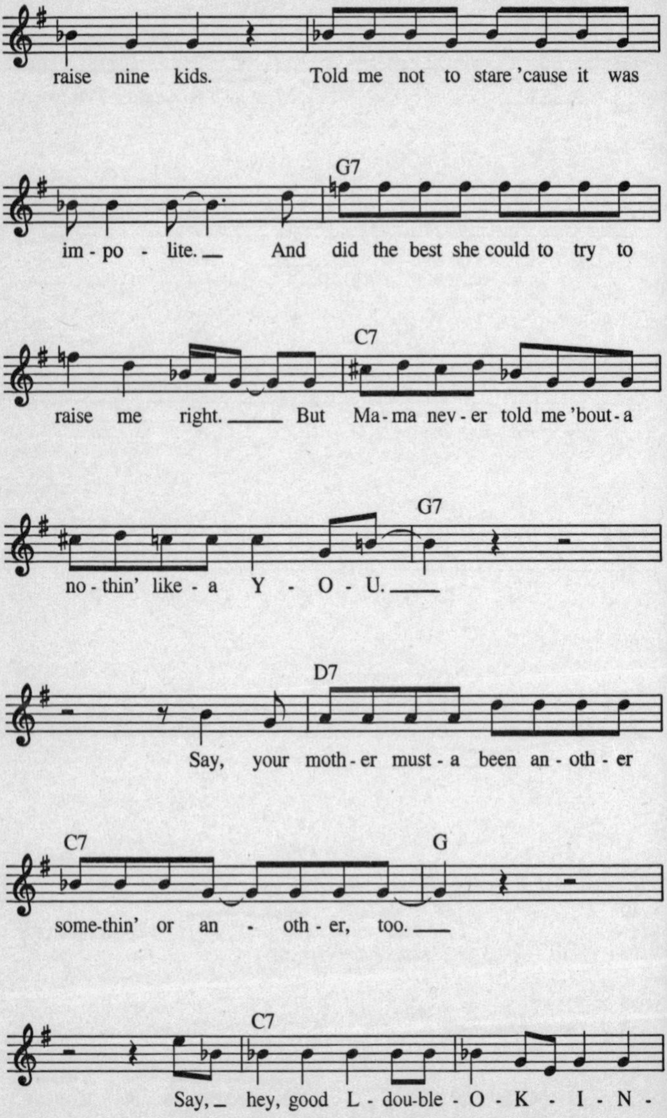
raise nine kids. Told me not to stare 'cause it was
G7
im - po - lite. And did the best she could to try to
C7
raise me right. But Ma - ma nev - er told me 'bout - a
G7
no - thin' like - a Y - O - U.
D7
Say, your moth - er must - a been an - oth - er
C7
G
some-thin' or an - oth - er, too.
C7
Say, hey, good L - dou-ble - O - K - I - N -

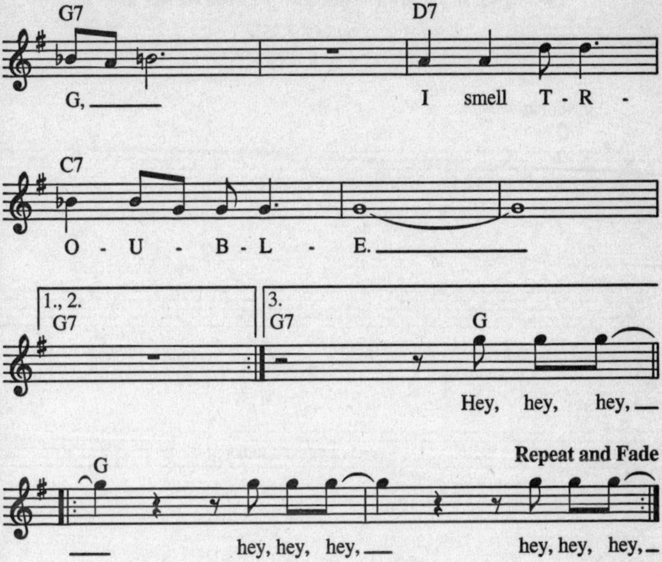
G7
D7
G,
I smell T - R -
C7
O - U - B - L - E.
1., 2.
G7
3.
G7
G
Hey, hey, hey,
Repeat and Fade
G
hey, hey, hey,
hey, hey, hey,

Additional Lyrics

3. Well, you talk about a woman, I've seen a lotta others
With too much somethin' and not enough of another,
Lookin' like glory and walkin' like a dream.
Mother Nature's sure been good to Y-O-U.
Well, your mother musta been another good lookin' mother, too.
Say, hey! Good L-double O-K-I-N-G, I smell T-R-O-U-B-L-E.

4. Well, you talk about a trouble makin' hunka' pokey bait
The men are gonna love and all the women gonna hate.
Remindin' them of everything, they're never gonna be,
Maybe the beginnin' of a World War Three,
'Cause the world ain't ready for nothing like a Y-O-U.
I bet your mother musta been another somethin' or the other, too.
Say, hey! Good L-double O-K-I-N-G, I smell T-R-O-U-B-L-E.

UNCHAINED MELODY

Lyric by HY ZARET
Music by ALEX NORTH

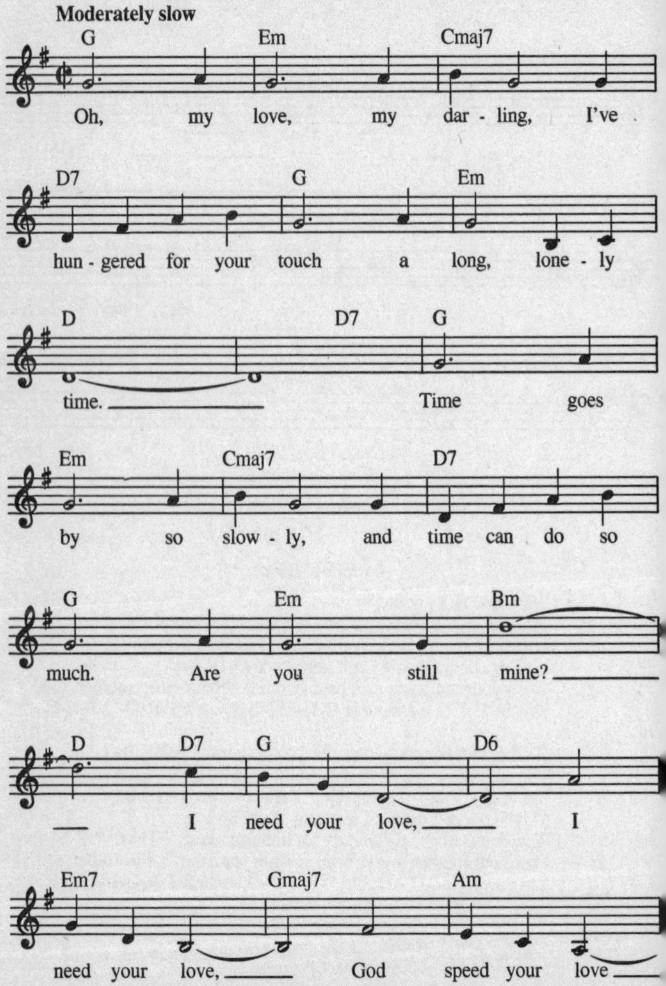
Moderately slow
G Em Cmaj7
Oh, my love, my dar - ling, I've
D7 G Em
hun - gered for your touch a long, lone - ly
D D7 G
time. Time goes
Em Cmaj7 D7
by so slow - ly, and time can do so
G Em Bm
much. Are you still mine?
D D7 G D6
I need your love, I
Em7 Gmaj7 Am
need your love, God speed your love

© 1955 (Renewed) FRANK MUSIC CORP.
All Rights Reserved

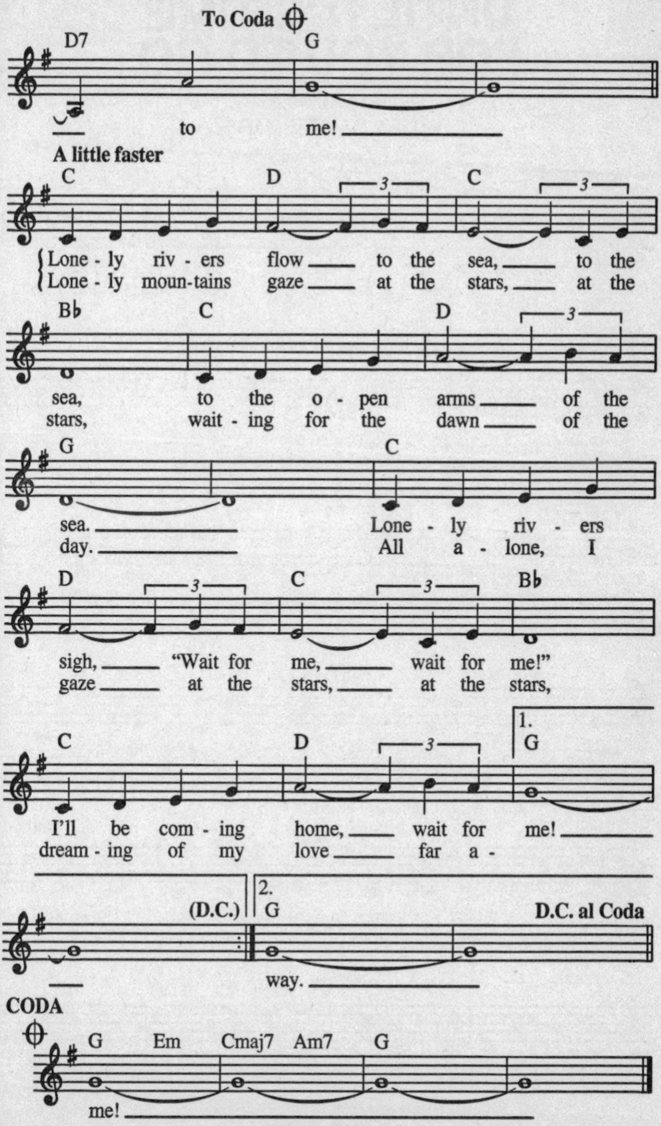
To Coda
D7
G
to me!
A little faster
C D C
Lone - ly riv - ers flow to the sea, to the
Lone - ly moun-tains gaze at the stars, at the
B♭ C D
sea, to the o - pen arms of the
stars, wait - ing for the dawn of the
G C
sea. Lone - ly riv - ers
day. All a - lone, I
D C B♭
sigh, "Wait for me, wait for me!"
gaze at the stars, at the stars,
C D
1.
G
I'll be com - ing home, wait for me!
dream - ing of my love far a -
(D.C.)
2.
G
D.C. al Coda
way.
CODA
G Em Cmaj7 Am7 G
me!

UNTIL IT'S TIME FOR YOU TO GO

Words and Music by
BUFFY SAINTE-MARIE

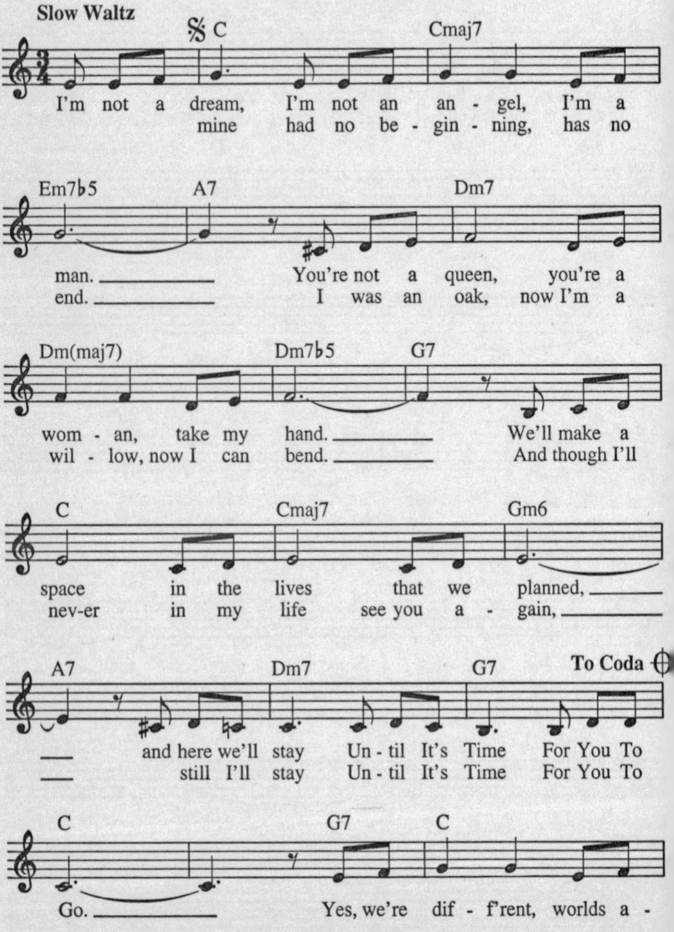
Slow Waltz
C
Cmaj7
I'm not a dream, I'm not an an - gel, I'm a
mine had no be - gin - ning, has no
Em7♭5
A7
Dm7
man. You're not a queen, you're a
end. I was an oak, now I'm a
Dm(maj7)
Dm7♭5
G7
wom - an, take my hand. We'll make a
wil - low, now I can bend. And though I'll
C
Cmaj7
Gm6
space in the lives that we planned,
nev-er in my life see you a - gain,
A7
Dm7
G7
To Coda
and here we'll stay Un - til It's Time For You To
still I'll stay Un - til It's Time For You To
C
G7
C
Go. Yes, we're dif - f'rent, worlds a -

Copyright © 1965, 1967 by Gypsy Boy Music, Inc.
Copyright Renewed
International Copyright Secured All Rights Reserved

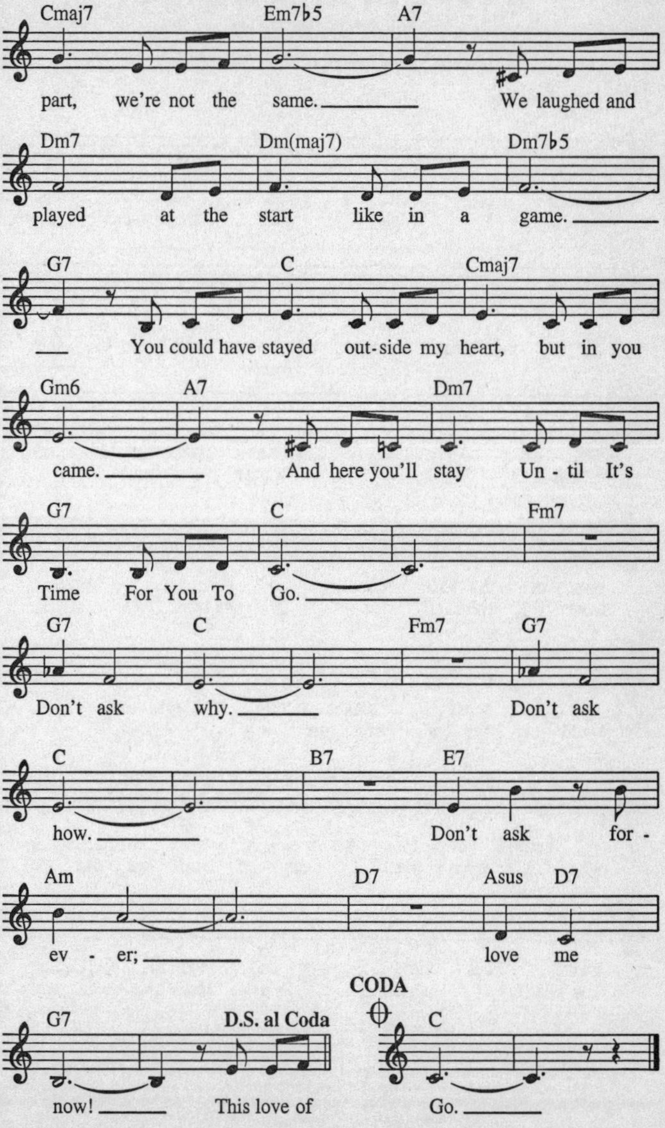
Cmaj7 Em7♭5 A7
part, we're not the same. We laughed and
Dm7 Dm(maj7) Dm7♭5
played at the start like in a game.
G7 C Cmaj7
You could have stayed out-side my heart, but in you
Gm6 A7 Dm7
came. And here you'll stay Un - til It's
G7 C Fm7
Time For You To Go.
G7 C Fm7 G7
Don't ask why. Don't ask
C B7 E7
how. Don't ask for -
Am D7 Asus D7
ev - er; love me
CODA
G7 D.S. al Coda C
now! This love of Go.

VIVA LAS VEGAS

Words and Music by
DOC POMUS and MORT SHUMAN

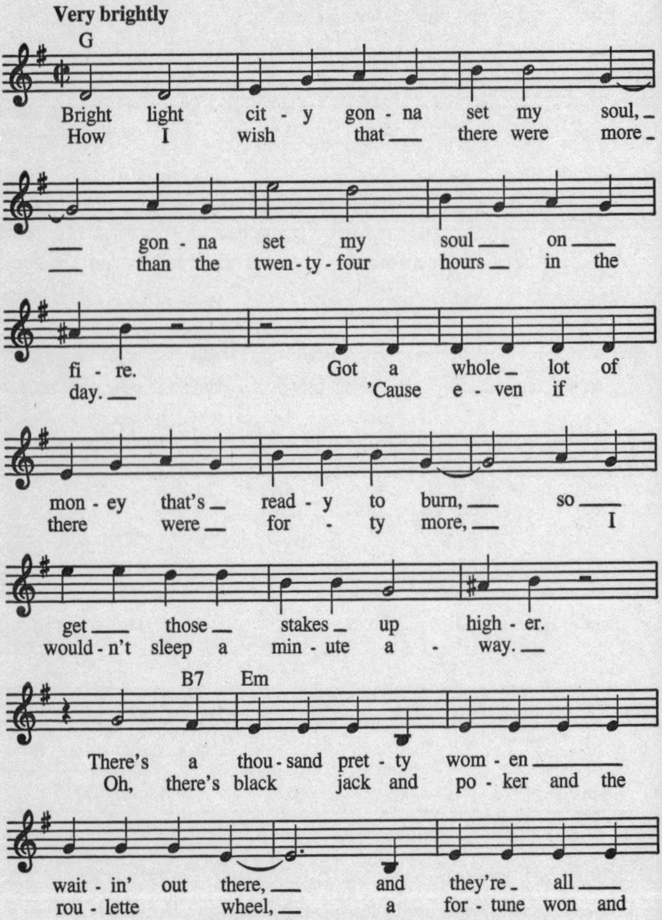
Very brightly
G
Bright light cit - y gon - na set my soul, gon - na set my soul on fire.
How I wish that there were more than the twen - ty - four hours in the day.
Got a whole lot of mon - ey that's read - y to burn, so get those stakes up high - er.
'Cause e - ven if there were for - ty more, I would - n't sleep a min - ute a - way.
B7 Em
There's a thou - sand pret - ty wom - en wait - in' out there, and they're all
Oh, there's black jack and po - ker and the rou - lette wheel, a for - tune won and

Copyright © 1964 by Elvis Presley Music, Inc.
Copyright Renewed 1992 by Sharyn Felder and Geoffrey J. Felder on behalf of Doc Pomus and Mort Shuman Songs on behalf of Mort Shuman
All Rights for Sharyn Felder and Geoffrey J. Felder in the United States Administered by Pomus Songs, Inc.
All Rights for Mort Shuman Songs in the United States Administered by Warner-Tamerlane Publishing Corp.
All Rights for the world outside the United States Controlled by Elvis Presley Music (Administerd by R&H Music)
International Copyright Secured All Rights Reserved

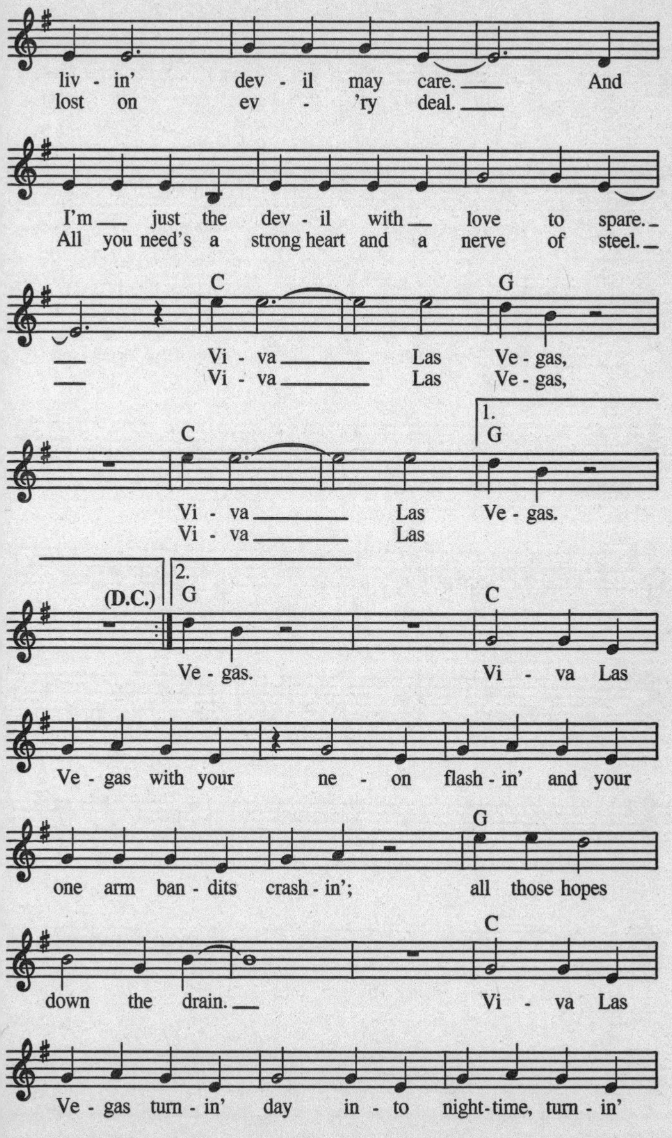
liv - in' dev - il may care. And
lost on ev - 'ry deal.
I'm just the dev - il with love to spare.
All you need's a strong heart and a nerve of steel.
C G
Vi - va Las Ve - gas,
Vi - va Las Ve - gas,
1.
C G
Vi - va Las Ve - gas.
Vi - va Las
(D.C.)
2.
G C
Ve - gas. Vi - va Las
Ve - gas with your ne - on flash - in' and your
G
one arm ban - dits crash - in'; all those hopes
C
down the drain. Vi - va Las
Ve - gas turn - in' day in - to night-time, turn - in'

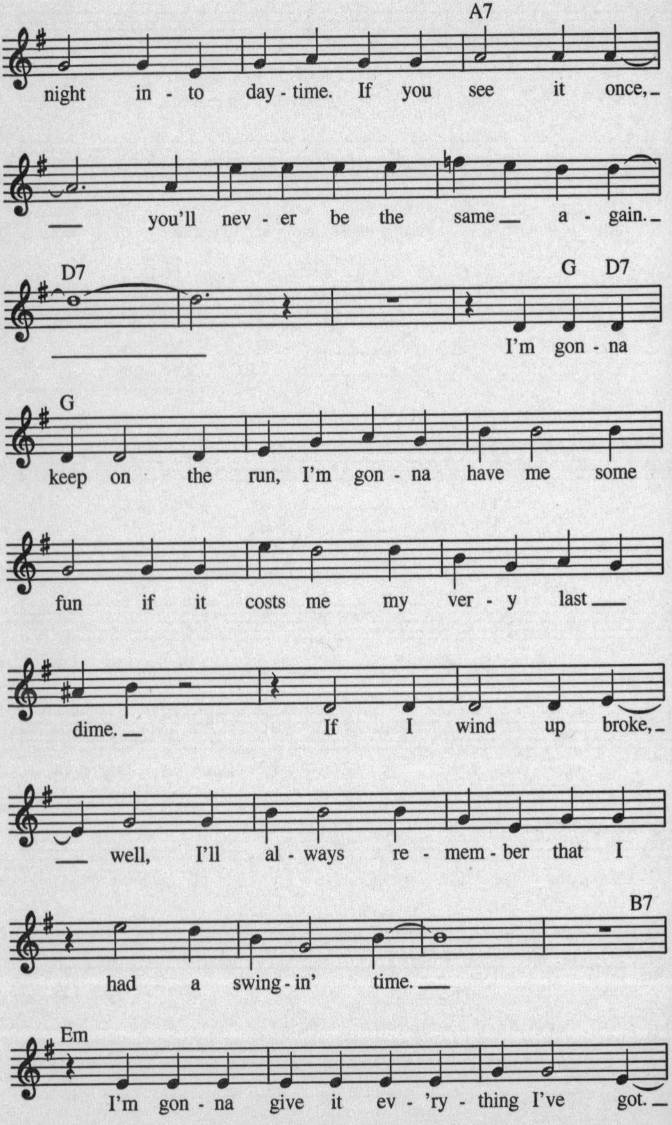
A7
night in - to day - time. If you see it once,
you'll nev - er be the same a - gain.
D7
G D7
I'm gon - na
G
keep on the run, I'm gon - na have me some
fun if it costs me my ver - y last
dime. If I wind up broke,
well, I'll al - ways re - mem - ber that I
B7
had a swing - in' time.
Em
I'm gon - na give it ev - 'ry - thing I've got.

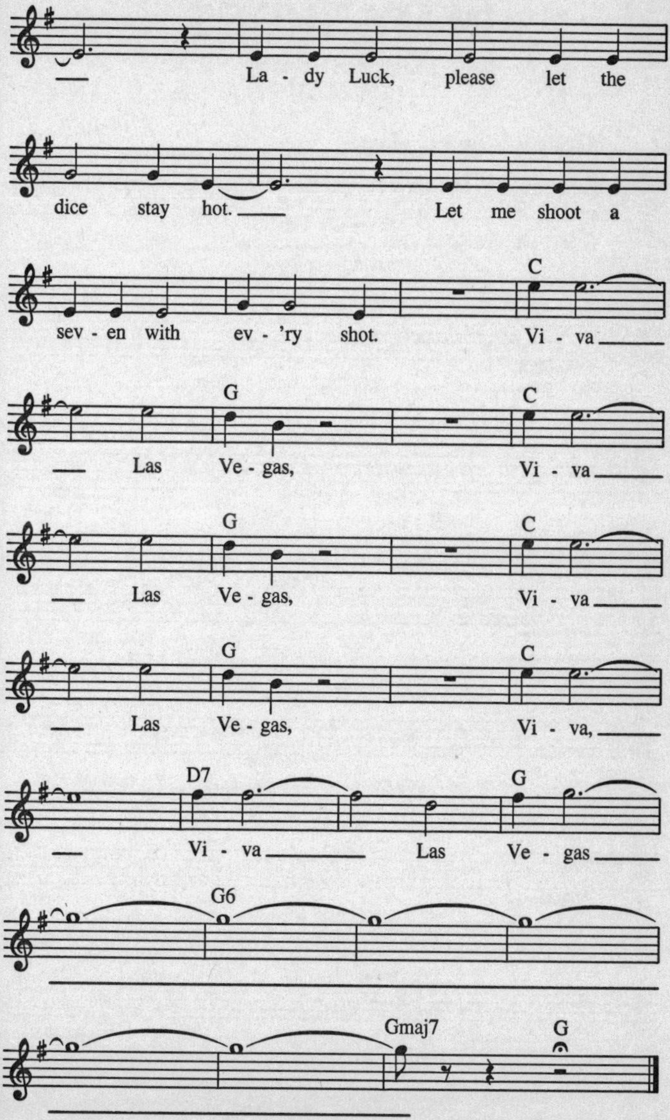
La - dy Luck, please let the
dice stay hot. Let me shoot a
sev - en with ev - 'ry shot.
C
Vi - va
G
Las Ve - gas,
C
Vi - va
G
Las Ve - gas,
C
Vi - va
G
Las Ve - gas,
C
Vi - va,
D7
Vi - va
Las
G
Ve - gas
G6
Gmaj7
G

WALK A MILE IN MY SHOES

Words and Music by
JOE SOUTH

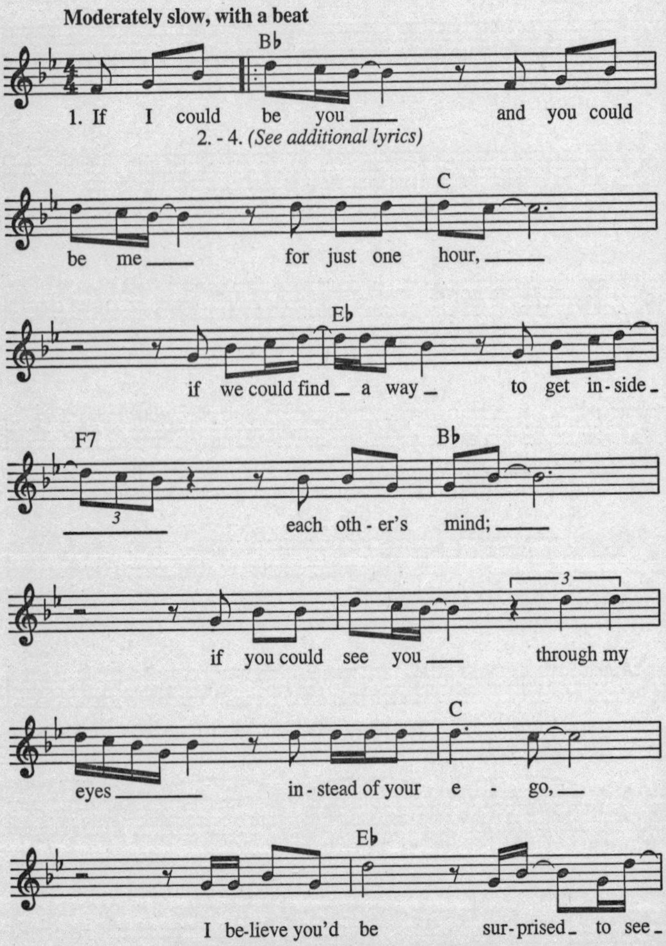
Moderately slow, with a beat
B♭
1. If I could be you ___ and you could
2. - 4. (See additional lyrics)
C
be me ___ for just one hour, ___
E♭
if we could find _ a way _ to get in-side _
F7
B♭
each oth - er's mind; ___
if you could see you ___ through my
C
eyes ___ in - stead of your e - go, _
E♭
I be-lieve you'd be sur-prised _ to see _

Copyright © 1969 by Lowery Music Co., Inc.
All Rights Reserved Used by Permission

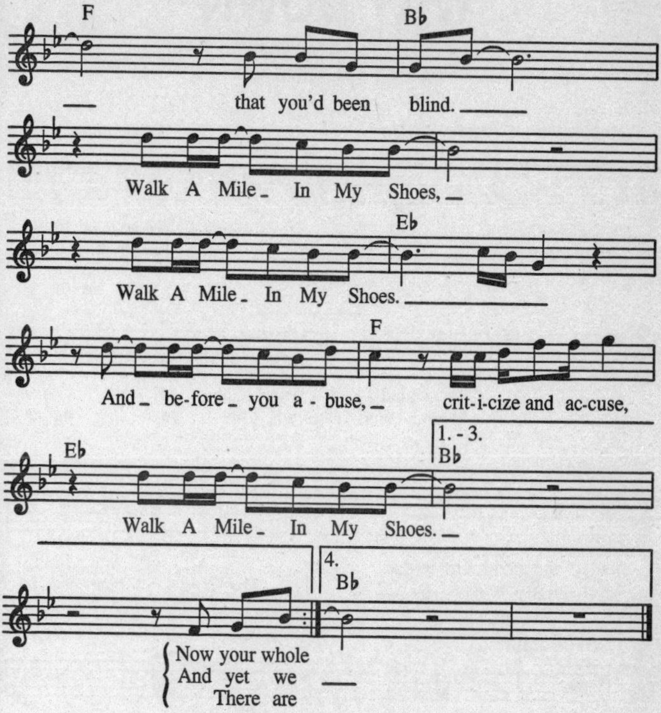
F
Bb
that you'd been blind.
Walk A Mile In My Shoes,
Eb
Walk A Mile In My Shoes.
F
And before you abuse, criticize and accuse,
Eb
1. - 3.
Bb
Walk A Mile In My Shoes.
4.
Bb
Now your whole
And yet we
There are

Additional Lyrics

2. Now your whole world you see around you is just a reflection,
And the law of karma says you reap just what you sow.
So, unless you've lived a life of total perfection,
You'd better be careful of every stone that you should throw.
(Chorus)

3. And yet we spend the day throwing stones at one another,
'Cause I don't think or wear my hair the same way you do.
Well, I may be common people, but I'm your brother.
And when you strike out and try to hurt me it's a-hurtin' you.
(Chorus)

4. There are people on reservations and out in the ghettos,
And, brother, there but for the grace of God go you and I.
If I only had the wings of a little angel,
Don't you know I'd fly to the top of the mountain and then I'd cry?
(Chorus)

WAY DOWN

Words and Music by
LAYNG MARTINE, JR.

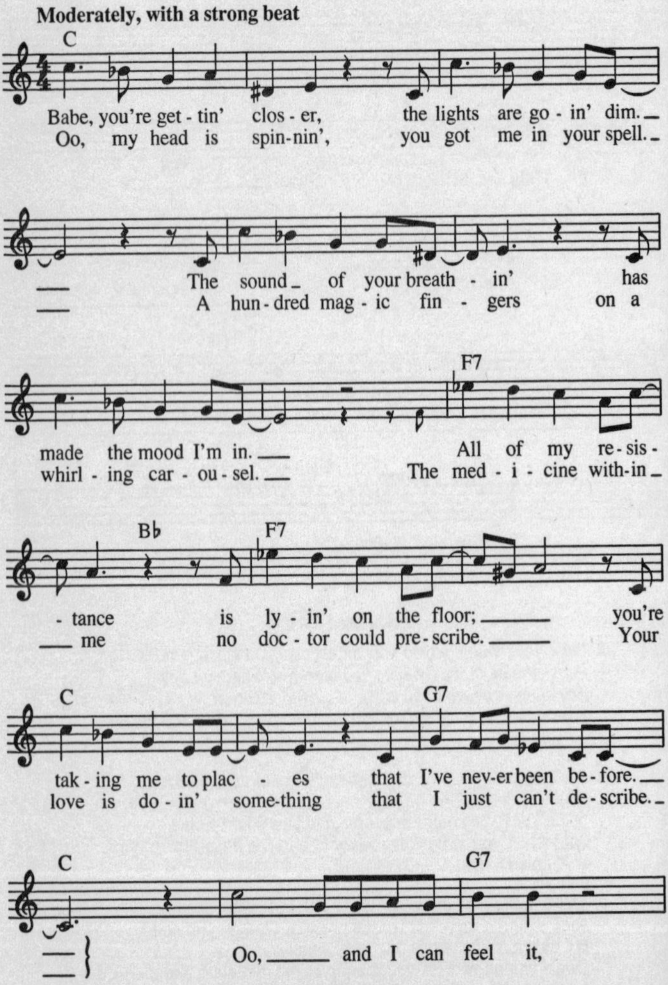
Moderately, with a strong beat
C
Babe, you're get - tin' clos - er, the lights are go - in' dim. _
Oo, my head is spin-nin', you got me in your spell. _
The sound _ of your breath - in' has
A hun - dred mag - ic fin - gers on a
F7
made the mood I'm in. ___ All of my re - sis -
whirl - ing car - ou - sel. ___ The med - i - cine with-in _
B♭
F7
- tance is ly - in' on the floor; ___ you're
___ me no doc - tor could pre - scribe. ___ Your
C
G7
tak - ing me to plac - es that I've nev - er been be - fore. ___
love is do - in' some-thing that I just can't de - scribe. _
C
G7
Oo, ___ and I can feel it,

Copyright © 1977 by Ray Stevens Music
International Copyright Secured All Rights Reserved

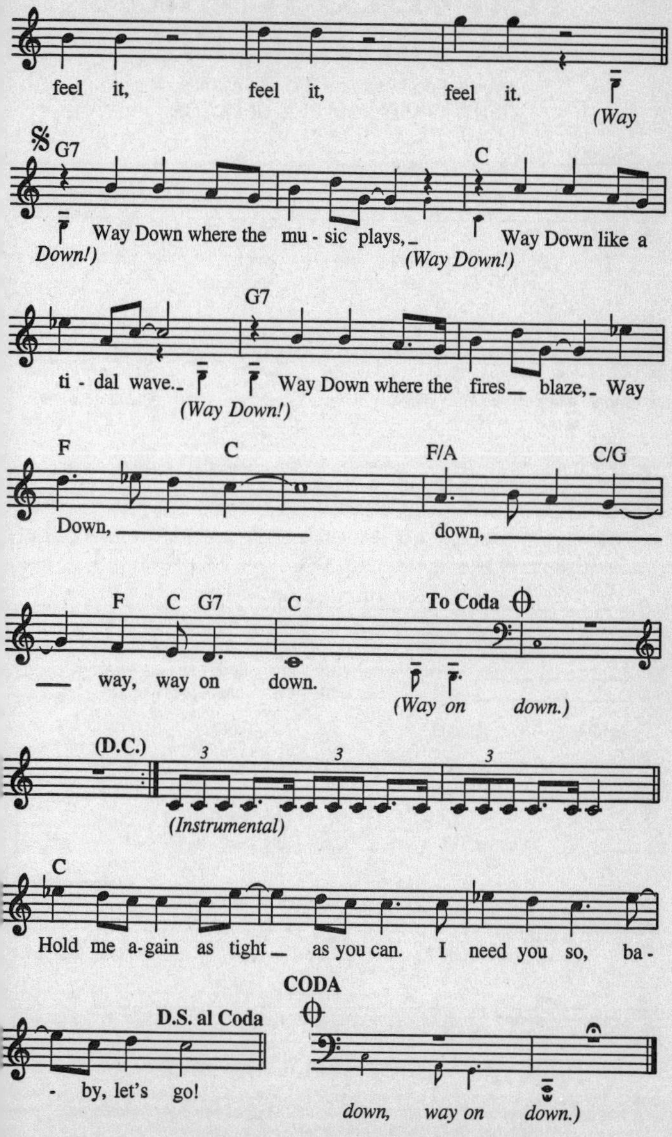
feel it, feel it, feel it.
(Way Down!)
G7
C
Way Down where the mu - sic plays,
(Way Down!)
Way Down like a ti - dal wave.
(Way Down!)
G7
Way Down where the fires blaze, Way
F
C
F/A
C/G
Down, down,
F
C
G7
C
To Coda
way, way on down.
(Way on down.)
(D.C.)
3
(Instrumental)
C
Hold me a-gain as tight as you can. I need you so, ba - by, let's go!
D.S. al Coda
CODA
down, way on down.)

YOU'VE LOST THAT LOVIN' FEELIN'

Words and Music by BARRY MANN, CYNTHIA WEIL and PHIL SPECTOR

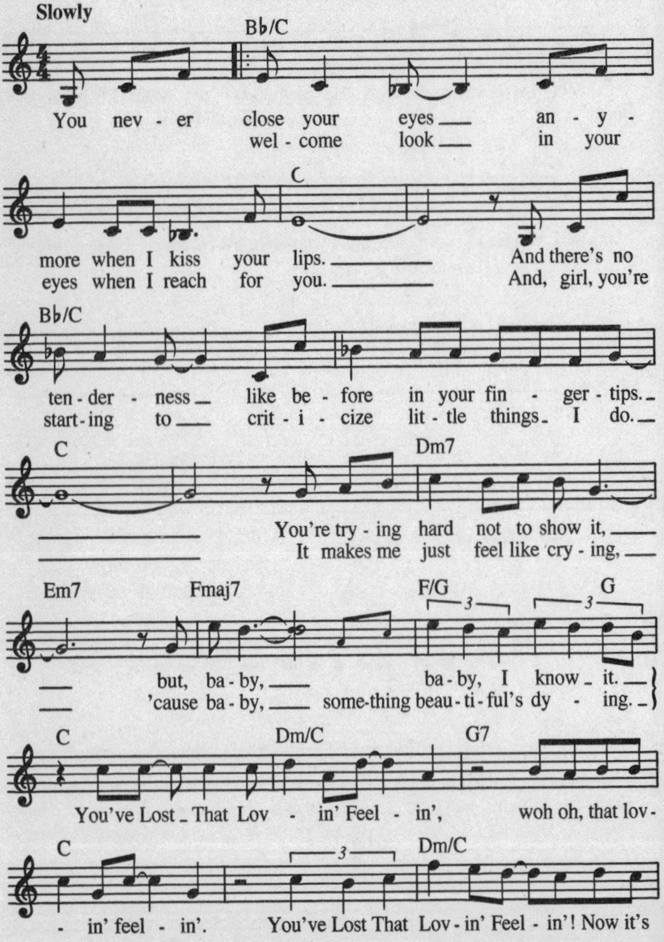
Slowly
Bb/C
You nev - er close your eyes ___ an - y -
wel - come look ___ in your
C
more when I kiss your lips. ___ And there's no
eyes when I reach for you. ___ And, girl, you're
Bb/C
ten - der - ness ___ like be - fore in your fin - ger - tips. ___
start - ing to ___ crit - i - cize lit - tle things ___ I do. ___
C
Dm7
You're try - ing hard not to show it, ___
It makes me just feel like cry - ing, ___
Em7
Fmaj7
F/G
G
but, ba - by, ___ ba - by, I know ___ it. ___
'cause ba - by, ___ some-thing beau - ti - ful's dy - ing. ___
C
Dm/C
G7
You've Lost ___ That Lov - in' Feel - in', woh oh, that lov -
C
Dm/C
- in' feel - in'. You've Lost That Lov - in' Feel - in'! Now it's

© 1964, 1965 (Renewed 1992, 1993) SCREEN GEMS-EMI MUSIC INC. and MOTHER BERTHA MUSIC, INC.
All Rights on behalf of MOTHER BERTHA MUSIC, INC. Administered by ABKCO MUSIC, INC.
All Rights Reserved International Copyright Secured Used by Permission

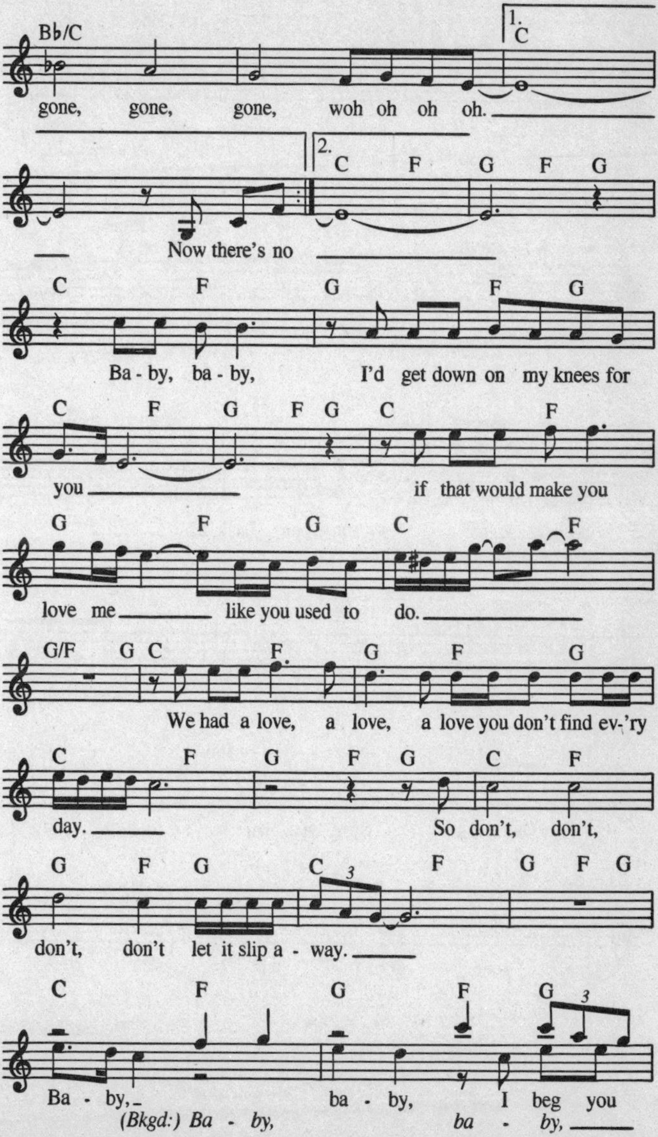
Bb/C
1.
C
gone, gone, gone, woh oh oh oh.
2.
C F G F G
Now there's no
C F G F G
Ba - by, ba - by, I'd get down on my knees for
C F G F G C F
you if that would make you
G F G C F
love me like you used to do.
G/F G C F G F G
We had a love, a love, a love you don't find ev-'ry
C F G F G C F
day. So don't, don't,
G F G C F G F G
3
don't, don't let it slip a - way.
C F G F G
3
Ba - by, ba - by, I beg you
(Bkgd:) Ba - by, ba - by,

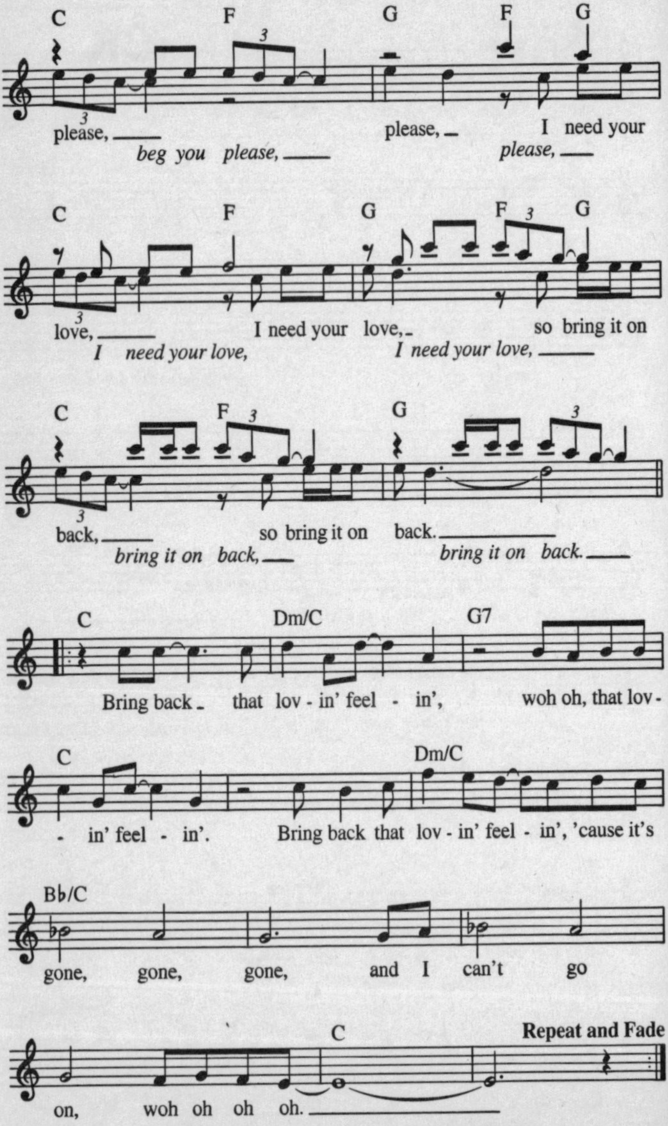
C F G F G
please, ___ please, _ I need your
beg you please, ___ please, ___
C F G F G
love, ___ I need your love, _ so bring it on
I need your love, I need your love, ___
C F G
back, ___ so bring it on back. ___
bring it on back, ___ bring it on back. ___
C Dm/C G7
Bring back _ that lov - in' feel - in', woh oh, that lov -
C Dm/C
- in' feel - in'. Bring back that lov - in' feel - in', 'cause it's
Bb/C
gone, gone, gone, and I can't go
C
Repeat and Fade
on, woh oh oh oh. ___

WEAR MY RING AROUND YOUR NECK

Words and Music by
BERT CARROLL and RUSSELL MOODY

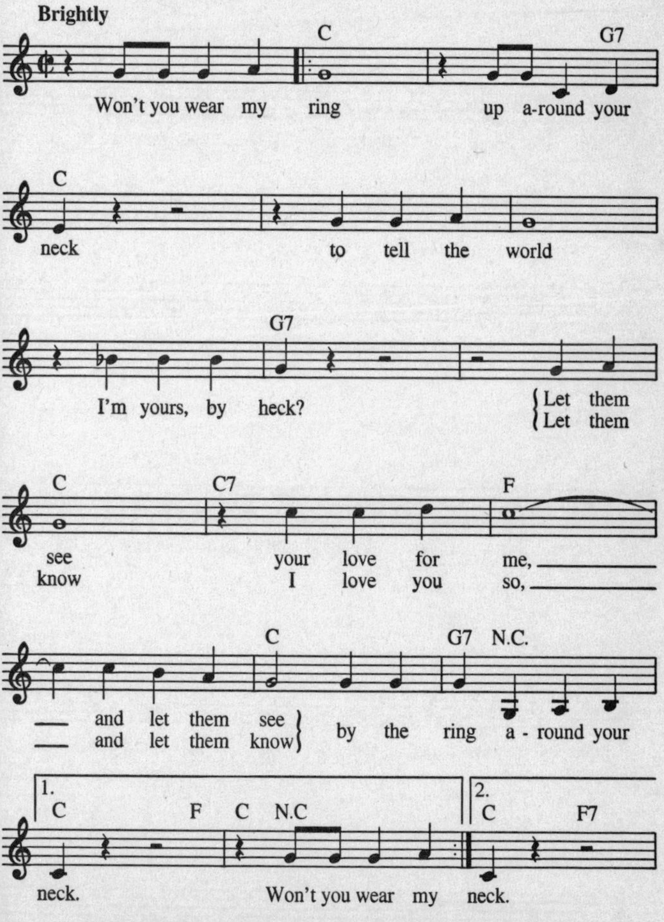
Brightly
C G7
Won't you wear my ring up a-round your
C
neck to tell the world
G7
I'm yours, by heck? Let them / Let them
C C7 F
see your love for me, / know I love you so,
C G7 N.C.
and let them see / and let them know by the ring a - round your
1. C F C N.C
neck. Won't you wear my
2. C F7
neck.

Copyright © 1958 (Renewed) and Assigned to Lollipop Music Corp. for the U.S.A.
All Rights for the rest of the world controlled by Elvis Presley Music, Inc. (administered by R&H Music), Pinelawn Music Publishing Co., Inc. and Tideland Music Publishing Corp.
International Copyright Secured All Rights Reserved

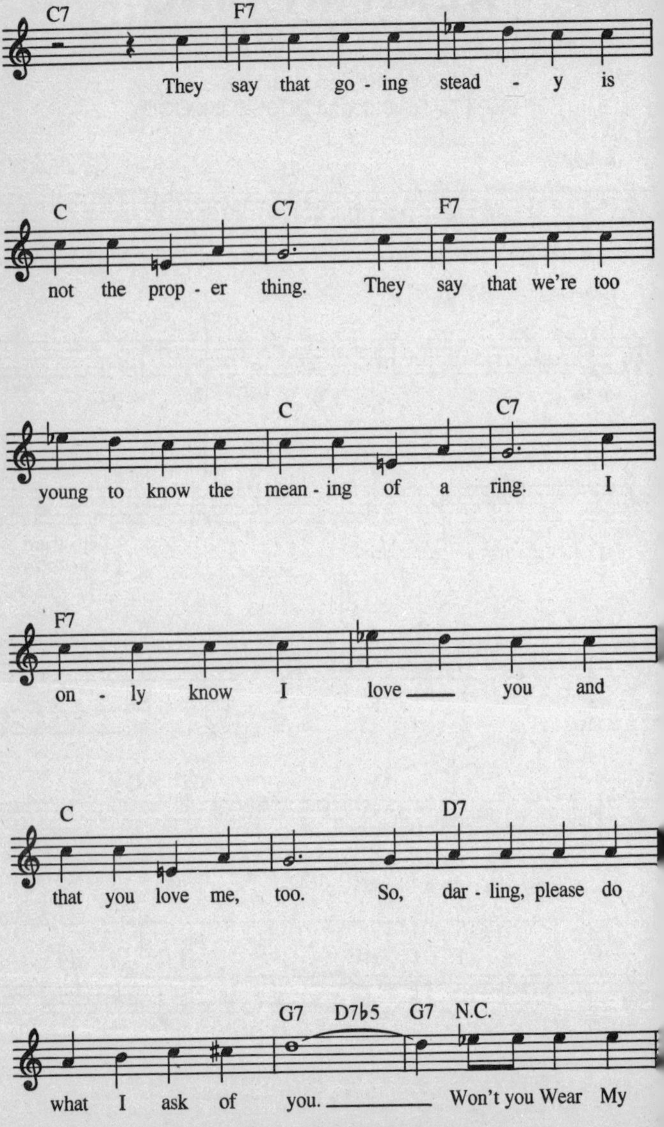
C7 F7
They say that go - ing stead - y is
C C7 F7
not the prop - er thing. They say that we're too
C C7
young to know the mean - ing of a ring. I
F7
on - ly know I love you and
C D7
that you love me, too. So, dar - ling, please do
G7 D7♭5 G7 N.C.
what I ask of you. Won't you Wear My

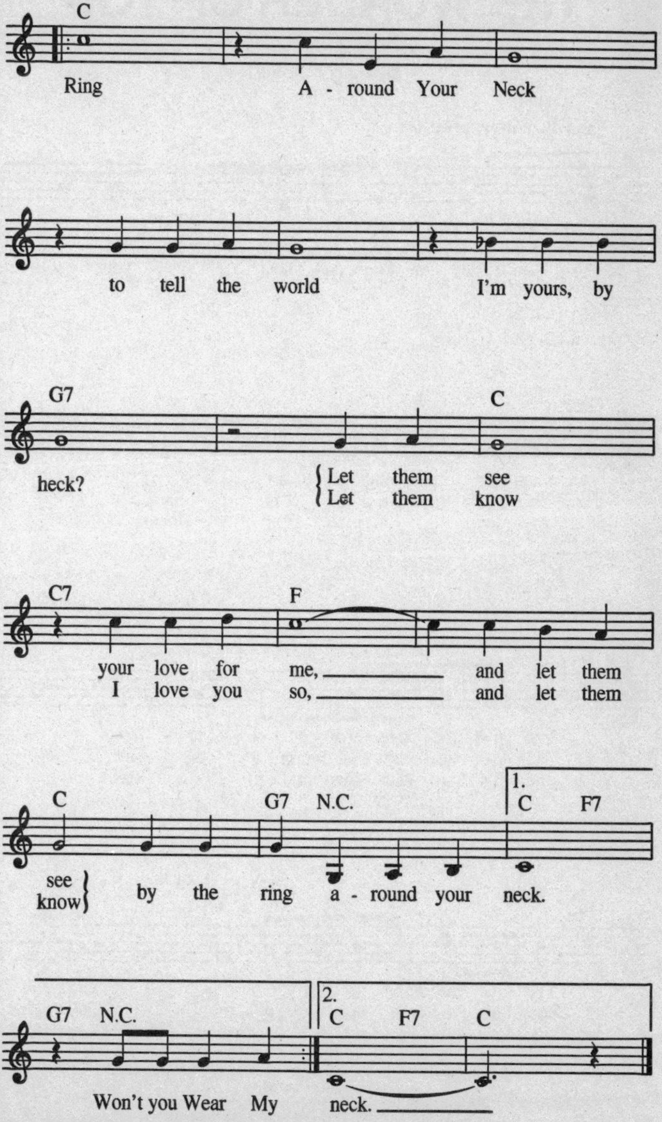
C
Ring A - round Your Neck
to tell the world I'm yours, by
G7 C
heck? Let them see
Let them know
C7 F
your love for me, and let them
I love you so, and let them
C G7 N.C. 1. C F7
see know by the ring a - round your neck.
G7 N.C. 2. C F7 C
Won't you Wear My neck.

THE WONDER OF YOU

Words and Music by
BAKER KNIGHT

Slowly, with expression

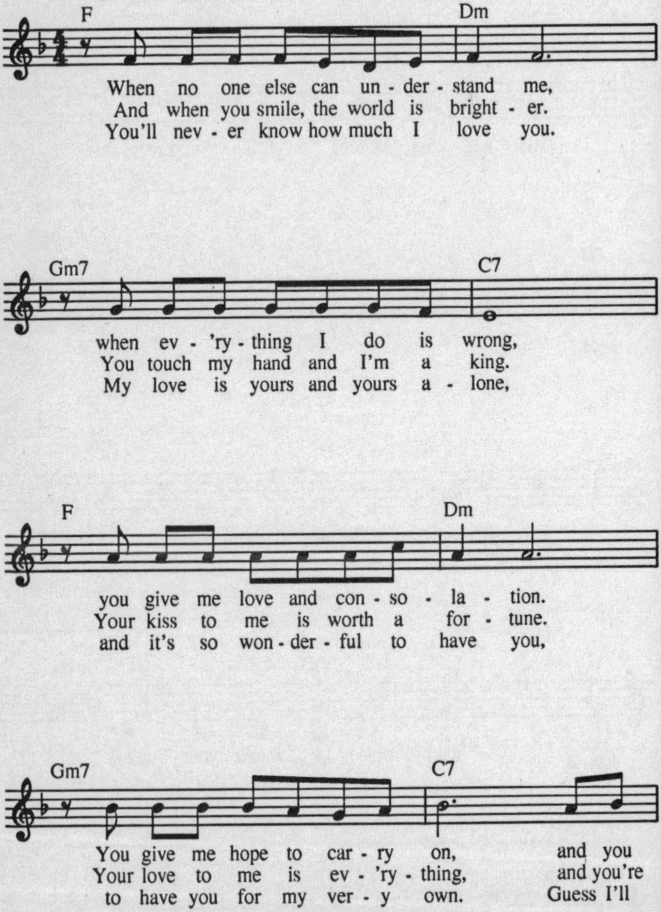
F
Dm
When no one else can un - der - stand me,
And when you smile, the world is bright - er.
You'll nev - er know how much I love you.
Gm7
C7
when ev - 'ry - thing I do is wrong,
You touch my hand and I'm a king.
My love is yours and yours a - lone,
F
Dm
you give me love and con - so - la - tion.
Your kiss to me is worth a for - tune.
and it's so won - der - ful to have you,
Gm7
C7
You give me hope to car - ry on, and you
Your love to me is ev - 'ry - thing, and you're
to have you for my ver - y own. Guess I'll

© Copyright 1958, 1964 by DUCHESS MUSIC CORPORATION
Copyright Renewed
DUCHESS MUSIC CORPORATION is an MCA company
International Copyright Secured All Rights Reserved
MCA music publishing

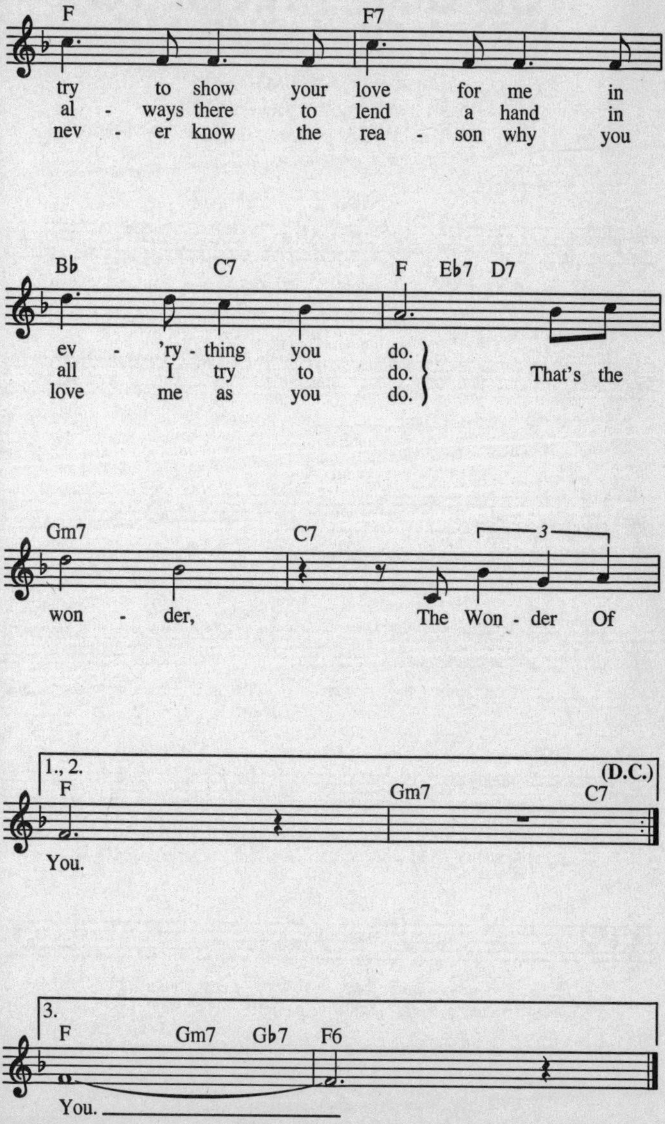
F
F7
try to show your love for me in
al - ways there to lend a hand in
nev - er know the rea - son why you
B♭
C7
F
E♭7
D7
ev - 'ry - thing you do.
all I try to do.
love me as you do.
That's the
Gm7
C7
3
won - der,
The Won - der Of
1., 2.
F
Gm7
C7
(D.C.)
You.
3.
F
Gm7
G♭7
F6
You.

YOU DON'T HAVE TO SAY YOU LOVE ME

Music by P. DONAGGIO
Italian Lyrics by V. PALLAVICINI
English Lyrics by VICKI WICKHAM and SIMON NAPIER-BELL

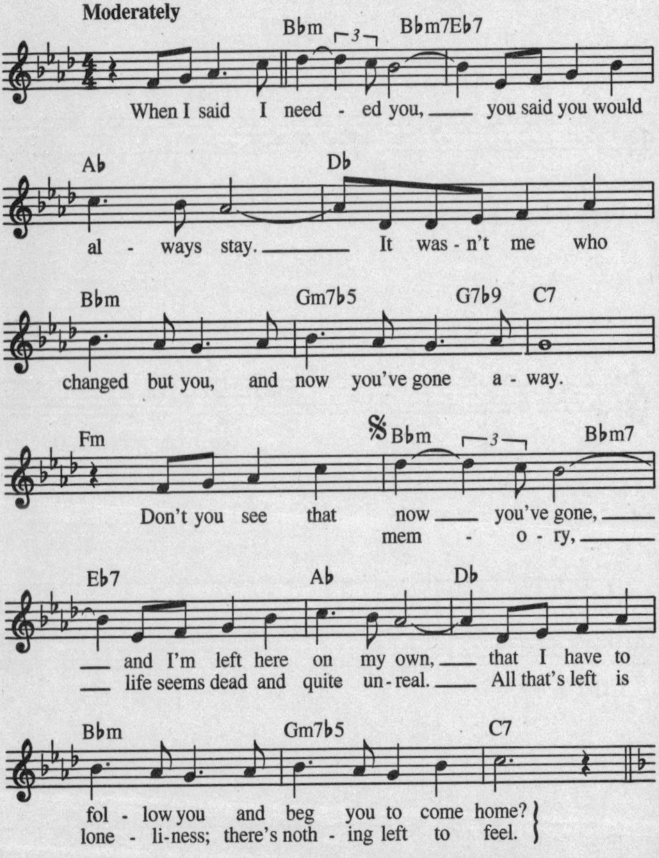
Moderately
Bbm Bbm7Eb7
When I said I need - ed you, you said you would
Ab Db
al - ways stay. It was - n't me who
Bbm Gm7b5 G7b9 C7
changed but you, and now you've gone a - way.
Fm Bbm Bbm7
Don't you see that now you've gone,
mem - o - ry,
Eb7 Ab Db
and I'm left here on my own, that I have to
life seems dead and quite un - real. All that's left is
Bbm Gm7b5 C7
fol - low you and beg you to come home?
lone - li-ness; there's noth - ing left to feel.

Copyright © 1965, 1966 ACCORDO EDIZIONI MUSICALI, Milan, Italy
Copyrights Renewed
Rights in the United States, Canada, British Commonwealth of Nations, South Africa, Korea, China and Taiwan Controlled by EMI MILLER CATALOG INC. (Publishing) and WARNER BROS. PUBLICATIONS U.S. INC. (Print)
All Rights Reserved Used by Permission

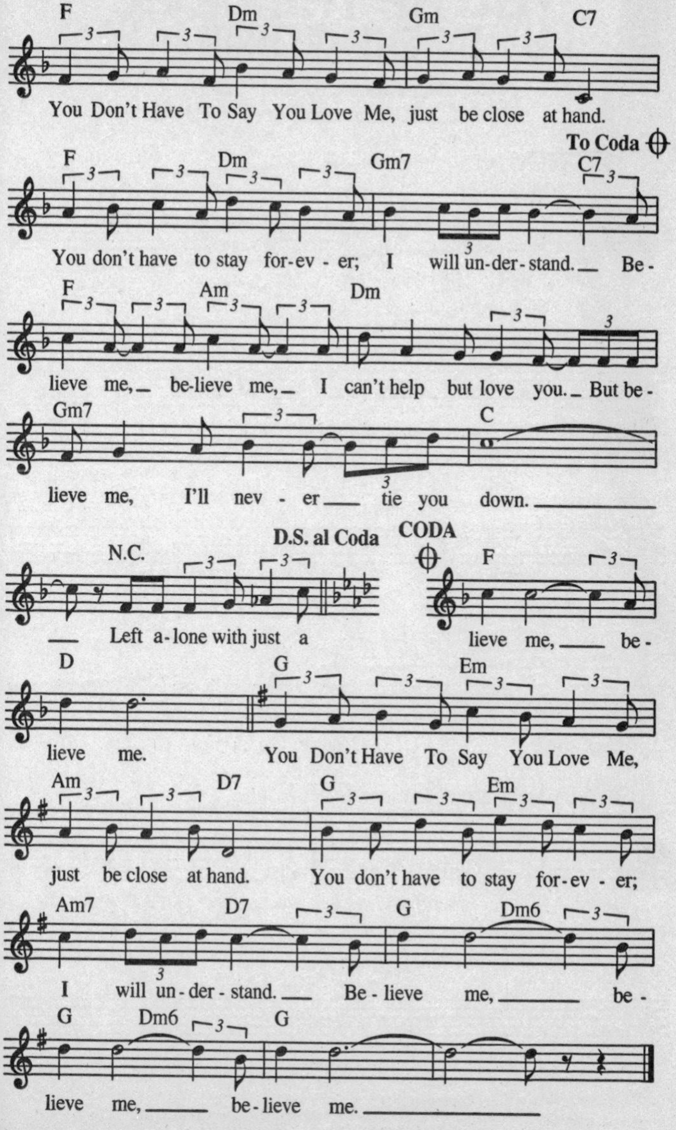
F Dm Gm C7
You Don't Have To Say You Love Me, just be close at hand.
To Coda
F Dm Gm7 C7
You don't have to stay for-ev - er; I will un-der-stand. Be -
F Am Dm
lieve me, be-lieve me, I can't help but love you. But be -
Gm7 C
lieve me, I'll nev - er tie you down.
D.S. al Coda
CODA
N.C.
Left a-lone with just a
F
lieve me, be -
D G Em
lieve me. You Don't Have To Say You Love Me,
Am D7 G Em
just be close at hand. You don't have to stay for-ev - er;
Am7 D7 G Dm6
I will un - der - stand. Be - lieve me, be -
G Dm6 G
lieve me, be - lieve me.

YOU'RE THE DEVIL IN DISGUISE

Words and Music by BILL GIANT,
BERNIE BAUM and FLORENCE KAYE

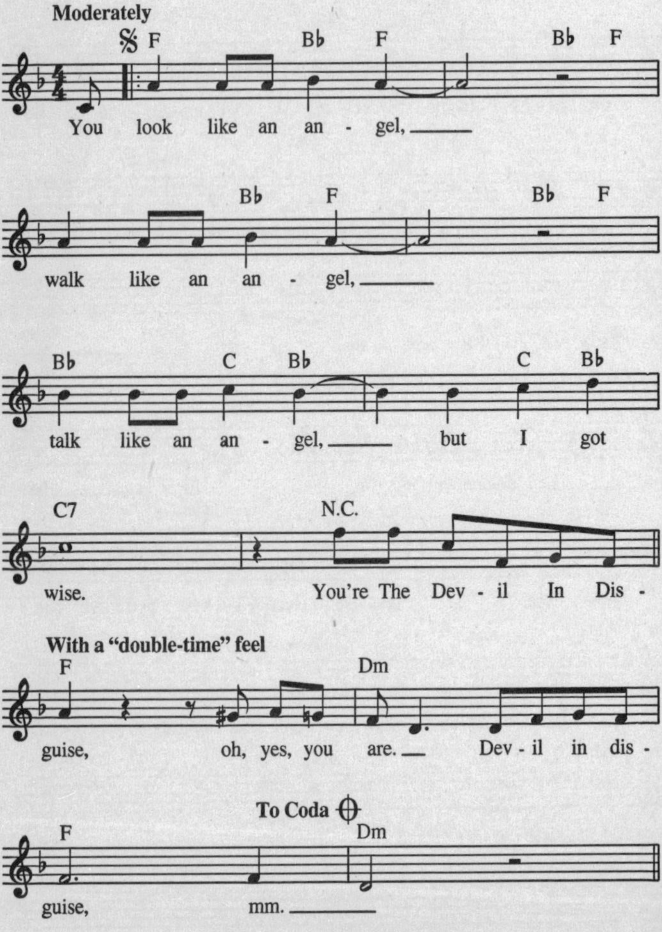
Moderately
F Bb F Bb F
You look like an an - gel,
Bb F Bb F
walk like an an - gel,
Bb C Bb C Bb
talk like an an - gel, but I got
C7 N.C.
wise. You're The Dev - il In Dis -
With a "double-time" feel
F Dm
guise, oh, yes, you are. Dev - il in dis -
To Coda
F Dm
guise, mm.

Copyright © 1963 by Elvis Presley Music, Inc.
Copyright Renewed and Assigned to Elvis Presley Music (Administered by R&H Music)
International Copyright Secured All Rights Reserved

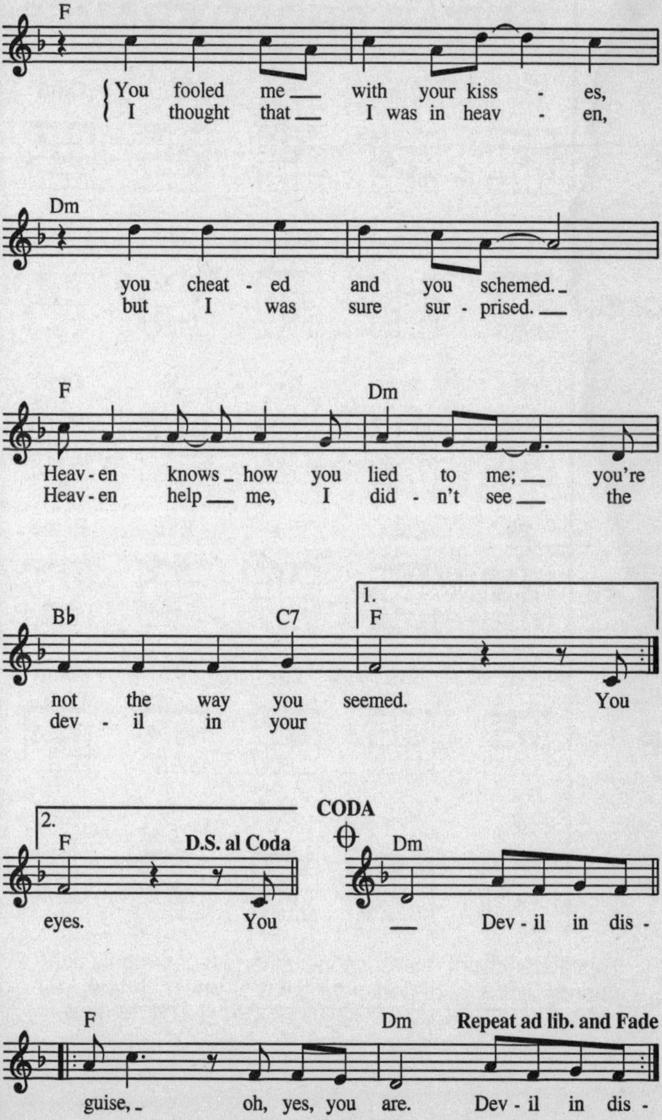
F
You fooled me with your kiss - es, you cheat - ed and you schemed.
I thought that I was in heav - en, but I was sure sur - prised.
Dm
F
Dm
Heav - en knows how you lied to me; you're not the way you seemed. You
Heav - en help me, I did - n't see the dev - il in your
B♭
C7
1.
2.
F
eyes. You
D.S. al Coda
CODA
Dm
Dev - il in dis - guise, oh, yes, you are. Dev - il in dis -
Repeat ad lib. and Fade

GUITAR CHORD FRAMES

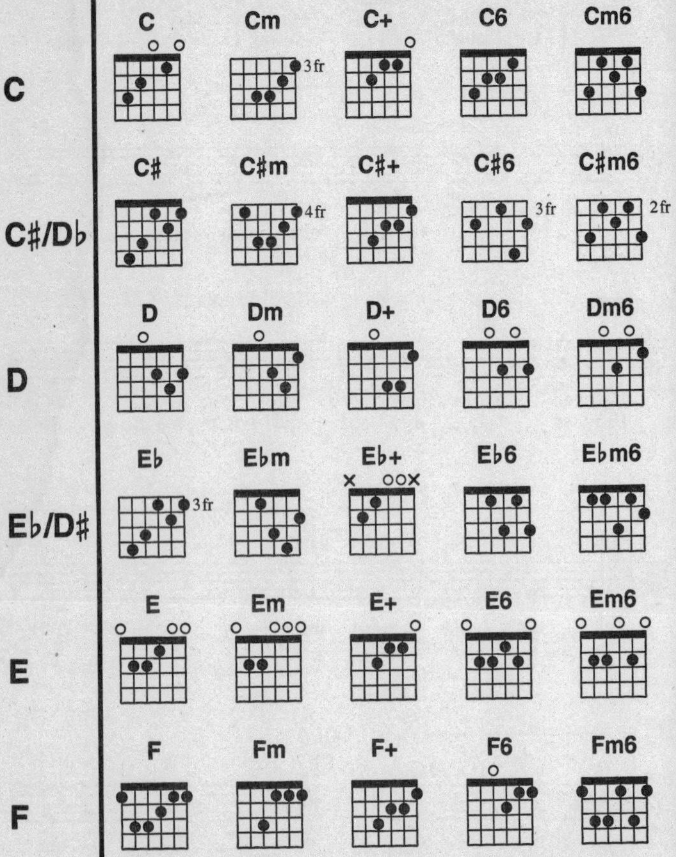
C
C Cm 3 fr C+ C6 Cm6
C♯/D♭
C♯ C♯m 4 fr C♯+ C♯6 3 fr C♯m6 2 fr
D
D Dm D+ D6 Dm6
E♭/D♯
E♭ 3 fr E♭m E♭+ E♭6 E♭m6
E
E Em E+ E6 Em6
F
F Fm F+ F6 Fm6

This guitar chord reference includes 120 commonly used chords. For a more complete guide to guitar chords, see "THE PAPERBACK CHORD BOOK" (HL00702009).

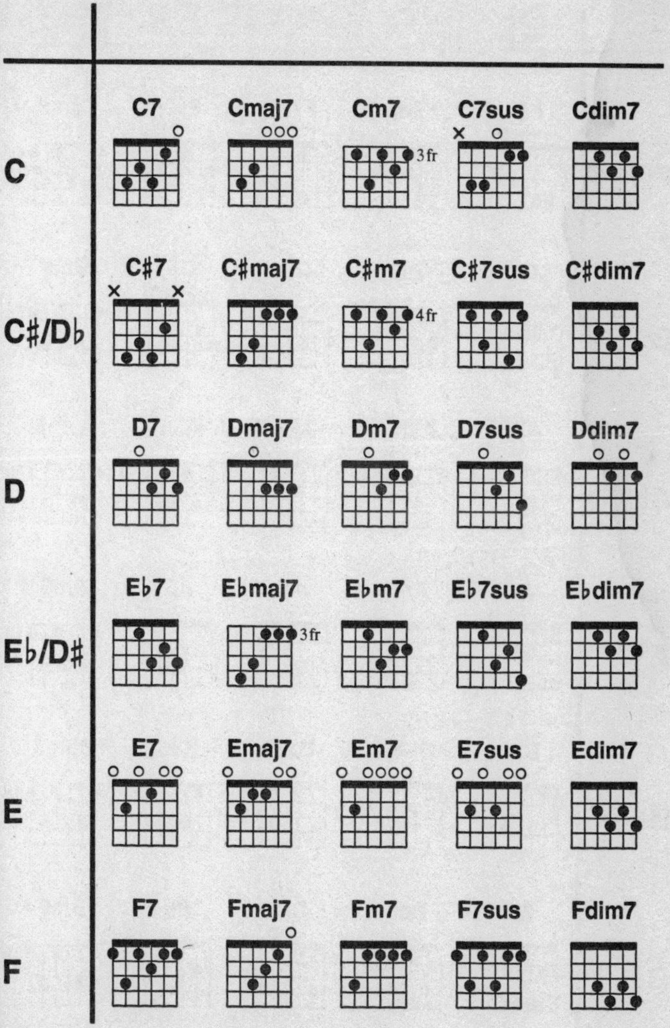
C
C7
Cmaj7
Cm7
3fr
C7sus
Cdim7
C♯/D♭
C♯7
C♯maj7
C♯m7
4fr
C♯7sus
C♯dim7
D
D7
Dmaj7
Dm7
D7sus
Ddim7
E♭/D♯
E♭7
E♭maj7
3fr
E♭m7
E♭7sus
E♭dim7
E
E7
Emaj7
Em7
E7sus
Edim7
F
F7
Fmaj7
Fm7
F7sus
Fdim7

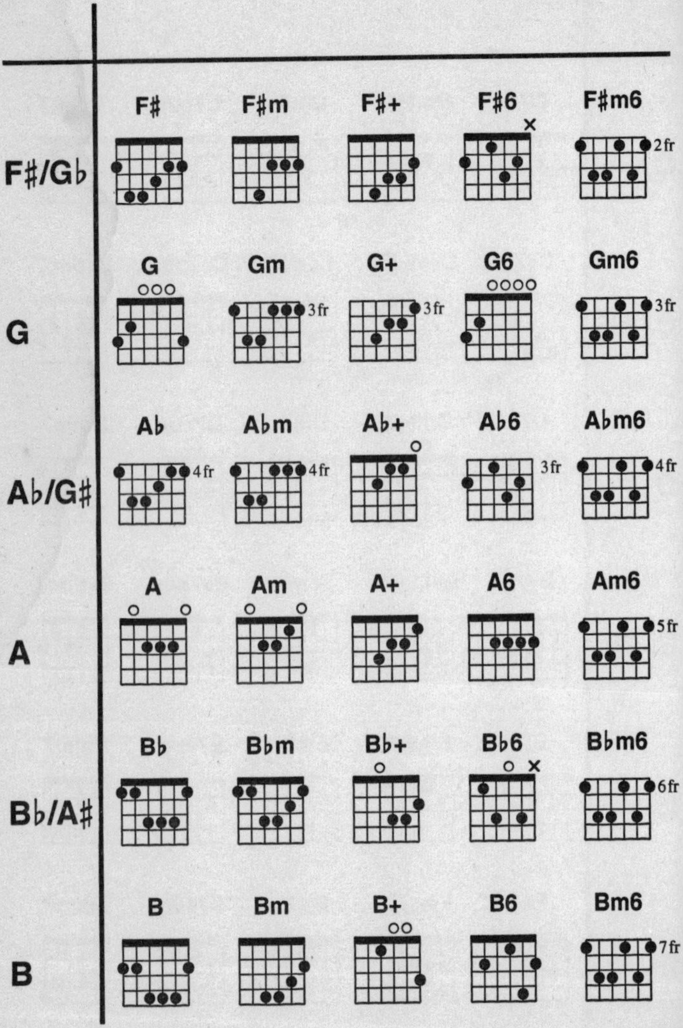
F♯/G♭
F♯
F♯m
F♯+
F♯6
F♯m6
2fr
G
G
Gm
3fr
G+
3fr
G6
Gm6
3fr
A♭/G♯
A♭
4fr
A♭m
4fr
A♭+
A♭6
3fr
A♭m6
4fr
A
A
Am
A+
A6
Am6
5fr
B♭/A♯
B♭
B♭m
B♭+
B♭6
B♭m6
6fr
B
B
Bm
B+
B6
Bm6
7fr

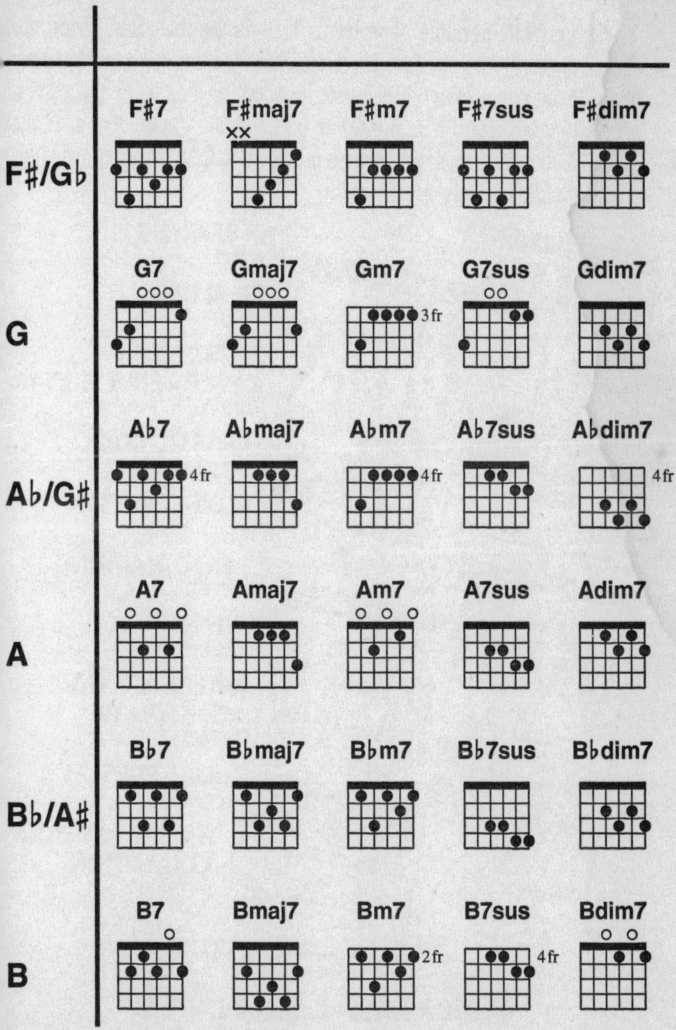
F♯/G♭
F♯7
F♯maj7
F♯m7
F♯7sus
F♯dim7
G
G7
Gmaj7
Gm7
3fr
G7sus
Gdim7
A♭/G♯
A♭7
4fr
A♭maj7
A♭m7
4fr
A♭7sus
A♭dim7
4fr
A
A7
Amaj7
Am7
A7sus
Adim7
B♭/A♯
B♭7
B♭maj7
B♭m7
B♭7sus
B♭dim7
B
B7
Bmaj7
Bm7
2fr
B7sus
4fr
Bdim7

THE PAPERBACK SONGS SERIES

These perfectly portable paperbacks include the melodies, lyrics, and chords symbols for your favorite songs, all in a convenient, pocket-sized book. Using concise, one-line music notation, anyone from hobbyists to professionals can strum on the guitar, play melodies on the piano, or sing the lyrics to great songs. Books also include a helpful guitar chord chart. A fantastic deal – only $5.95 each!

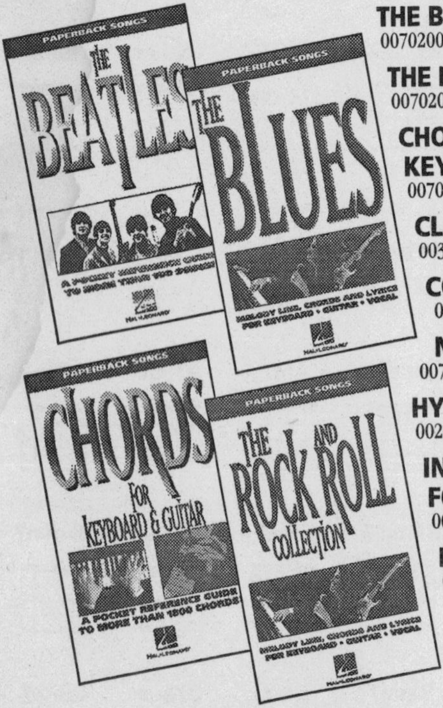
PAPERBACK SONGS
THE BEATLES
PAPERBACK SONGS
THE BLUES
PAPERBACK SONGS
CHORDS FOR KEYBOARD & GUITAR
A POCKET REFERENCE GUIDE TO MORE THAN 1500 CHORDS
PAPERBACK SONGS
THE ROCK AND ROLL COLLECTION
MELODY LINE, CHORDS AND LYRICS FOR KEYBOARD • GUITAR • VOCAL

THE BEATLES
00702008

THE BLUES
00702014

CHORDS FOR KEYBOARD & GUITAR
00702009

CLASSIC ROCK
00310058

COUNTRY HITS
00702013

NEIL DIAMOND
00702012

HYMNS
00240103

INTERNATIONAL FOLKSONGS
00240104

ELVIS PRESLEY
00240102

THE ROCK & ROLL COLLECTION
00702020

FOR MORE INFORMATION, SEE YOUR LOCAL MUSIC DEALER,
OR WRITE TO:

HAL•LEONARD®
CORPORATION
7777 W. BLUEMOUND RD. P.O.BOX 13819 MILWAUKEE, WI 53213

Prices, availability and contents subject to change without notice.
Some products may not be available outside the U.S.A.